Karla Bohmbach

:)

"Reading this book is like the best Bible study or class you ever— or never—attended. What distinguishes Clark-Soles's book from similar projects is that she doesn't just walk you through texts but introduces you to a whole range of different and often unexpected interpretations for each passage. Even difficult and painful texts become occasions for new pastoral, spiritual, and prophetic insights. Attending to the needs of preachers, teachers, and general readers, Clark-Soles has created an incomparable resource for encountering the full range of women in the Bible."

—Carol A. Newsom, Charles Howard Candler
Professor Emerita of Old Testament,
Candler School of Theology, Emory University

"Clark-Soles provides a format allowing readers to enter at their own pace and in their own space. While addressing a timeless topic, this work reimagines what the pursuit of 'women in the Bible' means in a time of gender fluidity. This is not another overview or mere summation. This is an opportunity to revisit and even disturb embedded biblical interpretations and social considerations for the sake of broader theological and ecclesial conversation."

—Stephanie Buckhanon Crowder, Academic Dean
and Associate Professor of New Testament,
Chicago Theological Seminary

"The rubric 'women in the Bible' suggests yet one more prosaic catalog of names and roles, chapters and verses. But Jaime Clark-Soles offers instead a fascinating account that ranges from rich consideration of individual characters to reflection on the feminine work of God. It's difficult to convey just how remarkable this book is in its scope and its treatment. Clark-Soles's diverse array of conversation partners and keen pastoral sensitivity make this an ideal volume for students and pastors alike. Simply first rate!"

—Beverly Roberts Gaventa, Distinguished Professor
of New Testament, Baylor University

"Jaime Clark-Soles's comprehensive and thoroughly engaging book about the varied roles of women in the Bible—seen and unseen—is an excellent antidote to the historical wrong of erasing women as protagonists in the story of God's engagement with the world. It is a feast that places biblical texts in dialogue with modern literature and culture to offer a careful and honest analysis of their liberative potential and pitfalls for faith communities. Scholars, pastors, and laity alike will see biblical texts about women and their implications for our times through a new lens."
—Raj Nadella, Samuel A. Cartledge Associate Professor
of New Testament, Columbia Theological Seminary

"Clark-Soles gives us the guide we need to the women of Scripture. For all kinds of today's readers (not just women!), Clark-Soles brings Old Testament and New Testament women springing from the page, full of righteous anger, wisdom, and power. They lived in fraught times, and so do we—Clark-Soles shows us how much they can teach us for the living of these days."
—Jacqueline E. Lapsley, Dean and Vice President
of Academic Affairs and Professor of Old Testament,
Princeton Theological Seminary

INTERPRETATION

RESOURCES FOR THE USE OF SCRIPTURE IN THE CHURCH

Samuel E. Balentine, *Series Editor*
Ellen F. Davis, *Founding Editor*
Richard B. Hays, *Founding Editor*
Susan E. Hylen, *Associate Editor*
Brent A. Strawn, *Associate Editor*
†Patrick D. Miller, *Consulting Editor*

OTHER AVAILABLE BOOKS IN THE SERIES

C. Clifton Black, *The Lord's Prayer*
Markus Bockmuehl, *Ancient Apocryphal Gospels*
Walter Brueggemann, *Money and Possessions*
Ronald P. Byars, *The Sacraments in Biblical Perspective*
Jerome F. D. Creach, *Violence in Scripture*
Ellen F. Davis, *Biblical Prophecy: Perspectives
for Christian Theology, Discipleship, and Ministry*
Robert W. Jenson, *Canon and Creed*
Luke Timothy Johnson, *Miracles: God's Presence
and Power in Creation*
Richard Lischer, *Reading the Parables*
Patrick D. Miller, *The Ten Commandments*

Women in the Bible

INTERPRETATION
Resources for the Use of Scripture in the Church

JAIME CLARK-SOLES

Women in the Bible

INTERPRETATION *Resources for the Use of Scripture in the Church*

WESTMINSTER
JOHN KNOX PRESS
LOUISVILLE · KENTUCKY

First edition
Published by Westminster John Knox Press
Louisville, Kentucky

20 21 22 23 24 25 26 27 28 29—10 9 8 7 6 5 4 3 2 1

Book design by Drew Stevens
Cover design by designpointinc.com

Library of Congress Cataloging-in-Publication Data

Names: Clark-Soles, Jaime, 1967– author.
Title: Women in the Bible / Jaime Clark-Soles.
Description: First edition. | Louisville, Kentucky : Westminster John Knox Press,
    [2020] | Series: Interpretation: resources for the use of scripture in the church |
    Includes bibliographical references and index. | Summary: "Women in the Bible
    investigates how women are presented in Scripture, taking into account cultural
    views of both ancient societies as well as our own. Jamie Clark-Soles treats well-
    known biblical women from fresh perspectives, highlights women who have been
    ignored, and recovers those who have been erased from historical memory"—
    Provided by publisher.
Identifiers: LCCN 2020042300 (print) | LCCN 2020042301 (ebook) | ISBN
    9780664234010 (hardback) | ISBN 9781646980390 (ebook)
Subjects: LCSH: Women in the Bible.
Classification: LCC BS575 .C53 2020 (print) | LCC BS575 (ebook) | DDC
    220.9/2082—dc23
LC record available at https://lccn.loc.gov/2020042300
LC ebook record available at https://lccn.loc.gov/2020042301

Most Westminster John Knox Press books are available at special quantity discounts when purchased in bulk by corporations, organizations, and special-interest groups. For more information, please email SpecialSales@wjkbooks.com.

PERMISSIONS

Mireille (Mimi) Mears. "Dedication." By permission of Mireille Mears. In chapter 2.

Love L. Sechrest. Excerpts from "Enemies, Romans, Pigs, and Dogs: Loving the Other in the Gospel of Matthew." In *Ex Auditu* 31 (2015): 71–105. Used by permission of Wipf & Stock Publishers. In chapter 1.

Irene Zimmerman. "Liturgy." In *WomenPsalms*, compiled by Julia Ahlers, Rosemary Broughton, and Carl Koch, 55–56. Winona, MN: St. Mary's Press, 1992. © Irene Zimmerman. Used with permission. In chapter 6. (A slightly different version of this poem appears in *Incarnation: New and Selected Poems for Spiritual Reflection*, by Irene Zimmerman [Lanham, MD: Cowley Publications, an imprint of Rowman & Littlefield Publishing Group, 2007].)

In honor of the generations, I dedicate this book to
Margot Clark, Jennifer Clark, Chloe Elizabeth Clark-Soles,
and Camila Zoe Clark-Soles

CONTENTS

SERIES FOREWORD

This series of volumes supplements Interpretation: A Bible Commentary for Teaching and Preaching. The commentary series offers an exposition of the books of the Bible written for those who teach, preach, and study the Bible in the community of faith. This new series is addressed to the same audience and serves a similar purpose, providing additional resources for the interpretation of Scripture, but now dealing with features, themes, and issues significant for the whole rather than with individual books.

The Bible is composed of separate books. Its composition naturally has led its interpreters to address particular books. But there are other ways to approach the interpretation of the Bible that respond to other characteristics and features of the Scriptures. These other entries to the task of interpretation provide contexts, overviews, and perspectives that complement the book-by-book approach and discern dimensions of the Scriptures that the commentary design may not adequately explore.

The Bible as used in the Christian community is not only a collection of books but also itself a book that has a unity and coherence important to its meaning. Some volumes in this new series will deal with this canonical wholeness and seek to provide a wider context for the interpretation of individual books as well as a comprehensive theological perspective that reading single books does not provide.

Other volumes in the series will examine particular texts, like the Ten Commandments, the Lord's Prayer, and the Sermon on the Mount, texts that have played such an important role in the faith and life of the Christian community that they constitute orienting foci for the understanding and use of Scripture.

A further concern of the series will be to consider important and often difficult topics, addressed at many different places in the books of the canon, that are of recurrent interest and concern to the church in its dependence on Scripture for faith and life. So the series will include volumes dealing with such topics as eschatology, women, wealth, and violence.

The books of the Bible are constituted from a variety of kinds of literature such as narrative, laws, hymns and prayers, letters, parables, and miracle stories. To recognize and discern the contribution and importance of all these different kinds of material enriches and enlightens the use of Scripture. Volumes in the series will provide help in the interpretation of Scripture's literary forms and genres.

The liturgy and practices of the gathered church are anchored in Scripture, as with the sacraments observed and the creeds recited. So another entry to the task of discerning the meaning and significance of biblical texts explored in this series is the relation between the liturgy of the church and the Scriptures.

Finally, there is certain ancient literature, such as the Apocrypha and the noncanonical gospels, that constitutes an important context to the interpretation of Scripture itself. Consequently, this series will provide volumes that offer guidance in understanding such writings and explore their significance for the interpretation of the Protestant canon.

The volumes in this second series of Interpretation deal with these important entries into the interpretation of the Bible. Together with the commentaries, they compose a library of resources for those who interpret Scripture as members of the community of faith. Each of them can be used independently for its own significant addition to the resources for the study of Scripture. But all of them intersect the commentaries in various ways and provide an important context for their use. The authors of these volumes are biblical scholars and theologians who are committed to the service of interpreting the Scriptures in and for the church. The editors and authors hope that the addition of this series to the commentaries will provide a major contribution to the vitality and richness of biblical interpretation in the church.

The Editors

ACKNOWLEDGMENTS

This book has been many years in the making, over a decade. A book on women in the Bible is no small undertaking. From Genesis to Revelation, women are there. From the beginning of time until now, women are there. From the books that did not make it into the various Christian canons to those that did, women arc there. We are here. And we are not going anywhere. Wait— yes, we are. We're marching to Zion, beautiful, beautiful Zion, we're marching upward to Zion, the beautiful city of God. We're on the way to the new heaven and new earth, where there are no more tears, no more death, where light reigns and women are clothed with the sun.

I cannot begin to acknowledge everyone who has contributed to this book, given its lengthy incubation and composition. Thus, I will only highlight a few and trust that those who remain unnamed know their part in this and my gratitude for it.

I thank Craig Hill, Dean of Perkins, for valuing rigorous scholarship that aims to serve the wider church and world. Both Associate Dean Hugo Magallanes and former Associate Dean Evelyn Parker support faculty research however they can, and this project benefited. I am grateful for grants received to complete this project, one from the Sam Taylor Fellowship Fund and another from the Perkins Scholarly Outreach Fund. Both entities care deeply about making scholarship accessible to as wide an audience as possible. I can only hope that this book helps to further the mission of both groups. Nothing would make me gladder, since that is my own goal as well.

I thank all those who have participated in my workshops on this in the Perkins Summit for Faith and Learning, whether in Alaska or Dallas. Special mention goes to Lonnie and Adriana Brooks and the Watson family—Susie, Ron, and Justin. Your support, insightful questions, observations, and critique, along with your faithfulness, have deeply encouraged and taught me. I also thank the many other groups who have invited me to share this topic: the Stalcup School for the Laity (especially Eileen Fisher for repeatedly inviting me back); St. Michael and All Angels Episcopal Church in Dallas, Texas; the Texas Annual Conference Clergywomen Retreat;

the Nevertheless She Preached conference (special thanks to the cofounders of this amazing gathering that brings me life and is always one of the highlights of my year—Natalie Webb and Kyndall Rothaus); and the Church of Christ Women in Ministry Conference. My own church, Royal Lane Baptist Church, led by the Rev. Michael Gregg, has buoyed me in this as in everything. It's just what they do, for everybody. For those who have participated in Educational Opportunities trips related to women in the Bible with me, I thank you for the chance to float ideas and get feedback. Special thanks are in order to the Montgomery women—Freda, Katie, and Jennifer, all astute from their different perspectives, who fearlessly investigate Scripture and raise important questions and considerations in a refreshingly frank manner.

I lead groups regularly to the Holy Land. Khalil Haddad, an extraordinary Holy Land guide (from Nazareth, no less) and an Orthodox Christian, has expanded my knowledge, tickled my intellectual imagination, engaged me in lively debate, and gifted me with his friendship and laughter. Everyone on the trips feels the same way. He has deepened my experience of the holy as it relates both to antiquity and to life in the current Israeli-Palestinian struggle.

Three biblical scholars served as research assistants over this decade of writing while pursuing their PhDs in the Graduate Program in Religious Studies at Southern Methodist University: the Rev. Dr. Michelle Morris, Dr. Leslie Cara Fuller, and April Hoelke Simpson, who will soon complete her PhD. No doubt, all have tales to tell about the challenges involved with taking everything I write and making it better, more thorough, and more . . . well, just more. April has done especially heavy lifting on this project as my research assistant for the last three years. Don't get me started on her gifts and graces and all the ways she improves anything on my docket (speaking, teaching, writing). Her scholarly range, attention to detail, standards of excellence, and perspicacity would be enough. But the fact that she combines all of this with unfailing graciousness is instructive. For instance, her phrase (that I've now adopted), "I'm not tracking with you here," is a much more understated way to say, "This make no sense!"

If it weren't for John Seddlemeyer, there would be no separate chapter dedicated to Mary, mother of Jesus. He insisted the book would be incomplete without it. He was right. Protestants diminish Mary, to their own detriment.

For a New Testament scholar, writing a book on women in the *whole* Bible is a special challenge that requires a hotline to Old Testament scholar buddies! Thus, special honors go to Anathea Portier-Young, Roy Heller, and Carolyn Sharp for being my OT resources on speed dial. Matthew Skinner and Greg Carey continue to be my New Testament speed-dial colleagues. Of course, all final decisions rested with me, so none of them are accountable for anything questionable in my arguments.

I have no idea how anyone writes a book (or an essay, even) without the expert assistance of reference librarians. Bridwell Library is unparalleled in both collections and staff. If you don't have a Jane Elder or David Schmersal in your life, I'm sorry for you. Both of these scholars have gone above and beyond the call of duty in assisting me. I owe David Schmersal for his work on the lectionary related to women in the Bible. It represents a vast number of hours. Both Jane and David have always come to my aid no matter where I am in the world, no matter what time it is, and no matter what subject I may be inquiring about at any given moment. Superheroes could learn a thing or two from them. Yet another Perkins staff person who makes my work possible, year after year, is Carolyn Douglas. I value her dedication, expertise, and friendship.

Regarding the lectionary, I also must acknowledge my colleague Mark Stamm, Professor of Christian Worship. For twenty years, he, a Methodist, and I, a Baptist, have gone round and round on the Revised Common Lectionary and its pros and cons (one con being the lack of a year devoted to the Gospel of John). I look forward to decades more of friendly debate about it and remain deeply grateful for his insight, faithfulness, humor, and expertise from which I continue to learn, change, and grow (if grudgingly at times). Dr. James Lee, my colleague here at Perkins, provided excellent input on the Mary chapter, especially related to Augustine and other church fathers on the topic of breast milk and virtue, mercy, and grace. I challenge anyone to find a student or colleague who would contest his personal example of virtue, mercy, and grace.

A special thanks goes to the wonderful staff of WJK, with whom I have worked on a number of books now. Along the way this has included Ellen Davis, Richard Hays, Sam Balentine, Julie Mullins, and Susan Hylen. Susan Hylen has borne the brunt of the work and has set a new standard for me with editing others' writing. She, like me, is a New Testament scholar. What's more, her own book,

Women in the New Testament World, came out while she was editing my manuscript. Nevertheless, she was able (against all odds) to let my book remain my book. You will see that I depend on her excellent work in places. In other ways, we diverge. Her meticulous attention and sheer time investment in this book humbles me. I cannot repay her, but I can hope that this resource serves as many people as possible to honor her time and commitment.

So many friends have supported me in this project over the years, but I name three here who have carried extra along the way. It would be difficult to describe the gift and role of Teri Walker in my life for these past twenty years. It's probably best just to say that she's the kind of *parthenos* (Matt. 25:1–13; KJV "virgin"; NRSV "bridesmaid") who would (a) most certainly have her oil ready for the bridegroom's arrival but (b) would one-up the biblical *parthenos* by actually sharing it with you if you foolishly ran out. In other words, Matthew could learn some grace from her. We all could. Enough said. The Rev. Mireya Martinez is my dear sister in the faith whose pastoral leadership is extraordinary. She preaches, teaches, and provides pastoral care equally well. And if I could make "friends" a verb, I'd add that to the list of her spiritual gifts. She reads my work (and my soul) attentively and offers suggestions grounded in intellect, faith, and grace. I and my offerings to the church are better for it. In addition to being OT adviser and dear friend, Anathea Portier-Young is my writing accountability partner with whom I meet weekly. She has provided motivation, feedback, and knowledge related to this book for the past two years. I have learned more from her than I could begin to tell, some of it related to the Bible, faith, productivity, leadership, and excellent teaching and the rest to life more generally and profoundly. I hope you have a Thea in your life. If you don't, I'd suggest you get one.

In writing a book on women in the Bible, it's natural to consider women who have inspired me, ancient and modern and in between. I'd invite you to stop for a moment and make your own list. If you're like me, you'll find that the list is long and spans centuries. From our ancient ancestors in the faith who appear in the biblical canon to those in the deuterocanonical or extracanonical materials, to the saints and mystics, ancient or modern, they surround us as the great cloud of witnesses, calling us forward into God's glorious future where it will be "on earth as it is in heaven."

So I'll dispense with history just now and focus on the present. My mom, Margot Clark, will always stand in a category all by herself in terms of both those who have shaped me and those I most admire. I am who I am mostly because of God and Margot (maybe in that order?). Born in 1947, raising a daughter born in 1967 (and another in 1974), she had her work cut out for her. She is smart, fierce, independent, an internationally renowned artist and teacher, resilient, resourceful, savvy, and gifted in hospitality to her students and friends. This includes, but is not limited to, chopping up fudge in her grandchildren's breakfast and serving it to them in the warm bathtub at night by candlelight, causing said children to exclaim: "Wow—you're so *lucky* you grew up with a mom like that!" I assured them, and I assure you all, that I most certainly *did not* grow up with that mom. But I did grow up with a mom who expected me to reach my potential and has helped me do that at every turn (especially the really sharp ones). My sister, Jennifer, is a chip off the old Margot block in terms of creativity and smarts. She's also an independent, successful businessperson with a passion for mentoring women in Habitat for Humanity's Women Build program. She is always a ready source of love, support, and calm for me (plus she's a great secret keeper, as all the best sisters are!).

All of this fabulousness has passed right down to my daughter, Chloe, who is named after the Chloe in 1 Corinthians 1:11. She was a preteen when I signed on to this book and is now a grown woman with a professional career who is her own person in every way and who inspires and teaches me regularly. She has especially schooled me in the area of gender, given that she was born when I was a grad student at Yale in New Haven, Connecticut, (ages 0–3) but then grew up in Dallas, Texas, where I've been a professor since. Let's just say we've had conversations ranging from pictures of the first three years of her life being all green, yellow, and orange clothing to cotillion classes in Texas.

My dad, Harold Clark, was the best father for a girl like me who was a "tomboy" growing up. He built me wonderful bikes and bike ramps to jump with them, took me fishing, didn't bat an eyelash when I was the only girl on the baseball team or the soccer team. He built me the coolest go-kart when I was ten and then kept me from near disaster the first day I drove it—he specializes in "coming in clutch." He also came to get me out of elementary school the day my first pet died and quietly let me soak his shirt with tears until I was all cried out. He's that winning combination.

My son, Caleb, has also been an important conversation partner all along and regularly helps me consider the issues that pertain to this book. The birth of his daughter, Camila Zoe Clark-Soles, on February 8, 2020, made me a grandma. You can be sure that with every word I have written in this book, I've had Mila in mind as I look forward to all the ways our rich biblical tradition will equip her to discern her place in the grand narrative, the Story of All Stories, of God with Us. I hope it will do the same for you.

Finally, as I've been saying for more than thirty years now, my deepest gratitude goes to my husband, Thad Clark-Soles, who quietly, consistently, and (often) patiently makes this life that I love so much not just possible, but exceptional.

Introduction

We begin this journey on a celebratory note for two reasons. First, today women are exercising leadership in churches across a number of denominations. Second, much scholarship has been published in the area of women in the Bible over the past two decades so that our knowledge has grown and the subject has become mainstream rather than ancillary. For example, we now have the *CEB Women's Bible*, a one-volume study Bible that combines excellent scholarship with attention to the complexity of contemporary lived reality. In addition, the new Wisdom Commentary series, an ongoing project that will cover the entire Bible in fifty-eight volumes through the lens of feminist scholarship, testifies to our explosion in knowledge, the refinement of interpretive approaches, and the exciting potential for individual, communal, and global transformation to which the gospel surely calls us.

Challenges remain, of course. First, many traditions still do not ordain women and continue to reinforce gender roles in ways that perpetuate inequality. In many Christian traditions today, women are not permitted to preach and teach the gospel in any formal capacity. Part of the "argument" against women in leadership comes from passages of the Bible, especially 1 Timothy 2, 1 Corinthians 14:33–36, and the household codes of Ephesians. Such authors drew upon their predecessors from both Jewish and non-Jewish sources. From Aristotle and Hippocrates, to the biblical texts, to Josephus, the church

fathers, Luther, Calvin, and so on down to today, one can adduce
an endless collection of choice quotations to prove that women have
been considered inferior to men. A few examples will suffice:

Quote	Source
"Males are warm, dry, and firm, and this is the norm. Females are cold, moist and spongy, these being defects."	Hippocrates, 5th–4th c. BCE (Dean-Jones 1991, 115–16)
"Females are weaker and colder in their nature, and we should look upon the female state as being as it were a deformity."	Aristotle, 4th c. BCE (Allen 1985, 98)
"The law says that the woman is in all things inferior to the man. Let her accordingly be submissive . . . for the authority has been given by God to the man."	Josephus, 1st c. CE (deSilva 2000, 183)
"The female sex is irrational and akin to bestial passions, fear, sorrow, pleasure and desire."	Philo of Alexandria, 1st c. CE (Allen 1985, 191)
"Praised be God that he has not created me a gentile; praised be God that he has not created me a woman; praised be God that he has not created me an ignorant man."	Tosefta Berakhoth 7, 8 (Swidler 1979, 155)
"It is not proper for a woman to speak in church, however admirable or holy what she says may be, merely because it comes from female lips."	Origen, 185–254 CE (Tavard 1973, 342)
"The rule remains with the husband, and the wife is compelled to obey him by God's command. He rules the home and the state. . . . The woman on the other hand is like a nail driven into the wall. She sits at home. . . . Just as the snail carries its house with it, so the wife should stay at home and look after the household."	Martin Luther, 16th c. CE (Tavard 1973, 174)
"[The woman] had indeed been subject to her husband [in Paradise], though this was an honest, and by no means harsh subjection, but now [after "the fall"] she is placed as it were in slavery."	John Calvin, 16th c. CE (Tavard 1973, 176)

Far from picking on any one tradition, my point here is to demonstrate the ubiquity of such attitudes toward women by movers and shakers across the board whose effects are felt to this day.

Second, there are many more women in the Bible than you may realize, but chances are that you have not heard of many of them because they are not mentioned in our teaching and preaching.

Third, when you do hear of a woman in the Bible, the woman is often presented as a sinner and is often associated with some kind of sexual immorality. Even Jesus's mother!

Fourth, rarely do we hear of women who lead and are moral or faith exemplars. Those we do encounter often have been so egregiously misinterpreted that it would be better if they had stayed ignored (e.g., Mary Magdalene and the Samaritan woman).

These patterns in the Bible raise some questions for us Christians and our witness. First, there is the issue of how God is described and portrayed: Does God believe that women are not equal to men and that most women are sexpots and seductresses? Second, based on the answer to the first question, do followers of God have license to constrain women on the basis of gender? Third, how do we entertain the issue of the unity and authority of the Bible? Not all texts agree; some are liberating for women and some appear to condone or engender oppression. How do we address this?

Goals of the Book

The Bible has been a resource in the struggle for gender equality and, by extension, people equality. The rising of women means the rising of the whole human family. When Christians talk about anything, including women, we are talking about the nature of the kingdom (or kin-dom, or dream) of God. Where does the Bible exemplify good news of abundant life for women and point the way to how life would look if things were "on earth as it is in heaven"? Since the Bible is Scripture for us, it has special authority. But how does that authority work, given the distance between the time and cultures in which it was composed and now? It is important to know how women were viewed in ancient society so that we can inquire about which aspects of that view inhere in the present and which aspects might be cast off. Paul asked women to veil in 1 Corinthians 11, but most

3

American women do not do that today. What was at stake then, and why do most of us not do it now? So, the Bible is authoritative, the Bible teaches us about the nature of God's kin(g)dom, and history can help us think about how we relate to the Bible today.

This book spotlights overlooked women and takes a fresh look at some of the most commonly referenced women. I address women who are astute theologians. I feature women who are active agents, those who are victims of forces beyond themselves, and those who are both. I try to be honest about what the texts do and do not say, whether we like it or not and whether we decide to agree or disagree with the author on any given point.

I also point out different types of family structures in the Bible. After all, neither Jesus nor Paul ever married or had children, and Paul patently calls Christians *not* to marry if they can at all resist it. Unmarried people in the Bible are whole people on their own. On the other hand, Peter is married. Some women are mothers, and some are not. Some are leaders in their communities—judges, warriors, prophets, apostles, ministers, leaders of prayer circles and churches. Others are "ordinary" people like the rest of us, trying to live faithful lives amidst sometimes difficult circumstances, celebrating and praising God for the joys that attend our lives (such as finding a coin or seeing a brother raised to new life).

The stated goals of this book are as follows:

1. Address well-known biblical women. Where necessary, reintroduce such figures from fresh perspectives using a variety of interpretive methods.

2. Lift up stories of women that have been ignored.

3. Reinstate biblical women who have been erased (rather than merely ignored) due to political moves in textual transmission (such as Junia) or through politically motivated translation moves of which the English reader may not even be aware (e.g., Phoebe).

4. Consider symbolic femininized figures such as Woman Wisdom in Proverbs, daughter Zion, and the "great whore" in Revelation.

5. Explore the ways the Bible employs feminine imagery and the ways it moves across or beyond gender. For example, God, Jesus, Paul, and the male disciples are depicted using feminine language. "When feminists speak of reclaiming the feminine aspects of salvation history, the common reaction is that one is somehow changing either scripture or tradition. In fact many feminists are merely asking that the fullness of the scriptures and tradition be

recognized within the public prayer of the church" (Fox, "Women in the Bible," 352).

6. Draw upon recent scholarship that addresses the status of women in ancient Israelite society, in Roman Palestine (and the empire more broadly), and in the early church.

7. Present insights from new perspectives that have emerged in the interpretive conversation through the growing attention to women in the Bible and the increasingly active participation of women in different social locations in the current global context.

8. Point the reader to excellent resources for further study.

Ideally, the book will cause readers to know more, incorporate the material into their faith life, and help others to do the same.

Texture of the Book

While the stated goals of the book have been enumerated above, the reader might fairly ask about some of the overarching commitments that undergird the project. First, I am a New Testament scholar, and the book is weighted more heavily in the New Testament direction as a result. Indeed, the longest, most detailed chapter is devoted to women in Jesus's ministry.

Second, of all the things I could have addressed, I have tried to choose what is most useful and urgent for those called to lead groups of people in engaging Scripture. How might engaging these texts deepen our discipleship and allow us to encounter God? How might we encounter the texts in different settings in the life of the church?

Third, I assume a stance of reading toward wholeness and liberation for everyone and everything in God's creation. This entails being honest about potential obstacles to said liberation. Patriarchy constitutes one such entrenched obstacle both in antiquity and in our contemporary society. Patriarchy, literally "rule by the father," is a system in which men rule by virtue of being male. The a priori assumption in this book is that patriarchy always disadvantages women and is inherently unjust insofar as political and economic power is not distributed evenly. Patriarchy is, by definition, sexist, and sexism is unjust. Thus, when I use the language of "equality" (or lack of) in this book, I refer to having agency and equal access to the power to shape societal structures that affect one's ability to survive and flourish.

It is the nature of scholarship itself for scholars to debate ideas and evidence in order to advance human knowledge. This book, however, is written not merely as a disinterested historical analysis or a summary of scholarly debate on women in the Bible; rather, as stated above, it is written for the sake of communities for whom these biblical texts are currently authoritative in some way, shaping the moral, intellectual, and emotional lives of contemporary people. Thus, I will spend very little time rehearsing arguments from every scholarly angle. Two specific examples may help.

Dr. Carol Meyers, a Hebrew Bible scholar whose work informs my own, suggests that we should use the word "heterarchy" rather than "patriarchy" in order to draw attention to the fact that women had a more active role and more agency in society during the Old Testament period than we generally imagine. Likewise, Dr. Susan Hylen, my esteemed New Testament colleague (and editor of this volume), tends to argue for a more optimistic view of women's power and agency in the biblical period than we generally imagine (while still noting that women were considered inferior and that the society was patriarchal). I respect, rely upon, and recommend the work of both scholars as they seek to nuance our historical knowledge.

Yet I remain concerned not to soften gender disparities in our own era, inherited from thousands of years of reading these very biblical texts. It may be that not all scholars are using the word *power* in the same way. On the one hand, I understand the argument that women have power when they influence their husband's choice about whom their daughter should marry or donate money to a civic organization. When I use the word "power," however, I mean the power of a woman to make and enforce laws that affect her and her children; self-determination with respect to her body and who has access to it and what kind of access; the same standards for morality that apply to men rather than a double standard; the same consequences (or lack of) for particular actions; and so on. One even reads arguments (not from Meyers or Hylen) trying to soften the inherently oppressive nature of patriarchy by appealing to "benevolent patriarchy" or something similar. I consider "benevolent patriarchy" an oxymoron in any century in any locale, and that assumption underlies the book. We have inherited patriarchy along with its concomitant dangers. To be sure, there have been moments of light, but then as now, trying to point out "bright spots" or to dull

6

the razor-sharp edges of patriarchy, far from making it safer, lulls us into obscuring the deadly force it has always been for women.

Given our subject, then, I address the potential promises and pitfalls of the biblical texts under consideration with respect to ancient audiences and later interpreters, including us. I ask: in what ways does the text have liberative potential, and in what ways does it present potential obstacles for those seeking abundant life (John 10:10)?

Challenges of the Book

Undertaking such a project requires addressing numerous complexities. Here are some of the issues that arose in conceptualizing and producing it.

1. Gender Constructs

One could argue that it is outdated to speak of "women in the Bible"; rather, it is now more common to speak of "gender in the Bible." To pull out "women in the Bible" draws attention to the fact that, even now, "male" is the normal, unmarked, unremarkable category. The norm. "Gender in the Bible" helps us to avoid reinforcing the masculine as normative and the feminine as some of kind of noteworthy exception to the norm. I want to avoid gender "essentialism," the idea that each gender is marked by inherent and distinctive traits or characteristics.

I find it curious that many books (including excellent ones that I adduce in this work) try to categorize ancient women: *Helpmates, Harlots, and Heroes* or *Goddesses, Whores, Wives and Slaves*, for example. There appears to be no urge to categorize men in this way. Such categorizing risks presenting females (in the literary texts and historical record) as flat, stereotyped characters without individuality.

Gender is a social construct. As Hylen explains: "What it means to be male or female is not a biologically given category that endures through time but is constructed by culture, often with political, social, and religious ramifications. In every culture, people make sense of their experiences and the world around them, and in doing so they construct understandings of what it means to be male or female" (*Women in the New Testament World*, 7). That

7

fact raises a question about where the category "women" fits into the LGBTQIA+ conversations about gender identity and performance, biological sex, and so on. (If such terms are new to you, consult the glossary in *A Brief Guide to Ministry with LGBTQIA Youth* by Cody J. Sanders.) For instance, we will find that God, Jesus, Paul, and the male disciples are depicted in categories that cross traditional gender notions; that is not to say, however, that the ancients did not have binary notions of male and female identity. In this book, we will understand the texts from the perspectives of the ancient authors and culture as well as raise questions related to our own contemporary appropriation of these texts.

To speak of "women" is to speak of gender and sexuality and personhood. It is to speak of procreation and family structures and social structures and embodiment and incarnation and choices and power (and lack thereof) and economics and race and ethnicity and anything else that pertains to the human condition. That's a tall order.

2. What about "Women in the Bible"?

The next issue is one of scope and focus. On the one hand, there are many women in the Bible—usually where we expect them, sometimes where we might not. There are hundreds of named and unnamed women in the Bible, and it would be impossible to treat them all. The indexes of named and unnamed women in the excellent *CEB Women's Bible* list 344 women (178 named, 166 unnamed). In choosing what to present, I must also choose what not to present, necessarily excluding other fascinating material.

On the other hand, women are missing, and the missing women should matter as much as the present women. None of the twelve named disciples is female. No females are depicted at the transfiguration, the Last Supper, or the Garden of Gethsemane. The story of the prodigal son names no females—was there no mother, were there no sisters? The special 144,000 in Revelation are all virgin males ("these who have not defiled themselves with women," 14:4). And Matthew tells us that the women and children at the feeding of the "five thousand" did not count, literally: "And the ones who ate were about five thousand men [*anēr*], not including [*chōris*] women and children" (14:21, my trans.). I am somewhat tempted to call this book *Women in the Bible . . . and Not.*

8

In addition to so much material to address in the biblical texts themselves, there are also now many good, useful books on women in the Bible. I direct the reader to a number of them. Given the availability of these resources, I have chosen to shape this volume according to the specific goals I provide in this chapter without trying to accomplish what has already been achieved elsewhere.

3. Nature of the Evidence

The type of evidence available presents challenges for those desiring a full picture of women's lives in biblical times. First, most of the evidence tells us only what elite men thought or imagined about women's lives, if they thought about them at all. It assumes certain notions of what constitutes an "ideal" woman for a given social context. When we do find the rare piece of evidence from a woman herself, it usually comes from a woman of the elite echelons of society. We have almost no direct evidence from the lives of ordinary women and only scant from elite women. Thus there is no easy answer to the common question "What was it like to be a woman in the biblical period?" It depended, in part, on a woman's social location—was she a wife, a widow, a slave, a queen, a judge, or an "ordinary woman"? We will consider women in those different categories.

Second, scholars do not all agree in their construal of the evidence. Third, we are working across a number of centuries, especially with respect to the Old Testament period, which covers about fifteen hundred years. Social conditions and norms can change over time, potentially altering some aspects of women's lives.

4. Audience

The danger of writing a book called *Women in the Bible* is that potential readers may think that the book is primarily for women. While it is primarily *about* women, the book is *for* everyone. I do not want this only to be a book by a woman, for women, about women; rather, I want people of all genders to use it. Material related to women or the feminine, like material related to other genders, should be considered a resource for addressing the "human" condition. Surely men are to imitate the behavior of faithful women, like the widow with her mite, the Canaanite woman, and the Samaritan

9

woman. As Ruth Fox avers: "Just as men are held up as spiritual models for women (how many sermons have we heard on the faith of Peter?), so, too, men's spirituality is enriched and aided with feminine patterns of holiness" (1999, 366).

Women have been using their "analogical imaginations" for centuries now. That is, they take material specifically addressed to men and translate it into their own lives. For instance, the Gospel of Matthew praises those who are "eunuchs for the kingdom" (19:12, my trans.). Eunuchs are castrated males. But women have worked by analogy to read this as a call to celibacy, which they have answered over the centuries. Are male readers also willing to use their analogical imaginations?

Structure of the Book

I begin the book by using Matthew 15 to display a variety of hermeneutical methods and considerations relevant to this project as a whole. It's an invitation into a world of rich conversations and a chance to turn the text around and around as if it were a diamond in the light in order to see the various facets. Then I move to God, consideration and experience of whom undergirds the whole interpretive process. I especially focus upon the ways God moves across gender in our Scriptures. Next I address a perennial issue for Scripture readers and people living in every age—women and violence. It was not an easy chapter to write, and I imagine it won't be the easiest to read. I kindly ask the reader, however, to stay with me through the "Women and Violence" chapter; I promise you will be rewarded and refreshed by the "Women Creating" chapter that immediately follows. Next, I address the book of Ruth as an example of one of books of the Bible named after a female. The complexities and beauty of life and relationships present themselves, with special attention to the relationships about women therein. Next I turn to the women who appear in Jesus's life and ministry, along with consideration of the ways that Jesus himself (and sometimes his disciples) moves across gender at certain places in our Scriptures. Likewise, I write about the women in Paul's life and ministry and the ways that he, too, is presented as one whose capacities defy ancient gender concepts. Finally, I explore the deutero-Pauline texts as they relate to the topic of women in the Bible.

In the spirit of Ralph Waldo Emerson's declaration that "a foolish consistency is the hobgoblin of little minds," I have not sought to subject the book or individual chapters to a contrived consistency. Rather, I have presented the content that I think is most useful laid out in an order that I think is most useful. Ideally, the reader would read the book in order from start to finish; however, I've tried to write the book in a way that would enable a person preaching or teaching in a specific area to use a relevant chapter on its own.

Assumptions about My Readers

You are people who are well-read and love learning. If you are clergy, you have probably gone to seminary. If you are a lay leader, you are that person who always goes deeper into the complexity of a subject. All of you care about the gospel of Jesus Christ and pray that God's will be done, on earth as it is in heaven. That is a big ask. But you have been called to work toward that vision and equipped to do so by God, Christ, and the Holy Spirit. Scripture is no small part of that equation. How might attention to women in the Bible help us to discern and enact God's will on earth, as it is in heaven?

You have been taught to consider both what the text *meant* in its original sociohistorical context, by its original author, for the original audience, and also what the text *means* today for the church in the world. You live in a time in which you and your community have unprecedented access to an overwhelming amount of information. It used to be that you could simply rely on the standard commentaries, written by a single author, from a single perspective, usually employing the historical-critical method undergirded by modernist assumptions. Notice that most commentaries in a library reference room are by males. Now you work in a postmodern context in which a plethora of methodologies have yielded new questions and approaches and insights, and voices from across the globe have entered the conversation.

You are tasked with helping others navigate a complex world where politics, religion, gender, sexuality, economics, race, technology, and global forces factor into everyday lives. The moral issues you address are weighty: sex trafficking, reproductive rights, end-of-life decisions, proper use of technology, pluralism, war, care for the least of these, the alien and sojourner in your land.

11

You do not have the luxury of burying your head in the sand and pretending that we live in "a simpler time" (if we ever did) and a small world where everyone thinks like "we" do. Your guidance and preaching and teaching are needed more than ever as unprecedented numbers of people have no knowledge of or connection to the life-giving power and genius that the Bible holds—wisdom from the ages, both pain and promise, breathtaking failures and astonishing moments of mystery and redemption.

The Lectionary

When we Christians gather for worship, how often do we hear biblical texts related to women? If one comes from a tradition that does not use a lectionary, the pastor chooses which texts are heard when the church gathers and can, therefore, choose whether to exclude or include women. It is my hope that pastors who use this book will review how often, in what ways, and to what ends the women of the Bible appear in the church's life with Scripture and will expand the exposure the congregations get to the wide variety of women who appear in our canon.

On the other hand, if one does follow a lectionary, one may encounter some women, but there are real obstacles to presenting the full picture of women in the canon.

The Challenge of the Lectionary

In the biblical text, women are rarely central in the stories, compared to men. The problem is exacerbated by the lectionary tradition. In this book I refer to both the Revised Common Lectionary (RCL) used by Protestants and the Roman Lectionary (RL) used by Catholics. The lectionaries differ.

J. Frank Henderson's *Remembering the Women: Women's Stories from Scripture for Sundays and Festivals* is a great starting point for an in-depth review of problems with the lectionary. It provides some history of the lectionary (both the RL and the RCL), especially as it pertains to the presence and absence of women's stories therein. Women's stories are more absent than present, to the detriment of both women and men whose faith lives are shaped by the liturgy of the church. This absence of women includes the following:

12

1. Including only a limited selection of the "women's books," especially in Sunday readings
2. Omitting many stories of the Bible that feature women
3. Omitting verses featuring women from passages used as lectionary readings
4. Listing some passages that feature women only as "optional" or "alternative" readings

Other problems with the presentation of women in the lectionary relate to how women are portrayed in biblical passages and whether their inclusion or exclusion from the lectionary is helpful or dangerous. When negative stories about women are included and positive stories omitted, surely this inhibits the celebration of women in ministry doing the work of God and reinforces negative stereotypes about women. On the other hand, if some of the Bible's challenging passages about women are omitted from the lectionaries—and especially Sunday readings—when will the corporate body of believers ever deal with these difficult passages, speaking honestly about the harm they have done and can do? Will believers simply have to decide how to interpret such texts on their own?

Solutions for the Problems with the Lectionary

To help solve the problem of women's absence from the lectionaries, Henderson's book is arranged according to the logic of the lectionaries (which is explained in detail in the introduction). Women's stories that already are part of the lectionary are capitalized upon and expanded. Those that have been omitted are now included, according to a set of four principles:

1. Stories taken from the same biblical book or closely related material from other books
2. Theological relationships with the festival or season
3. Passages that employ feminine images of God
4. Passages that refer to holy Wisdom

The book provides an appendix with excerpts from some psalms that use feminine images of God. Another appendix is an index of Scripture readings in three columns. Column 1 lists the Scripture readings in canonical order. Column 2 names the Sunday

13

or festival on which *Remembering the Women* suggests use of the passage. Column 3 shows the relationship with the RL and RCL (and, on occasion, other lectionaries). A third appendix includes three essential essays related to women in the lectionary by Jean Campbell, OSH; Ruth Fox, OSB; and Eileen Schuller, OSU. In their essays, Fox and Schuller suggest the following ways to include more women in Christian engagement of the Bible (1–4 below are in Fox, "Women in the Bible," 366):

1. Choose to read the long versions of the Gospel.
2. Preach on the full text, including omitted texts.
3. Use texts including women on other occasions. For example, if anointing the sick, read from the story of the woman anointing Jesus. When commissioning music ministers, use the example of Miriam or Judith leading singing.
4. Open and close meetings with Esther or Judith's prayers or portions of the Magnificat.
5. Expand opportunities for Bible study. "The Sunday readings at Mass can never be the only context in which we experience the Bible. There is a real need for small group Bible study, catechetical and adult-learning programs to provide an arena for people to explore the full scope of what the Bible says about women; here we can bring our own experiences to interact with the text in ways which are not possible with the parameters of the Sunday eucharist" (Schuller, "Women in the Lectionary," 373).

In addition to reading the essays in *Remembering the Women*, I recommend that the reader who wants to counter the problems with the lectionary learn what is excluded or relegated to a basically unheard status. Make use of resources that mind the gap for you, such as *WomenPsalms* and *In Her Own Rite*. In preaching and teaching, engage difficult texts about women creatively and by pairing them with positive texts. Speak boldly about what is excluded—whether those texts have positive or negative images— to reinforce life-giving perspectives about women in the Bible and beyond.

In this volume, I direct readers to material related to women in the Bible so that they can choose to present those passages in sermons and liturgical events. That is, I highlight material already in the lectionary. In addition, I present some of the important women or aspects of womanhood in the Bible that are excluded from the lectionary. This two-way method should, God willing, make it easier for those who lead worship or education to find ways to include more of the material related to women in the Bible in the life of the church and in their own personal study.

Conclusion: Truth, with Hope

Of all the women in the Bible, Pollyanna is not one of them. So in the pages that follow, I aim to have an honest conversation with you about what kinds of things the Bible says and does not say about women; who is present and who is absent; what the text actually says and what interpreters have said it says. I want to provide information and point you to some excellent resources for further study. In many ways, I want to stoke your imagination and inspire you to come at the subject from a variety of angles, each yielding different fruit for different seasons. It will have to be done in a representative, not exhaustive, fashion, of course.

If I am successful, you may learn something new about particular women or groups of women in the Bible; more importantly, I hope that you will be equipped to imaginatively consider these women from more angles than you might have before and, as a result, that the scriptural text will spark your imaginations about how we might live better, more just (or righteous) lives today. I suppose I consider myself the scribe of whom Jesus speaks in Matthew 13:52: "Therefore every scribe who has been trained for the kingdom of heaven is like the master of a household who brings out of his treasure what is new and what is old." Something old, something new—may you find some of each in the pages that follow.

Recommended Resources

Ahlers, Julia, Rosemary Broughton, and Carl Koch, compilers. 1992. *WomenPsalms*. Winona, MN: St. Mary's Press.

Baughman, Rachel, Christine Chakoian, Jaime Clark-Soles, Judy Fentress-Williams, and Ginger Gaines-Cirelli, eds. 2016. *The CEB Women's Bible*. Nashville: Abingdon Press.

Henderson, J. Frank, compiler. 1998. *Remembering the Women: Women's Stories from Scripture for Sundays and Festivals*. 2nd ed. Chicago: Liturgy Training Publications.

Hylen, Susan. 2019. *Women in the New Testament World*. Essentials of Biblical Studies. Oxford: Oxford University Press.

Procter-Smith, Marjorie. 2000. *In Her Own Rite: Constructing Feminist Liturgical Tradition*. 2nd ed. Cape May, NJ: OSL Publications.

Reid, Barbara E., ed. 2015–. Wisdom Commentary series. Collegeville, MN: Liturgical Press.

Sanders, Cody J. 2017. *A Brief Guide to Ministry with LGBTQIA Youth*. Louisville, KY: Westminster John Knox Press.

CHAPTER 1

Of Canaanites and Canines

Matthew 15

So many passages in the Bible are relevant to our topic that it is impossible to cover each one or even all possible interpretations of a single passage. However, I want readers to have a sense of the variety of approaches that are available to a contemporary interpreter. There isn't a single "right" answer for a given passage, so the task isn't to make one correct interpretation. Rather, we readers can learn to make various interpretive decisions, understanding that we might revisit and revise those conclusions at a later reading.

The story of the Canaanite woman in Matthew 15:21–28 admits of polyvalent interpretation to a stunning degree. One-fourth of the essays in *The Feminist Companion to Matthew* are devoted to it. In what follows we

- review the story, offering some comments along the way,
- note varieties of interpretations,
- draw conclusions about the significance of the variety of interpretations, and
- tie the chapter into the stated goals of the book.

The Story
17

Immediately preceding this story, Jesus is in Gennesaret (northwest corner of the Sea of Galilee; Matt. 14:34), where he addresses the issue of defilement. It's not what goes into the mouth that defiles but rather what comes out, Jesus says, because "what comes out of the mouth proceeds from the heart" (15:18)—the heart is the gold standard for judging. Notice that the offenses he names, including slander, involve mistreating others. This is something to keep in mind when Jesus calls the woman a dog later in Matthew 15. In the two passages that follow ours, Jesus heals and feeds. His experience with the woman is catalytic.

Jesus leaves Gennesaret and proceeds to the area of Tyre and Sidon, which is significant because that is predominantly Gentile territory. Not only is the woman who approaches Jesus a Gentile, then, but Matthew further labels her a Canaanite, an extremely loaded, if anachronistic, term. The Canaanites were among the most hated enemies of ancient Israel, although there were no longer any "Canaanites" per se in the first century. The term is a slanderous one, a point made more starkly if one compares Matthew's version to its source, Mark, which simply calls her "Syrophoenician." First, as Gail O'Day suggests, Matthew lumps Tyre and Sidon together as a region (Mark mentions them separately in 7:24 and 7:31) to evoke the Old Testament vitriol against Israel's old enemies: "In the prophetic literature of the Old Testament, Tyre and Sidon are more than place names; they were Israel's dangerous and threatening enemies (e.g., Isa. 23; Ezek. 26–28; Joel 3:4)" (O'Day 2001, 115). Second, Matthew employs the Canaanite slur (though Tyre and Sidon were real Gentile places in the first century, unlike Canaan). So, Matthew is maximizing the "unclean Gentile" theme here. The woman is not simply "other"; she is intensely "other."

And she's a loud mother "other." She shouts a command to Jesus using some of Matthew's favorite words: "Have mercy on me, Lord" (*eleēson me, kyrie;* Matt. 15:22). Eight of the fifteen occurrences of "mercy" in the Gospels occur in Matthew (four in Luke; three in Mark; zero in John). And "Lord" is a christological confessional title in Matthew. In fact, often where Mark has someone call Jesus "Teacher," Matthew changes it to "Lord."

Next, the woman calls Jesus "Son of David." Why is this important? Matthew alludes to David and his relationship to Jesus far more than any other Gospel; "Son of David" is one of the most important christological titles in Matthew. So this woman "gets it" with her doubly correct christological confession.

The title "Son of David" links this Canaanite woman to the understanding of Jesus expressed back in Matthew's genealogy, which ties Jesus directly to David, through an ancient *Canaanite woman*—Rahab. That is, Rahab and Salmon begat Boaz; Ruth and Boaz begat Obed; Obed begat Jesse with an unnamed woman; Jesse begat David with an unnamed woman. A lot of begetting, which takes two of course, even though the genealogy focuses on men. That's all the more reason to take note of the exceptional spots where women are named, including the Canaanite Rahab, the foremother of Jesus himself and also, in some ways, the Canaanite woman in the story, given that only Matthew insists that the woman who engages Jesus is a Canaanite. In fact, the genealogy is one of the most important and rich texts in the New Testament for appraising the topic of women in the Bible. (For more on Matthew's genealogy, consult chap. 7, "Women in Jesus's Life and Ministry.") I particularly appreciate Stuart Love's treatment of the ways the genealogy connects to our passage (as well as the ways our passage is inextricably tied to the hemorrhaging woman in Matt. 9). He argues, "The Canaanite woman's story remains a significant memory for the Matthean community. Old external/internal boundaries have been crossed or are being challenged." Further, he asks, "But what can be said about marginal, non-Israelite women in this contentious, polemical, fluid and uncertain period? Does the Canaanite woman's story provide a social transparency of a gender issue being faced by Matthew's community?" (Love 2009, 158). After rehearsing some of the history of scholarly interpretation of the genealogy, Love suggests that the four women in the genealogy have more in common with the Canaanite woman in Matthew 15 than they have in common with Mary. He also asserts:

> We believe the inclusion of these women in the genealogy anticipates the "surprise and scandal" of the Canaanite woman's story. But as in the time of Jesus who as an Israelite healer had difficulty negotiating his own defined boundary limits (only to Israel), so now, the Matthean community must pass through its own boundary taboos by accepting outcast non-Israelite women. Following the model, her example upsets the "order of the social system." (160)

In this view, then, the Canaanite woman represents women who are "out of bounds" in some way and the conversation taking place

19

in Matthew's own late-first-century community about where such women fit into the new community.

After she calls Jesus "Son of David," the NRSV has the Canaanite woman telling Jesus that her daughter is "tormented by a demon" (15:22). That translation does not convey the full force of the language here. "Evilly demonized" would be better. This is deeply harrowing, excruciating language. The adverb (*kakōs*) comes from the adjective that means evil or wicked. The verb (*daimonizomai*) shows that the daughter is a victim who is acted upon; the Greek present tense emphasizes the ongoing nature of the situation such that we could justifiably add the word "constantly." Notice that the woman asks for mercy on herself, not her daughter. Anyone who has watched someone who is their very heart suffer will understand her choice of words. Is there a more heart-wrenching scene in the Bible?

How does Jesus react to the mother's cry for mercy? The text says: "But he did not answer her a word" (15:23, my trans.). Period. While we may want to fill in felt "gaps" here, to do so is to add to the text, and that move should be overtly acknowledged. Jesus remains silent.

How do the disciples react to the mother's cry for mercy? They do not talk *to* her at all; rather, they talk *about* her, presumably right *in front of* her. They, unlike the woman, approach Jesus with no honorific title, just a command of their own: "Send her away." Why? "Because she is [repeatedly] crying out after us" (my trans.).That is the sole reason given. They find her an annoying bother.

Finally, she gets a response from someone: Jesus. He delivers the unfortunate (for her as a Gentile) news: "I was sent only to the lost sheep of the house of Israel" (15:24). When you picture the exchange, is Jesus saying this to the woman, to himself, to the disciples, to some or all of the above? The text does not specify. At any rate, the statement is entirely in keeping with Matthew's understanding of both Jesus's and his disciples' mission, as the reader recalls from Jesus's command to his disciples in 10:5–6: "Go nowhere among the Gentiles, and enter no town of the Samaritans, but go rather to the lost sheep of the house of Israel." Indeed, Matthew's genealogy squarely ties Jesus to Judaism, from King David all the way back to father Abraham. Only Matthew specifies that the child is to be named Jesus because "he will save *his people* from their sins" (1:21; emphasis added). Jesus is a Jewish Messiah for Jewish people.

20

After Jesus's pronouncement, he stops speaking to the woman or about the woman. Nevertheless, she persists. She approaches Jesus, prostrates herself before him (*proskyneō* has a number of meanings, including "worship"), calls him by an honorific title (Lord) again, and issues another imperative from beneath him: "Help me!" (15:25).

The text then says that Jesus answers. Again, it does not specify to whom Jesus is speaking. Is he speaking to her directly or to someone else (the disciples; himself)? Pay attention to what he says: "It is not good to take the children's bread [*artos*] and cast it to the little dogs" (15:26, my trans.). The children are those belonging to the house of Israel. The dogs are non-Jews.

She takes the comment as directed to her and responds, for the third time calling him "Lord." She absorbs the slander of being called a dog and rolls with Jesus's logic in order to defeat his argument: "Yes, Lord [*kyrie*], but even the little dogs eat the scraps of the things that fall from the table of their lords [*kyriōn*]" (15:27, my trans.). Note that the children sit at the table; the proper place for a dog is on the ground, where she is as she says this.

For the first time since the story began, the text notes that Jesus answers her directly. In 15:28 he calls her "Woman" (the only place in Matthew where he does this) and extols her: "Great is your faith!" He then issues a command: "Let it be done for you as you wish." The story ends thus: "And from that hour her daughter was healed [*iaomai*]" (my trans.).

In the chapter before ours, Jesus feeds bread (*artos*) to a multitude and heals many people in his own Jewish territory. Immediately following, the reverse happens— Jesus heads back to his own Jewish territory and heals (*therapeuō*) innumerable people who are at his feet. He also gives them bread (*artos*). Jesus heals many people and then feeds a multitude. This pattern, called chiasm, puts the attention on the center element, C, highlighting it as crucial:

A. Feeding bread to thousands in Galilee

B. Healing many in Galilee

C. Canaanite woman and her daughter in Tyre and Sidon: Who should receive bread and healing?

B1. Healing many in Galilee

A1. Feeding bread to thousands in Galilee

The story is a watershed moment in the narrative where we learn that, in fact, the ministry of Jesus (and the church) extends across boundaries of many sorts.

Traditional Interpretations

Traditional interpretations of this passage fall into the following categories.

1. This Is a Test. It Is Only a Test.

The first line of interpretation sees the episode as Jesus testing the woman's faith and often attempts to downplay Jesus's harshness. According to this approach, Jesus intended all along to respond to her; furthermore, the point is made that Jesus calls her a "little dog," more like a "puppy," such that it is a term of affection. A variation of this approach claims that Jesus is testing the disciples in the episode.

2. Faith as a Prerequisite for Healing

The second approach focuses upon the importance of faith for healing to occur. Jesus praises the woman's faith and grants healing on the basis of her faith. (We return to this line of reasoning in the section on disability below.) Often, her faith is seen as a foil for the lack of faith of the scribes and Pharisees, with whom Jesus is wrangling in this part of the narrative.

3. Jesus Includes Gentiles

In the third approach, "the point" (because many interpretations assume that there can be only one point) is that the woman is a Gentile, and Jesus, unlike the scribes and Pharisees, accepts her as part of the people of God. The eventual inclusion of Gentiles is foreshadowed at certain places in the Gospel, including, perhaps, the genealogy; the arrival of the magi (Zoroastrian priests; Matt. 2); the healing of the centurion's servant (Matt. 8); and the encounter with this woman. The earthly Jesus primarily came to the Jews as the promised Messiah; in this way it can be said that God kept God's covenant with God's elect people. The resurrected Jesus (and his disciples, in his name) have all nations as their scope. This would help Matthew's own church understand and explain why the church has both Jews and Gentiles in it.

Whenever contemporary Christians take up the issue of how Gentiles fit into God's plan of salvation history, it becomes important to notice the potential for the interpretation to go off the rails in a variety of ways, including promoting anti-Semitism. Thus, a brief word is in order. Matthew's own historical context made for a variety of tensions between his church and the surrounding world. Usually thought to be in Syrian Antioch where there was a substantial Jewish community, Matthew's own church contained both Jews and Gentiles near the end of the first century. Presumably, it was *at least* bilingual and bicultural. The first tension exhibited in Matthew, then, is that while Jesus is the fulfillment of the promises to Israel, his chief opponents are from that group. Perhaps Matthew's most vitriolic moment in this regard occurs at 27:25: "Then the people *as a whole* answered, 'His blood be on us and on our children!'" (emphasis added). I imagine that Matthew, himself most likely a Jew speaking to a largely Jewish audience about a Jewish Messiah, would be horrified to discover that his love of hyperbole has resulted in a terrible history of anti-Semitism on the part of Christians over the centuries. Words matter and sometimes have unintended consequences.

How might this play out in some interpretations of Matthew 15:21–28? Let me overstate the case for illustrative purposes. One might argue: "Jews were ethnocentric and did not have dealings with Gentiles, especially Canaanites, the worst of Jewish enemies." Jesus, though a Jew, overcame his "natural" Jewish proclivities toward ethnocentrism and was more expansive and inclusive; he overcame (and dissociated from) his "narrow" Judaism and left it behind to become something totally different—a Gentile-accepting Christian. For a further analysis, I would point the reader to A.-J. Levine's comment:

> Rather than view the narrative as hopelessly colonial or employ it to advance a supersessionist agenda, we might see the woman as another Rahab or Ruth: she recognizes her salvation is with Israel's representative, yet she retains her Canaanite identification; she proves more faithful than insiders (the spies in Jericho; the disciples); and she does what she must to save her family. (2012, 474)

4. The Importance of Humility

In this interpretation the woman's humility, expressed by prostrating herself and allowing the canine slur, gives all Christians a model to live by.

At the granular level within each of these categories, one could include more detail or shades of nuance within these interpretive trajectories. These four, however, provide enough background for our purposes at present. We now turn our attention to newer interpretations.

Newer Interpretations

In most traditional interpretations, Jesus is the protagonist and hero of the story. Where the woman is highlighted, she is often painted as one who is acted upon by Jesus, rather than the one acting upon Jesus. Citing numerous commentaries, Gail O'Day notes: "There seems to be a resistance in scholarship on this text to credit the Canaanite woman with much more than submission to Jesus. . . . Such a view of the Canaanite woman, however, is more determined by preconceptions about the relative positions of Jesus and the woman than by the details of the text itself. This woman does not quietly submit to Jesus, but takes him on directly. Her faith moves beyond stereotypes of female passivity" (2001, 124 n. 24).

Innumerable articles on this passage take a newer interpretive approach, especially since 2000. In what follows, I acquaint the reader with some of the current interpretive trajectories. (If you are looking for a single book that brings you relatively up-to-date on the recent productive lenses through which to view biblical texts, I recommend *Mark & Method: New Approaches to Biblical Studies*, edited by Janice Capel Anderson and Stephen D. Moore, second edition.)

Sample of Feminist Interpretations

Feminist biblical interpretation has led interpreters to investigate the Canaanite woman from new angles. For instance, many would argue that the woman, not Jesus, is the protagonist and hero of the story. She helps Jesus imagine a wider scope for his ministry and thus helps to shape his understanding of his vocation. Countless feminist interpretations have been conducted on this passage; in what follows I sample only a few. Each one is an act of recovering the voice and significance of the woman, who is seen as strong,

24

savvy, and even subversive. These interpretations do not feel a need to "rescue" Jesus from his humanity, and they do not sugarcoat his harsh treatment of the woman.

As if stories involving gender were not complicated enough, ethnicity is a primary factor in the story as well. In fact, if one surveys feminist essays on this passage, one notices stages of interpretation. First are moves of recovery and reinterpretation. Then interpreters notice that the issue is far more complex than gender alone and includes considerations of class, of ethnicity, and, more recently through postcolonial contributions, of empire. Make no mistake—empire is at least as alive and well in our century as it was in Jesus's and Matthew's.

Another move that feminists make in their recovery effort is to take note of who and what information is *not* in the story. Is there a father? How old is the daughter? Is she there? Feminists pay close attention to children (or lack thereof) in the narratives because in antiquity, as now, there was a tight connection between the fate of women and the fate of children. In fact, in two different places just before and just after our passage (the feedings of the five thousand and the four thousand), Matthew overtly states that the women and children, unlike the men, are not even important enough to count:

> And those who ate were about five thousand men, not counting (*chōris*) women and children. (Matt. 14:21, my trans.)

> Those who had eaten were four thousand men, not counting (*chōris*) women and children. (Matt. 15:38, my trans.)

One act of recovery, then, would be to start *counting* and *naming* women in the Bible.

Megan McKenna writes about this issue in her book *Not Counting Women and Children: Neglected Stories from the Bible*:

> "Not counting women and children." People react to that phrase in different ways—some with laughter, others with anger, sadness, or disgust. Especially when read aloud, that phrase hangs suspended in the air, like bait on a hook for a fish. One person responds, "I feel excluded." Another complains, "Women and children are put in the same category." Such responses are countered, "But we are all the children of God" (theological reaction to emotion). Or, "But they all were fed and everyone was satisfied, full."

25

> ... It is amazing that in a culture where we characterize men as the dominant group—and men are still dominant in the church in many ways—that that line is even in the text.... Furthermore, sociologists say that when you gather a crowd of men, women, and children, the ratio of women and children to men can be as high as five or six to one. *So, the story is really the feeding of the thirty-five thousand!* (1994, 7–8; italics added)

Thus if we are going to count honestly, let's start calling this feeding story "The Feeding of the Thirty-Five Thousand." In all of these stories about handing out divine bread—Matthew 15 and the feeding miracles—the women and children stand on the margins.

The Woman as a Paradigm of Faith

New interpretations of the Bible also note that, in addition to being charged with the care of children (usually without pay), women have historically been tasked with caring for the ill as well (usually without pay). Matthew 15, then, features a woman suffering a double burden—caring for a child who is ill. If there is no male provider, she is further disadvantaged. In this story, she attempts to get help from some powerful males, and that becomes, in large part, a harrowing experience of humiliation.

Like the woman with the flow of blood in Matthew 9, the Canaanite woman is unnamed and not explicitly tied to a male. Her social standing is not given. Is she what we would call a single mother? Martina Gnadt sees the woman as a proselyte or God-fearer, because she knows and subscribes to the traditions of the Jews (Son of David, etc.). She is said to have great (*megas*) faith. Conversely, the disciples are designated as having "little" faith (*oligopistos*).

> The woman sees more than Jesus does. ... In contrast to Jesus, the woman has an inclusive vision of the wholeness God offers, and she holds it fast in the face of persistent attempts to get rid of her—and in the end she is proven right. Jesus makes a fundamental change in his attitude. He has been shown the better way. ... What is so striking about this story is that here Jesus is espousing a position that in the course of the discussion is shown to be "short on faith" and is overcome. That confers authority on the woman's point of view. It cannot be set aside without further

ado. On the contrary, it has such an inner weight that it must be wrestled with. (Gnadt 2012, 622)

In this interpretation, the woman is a paradigm of faith to be emulated whose persistence and courage benefit many, including at least her daughter, Jesus, the disciples, the early church, and us, the contemporary readers.

A Jewish Lament

O'Day's treatment of Matthew 15:21–28 focuses upon three aspects of the story: (a) the irony of the Canaanite woman as the quintessential Jew in the narrative; (b) the way the woman shapes Jesus; and (c) how the reader might be shaped by the narrative. Irony is subversive in its own way.

O'Day seeks to show that our passage "is a *narrative embodiment of a lament psalm*" (2001, 119). In the lament psalms (such as Ps. 13), Israel boldly approaches God in the midst of her pain, need, and despair and implores God to rise to the occasion of assisting her, to remain actively faithful to the promises made long ago. O'Day analyzes the eight moves made in a traditional lament psalm, starting with address and concluding with praise. She then maps the story of the Canaanite woman onto this model and argues that, ironically, it's the Canaanite woman who plays the role of Israel in her bold entreaty and her faithful conviction that she deserves to be helped and that she will be helped by the Lord. "This Canaanite woman is more faithful, indeed, more authentically Jewish, than many of the Jews whom Jesus encounters. She is a fuller embodiment of Jewish traditions than Jesus's own disciples who want to dismiss her because she is a foreigner and an irritant. . . . She is not a Jew; she is, nevertheless, fully Jewish" (124).

O'Day stresses not only that the woman is a Gentile female, but, again, even a Canaanite. Furthermore, her faith is anything but submissive. On the contrary, "Jesus was changed by this woman's boldness. . . . She insists that Jesus be Jesus, and through her insistence she frees him to be fully who he is." O'Day concludes by calling us readers to, "like Jesus himself, listen to her and be transformed through a faith like hers: persistent, vigorous, and confident in God's faithfulness to God's promises" (2001, 125; for

27

a similar interpretation of this passage in Mark's Gospel, consult Pablo Alonso, *The Woman Who Changed Jesus*, esp. 287–343).

Introducing Justa

Elaine Wainwright's passion for this passage shows in the fact that she has reconsidered it from various angles over her career. (Consult, for example: *Shall We Look for Another?*; "The Gospel of Matthew"; and "Not Without My Daughter.") She reminds us of the importance of naming, reclaiming, and remembering. For her, Matthew evinces numerous tensions. First, Matthew presents Jesus as being in tension with his own tradition. Jesus is the fulfillment of promises made to Israel, but he is opposed by the leaders of Israel who seek to kill him. As seen earlier, at one point "all" of Jerusalem cries out, "His blood be on us and our children" (Matt. 27:25).

Second, there is ethnic tension in the Gospel of Matthew. On the one hand, Jesus came to make disciples of all nations (*ethnē*; Matt. 28:19). On the other hand, he says he came only to the lost sheep of the house of Israel. This tension inheres not only in the Gospel of Matthew as a whole, but also in our passage.

Third, there is gender tension:

> The tension is also visible, on the other hand, in relation to gender, which is the significant concern in this commentary. Indications have already been given of the inclusion of women within the *basileia* vision and praxis of Jesus. Yet the Matthean Gospel constructs a symbolic universe that is androcentric and encodes the patriarchal constructs present in its sociohistorical location. The text creates a world in which the male norm is coterminous with the human, and this presupposition finds expression in the grammatical and narrative strategies of the text resulting in the marginalization of women. (Wainwright 1997, 637)

The use of masculine language and examples (sons, fathers, men, brothers) obscures women and makes the male the norm for discipleship. Only four women appear in Matthew's genealogy; that is, they are "exceptions." Jerome calls them sinners, and Luther calls them outsiders. So, not only Matthew, but also later interpreters obscure the place of women in Jesus's ministry.

In her essay "Not Without My Daughter: Gender and Demon Possession in Matthew 15.21–28," Wainwright highlights the importance of naming. She insists that we should refer to the Canaanite woman as Justa, the name given her in the afterlife of the story:

> The *Pseudo-Clementine Epistles* give the name "Justa" to the Canaanite woman. I have chosen to use this name throughout this paper in order that in the reclamation of this story, the naming of the woman may lead to her story being remembered in contemporary Christian telling of the story. Unnamed characters tend to be forgotten more easily than those who have been given names, and female characters in the gospel story, especially; named female characters are fewer than named male characters. The naming of women characters, especially when that naming belongs within the Christian tradition, can assist in bringing them to the center of the Christian re-membering. (Wainwright 2001, 126 n. 2)

Wainwright turns to an analysis of the daughter by attending to the interconnection of gender and ethnicity. She determines that demon-possession, which is more prevalent in Greco-Roman sources than Jewish, does not tend to be gendered. While the healer/exorcist is usually male, the afflicted person can be either gender. What stands out in Matthew is that those who have a demon exorcised from them and are then declared as healed using the Greek word *iaomai* (as in our case) are Gentiles. That is, this is the same word used for the centurion's servant in Matthew 8. Thus the focus on the *ethnicity* of Justa and her daughter stands out.

Woman Wisdom

Stuart Love connects the Canaanite woman to Israel's wisdom tradition through the ideal woman of Proverbs 31 as well as Ruth. He treats each figure in turn. He argues in reference to the Canaanite woman:

> She, too, should be given "an everlasting name" as a foreigner who honors the God of Israel even if her status is that of a liminal person. She, like the women of the genealogy, wise women in their life settings, courageously speaks and behaves as a capable, worthy woman whose strength is manifest in her persistence with Jesus. Wisdom is seen in her behavior. . . . Wisdom is revealed in her language. There is no other such example in Matthew. . . .

29

She is a capable, worthy, and wise person who teaches Jesus. (Love 2009, 161–62)

Given that Matthew depicts Jesus himself in terms of Woman Wisdom in Matthew 11:28–30 (consult chap. 8, "Jesus across Gender"), interpreting the Canaanite woman within that trajectory elevates her and her powerful witness to the gospel in the Gospel.

Critique from Jewish Feminists

Jewish feminists take issue with some Christian feminist interpretations of the passage as anti-Jewish on a number of counts. They argue that it is wrong (a) to present Judaism as particularly biased against women, Gentiles, and the sick (as impure) and (b) then to depict Jesus as uniquely "overcoming" the biases of his native Judaism. It leaves the impression that Judaism and Christianity were both in existence at the time of Jesus (they were not) and that Jesus was more a Christian than a Jew. That is, it inappropriately suggests that all the "bad" behaviors or motivations ascribed in Matthew to characters such as the scribes and Pharisees (for example) are representative of Judaism, while Jesus goes against his native Judaism when he interacts graciously with women, Gentiles, and ill people (for more on this topic, consult Gnadt 2012, 621).

Amy-Jill Levine raises some questions along these lines:

> Some readers understand the woman as the (postcolonial) Christian who must subjugate herself and her culture to obtain the West's benefits. For others, the story shows Jesus moving beyond the ideology of chosenness, to embrace (Christian) universalism. However, chosenness need not be an oppressive ideology: it is precisely that ideology that helps groups persevere despite persecution, and it is how the church saw itself. . . . Also, Jesus does not insist that the woman become Jewish to receive the healing. This is an ironic difference from the so-called universalism of those claiming salvation only through Jesus. Rather than view the narrative as hopelessly colonial or employ it to advance a supersessionist agenda, we might see the woman as another Rahab or Ruth: she recognizes her salvation is with Israel's representative, yet she retains her Canaanite identification; she proves more faithful than insiders (the spies in Jericho; the disciples); and she does what she must to save her family. (2012, 474)

LGBTQIA+ Readings

Women are not the only minoritized group who find hope in this passage. For LGBTQIA+ interpreters, the story inspires in at least two ways. First, those who are currently marginalized as "outsiders" are encouraged to fight for inclusion: "A queer interpretation of this story remembers that often the Christian Church, like Jesus in the story, is reluctant to give queer folk our just deserts; frequently queer activists must resort to extraordinary means to get a hearing" (Bohache 2006, 513).

Second, the Canaanite woman models Acting Up. (Here I allude to the ACT UP movement, AIDS Coalition to Unleash Power, an advocacy group that operated in legal, medical, and social realms.) The woman's assertive faith leads to inclusive justice for all of God's children. Thus, in addition to calling for bold activism on behalf of the marginalized, the story shows that Jesus himself ordains inclusivity beyond our (and originally his) wildest imaginations. "A queering of Matthew sees hope in this radical inclusivity that pushes the justice of God beyond human conventions and comfort levels and will thus even overcome the predisposition of many toward intolerance and homophobia" (Bohache 2006, 513).

We could multiply examples of minoritized readings, but at this point the reader can see the interpretive strategies involved, which include pressing the Christian community in all times and places to widen the net of inclusion.

Postcolonial Readings

Postcolonial critics have much to work with in this passage. (Warren Carter has done much good work on postcolonial criticism as it illuminates the New Testament, especially the Gospels. Consult his *Matthew and Empire.* For a general primer, consult Carter's *The Roman Empire and the New Testament.*) In both Jesus's and Matthew's time, Palestine was occupied by Rome. Rome crucified Jesus (and many other Jews as well). After Jesus died but before the Gospel of Matthew appeared, Rome burnt the Jewish Second Temple to the ground and expelled the Jews from Jerusalem. In addition to operating under Gentile Roman rule (no matter where the Gospel of Matthew was composed), Matthew's community had to address ethnic tensions in its midst between Jews and Gentiles. How is a

Christian community supposed to relate to the government at any given moment? How is a Christian community supposed to define its boundaries and establish its identity, especially when it is at odds with both its parent tradition (Judaism) and the ruling government? How does one live in and for God's empire while Caesar and his systems are alive and well?

How is Matthew's community a subversive community with a counternarrative? Caesar Augustus claimed to be a divine savior who brought healing, salvation, and peace (*Pax Romana*); the whole system, of course, was built on power, violence, injustice, and oppression. Christians told a counternarrative about a Messiah who brought *true* healing, salvation, and peace. Part of that involved healing stories. Thomas Bohache notes: "A postcolonial reading of Matthew sees his exorcisms as a way of overcoming the evils of imperialism and colonialism that seem incurable" (2006, 512). For most of the history of scholarship, interpretation has been done by Western males. With the rise of feminism, female Western voices were added. Finally, we are hearing from global voices, many of whom have lived under imperial rule. They have shed new light on the ways the Gospels resist and undermine empire and the ways they inadvertently collude with and propagate the values of Caesar.

I have preached on Matthew 15:21–28 a number of times from various angles and find it endlessly fascinating. I also used it as a test case for an exercise in "the politics of biblical interpretation" in *Engaging the Word*. In that chapter I touch on various interpretive lenses and wrote this concerning aspects of postcolonial interpretation:

> The passage is rich with potential for postcolonial analysis as it is rife with political, economic, racial, and ethnic boundary issues. Clearly Israel is privileged in this story, and the unnamed woman is painted as the "undeserving other," a foreigner (even though Jesus is outside of his own country), someone who is "lesser than." She brings nothing to the table; Jesus deigns to provide a handout from his abundance. It's not enough, apparently, for Matthew to call her a Gentile; rather, he designates her a "Canaanite." This is, of course, a historical anachronism since the Canaanites lived many centuries ago and were driven out (killed, assimilated) by the imperializing conquerors, in this case the Israelites. Hence, to call the woman a Canaanite is to further degrade and marginalize her. Furthermore, Jesus tells her flat out that his power and

product is to be used to benefit *only* those of his own nation. This should not surprise the reader since he has already told the disciples in the Missionary Discourse of chapter 10 to "Go nowhere among the Gentiles, and enter no town of the Samaritans, but go rather to the lost sheep of the house of Israel" (10:6).

Not only is this woman not a member of the "house of Israel," she also is male-less, which in her culture (and perhaps in most cultures today) leaves her exceedingly vulnerable. Without a male, there's no money; without money, there's little access to health care. Without a male of her own, a woman is often left no choice but to get on her knees and throw herself upon the mercy of another male. How terrifying, then, when Jesus, the foreign male she is desperately and shamefully begging from (and not even for her own sake but for the sake of one even more vulnerable than she, a female child), first rebuffs her with silence. What does his silence mean? Will he harm her, kick her as she's down in the dirt debasing herself, groveling, making herself as small as possible so that he is bigger and taller and can look down upon her as she piles up honorific titles fit for an emperor or a king (note the reference to David)? Will he simply ignore her and thereby destroy her last hope?

As if that weren't threatening enough, now a whole pack of males (Jesus' disciples) turn against her, and Jesus makes the comment about his patriotism to Israel. Still, she presses on, having nothing left to lose. Jesus then makes another racial slur that literally dehumanizes her. Israelites are children; her kind are mere curs. Sometimes interpreters try to soften Jesus' words by noting that the diminutive form of the word dog is used here. But as one scholar said, there's not a lot of difference between "bitch" and "little bitch" (Levine 2001, 32). The context in which Jesus makes the comment is polemical, not warm and cuddly. Another commentator notes: "'[D]og' was an insult in the earliest extant pagan tradition, as was its female derivative form. . . . Dogs were known for their attachment to dung and sniffing other dogs' rear ends . . . ; more commonly they were linked with birds as scavengers that devoured unburied corpses" (Keener 2009, 416–17).

For the sake of her daughter, she absorbs the slur and even adopts it so as to protect herself and her daughter. She has no power and is in an extremely compromising situation—now is not the time to fight back.

But as a matter of fact, she is fighting back by "using the master's tools to dismantle his house." Hers is a subversive approach, and women worldwide as well as groups like African Americans

33

who were enslaved in America have been relying on such techniques for centuries. And sometimes it works. By the end of this story, this woman has taught Jesus a lesson about his own identity and mission that even he himself didn't know (let alone his ill-mannered disciples), that his mission was broader than he had realized. Jesus, it turns out, is not a flat literary character; he develops, with her help. Her grit and wit literally saved her and her daughter. She is the only hero in the story. You might say she is a protofeminist. (Clark-Soles 2010, 145–46, revised slightly)

Disability Studies

Disability studies has taught us to ask other good questions as we interpret biblical texts and seek to learn how they might inform our current lived reality. Continuing from the section in *Engaging the Word* that began above, I wrote:

Women and children have always been disproportionately represented among the poor. Women still do the majority of the world's labor and own hardly any of the world's goods. In this story, gender, race, ethnicity, culture, politics, and disability intertwine. The woman has a sick child and seems to have no one to rely on. Women tend to be assigned the care of those who are sick, thus further inhibiting their ability to sustain a profitable job that could lead to independence and agency. In this story, the daughter is said to be "tormented by a demon." Disability theorists would have us unpack this. What did it mean in its own context? Certainly ancient medical models have little in common with current ones. Does she have a sickness, an illness, a disease (these are not synonyms)? Is this a physical ailment? A mental illness? Is it a short-term or chronic condition? Does it incapacitate the daughter such that she cannot easily be integrated into society, be a "productive" citizen, hold a job, or have a family? How old is this daughter? Can she worship with her community, or must she remain sequestered according to her society's mores?

Just as the language of illness is debated, so is the language of health. What does it mean to be healed or cured? How is that different from being saved, if at all? When the woman with the issue of blood was made well in Matthew 9:22, Matthew uses the Greek word *sōzō*, typically translated as "save." Indeed, Jesus was to be named "Jesus" because he was to "save [*sōzō*] his people from their sins" (Matt. 1:21). Why, then, do we hear in 15:28 that the woman's daughter was "cured" (Greek: *iaomai*)? Was there something different about the result of the miracle in chapter 9 versus chapter 15? Furthermore, can one be saved without being cured? Can one be both "whole" and disabled? Is the language literal, metaphorical, both? How did her being healed affect her life on the ground—her relationships with friends, enemies, family; her sense of self; her identity; her relationship with God; her place in her religious community; her place in her society and its economy? And, importantly, what does her story teach us to ask about our own context with respect to persons with disabilities? (Clark-Soles 2010, 146–47)

While Elaine Wainwright began to explore exorcism and healing in terms of health care, the full force of that line of questioning was not to come until postcolonialism and disability studies further developed, which they have enormously since Wainwright wrote and even since I wrote the above in 2010. We now have the excellent *The Bible and Disability: A Commentary* (Melcher, Parsons, and Yong 2017). Disability studies teaches us to ask a number of new questions. (For those who regularly preach, I recommend Kathy Black, *A Healing Homiletic*. In addition, I highly recommend taking advantage of the resources provided by the Institute on Theology and Disability; consult the Collaborative on Faith and Disabilities, https://faithanddisability.org.)

As part of the good news that the kingdom of God has come near in Jesus, the Gospels narrate numerous stories of miraculous cures. While healing is a worthy goal of Christian practice, to be celebrated whenever and wherever it occurs, the cure stories are not necessarily unmitigated good news for faithful people who live with chronic disabilities. As Kerry Wynn notes: "The two most common assumptions in popular theology that marginalize people with disabilities are (1) disability is caused by sin, and (2) if one has enough faith, one will be healed" (2007, 61). In our passage Jesus says: "Woman, great is your faith! Let it be done for you as you wish." We are then told, "And her daughter was healed instantly" (Matt. 15:28). Did the healing of the daughter depend upon the faith of the mother? What about those who are not healed—do they or their advocates simply not have enough faith? Does the burden of healing rest upon the afflicted individual and their family, or is the situation more complex than that?

Matthew 15 as a Model of Allyship

In her essay "Enemies, Romans, Pigs, and Dogs: Loving the Other in the Gospel of Matthew," Love Sechrest writes as a "female African American NT [New Testament] scholar who is well read on the dynamics of race and gender in American society" (2015, 71). Through her work, she aims to "construct a Christian ethic of allyship" (73). Though the language of "allies" arose in the context of LGBT activism, it applies to other instances in which a person from the majority group works to end the oppression of minority populations. In terms of race in America, allyship entails whites, who constitute the powerful majority, working to interrupt racism and eradicate oppression of people of color.

How does Matthew help us? Sechrest first addresses Matthew's ambiguous attitude toward Gentiles. She assumes that Matthew writes from a Jewish perspective that reflects the tensions found in the Old Testament "with respect to ancient Israelite ethnocentrism on the one hand and a welcome of outsiders through conversion on the other hand" (83). Sechrest also assumes that the author of Matthew was "ethnically Jewish" (83 n. 58). Matthew evinces positive examples of Gentiles, including the magi (2:1–12); the Roman centurion (8:5–13); the Canaanite woman (15:21–28); and the Roman soldiers who confess at the cross (27:54). On the other hand, there are passages that derogate Gentiles. Having presented concerns from Jewish feminists above, it is appropriate to include these words of Sechrest here: "Jesus's encounter with the Canaanite woman . . . triggers a firestorm of protest about sexism and hierarchy and ethnic discourse. Interpreters recoil at the evangelist's portrait of a woman who seems to participate in her own denigration, while other readers resent the subtle anti-Semitism that emerges when critics label Jesus's behavior as racist and then suggest that it was typical of Jewish thought of the time" (86).

Sechrest depicts Matthew's sociohistorical milieu as a community pressured from all sides: Gentile persecution in Syrian Antioch; conflict with Pharisees in the wake of the Jewish War; and pressure to accept local Gentile converts into a Torah-observant mission. Thus, Sechrest operates from the assumption that Matthew is a Torah-observant Jew who is faced with the challenge of inviting into his community those who had traditionally opposed him and his community, including neighboring Gentiles as well as the Gentile occupying government of Rome. Thus Matthew's willingness to depict a Roman centurion and a Canaanite woman, both traditional enemies of Israel, as persons who model faithful Christian discipleship is astonishing.

These are the only two Gentiles in the Gospel who converse with Jesus. In a poignant statement, Sechrest notes that the Canaanite woman represents the "old" enemy and the centurion the "new" enemy—enemies all the same: "the Canaanite and the centurion are both enemies who reach out to Jesus for grace across the lines of profound enmity" (2015, 97).

> The Roman represents the oppressive military force that has within living memory of the community receiving this Gospel devastated the Jewish people, temple, and capital city, inflicting horrific losses that threatened to crush the very heart of the people. The Canaanite represents a different kind of enemy but one no less potent, embodying deep-rooted, longstanding, and entrenched hostility that is intertwined with a peculiar kind of intimacy that is anchored in shared life, shared land, and even shared ancestry. (95–96)

Both gender and race come into play here. Regarding gender, certainly the woman is treated more harshly than the male. Regarding race, there are numerous points to be made. For instance, since Sechrest's article focuses upon race, it is important to highlight that "race," of course, is patently a construct of modernity. As part of that factual conversation, it is important to include this comment from Sechrest:

> Further, we should reflect on the fact that Jesus's Canaanite ancestry [recall that Rahab the Canaanite appears in his genealogy] problematizes the racial purity aspect of the ethnocentric message in Matt. 10:5–6. Just like the findings of modern genetics that renders the idea of pure races dubious, Matthew's genealogy suggests that the icon of Judaism, the Davidic Messiah-King Jesus, is himself "mixed race" (96 n. 93).

Matthew, following Old Testament precedent, presents dogs as negative—ferocious and antagonistic: "Do not give what is holy to dogs; and do not throw your pearls before swine, or they will trample them under foot and turn and maul you" (Matt. 7:6). Thus, when he refers to the woman and her daughter as dogs, it raises the

37

specter of racialized stereotypes. The woman, however, deals with the affront astutely:

> Yet rather than trying to resist the categorization, the woman accepts the image and channels it in a way that advances her plea. If it is possible to characterize this acceptance as something akin to internalized racism, a more generous understanding is that she recognizes that the label is a part of the cost of seeking a relationship with a long-time enemy. She understands that she lives in a world that she did not construct and which does not facilitate entering into the relationship she seeks. Her only way forward is to trust that Jesus's love can transform the terms of this encounter. (Sechrest 2015, 98)

Powerful words.

The way that Sechrest brings together the ancient text with modern analogies of allyship is creative and thought provoking. Jesus, representing Judaism to some degree, is aligned with modern oppressed groups, while the woman, as an outsider and historic enemy, is depicted in the role of an ally who shows humility and deference to the oppressed minority that Jesus represents. One analogy is that white Christians should recognize "that communities of color are endowed by their Creator with all the resources of agency and co-regency in creation when it comes to leading work that participates with Christ in bringing justice and healing to earth as it is in heaven" (Sechrest 2015, 100–101). Another is to recognize that the Canaanite woman represents the white ally who understands that we do not live in isolation from one another. Everyone gets hurt and becomes less than God intended them to be when we participate in racism. White allies will recognize that, though they individually may not subscribe to racism, they "must squarely face the lack of trust and conflict bequeathed on them by history" while simultaneously boldly daring to dream of and work toward "the new creation that Jesus represents" (103). "They listen and learn, and like the Canaanite, they engage deeply with what the oppressed say, even when it hurts. 'When criticized or called out, allies listen, apologize, act accountably, and act differently going forward.' In solidarity with those who have no respite from racism and prejudice, allies are endlessly persistent and refuse to back down, take breaks, or retreat back into privilege" (103).

In Sechrest's proposal, then, Jesus represents African Americans and the Canaanite woman represents the model white ally. Hear her call:

> The goal of allyship is not for people in privileged groups to be shamed, punished, or retaliated against but to eliminate the conditions that dehumanize us all, to restrain evil in our midst, and to seek our common good. Each and every one of us needs to be able to see what and who have been previously invisible as we cautiously move towards inhabiting the kinds of relationships that give honor to the gospel, risking pain but persisting in our desire to build the beloved community. (Sechrest 2015, 105)

The Lectionary

The story of the Canaanite woman in Matthew 15 appears in the Roman Lectionary (RL) on the 20th Sunday in Ordinary Time in Year A, and it is also a weekday reading for Wednesday of Week 18 of Ordinary Time. According to the Revised Common Lectionary (RCL), the passage is to be read in Year A on Proper 15 (20), in the season after Pentecost. The parallel in Mark 7:24–30 is designated by the RCL to be read in Year B on Proper 18 (23), in the season after Pentecost. According to the RL, it is a weekday reading for Thursday of Week 5 of Ordinary Time.

The inclusion of the story in the lectionary readings provides congregations the opportunity to share (even emphasize) some of the newer interpretations now available, to recover and lift up women and any who are marginalized, to seek ways that we can become allies to those in need of healing or liberation.

Conclusion

In keeping with the goals of the book presented in the introduction, a major purpose of this chapter has been to provide readers with a sense of the variety of approaches that are available to a contemporary interpreter. We have heard from interpreters who occupy diverse social locations. We have drawn upon scholarship that illuminates the ancient sociohistorical context within which the narrative is set. We have provided further resources for study. For those who previously were unfamiliar with this woman, or who had in mind only Mark's version, I hope you have added a new sister to your great cloud of witnesses who sustain you.

We have allowed this fascinating woman—Justa, if you will—to take her rightful place at center stage with the spotlight shining upon her. As a result, we have had the opportunity to engage her more fully, spot details that had previously escaped our notice, and ask questions that may have never occurred to us before. We have marveled at her courage, tenacity, wit, and willingness to fight boldly for her daughter in an oppressive system or systems (since both the religious system as well as the political system of Rome were deeply patriarchal). We have interrogated the text.

In the end, however, the real force of the story may reside in its power to interrogate us. Who are we in this story? Are we the woman, the daughter, Jesus, the disciples, or someone else? Do we long for healing and inclusion? Do we offer it? Do we obstruct it? And if so, do we obstruct it because of our individual attitudes and practices or because we are part of a larger system that inhibits healing and inclusion? As Christians, do we understand or care to understand the culture we live in enough to assess honestly where we need to work within a given system and where we need to promote change in the system? If this text were to have its way with us, what would happen? Would we more closely represent the kin-dom of God as God envisions it, "on earth as it is in heaven"? If we did, that would be good news, the gospel, indeed!

Recommended Resources

Alonso, Pablo. 2011. *The Woman Who Changed Jesus: Crossing Boundaries in Mk 7,24–30.* Biblical Tools and Studies 11. Leuven: Peeters.

Anderson, Janice Capel, and Stephen D. Moore, eds. 2008. *Mark & Method: New Approaches to Biblical Studies.* 2nd ed. Minneapolis: Fortress Press.

Black, Kathy. 1996. *A Healing Homiletic: Preaching and Disability.* Nashville: Abingdon Press.

Bohache, Thomas. 2006. "Matthew." Pages 487–516 in *The Queer Bible Commentary*. Edited by Deryn Guest, Robert E. Goss, Mona West, and Thomas Bohache. London: SCM Press.

Carter, Warren. 2001. *Matthew and Empire: Initial Explorations*. Harrisburg, PA: Trinity Press International.

———. 2006. *The Roman Empire and the New Testament: An Essential Guide*. Nashville: Abingdon Press.

Clark-Soles, Jaime. 2010. *Engaging the Word: The New Testament and the Christian Believer*. Louisville, KY: Westminster John Knox Press.

Collaborative on Faith and Disabilities. https://faithanddisability .org.

Gnadt, Martina. 2012. "Gospel of Matthew: Jewish-Christian in Opposition to the Pax Romana." Pages 607–25 in *Feminist Biblical Interpretation: A Compendium of Critical Commentary on the Books of the Bible and Related Literature*. Edited by Luise Schottroff and Marie-Theres Wacker. Grand Rapids: Wm. B. Eerdmans Publishing Co.

Levine, Amy-Jill. 2012. "Gospel of Matthew." Pages 465–77 in *Women's Bible Commentary*. Edited by Carol A. Newsom, Sharon H. Ringe, and Jacqueline E. Lapsley. 3rd ed. Louisville, KY: Westminster John Knox Press.

Love, Stuart L. 2009. *Jesus and Marginal Women: The Gospel of Matthew in Social-Scientific Perspective*. Eugene, OR: Cascade Books.

McKenna, Megan. 1994. *Not Counting Women and Children: Neglected Stories from the Bible*. Maryknoll, NY: Orbis Books.

Melcher, Sarah J., Mikeal C. Parsons, and Amos Yong, eds. 2017. *The Bible and Disability: A Commentary*. Waco, TX: Baylor University Press.

O'Day, Gail. 2001. "Surprised by Faith: Jesus and the Canaanite Woman." Pages 114–25 in *A Feminist Companion to Matthew*. Edited by Amy-Jill Levine with Marianne Blickenstaff. Sheffield: Sheffield Academic Press.

Sechrest, Love L. 2015. "Enemies, Romans, Pigs, and Dogs: Loving the Other in the Gospel of Matthew." *Ex Auditu* 31:71–105.

Wainwright, Elaine M. 1997. "The Gospel of Matthew." Pages 635–77 in *Searching the Scriptures*. Vol. 2, *A Feminist Commentary*. Edited by Elisabeth Schüssler Fiorenza. New York: Crossroad.

————. 1998. *Shall We Look for Another? A Feminist Rereading of the Matthean Jesus*. Maryknoll, NY: Orbis Books.

————. 2001. "Not Without My Daughter: Gender and Demon Possession in Matthew 15.21–28." Pages 126–37 in *A Feminist Companion to Matthew*. Edited by Amy-Jill Levine with Marianne Blickenstaff. Sheffield: Sheffield Academic Press.

Wynn, Kerry H. 2007. "Johannine Healings and the Otherness of Disability." *Perspectives in Religious Studies* 34:61–75.

CHAPTER 2

God across Gender

In recent years the use of inclusive language to refer to God has been debated. As Ludwig Wittgenstein, the philosopher of religion, noted long ago, *"The limits of my language* mean the limits of my world" (1922, 5.6; italics original). While we need language to communicate, human language can never, of course, fully describe or define the full reality and nature of God. Apophatic theology (that of negation) exemplifies this fact starkly by choosing only to say what God is not, since, finally, God is ineffable.

When Jesus says God is a vine grower, Jesus is a vine, and we are branches (John 15:1–5), we know that the language is metaphorical—it functions to convey meaning about the relationship between God, Jesus, and us (and about our relationships with each other). When Paul says he was a wet nurse among the Thessalonians (1 Thess. 2:7), he does not mean that he has actual breasts that produce breast milk. When he says to numerous Christians that he is like their father (1 Thess. 2:11; 1 Cor. 4:15; Phil. 2:22), he is not referring to his biological sex; it is, again, metaphorical language to express his sense of how he relates to his people—in both cases, as a parent.

Likewise, God is not literally gendered with hormones, chromosomes, and reproductive genitalia. Biblical authors employ both feminine and masculine metaphorical language for God. Some interpreters, however, have reified the dominant masculine

43

language for God in the Bible and have come to believe, at some level, that God is literally of the male gender and thus must be referred to with exclusively male language. This calls for a few words of consideration.

First, there is an issue of distorted, even idolatrous, power. When maleness is seen as reflecting the image of God more than femaleness is, then males reign supreme in the so-called natural order (although, as anthropologists and sociologists have shown, maleness and femaleness are actually socially constructed categories that vary across societies in different times and locations). As Mary Daly put it, "As long as God is male, then the male is God" (1973, 19). It is analogous to when white people assume that they are somehow superior (typically assuming that they are closer to God, understand God better, or have been deputized by God) to people of color. It is called white supremacy, and it is a wrong idea, though it has been considered normal for centuries now in many places. Most people probably adopt such wrong ideas reflexively as members of their society and even their churches. Others have been shown a more excellent way but, since the status quo "works" for them, they are not motivated to operate with the still more excellent way. Neither ignorance nor ill will should be allowed to carry the day. Thus in attending closely to the ways that the Bible depicts God as feminine, we hope to change minds, hearts, and actions.

Second, we must concern ourselves with *essentialism*. Essentialism is an approach to gender that links certain traits, behaviors, inclinations, talents, challenges, ways of expressing oneself physically in society (how one carries one's body in space, what color and style of clothes one wears, etc.) to one of two categories: male or female. This happens when people insist upon dressing boys in blue and girls in pink (or perhaps more often insist that boys cannot be dressed in pink and girls cannot be dressed in blue); when they consider nurturing a feminine trait in a girl and discouraging a masculine one, or vice versa with boys. When a man exhibits attributes that society has deemed to be essentially female traits, he is called "effeminate." When a girl refuses to wear "girl clothes" or prefers sports to the exclusion of primping or playing dolls, she is called a "tomboy." And so on. In what follows, I present biblical material that depicts God in feminine terms, all the while remaining cognizant of the problems and fallacies of essentialism. I do not aim to perpetuate these static categories of what counts as masculine

44

or feminine. Rather, I consider assumptions about gender in the ancient world in which these texts were composed to show when and where the authors patently choose to depict God with traits that they would have identified as "feminine."

This brings me to the third consideration: the biblical texts were composed in a particular social context in a certain time and place by people of a particular gender (all or mostly male) and social class (elite and educated). They, like us, were affected by essentialist thinking and tied particular traits and behaviors to women. It is important for us to understand what meaning they were conveying in their own context for their own society, whether it coheres with our own values or not. However, it is entirely appropriate, after understanding the text in its context, for us to question the texts (as they question us). That is to say, we can notice what they were doing and saying and then ask how we, as modern interpreters, should appropriate any given text. Should we adopt it wholesale? Learn from the ancient authors' mistakes? Resist the text? Augment it? Reject it? Value the principle that generated a particular rule (e.g., "we should have certain behaviors that clearly identify us as part of God's people") but reject the rule itself (e.g., "you cannot marry someone from another religion"; "you must circumcise your sons")?

We do not live in the eighth century BCE with Amos the shepherd-prophet or even in the first century CE with Jesus, and we should not pretend that we do. Yet it is they and their communities who bequeathed these sacred texts to us. We do not want to be so lazy as to adopt the texts mindlessly or to reject the texts mindlessly. Substantial conversations require work, but it is good work and, when it comes to the Scriptures, an act of devotion to the very God we are called to know, in part, through these texts. In what follows, then, I lift up the texts that depict God with female imagery, texts that may be unknown or currently undervalued by many Christians.

Examples from the Old Testament where God is referred to or imaged in female terms are ample. There are those designations that are biologically female, such as God giving birth and nursing, and those that are based on "sex role stereotypes. That is, these things could be done by fathers or other males, and sometimes are done by men in our culture. But sex roles in biblical times and places assigned these jobs as exclusively 'women's work,' so their

45

proper effect is to picture God as female" (Mollenkott 2014, 26). In this category one could list seamstress (Gen. 3:21), mistress of a household, midwife, nurse, and mother. Mother bears in the Bible are fierce (2 Sam. 17:8 and Prov. 17:12); in Hosea 13:8, God is likened to both a lion and a mother bear. God is a baker woman (Luke 13:20–21), a mother eagle (Deut. 32:11–14), a mother hen (an image from 2 Esd. 1:30 and elsewhere that Jesus uses of himself in the Gospels; consult Matt. 23:37). God and Lady Wisdom are often equated (we say more about Lady Wisdom in chap. 4), as are God and Spirit, *Rûaḥ* (feminine).

One should also note the many places in Scripture where God is presented with both male and female images in the same verse. For example, in Psalm 123:2, God is depicted as both a master and a mistress of a house. In 2 Esdras 1:28–30, which all New Testament authors would have used as Scripture, God is a father, mother, nurse, and hen: "Thus says the Lord Almighty: Have I not entreated you as a father entreats his sons or a mother her daughters or a nurse her children, so that you should be my people and I should be your God, and that you should be my children and I should be your father? I gathered you as a hen gathers her chicks under her wings." God is described in various ways, even within a single verse.

Women at Work

To better understand how feminine imagery for God functions in the Bible, it is useful to know something about the kinds of work women did in antiquity. For this we draw primarily upon Carol Meyers's acclaimed book *Rediscovering Eve*. Women produced and reproduced.

Food Production

The mainstays of food production were bread, wine, and olive oil. Meyers estimates that 75 percent of people's diet in antiquity was bread; women were important in this production. During the Old Testament period, grains were the foundation of the Israelite diet. For the most part, men carried out the seasonal tasks of plowing, sowing, reaping, threshing, and winnowing. On the other hand, it was primarily women who carried out the daily, year-round task of converting grain into something edible (most often bread), which involved parching, soaking, grinding, kneading, heating, and leavening.

So important was bread to the ancient household that it became a synonym for food itself. Producing ample amounts of flour, women would have performed the "daily grind" together in shared space. The kingdom of heaven is compared to yeast that (positively, in this case) leavens the bread. God is compared to a baker woman who works with the yeast (Matt. 13:33; Luke 13:20–21). In John, Jesus, of course, is the Bread from Heaven, the Living Bread. God is the provider. Jesus is both the gift and the giver. Jesus is described as God's bread. God gives, and Jesus gives his body to his disciples as bread to eat (John 6).

Women made other foods and drinks as well, including beer. While both male and female youth tended flocks, women also performed textile activities—spinning, weaving, sewing. Again, they did it together. Women were also potters. This gives new meaning to the biblical metaphor of God as potter, a female role. In addition to clothing, women made baskets and items for household use, such as ovens. Women helped in other construction activities as well. Notice the Nehemiah 3:12 reference to Shallum "and his daughters" helping to build the wall. Meyers indicates that some scholars, unfamiliar with the evidence of women construction workers, assume it to be an error and argue that it should read "sons" instead of "daughters" (2013, 135).

Reproduction

Women worked hard and had babies—they produced and reproduced. Women worked throughout pregnancy and after:

> The idea of work and motherhood as oppositional alternatives for women is a relatively recent phenomenon, a product of industrialization and the separation of the workplace from the home. . . .
>
> Israelite women in agricultural households—like women in traditional peasant societies everywhere—performed an endless succession of tasks . . . along with bearing children. Everywoman Eve would have been astonished at our contemporary career-family dilemmas. Even elite women were rarely relieved of a significant number of tasks. (Meyers 2013, 52)

47

Pregnancy and childbirth were extremely risky for both mother and child, given the lack of sanitation, knowledge about pathogens, and medical capacity. Food shortage was common. With a high infant mortality rate, it took multiple pregnancies to produce a viable number of children to help with labor in this agrarian society and to care for elders. Life expectancy was short by modern Western standards.

Women bore children and raised them, named them and taught them. Teaching and socializing children was integrated into daily life. Is it any wonder that Wisdom is depicted as female in the Bible?

Women served as ancient doctors, if you will, from dealing with fertility issues to delivering babies and devising medicines to heal the ill. The healing arts and religion were intermingled. In a culture that depended upon women birthing children, infertility was considered a problem. Demonic forces were thought to prey upon women who were pregnant and nursing and upon newborns. Various protective strategies and religious rituals were employed. People might be ill because they sinned, because God wanted them to learn something (Job), or because demons were active. Medical care largely took place in the home and was handled by women using various remedies, many of them plant-based. A number of biblical texts point to women as healers. Notice especially that when Hosea (11:3–4) depicts God as a mother, it includes attention not just to teaching and feeding the children, but also to healing them.

Women served important functions at the time of death and beyond. They often tended to the dying and prepared the dead body for burial. In addition, they were mourners, lamenting and wailing (if you've been to the Wailing Wall in Jerusalem, you have likely experienced this activity even today). Some were professional mourners, for hire by those with the resources.

It is clear, then, that women were religious leaders insofar as most religion took place in the household. We have seen women active in life-cycle events, feasts and festivals, and health care. "Everywoman Eve clearly had a prominent role in many household religious practices" (Meyers 2013, 168). The leadership of women in religion in this period has been belittled by what Meyers refers to as the "masculinized approaches to the study of Israelite religion. Until relatively recently male religious professionals or scholars were the chief interpreters of Israelite religion, and their perspectives

48

generally marginalized women's experiences and practices as not being the 'real religion' carried out by male priests" (169). Meyers laments that even feminist biblical scholars have allowed an androcentric stance to dominate by adopting the approach that focuses only on formal religious practices where women are largely absent. She asks, "Could the seemingly mundane food-preparation or lamp-lighting tasks, among others that were part of household religious practice, really have been as important as the explicitly sacral actions of priestly officiants at community shrines?" (169). She goes on to answer in the positive, noting that women had very rich religious lives.

Beyond Home

Some women's skills led them to being hired beyond their own households. What were some of these jobs, beyond the proverbial prostitute? Archaeologists have discovered seals and ostraca with the names of women on them, indicating that some were business-women. Women were textile workers, midwives, and wet nurses. They served in cultic roles (for instance, Exod. 38:8 depicts women serving at the tent of meeting, and Meyers suggests that they were relating information from God). Women were prophets. We know of Miriam, Deborah, Huldah, and Noadiah, along with unnamed female prophets in Isaiah, Joel, and Ezekiel (we address female prophets in chap. 4). If these few manage to appear in an androcentric text like the Hebrew Bible, it may imply that many more existed. The biblical text lists diviners who were involved in dream analysis, augury, necromancy, and so on; some of these practitioners were female.

Women also appear as musicians. Songs are associated with Miriam, Deborah, and Hannah; some involve dancing and instruments as well. Each song conveys theology, much like hymns in modern Christian worship.

Some women served as community leaders. Those named are quite rare in the Hebrew Bible, Deborah of course being a famous judge. Note also the wise women of Tekoa (2 Sam. 14) and Abel of Beth-maacah (2 Sam. 20), who help resolve issues during David's reign. (The figure of the wise woman is taken up in chap. 4.) Meyers argues that royal women had what she calls "managerial roles on a national level" (2013, 177). Thus, we see professional women

49

serving their households, their communities, and even the nation of Israel.

Knowing that women's expertise ranges from mothering to medicine, food provision to pottery production, and plenty more opens up much more meaning for the ways the Bible presents God in feminine terms. Given our limited space, in this chapter I trace only three of the many feminine images for God mentioned above. Each one is particularly useful for understanding God and for encouraging readers in their Christian journeys, and each one is found in the Old Testament and carries over into the New Testament in some way.

The Work of L. Juliana M. Claassens

We are greatly helped in this endeavor by L. Juliana M. Claassens's work. In her book *Mourner, Mother, Midwife: Reimagining God's Delivering Presence in the Old Testament*, she begins with the image of God as a Warrior-Deliverer, which is the default image when speaking of God as Liberator in the Old Testament. When God is depicted as a Warrior-Deliverer, God is depicted as male. Male and warrior go together in people's minds.

There are, however, women warriors—think of Deborah, Jael, Judith (in the Apocrypha), and the woman of Thebez in Judges 9. It can be helpful to consider such characters insofar as they disrupt our stereotypes and remind us that "gender constructions cannot be assumed to be universally true; rather, they reflect the reigning values in particular cultural and temporal locations" (Claassens 2012, 5). Claassens notes that some readers relish the biblical stories of warrior women because these stories depict empowered women using their strength to fight against male domination and to resist gender norms.

Claassens, however, highlights the problematic aspects of these examples. First is the question of whether they actually disrupt our stereotypes, since the stories really "work" only because of the stereotypes. That is, Deborah and Jael are "an exception to the rule," an "anomaly." Furthermore, they are tools to shame the males—if the males had been doing their job properly, they would not have had to be rescued by females. Another problem, from Claassens's perspective, is that, whether the warrior is male or female, liberation through violence and war is not the most helpful imagery to glorify and emulate.

Claassens wants to keep the God-as-Deliverer metaphor, but she challenges our violence-loving, warmongering selves to consider God as Mourner, Mother, and Midwife. "These metaphors offer rich possibilities of an alternative image of God that is rooted not in death and destruction, but in engaged, life-enhancing acts as well as a deep-seated compassion for the suffering, the vulnerable, and the power-less" (2012, 7). Such a view of God might motivate us, who long to be more godly, to orient our hearts in that same direction.

Claassens chooses these three images for three reasons; each connects concerns of the past with our concerns in the present. First, each image occurs in texts related to the Babylonian exile—a traumatic, watershed moment in every aspect of Israelite life, the-ology, and piety. The exiles had to rethink a lot of their theological assumptions, they suffered, and they found no quick solution to their complex situation and experiences. "The task of doing the-ology is, therefore, a continuing process of seeking to include into our conversations the ways we talk about God in light of the reali-ties of life that are sometimes far more messy and tragic than we would like them to be" (Claassens 2012, 8–9).

Second, Israel had to work out its theology in the midst of empire. Revisiting these practically hidden metaphors of mourner, mother, and midwife may equip us to embody "values such as mercy, commitment to life, and concern for the other"; such values directly oppose "the empire's drive to show no mercy, to humiliate, and to destroy" (Claassens 2012, 9).

Third, all three of the metaphors are related to females. It behooves us to pay attention to the muted, "minor" voices and metaphors in Scripture; it may train us to do the same in real life with real people. They are all there.

Claassens notes that all three images are deeply relational (for me this invokes thoughts about the nature of the Trinity), express-ing concern for the other. The wailing woman weeps over a person; the mother gives birth to and cares for a child; the midwife helps the mother and infant (2012, 10). Again, for the ancients, these roles were filled by women. We want to honor that fact and, as modern interpreters, break open the gender stereotypes so that the features of each of these metaphors are expected of men as well—men can be and are nurturers too.

51

God as Mourner

I first saw a "tear bottle," a glass jar to catch tears, and hearing legends associated with it when I was in Bethlehem. Such legends abound in Bethlehem. Some believe they were used as part of funerary rites. They were common in antiquity. I was struck soon afterward, while preparing this book, to discover this verse in which the psalmist refers to God's own tear bottle:

> You have kept count of my tossings;
>   put my tears in your bottle.
>   Are they not in your record?
>   *(Ps. 56:8)*

God is a crier. For our purposes, it is important to emphasize that in antiquity that role was reserved for women.

A modern tear bottle made of glass purchased in Bethlehem in 2019.
Thank you to Margot Perez Greene for helping me obtain such a beautiful bottle for the purposes of this book. Photo by Jaime Clark-Soles.

Women as Mourners

If you have ever visited the Wailing Wall in Jerusalem, you likely noticed that it is divided by gender (the males are closer to the area where the Holy of Holies once stood). If you go to the women's section, you will find women wailing, rocking or swaying, often holding a prayer book, dressed in black, heads covered. People write their prayers on a piece of paper and fold it up and stick it in the cracks in the wall. These women, in a sense, express our collective crying. Even my students who are most resolved to be unmoved find themselves moved. There are generations of females there; I have no doubt the daughters are being taught a dirge on that very spot.

Women in antiquity worked as professional, expert mourners. Referring to the details of Jeremiah 9:17–20, a text also adduced by Claassens, Meyers discusses the reference to skilled women who are to come and mourn and are to teach a funeral dirge to their daughters. (Consult the Jeremiah passage in the next section.) Meyers notes that "skilled" indicates an acquired ability. It may be that skilled women taught their biological daughters such skills, but Meyers suggests that we should consider the term "daughter" in the passage as extending beyond biology: "It perhaps is used in an extended sense to represent an association or professional 'guild' of women lamenters (cf. 2 Sam 1:24)" (2013, 175). Already we might consider the role these professional keeners will play in the story of Jesus's raising of Lazarus in John 11.

Claassens explores four functions served by the ancient wailing women. First, they served a therapeutic role for society by giving voice to suffering, refusing to dismiss or minimize the pain. Giving voice is the first step to healing. "Trauma often leaves people numb and confused, unable to express their emotions" (Claassens 2012, 27). I cannot help but think of Mary Magdalene here—the first at the tomb, weeping, testifying to the trauma of the loss of Jesus on Good Friday but facing the emotion directly and abiding anyway rather than retreating as the other disciples did.

Second, the wailing women serve a communal function, gathering the people into shared lament. Third, they testify or witness and therefore help the community to remember the story, even the most painful parts. "The tears and laments of the wailing women as represented in literature form in Jeremiah 9 can best be understood in terms of a testimony to what has transpired, calling on the

53

rest of the community not to forget but to honestly and bravely name their pain. Thus, the wailing women play a significant role in helping the people of Judah to come together in their grief, and so to participate in the 'survival of their story'" (Claassens 2012, 29).

Finally, the wailing women serve a prophetic role. Notice in Jeremiah 9:20 that the women received the word from God's mouth as prophets always do, serving as spokespeople for God, and they call for justice, as prophets always do. "As the prophet challenged the community by saying, you say 'peace, peace, when there is no peace,' . . . the wailing women challenge complacency that ignores the many social injustices threatening the well-being of their society as a whole" (Claassens 2012, 30).

God as a Wailing Woman

God is the first to weep in Jeremiah 8:

> For the hurt of my poor people I am hurt,
>   I mourn, and dismay has taken hold of me.
>
> Is there no balm in Gilead?
>   Is there no physician there?
> Why then has the health of my poor people
>   not been restored?
>
> O that my head were a spring of water,
>   and my eyes a fountain of tears,
> so that I might weep day and night
>   for the slain of my poor people!
>   (*Jer. 8:21–9:1*)

Then in Jeremiah 9, God calls the women to do the same, in God's image:

> Thus says the LORD of hosts:
> Consider, and call for the mourning women to come;
>   send for the skilled women to come;
> let them quickly raise a dirge over us,
>   so that our eyes may run down with tears,
>   and our eyelids flow with water.
> For a sound of wailing is heard from Zion:
>   "How we are ruined!
>   We are utterly shamed,

because we have left the land,
    because they have cast down our dwellings."

Hear, O women, the word of the LORD,
    and let your ears receive the word of his mouth;
teach to your daughters a dirge,
    and each to her neighbor a lament.

                                        (Jer. 9:17–20)

Claassens argues that the imagery of the women in Jeremiah 9 plays a crucial role in understanding Judah's traumatic experience. "The wailing women's tears, which represent the depth of the community's emotion in the face of extreme trauma, are closely connected to the tears of God in Jeremiah 8:21–23 . . . —to the extent that we can say God's tears are embodied in those of the wailing women" (2012, 20). Jeremiah is full of tears: heaven and earth mourn; Rachel weeps for her children; the prophet and God cry.

As is typical in prophetic speech, God's pathos and words coalesce with those of the people through whom God speaks, in this case the vocal women.

> God is leading the people in mourning. In this way God is providing the wailing women with the cue that now is the right time to lament. The messenger formula—"thus says the Lord" . . . — indicates that the divine word is coming to the wailing women, who are implored to "hear the word of the Lord" and to receive the teaching from God's mouth. . . . Viewed in this way, God becomes a Wailing or Mourning Woman. (Claassens 2012, 31)

Claassens explores the advantages of focusing upon this metaphor. First, it provides us with a metaphor of God as Deliverer that does not depend on violence. More typically, biblical traditions privilege texts that depict God as a warrior liberator, violently crushing Israel's opponents, annihilating whole people groups (such as Canaanites in Deut. 20:16–17). Highlighting more constructive metaphors in the scriptural text is in order.

Second, viewing God as a mourner gives hope to those who suffer by reminding them that God understands their plight and cares deeply about it. This is what Christians would consider *incarnational theology*. It is a path to healing and redemption. It calls us to speak honestly about how complicated our experiences are and, in speaking it, to imagine moving into a future story.

Third, this metaphor offers a better theodicy than any theory of retributive justice ever could and ceases victimizing victims of trauma. Theodicy refers to God's justice; it comes from the Greek words for "God" (*theos*) and "just" (*dikaios*). Where is God in suffering? David Hume's classic statement of the issue posits two possibilities. God is omnipotent, but malevolent, or God is benevolent, but impotent. Put another way, is God able to prevent suffering but chooses not to (in which case God might be seen as malevolent, not willing the good) or does God will the good but is not able to accomplish it (in which case God might be seen as impotent)? Many others after Hume have suggested answers to this question. Some, like the "friends" of Job, imagine that all suffering stems from the sin a person or a people group has committed; thus, the suffering is deserved. This is a theology of blame, and this approach is castigated by the author of Job insofar as the friends are shown to be egregiously wrong. In their case, they did well only when they said nothing.

Things happen that break the heart of God. Those are the very things that should break our hearts as well. If God cries about it, shouldn't we? A theology of compassion replaces a theology of blame. Another way to say this is: David Hume has given us a false dichotomy in forcing us to choose either "God as omnipotent" or "God as benevolent." The categories are erroneously construed. God is less doctrinaire than we are, it turns out.

Fourth, though men occasionally weep in the Bible, across cultures the role of mourner or "keener" has fallen to women. Depicting God as Mourning Woman balances out male images and metaphors of God. Finally, Claassens argues that this metaphor allows us to inscribe the language of power with new meaning: "The image of God as Mourner resonates with biblical imagery of power in vulnerability, e.g., Deutero-Isaiah's use of suffering servant imagery, and God as Mother in Labor . . . , culminating in the image of the Crucified God on the cross" (2012, 35).

Claassens closes the chapter by drawing upon authors and poets in addition to the biblical ones to help us to imagine how this metaphor can speak into our own communities today (she herself is South African). It can break, or at least soften, our hearts: "The tears of God and the wailing women challenged the Judean community at the time of the exile—and communities ever since—to have the same broken heart as God and to work for change wherever change is possible" (2012, 36). It can bring together people, even former enemies, such that cycles of revenge might cease. Finally, it serves "as a symbol of hope," since the "way of weeping" is the road to healing and restoration (39).

Many can relate to these words that recur in Jeremiah: "Terror is all around" (20:10; 46:5; 49:29). If you want to know *why* the women should wail, chapter 9 continues with these words:

> "Death has come up into our windows,
>   it has entered our palaces,
> to cut off the children from the streets
>   and the young men from the squares."
> Speak! Thus says the LORD:
> "Human corpses shall fall
>   like dung upon the open field,
> like sheaves behind the reaper,
>   and no one shall gather them."
>   (*Jer. 9:21–22*)

Many contemporary analogies could be drawn, including the Holocaust. I am reminded of Markus Zusak's *The Book Thief*, in which Death is also personified, though it becomes a sympathetic character of sorts, thus highlighting all the more that *human beings* terrorize and kill one another. Before developing her argument about God as a Mourning Woman, Claassens confronts the dominant metaphors of God as Aggrieved (even abusive) Husband of Judah (Jer. 2–3) and God as Architect of War.

This violent story line is interrupted by the tears of God and of the prophet in Jeremiah 8. Scholars debate whether the tears come from the prophet or God. Claassens notes, "The prophet's tears merge with the tears of God, who ultimately functions as the principal speaker in the poem in 8:22–9:3" (2012, 23). Claassens writes beautifully about the hope and comfort inherent in a God who weeps in solidarity with God's people. Why does God cry? Claassens offers various possibilities. Perhaps because of the rampant social injustice wherein the least of these are not cared for. God feels their suffering. The same kinds of questions arise when scholars debate John 11:35 and the reasons behind Jesus's tears there.

New Testament Tears and Our Tears

What is good enough for God and the Old Testament prophets is clearly good enough for Jesus and the two apostles Mary Magdalene and Paul, all of whom are shown crying in the Bible. In fact, Paul references an epistle he calls the "letter of tears," which many scholars take to be the material in 2 Corinthians 10–13: "For I wrote you out of much distress and anguish of heart and with many tears, not to cause you pain, but to let you know the abundant love that I have for you" (2 Cor. 2:4). Luke also depicts Paul as crying (Acts 20:19, 31). In John, Jesus tells the disciples they will weep (16:20). Elsewhere he says, "Blessed are those who weep *now*" (Luke 6:21), just before the story of the woman who bathes his feet with her tears (Luke 7:38). Thus, when we Christians cry, we may be "womanly" in an Old Testament sense, but at that moment we are particularly "godly." Robert Pierce, founder of World Vision, is credited with the saying, "Let my heart be broken with the things that break the heart of God."

Tears and weeping are not the last word, however. What the prophet Isaiah proclaimed centuries before—"He will swallow up death forever. Then the Lord GOD will wipe away the tears from all faces, and the disgrace of his people he will take away from all the earth, for the LORD has spoken" (Isa. 25:8)—John declares in the closing section of the canon: "He will wipe every tear from their eyes. Death will be no more; mourning and crying and pain will be no more, for the first things have passed away" (Rev. 21:4).

The biblical references give us freedom to name the things that bring us to tears. In the stunning novel *The Secret Life of Bees*, May has the gift of deep empathy—she feels the pain of others. As we all know, you cannot carry all the pain of those around you and still thrive. So May builds her own stone Wailing Wall in her backyard, and she writes all of the prayers on pieces of paper and sticks them in the cracks—an idea we might want to borrow for ourselves. When I lead retreats that include reference to tears in the Bible, I have each person take a small tear jar and a piece of paper. I play the song "I Have This Hope" by Tenth Avenue North, which contains a stanza that references God's tear jar. After voicing the anguish of seemingly unending trying times, the singer asks:

58

Will You catch every tear
Or will You just leave me here?

I then give people time to pray and reflect using the following questions as prompts.

Tears

How do you feel about crying?
When is the last time you cried?
What kinds of things tend to make you cry?

Hurting, Healing, and Hope

What hurts right now?
What deserves lamenting?
Do you imagine God's tears as healing?
What if you mixed your tears with God's?
Do you see hope beyond the hurt yet?
Does anything stand between the hurt and the hope?

The Lectionary

For those who want to lift up these tearful texts, note that while Jeremiah 8:18–9:1 appears in the Revised Common Lectionary (RCL), in Year C, on Proper 20 (25), in the season after Pentecost, Jeremiah 9 does not. The Roman Lectionary (RL) contains neither Jeremiah 8 nor 9. Surely we want to invite our people to reflect upon all of these implications of a God who weeps with God's people?

With respect to the New Testament texts, in the RCL, Luke 6:20–31 appears in Year C on All Saints' Day, in the season after Pentecost; according to the RL, Luke 6:20–26 is read on Wednesday of Week 23 of Ordinary Time and during Year C on the 6th Sunday in Ordinary Time. Unfortunately, the RCL omits most of the passages discussed above other than Luke 6; however, the RL includes several of them. I encourage teachers and preachers to find ways to lift up these various texts, inviting our communities to celebrate the connection between crying and godliness and to celebrate that women have traditionally carried out this role and that men can carry it out as well.

59

God as Mother

The Babylonian conquest and exile devastated Israel and left a traumatized people forced to reexamine everything, including their theology. Claassens explores Second and Third Isaiah (Isa. 40–66, written in the sixth century BCE) as survival literature. She finds the prophet moving his people forward by bringing out something old and something new. God continues to be the Deliverer, but we also get wonderful maternal imagery for God. In particular, Claassens treats Isaiah 42:13–14; 45:9–10; 49:13–15; and 66:10–13. Within these passages she finds images of God as a Mother in Labor and God as Nurturing Mother.

God as Mother in Labor

Isaiah 42 and 45 both depict God as a Mother in Labor to highlight God's ability to create something new—a new life, a new nation, a way out of no way. Both passages combine the image of a mother in labor with other imagery:

> The LORD goes forth like a soldier,
>   like a warrior he stirs up his fury;
> he cries out, he shouts aloud,
>   he shows himself mighty against his foes.
>
> For a long time I have held my peace,
>   I have kept still and restrained myself;
> now I will cry out like a woman in labor,
>   I will gasp and pant.
>   *(Isa. 42:13–14)*

> Woe to you who strive with your Maker,
>   earthen vessels with the potter!
> Does the clay say to the one who fashions it, "What are you making"?
>   or "Your work has no handles"?
> Woe to anyone who says to a father, "What are you begetting?"
>   or to a woman, "With what are you in labor?"
>   *(Isa. 45:9–10)*

60   A mother and a potter (also a female role in antiquity), through their effort, bring forth something new in the world. For nine months,

the woman quietly and steadily grows this new creation. Then the time comes for the new creation to burst forth in a heaving effort of hope. Likewise, the potter conceives of the pot's design, prepares and gathers all that is necessary to bring into being this new creation, and then expends valuable life energy shaping it into existence in accordance with the potter's intentions.

In Isaiah 42:13–14 the Mother in Labor metaphor is combined with the Divine Warrior metaphor. As a result, the metaphors shape each other in new ways that may help Isaiah's people think about power, especially God's power, in different ways after exile. Most certainly it can help modern readers do so. The "mother in the violent throes of birth pangs" language counters or subverts the militaristic "deliverance through death and destruction" trajectory. Likewise, the warrior imagery makes us reconsider the Mother in Labor image. Claassens points out that, as did war, the danger of childbearing left women vulnerable. At the same time, both war and childbearing required strength and determination.

> We should not forget that childbearing was a treacherous affair in those times; women all too often died in labor, just as warriors died in battle. Using these provocative metaphors for God contributes to an understanding of the vulnerability of the people who dared to depict the vulnerability of God. However, even though both the mother and the warrior are in danger and hence quite vulnerable, both are exceedingly strong. The cries and panting of a woman in labor is not a sign of weakness but of strength; a sign of her determination to ensure that her child enters the world alive and healthy. Similarly, God's willingness to enter into the people's suffering, which is evidence of God's great love, is coupled with God's resolve to act by bringing forth new life. Thus, the metaphor of God as Mother in Labor offers an extraordinary mixture of active power in the midst of vulnerability; that is, of a God who is as vulnerable, and at the same time as powerful as a woman giving birth. (Claassens 2012, 56)

The second instance of the Mother in Labor metaphor occurs in Isaiah 45:9–10, in which Isaiah piles up metaphors for God, adding God as Potter and God as Father. Again, the focus is upon God's ability to create that which is new.

61

God as Nurturing Mother

The metaphor of God as Nurturing Mother appears in Isaiah
49:13–15 and 66:10–13.

> Sing for joy, O heavens, and exult, O earth;
>> break forth, O mountains, into singing!
> For the LORD has comforted his people,
>> and will have compassion on his suffering ones.
>
> But Zion said, "The LORD has forsaken me,
>> my Lord has forgotten me."
> Can a woman forget her nursing child,
>> or show no compassion for the child of her womb?
> Even these may forget,
>> yet I will not forget you.
>
> *(Isa. 49:13–15)*
>
> Rejoice with Jerusalem, and be glad for her,
>> all you who love her;
> rejoice with her in joy,
>> all you who mourn over her—
> that you may nurse and be satisfied
>> from her consoling breast;
> that you may drink deeply with delight
>> from her glorious bosom.
>
> For thus says the LORD:
> I will extend prosperity to her like a river,
>> and the wealth of the nations like an overflowing stream;
> and you shall nurse and be carried on her arm,
>> and dandled on her knees.
> As a mother comforts her child,
>> so I will comfort you;
>> you shall be comforted in Jerusalem.
>
> *(Isa. 66:10–13)*

The Nurturing Mother provides food and drink from her own
body, ensuring the well-being and thriving of that child. Again, this
is a profoundly embodied, intimate image of the way God cares
for us that, for me, immediately connects with the Eucharist as
Christ's body and his blood as "true drink," as John will say. Jesus
is always feeding people, literally and figuratively nourishing them,
just as the mothers of his own time did. (On this note, consult also

62

Claassens's book *The God Who Provides: Biblical Images of Divine Nourishment*.)

I appreciate that Claassens is careful to keep us from naiveté. Metaphors can be transformationally powerful but also complicated. Many are accustomed to using the metaphor of God as Father. For those who have fathers, especially good ones, the image can be helpful. But it can also fill in some holes left by absent or injurious fathers. The same is true of God as Mother. For those who have experienced good mothers, the metaphor can celebrate that. For those who were not so fortunate, it can fill in holes left by absent or injurious mothers. There is no difference in the metaphors in that way. Here, though, we are addressing only maternal metaphors. As with the paternal ones, the biblical author depicts God as even more faithful than earthly parents, acknowledging that the author knows of those who have had faithless earthly parents. "Is there anyone among you who, if your child asks for bread, will give a stone? Or if the child asks for a fish, will give a snake? If you then, who are evil, know how to give good gifts to your children, how much more will your Father in heaven give good things to those who ask him!" (Matt. 7:9–11).

Such trauma may be especially pronounced in times of war when people are made refugees and exiles, as were the Israelites in the Babylonian exile:

> The female metaphors that are used for God in these Deutero-Isaianic texts offer a means of acknowledging these horrors and pain before moving on, and so allowing this important phase in the grieving process. The confession that God is the capital mother whose love knows no bounds serves the function of naming the pain and rebuilding the bond between God and God's traumatized children who have suffered from the fear of being forsaken by God. It is by remembering the horror of mothers abandoning their children and then invoking the metaphor of God as Nurturing Mother, that the pain of abandoning and being abandoned is confronted. (Claassens 2012, 53)

Claassens also connects the God as Mother imagery with the Suffering Servant imagery. This too provokes new thinking about power, the kind of power that reaches out in "compassion rather than in self-defensive violence" (2012, 58). When God is portrayed as a compassionate, nurturing mother who focuses upon creating

63

and sustaining life, those who worship that God might follow suit in their own contexts.

Male Mothering in the New Testament

We noted above that the mourning motif carries through into the New Testament. So does the mothering motif. God, Jesus, and Paul are depicted as nursing, nurturing mothers. In 1 Thessalonians 2:7, Paul compares himself and the other apostles to a wet nurse: "But we were gentle among you, like a wet nurse tenderly caring for her own children" (my trans.). In 1 Corinthians 3:1–2, he refers to providing milk: "And so, brothers and sisters, I could not speak to you as spiritual people, but rather as people of the flesh, as infants in Christ. I fed you with milk, not solid food, for you were not ready for solid food." At Galatians 4:19 he writes as their mother, "My little children, for whom I am again in the pain of childbirth until Christ is formed in you." Jesus, too, is depicted with maternal terms (just as he rests on the breast of God, so the Beloved Disciple rests on Jesus's breast in a feeding scene in John 13). Jesus is depicted as having a "womb" in John 7:38. All of this is explicated more fully in later chapters in this book.

An Overdue Metaphor

The maternal metaphors in Isaiah remind us, once again, that God cannot be reduced or defined, finally, by our attempts to name and describe God. Rather, the wild array of God-language reminds us to celebrate the richness and complexity of God and, honestly, ourselves and our different situations. We are reminded, once again, that now we see through a glass darkly; only then will we see God face to face (cf. 1 Cor. 13:12). The maternal metaphors related to gestation remind us that new growth and development can take time, but that we might try some patience. Recall the seed that grows automatically in Mark 4, quite apart from any human tinkering, appearing in the fullness of time, God's own time. Or maybe you are more of a James 5:7 person: "Be patient, therefore, brothers and sisters, until the appearing of the Lord. Behold, the farmer awaits the precious fruit of the earth, being patient about it, until it receives the early and late rains" (my trans.). Six of one, a half dozen of the other—patience and humility are in order.

64

We live in a period of unprecedented migration, most of it forced. Many individuals and communities find themselves in a place of actual exile, torn from their homes, their cultures, their families, and their traditions. To be reminded that God brings forth new life and faithfully nurtures that life can inspire hope where the promises of war and revenge do not.

If you have followed Father Greg Boyle (and you should), founder of Homeboy Industries and author of *Tattoos on the Heart*, you know that many gang members have a history of absent parents. The church does well to use familial language of father and mother for clergy who fill in as the substitute human parent trying to reflect the kind of parenting that God does.

By meditating upon the maternal imagery in Isaiah, we might imagine a different way of working and waiting in this world, one that is marked by "compassion and not by coercion" (Claassens 2012, 62). As we turn in the next section to feminine imagery for God in Psalms, I close with a resource from Bobby McFerrin that I use in various liturgical settings. His stunning song "The 23rd Psalm" is a moving tribute to his own mother, depicting God in feminine terms. It moves me deeply every time I hear it. Once McFerrin has us walking in the valley, he beautifully, gently, and convincingly sings, "There is nothing that can shake me, She has said She won't forsake me," and asks us to feel what it's like to be held in her hand.

The Lectionary

Sadly, neither of these passages in Isaiah 42 and 45 is read in public worship as prescribed by either the Roman Lectionary (RL) or the Revised Common Lectionary (RCL). Isaiah 42:10–18 is a Friday reading in Year C in preparation for the 4th Sunday of Advent, according to the RCL.

Happily, though, both of the texts in Isaiah 49 and 66 that promote maternal imagery are given Sunday readings in both lectionaries. The RL assigns Isaiah 49:14–15 during Year A, on the 8th Sunday in Ordinary Time, and Isaiah 66:10–14c during Year C, on the 21st Sunday in Ordinary Time. The RCL calls for Isaiah 49:8–16a to be read twice in Year A, on the 8th Sunday after the Epiphany and on Proper 3 (8), during the season after Pentecost. It calls for Isaiah 66:10–14 to be read in Year C, on Proper 9 (14), during the season after Pentecost. Perhaps the lectionary-based preacher and teacher can start with the maternal imagery that does appear and supplement it with Isaiah 42 and 45, enlarging the repertoire of the hearers and showing that such imagery is not singular in appearance.

God as Midwife

The image of God as Midwife appears in Isaiah 66 and two lament psalms, 71 and 22. In lament psalms, the individual or community hovers over the pit of despair, crying out to the God whom they fear has forsaken them in their darkest hours. One of the most powerful aspects of the psalms of lament lies in their drawing upon their tradition, accessing the community's memory of God's acts of deliverance in the past. Psalms 22 and 71 do just that, but they add a new twist—the metaphor of God as Midwife. Consider the following verses: "Yet it was you who took me from the womb; you kept me safe on my mother's breast. On you I was cast from my birth, and since my mother bore me you have been my God" (Ps. 22:9–10). "Upon you I have leaned from my birth; it was you who took me from my mother's womb. My praise is continually of you" (Ps. 71:6). God as Midwife acts as deliverer and protector, both politically and physically, as do human midwives in the Bible. We do well to train our attention on the important work of these females whose work the biblical authors highlight by depicting God in that role.

The names Shiphrah and Puah might not roll off your tongue or ring a bell right away, but they are two of the heroes of the story of the exodus and should be celebrated (consult Exod. 1:15–21). Unfortunately, they appear nowhere in the RL; they almost do, since Exodus 1:8–14, 22 appears on the Monday of Week 15 of Ordinary Time, but their verses are cut out and skipped over. In the RCL they appear once: Year A, Proper 16 (21), in the season after Pentecost. When Pharaoh orders the death of the male infants, these women engage in nonviolent resistance by refusing to obey; rather, they assist the Hebrew women in bearing the children and keeping them alive. It is not clear whether they are Egyptian or Hebrew themselves. In an empire that demands death, they insist on life. One is reminded of Peter's response to empire when the

66

apostles engage in civil disobedience of their own: "Whom shall we obey, God or human beings?" (Acts 5:29). Different century, different empire, same conundrum. Empires are never original in their tactics.

The midwife does not do all the work for the mother; the mother is called to participate fully in the process of delivery and care for the infant, with the help of the strong hands and wisdom of the midwife. The laboring mother and midwife are also assisted by others in the work of delivery. They undermine empire, they work together with others to bring deliverance, and they spend their lives protecting society's most vulnerable people. As God does.

We learned earlier that women were the primary healers in Old Testament times. It is unfortunate that this thread gets lost by the time the New Testament texts are composed. As Claassens notes:

> In the portrayal of Jesus as healer, for instance, "the midwife, the wise woman, the folk healer, the mothers, wives, sisters, and daughters who routinely nurse the ailing members of the traditional household" are glaringly absent. . . . I propose that the image of God as Midwife that found its way into the psalms presents us with the opportunity to re-envision or reimagine the conventional understanding of God as the One who delivers or heals by referring to the suppressed memories of midwives. (2012, 70–71).

I doubt that most Christian readers think "midwife imagery" when they think of Psalm 22, but there, too, God is depicted as the midwife who protects and delivers during the difficult, painful process of birth. Christians know Psalm 22:1 because Jesus quotes from it on the cross when he cries out, "My God, my God, why have you forsaken me?" They may know 22:18 as well ("They divide my clothes among themselves, and for my clothing they cast lots"), because it is quoted in the passion narratives, but not by Jesus. Jesus quotes only 22:1, thus leaving the matter with a Good Friday feel, experiencing the true depths of human misery and not rushing to gloss over the horror and anguish.

The psalm itself moves from anguish to hope, however, and that movement depends in part on the depiction of God as a midwife. Early in the psalm, the author mentions "our fathers" (v. 4); in vv. 9–10 attention is given to the mother: "Yet it was you who took me from the womb; you kept me safe on my mother's breast. On

67

you I was cast from my birth, and since my mother bore me you have been my God."

> The psalmist addresses God with the personal pronoun "you," saying that God was the one who assisted at her birth, who drew her out of her mother's womb, and who kept her safe on her mother's breasts. From that moment on she was cast upon God, whom she boldly calls "*my* God." Verses 9–10 end with a statement of faith ("You are my God"), transforming the initial cry of despair in verse 1 ("My God, My God, why have you forsaken me?") into a declaration of trust. (Claassens 2012, 72–73)

God as Midwife pulls the psalmist (and later, Jesus) out of dread and into hope.

The author of Psalm 22 does not sugarcoat the experience of suffering, which makes for a harrowing read; it is the same as when one reads the story of the cross. John 19 singularly depicts Jesus's mother at the foot of the cross; John, like Luke, does *not* have Jesus quote Psalm 22:1. I now cannot help but wonder if, as Jesus hung there in the crucifixion depicted by John, with his mother right there, he was reminded of this part of the psalm and was encouraged and emboldened and held by his mother and his Midwife God, both of them standing with Jesus as he traveled the difficult journey through the birth canal to be born again / from above (à la John 3), moving from death to new life. Again, only in John's Gospel do blood and water come out of Jesus's belly (cf. John 7:38); clearly this is birth imagery. It is not to say that this is not sacramental language referring to baptism and Eucharist. Quite the opposite; baptismal and eucharistic language are tied to birth imagery in the Gospel of John. In John, Jesus births the church at the foot of the cross and creates a family as a result. Thus, Jesus is depicted as a woman in the Bible—giving birth to the church. He is born, and he births. All the while, the psalmist would assert, God midwifes.

As does Psalm 22, Psalm 71 relies on the memory of the past. It even quotes from other psalms of lament and thanksgiving. As is the case with many psalms, in Psalm 71 the psalmist wrestles with the issue of theodicy. Will God deliver God's people? This psalm uses graphic, emergency language to depict God as deliverer. In this case, when home (the womb) becomes a death trap, it is necessary to cut the baby out, lest both mother and child die. Such is the action the midwife is called upon to take. Claassens notes that whereas in Psalm 22:9 the midwife/God "draws out" the child (representative of one of God's followers), in Psalm 71:6 the midwife/God has to "cut" the child from the womb. God takes drastic measures to deliver the child; the experience may be traumatic, but the child survives and, with God's help, grows up and grows strong. If the child's mother dies, the midwife/God will connect the child with other caregivers or a surrogate mother; in this way, the metaphor emphasizes the importance of community as part of deliverance from near death in any of its forms (consult Claassens 2012, 75–77).

The Lectionary

The Revised Common Lectionary (RCL) includes the beautiful midwife imagery in Psalm 22:9–10 as a Sunday reading in Year B, on Proper 23 (28), in the season after Pentecost; it is also a weekday reading for three days during that week. Psalm 22 is a reading on every Good Friday. With respect to the Roman Lectionary (RL), although Psalm 22:8–9, 17–18, 19–20, 23–24 is read in Palm Sunday Mass every year, Psalm 22:10 never appears.

Psalm 71:6 appears in both lectionaries in both Sunday and weekday readings. The preacher and teacher have ample opportunity, then, to help people experience this rich imagery for God.

Conclusion

In keeping with the goals stated in the introduction, this chapter has explored the ways the Bible employs feminine imagery and the ways it moves across or beyond gender; God, Jesus, and Paul are depicted in feminine terms. The chapter has also presented recent scholarship that addresses the status of women in antiquity. We have lifted up ignored women (Shiphrah and Puah) and provided resources for further study.

Through each of these metaphors—Mourner, Mother, and Midwife—we are invited to focus upon aspects of God that usually go unnoticed or are undervalued. Claassens expands our understanding of who God has always been and, in so doing, provides us rich resources for connecting with God in new ways. Her work shows special concern for those who have survived trauma and are trying to piece together a life; these metaphors may be a lifeline for those on the slippery edge of Sheol.

In addition to exhibiting compassionate concern for those in such precarious places, Claassens sounds a call to the rest of us—all of us, no matter our gender—to imitate these aspects of God. We can all name famous people who have sacrificed much to serve as what we might call "midwives of peace and justice." But Claassens does not let us off the hook when she notes that the midwives in Exodus, those who helped to birth the liberation of God's people, were ordinary human beings.

I close by honoring two midwives of peace and justice whom I know, while inviting you to do the same. First, I was fortunate to participate in a certain weekly liturgical ritual, a yoga class taught by my gifted teacher, Mireille (Mimi) Mears. She is from Belgium, which you may recall was bombed by terrorists in March 2015. All of her classes except the one I went to were for prenatal or postpartum women. She exemplifies well Claassens's call for us to be midwives of peace. Midwife Mimi always closed our class with this dedication, which was especially moving in the class session right after the bombing:

> As you bring your hands together in front of the heart, take a moment to congratulate yourself for taking the time and the energy to be here today. We dedicate our practice to those who couldn't be here, that they may benefit from the energies we have nurtured together. To those who are suffering, that they may find Peace and Relief, and for the healing of our species and our planet, knowing that it starts with each one of us taking responsibility for the choices that we are making on a day-to-day basis. Honoring the light within yourself and each other, that connects us all, we say: "Namaste."

Second, the late Bishop David Lawson was the bishop-in-residence at Perkins School of Theology when I arrived long ago. He courageously labored to serve God without counting the cost, and he most certainly journeyed through many a harrowing moment. He playfully held onto hope, though, and infected others with it, as he did for me when he sent me this poem by Kaylin Haught, which I now offer to you as we close this chapter on "God across Gender."

God Says Yes To Me

I asked God if it was okay to be melodramatic
and she said yes
I asked her if it was okay to be short
and she said it sure is
I asked her if I could wear nail polish
or not wear nail polish
and she said honey
she calls me that sometimes
she said you can do just exactly
what you want to
Thanks God I said
And is it even okay if I don't paragraph
my letters
Sweetcakes God said
who knows where she picked that up
what I'm telling you is
Yes Yes Yes
      (Kaylin Haught, "God Says Yes To Me")

Recommended Resources

Claassens, L. Juliana M. 2004. *The God Who Provides: Biblical Images of Divine Nourishment*. Nashville: Abingdon Press.

———. 2012. *Mourner, Mother, Midwife: Reimagining God's Delivering Presence in the Old Testament*. Louisville, KY: Westminster John Knox Press.

Daly, Mary. 1973. *Beyond God the Father: Toward a Philosophy of Women's Liberation*. Boston: Beacon Press.

Haught, Kaylin. 1995. "God Says Yes to Me." Page 6 in *In the Palm of Your Hand: The Poet's Portable Workshop*. Edited by Steve Kowit. Thomaston, ME: Tilbury House.

Johnson, Elizabeth A. 2002. *She Who Is: The Mystery of God in Feminist Theological Discourse*. Anniv. ed. New York: Crossroad.

Meyers, Carol. 2013. *Rediscovering Eve: Ancient Israelite Women in Context*. Oxford: Oxford University Press.

Mollenkott, Virginia Ramey. 2014. *The Divine Feminine: The Biblical Imagery of God as Female*. Eugene, OR: Wipf & Stock.

Smith, Paul R. 1993. *Is It Okay to Call God "Mother"? Considering the Feminine Face of God*. Ada, MI: Baker Academic.

Trible, Phyllis. 1978. *God and the Rhetoric of Sexuality*. Overtures to Biblical Theology. Philadelphia: Fortress Press.

CHAPTER 3

Women and Violence in the Bible

Truth Telling, Solidarity, and Hope

Women in the Bible, like women today, suffered various kinds of gender-based violence. Given the staggering statistics on violence against women globally, I have no doubt that some of you reading this right now have experienced it yourselves or journeyed with those who have. The expressions of violence against women are numerous and overlapping: war, forced migration, rape, human trafficking, domestic violence (including marital rape), and economic inequality and precarity. As long as we are born and socialized into patriarchal systems (which all of us are at present), violence against women will continue.

Because gender-based violence remains prevalent both in our own lives and in the biblical texts, it is crucial that we address it here. As Christians, how do we navigate our own experiences of it, and how do we lead others in faithful discipleship around this heinous many-headed beast? How do our sacred texts encourage, equip, and embolden us to be a gospel people? By calling us to live out the virtues of truth telling, solidarity, and hope.

Taming Violence with Virtues

73

Would that the Bible baldly, expressly stated that violence against women is wrong; it doesn't. It does address the problem, however, by means of the virtues it has the potential to cultivate in us should we allow it. Duly formed as virtuous Christians, we will avoid perpetrating violence, we will dismantle systems that perpetuate it, and we will join with others to heal the brokenness we encounter in this world that God deigned to create, sustain, and redeem. In what follows, I address three relevant virtues repeatedly exhibited by our sacred texts: truth telling, solidarity, and hope. If we adopt these virtues, we will be agents of healing resembling Jesus.

Truth Telling

We start with the virtue of truth telling, transparently testifying to the gendered violence in our texts and in our world, including our own lives. Here I lift up examples of the kinds of violence on display in the Bible so that we can become familiar with the existence of such texts and practice shining a light on them as the church in our teaching and preaching and theologizing, rather than ignoring, denying, or hiding them. Carolyn Sharp's exceptional commentary on Jeremiah, which shares many of the same values and assumptions of this book, states this principle as "making violence visible" (2021, forthcoming). So, first, we as readers of Scripture need to *name texts* that deal with women and violence.

Second, we need to wrestle with the fact that there are places where Scripture itself may condone or encourage violence against women either by its *deafening silence* where we would expect outrage in the name of justice and all that is holy or by its normalizing of violence against women. (For example, violence has been normalized when someone can say, "It's to be expected that women get abducted and raped in war. That's 'normal' and just the way things are.") Worse yet, some texts depict God demanding violence against women. In response to such texts, Hebrew Bible scholar Anathea Portier-Young charges, "I call on all biblical theologians and the project of biblical theology to embrace concern for wounded bodies, shattered psyches, and the texts that portray and promote their wounding" (2012, 394–95).

Third, we need to attend not only to the ethics *in* the text but also to the ethics we derive *from* the texts today based on our sense of their authority. *How* are they authoritative? We must attend to strategies and tactics of ethical interpretation.

74

Solidarity

The second virtue I want to cultivate is solidarity, the will and capacity to listen to the experiences of women in our texts and in our lives who have suffered violence, to believe them, and to walk through the fire with them rather than running away for fear of being burnt or reminded of the burn scars hiding under our own clothes. The first injury suffered by the person is the violence itself. The second is the potential isolation and paralyzing shame that comes from people blaming or avoiding the sufferer. As Thomas Tracy writes in his essay "Why Do the Innocent Suffer?" (1998, 46):

> Suffering frightens us, and we typically respond by looking for differences between ourselves and the sufferer. If you are in some way responsible for your misfortune, then I can hope to avoid what has befallen you. I can explain why you suffer as you do (and, by implication, why I do not), and in this way I can avoid admitting the unsettling fact that you and I are alike in our vulnerability. The price of compassion is acknowledgment of this unwelcome truth, and so we often draw back physically and morally from the one who suffers, as though suffering is contagious and can be avoided if we keep a safe distance. As a result, part of the sting of suffering is loneliness:
>
> > All my friends have forgotten me;
> >   my neighbors have thrown me away.
> > My relatives look through me
> >   as though I didn't exist.
> >   *(Job 19:13–14)*

Confronting the suffering of others is a difficult task that requires our attention.

In addition to attention and compassion at the personal level, our commitment to solidarity could include insisting upon and effecting systemic change in institutions and society itself, since systems are in place that perpetuate violence against women. Tarana Burke began the "me too." movement in 2006 to empower and be in solidarity with women who have suffered sexual abuse. In 2017 the movement came to national and international attention when the hashtag #MeToo went viral on social media as women courageously shared their experiences, often for the first time. The

75

movement has certified that our social, legal, and economic systems still harbor features that obstruct women's safety and wholeness. Our religious institutions do the same at times with our language, our metaphors, our gender binaries, and our hierarchies. To take seriously the problem of women and violence necessitates commitment to action, not simply warm wishes and words: "If a brother or sister is naked and lacks daily food, and one of you says to them, 'Go in peace; keep warm and eat your fill,' and yet you do not supply their bodily needs, what is the good of that? So faith by itself, if it has no works, is dead" (Jas. 2:15–17). When we actively enter the struggle, we fulfull Galatians 6:2: "Bear one another's burdens, and in this way you will fulfill the law of Christ." We are better together. The "me too." movement has proven that when people stand in solidarity with and take action on behalf of victims, concrete changes can occur.

Hope

The third essential virtue that we remain staunchly committed to and shaped by is hope. It is the essence of the gospel. We engage the difficult subject of violence against women—as we do all difficult subjects—firmly grounded in hope. Hope that heals and endures allows suffering to speak, stares at suffering directly without shrinking back, and only then declares, "And yet, hope calls us into our future story with God." We follow a Messiah who went to the cross, not around it, on the way to resurrection. On the cross, Jesus's body was publicly exposed in shame, violently beaten, tortured at length, penetrated, and murdered. In the Synoptics, he is deserted by the men closest to him (Mark 14:50), while the women look on from a distance (Mark 15:40–41; John's version is quite different). He was dead for days, shut up in a dark, dank tomb. Some traditions face these difficult truths by celebrating Maundy Thursday, Good Friday, and a Saturday vigil before moving to the resurrection. Thus, we will speak the truth about women and violence. On the other hand, Scripture insists, and Jesus's own experience demonstrates, that suffering does not have the final word. We are called not only to solidarity but also to hope. We will not turn away, but jump into the fray to help make it on earth as it is in heaven. I consider Revelation 21:3–4 the pinnacle of biblical hope language and the sure promise upon which faith rests: "And I heard a loud voice from the

76

throne saying, 'See, the home of God is among mortals. He will dwell with them; they will be his peoples, and God himself will be with them; he will wipe every tear from their eyes. Death will be no more; mourning and crying and pain will be no more, for the first things have passed away.'"

Naming and Unmasking Violence in the Texts: Rape and Other Sexualized Violence

The Bible is long on stories of rape but short on critiques of it. In fact, biblical Hebrew has no word for rape. Please linger over that telling fact for a moment—the language of the Old Testament has no word for rape. When there's no word for something, it can be hard to identify and articulate one's experience of it. As the philosopher of language Ludwig Wittgenstein said, *"The limits of my language* mean the limits of my world" (1922, 5.6; italics original). Who gets to define what constitutes rape? How does the fact that our ancient texts were written by men for a primarily male readership affect the construal of the experience of rape?

In *Sacred Witness: Rape in the Hebrew Bible*, Susanne Scholz uses the following categories, with attendant biblical passages for each: acquaintance rape (including Tamar and Dinah); rape of enslaved women (including Bilhah, Zilpah, and Hagar); marital rape (Bathsheba); war rape and gang rape (the Levite's *pîlegeš*, or secondary wife, usually translated as "concubine"); and rape metaphors in the prophetic literature. Scholz is particularly interested in engaging these stories in light of the experience of contemporary rape victims.

Leah Schulte's *The Absence of God in Biblical Rape Narratives* expresses appreciation for works like Scholz's but notes ways that modern definitions of rape (about which there is no agreement, as she makes painfully, astonishingly clear) differ from those of the ancients. That is, for modern readers, rape is seen as an offense against a woman and her power and agency—a woman is penetrated by a male against her will. But this notion does not cohere with the view of the biblical authors.

77

> The problem with concepts of power, agency, and control is that they are contemporary modes of analysis from feminist

scholarship that did not play a role in the patriarchal context of biblical Israel. An Israelite virgin lacked power over her own sexuality; her father was the owner/protector of her virgin status. A feminist model that applies lack of individual agency to a rape victim assumes that a daughter of Israel had sexual agency at all, which she did not. (Schulte 2017, 17)

Schulte also explains that the male family members were more likely to be viewed as the victims of ancient rape, because of the monetary value of a woman's virginity. "Therefore, a key component of an ancient or biblical rape is not sexual activity that is *unsolicited* (a violation of the rights of the victim) but instead activity that is *unauthorized* (a violation of the property rights of the one who acts as owner/protector of the victim's sexuality)" (10–11). The question of a woman's consent was not a primary consideration in determining whether rape occurred.

By Schulte's definition, many of Scholz's instances do not count as rape because the sex involved was authorized by the person in charge of the female's body. For instance, marital rape was not a recognized category for the biblical authors. Schulte's own project involves addressing the rape scenes in Genesis 34, Judges 19, and 2 Samuel 13. She argues that God's absence from the rape scenes is tied to a rupture in the covenantal relationship between God and Israel. God's absence from these narratives signals that Israel is in a covenantal breach space.

While you will find the English word "rape" in some versions of the Old Testament (such as NRSV, NASB, CEB), translating various Hebrew words or phrases, the New Testament never mentions the word rape. The closest it comes may be Revelation's imagery of what Jesus is going to do to "Jezebel" and the "whore." We discuss this further below.

To add to the confusion, obscurity, and danger for ancient women, "in biblical law there is no categorical distinction between rape and adultery as in modern vocabulary and definitions" (Schulte 2017, 11). In part, defining rape in biblical law involves whether the woman cries loudly enough or resists fiercely enough. For instance, Deuteronomy 22:23–24 considers a betrothed female virgin having sex with a male (we don't know if he's a virgin, and the text doesn't care) in a town. In this case, it's considered adultery, not rape, since the woman doesn't cry out for help, thus implying she is complicit.

In verses 25–27, if the same thing happens in a rural setting, only the man is liable to death because the woman might have cried out without anyone hearing. In verses 28–29, if a man has sex with an unbetrothed virgin, he has to pay her dad fifty shekels and marry her and can't divorce her. We can imagine how that would go for the woman.

While some have argued that the Deuteronomic laws are "humane," Schulte disagrees. "The laws depend on four factors present in patriarchal contexts," she writes (14–15), based on a list from Carolyn Pressler (1993, 5):

> 1) women are dependent on male-headed households for security and social status; 2) the marriageability of a woman is defined in terms of her virginity; 3) men normally were able to divorce their wives easily . . . 4) the woman's consent or lack of consent to sexual intercourse was a negligible factor in determining the gravity of a sexual offense.

It's not clear, of course, how the texts relate to real life, whether these laws were enforced, or whether they present the "ideal" society. It doesn't really matter for two reasons. First, the fact that this would be considered ideal gives enough context to show that patriarchy prevailed. Second, these texts, as sacred Scripture (as opposed to merely a window on the past), have shaped and continue to shape notions of gender dynamics and what "counts" as sexual assault today, even when people cannot name where the texts are in their Bibles.

This volume is concerned with these texts as they are read in Christian community, not simply a historical investigation of antiquity. For that reason, I present this definition of sexual violence, from Elaine Heath's important, compelling work *Healing the Wounds of Sexual Abuse: Reading the Bible with Survivors*:

> Sexual violence refers to harmful behaviors that use sex or sexuality as a weapon to control, intimidate or violate others. Whether it is viewed clinically or legally, objectively or subjectively, violence is the common denominator. Sexual violence is about violence that misuses sex and sexuality to exert power over or exploit others. It encompasses rape, incest, assault, date rape, sexual exploitation, misconduct and abuse, as well as inappropriate touching and harassing jokes and comments. The injuries may be psychological or physical, and frequently are both. (2019, 185)

79

The Bible includes many stories of and references to rape. We begin with attention to a single illustrative story about the rape of an individual woman, Tamar, though we could name others (e.g., Dinah). Next, we address the multipronged issue of violence against women on a more generic, global scale, with special attention to women in war zones (and these days, war is a constant reality for many people).

This chapter is far from being exhaustive. Its goal is to inform the reader that there is ample material for addressing the topic of sexual assault, an ever-present concern for most women. It is my sincere hope that reading this chapter, rather than overwhelming or paralyzing the reader, will catalyze much-needed conversation, action, and healing.

Rape of a Named Individual: Tamar, Raped by Her Brother Amnon

David's son Amnon rapes his sister (and David's daughter), Tamar (2 Sam. 13:1–14). It's a horrifying read, as one goes from the claim in verse 1 that Amnon "loved" her to verse 14, "However, he would not listen to her; since he was stronger than she, he violated her and lay with her" (NASB). Tamar is the only female mentioned in this story, which involves a number of men; her welfare is the least of anyone's concern. Amnon desires her and fakes illness. David is so concerned about Amnon's fake illness that he visits him and feels sorry for him. David, a man used to doing whatever necessary to have the women he wants when he wants them for his purposes (Bathsheba, Abigail, e.g.), sends Tamar to tend to Amnon's physical needs. Amnon promptly rapes his sister as she protests in vain.

Given his own selfish use of women, it's hard to imagine that David wouldn't suspect his son or worry about sending a female into private physical space like that. But that's the point; David does not give a thought to the safety or well-being of women—they are tools for men. "He does not come to see the screaming Tamar as he has the scheming Amnon" (Gafney 2017, 231). David is certainly capable of crying and showing grief throughout Scripture, including when Absalom kills Amnon. He may *seem* to show concern for Tamar in 13:21, when he becomes "very angry." Yet this concern is merely a facade, as "he would not punish his son Amnon, because he loved him, for he was his firstborn." Favoritism and privilege

80

dissuade David, the precise person in a position of power, from doing anything for Tamar; concern unbacked by action is not true concern. Thus, any argument that attempts to defend David's concern for Tamar does not stand. Further, "concern" that leaves the rape victim unattended to while people focus on how unfortunate it is that the home-town boy committed an act that may hurt his chances to fulfill the perfectly bright future toward which he was headed simply adds insult to injury for the victim.

David's son Absalom kills Amnon, potentially appearing to be a man who cares about the safety of women. But lionizing Absalom is not in order. First, Absalom may be complicit in the rape (consult Gafney 2017, 230). Second, Absalom himself is a rapist, raping his father David's wives in 2 Samuel 16:22.

Note also that the brothers' cousin, Jonadab (David's nephew), helps Amnon arrange the rape. For a fuller treatment of this layered, crucially relevant story of family sexual violence, I highly recommend reading at least Phyllis Trible's stellar essay "Tamar: The Royal Rape of Wisdom," in *Texts of Terror*, and Gafney's treatment in *Womanist Midrash*, where she writes: "The specter of a family member enabling the sexual abuse of a relative is unfortunately a well-known and enduring phenomenon" (228). The story also reminds us that rape cuts across all social classes; being a member of the royal household offered Tamar no special protection.

Tamar's story is told as a lone woman surrounded by men who believe in violence against women. We never even read of women comforting her at any point. The texts are not written from the viewpoint of women. That does not mean, of course, that it is too late for modern readers to respond appropriately to her story. We can lift up the story, turn it around like a prism in the light, and learn from it in ways that make us a more gospel-invested people. No one listened to her then, but we listen to her now, and we listen to all those who are caught up in sexual violence, especially at the hands of family members. "*The Tamar Campaign*, an African Bible study that explores the roles of women and men in this text, in conversation with domestic and sexual violence in their own contexts, uses both feminist and womanist approaches. Specifically, *The Tamar Campaign* provides a framework for women to talk about sexual violence, using its inclusion in the Scriptures as authority to discuss it in their own communities" (Gafney 2017, 232). It's a new day; we as Christians stand ready to help usher it in.

81

Females as "Spoils of War": Mass Abduction, Rape, Genocide, and Human Trafficking

War breeds gender-based violence for women in the Bible, including the overlapping categories of murder, rape, abduction, forced migration, forced marriage, forced breeding, and human trafficking or sexual enslavement. In war, women are especially targeted for violence that is layered as a result of patriarchy. For instance, violence against the females of one's enemies is conceived of not only as violence against women, but also (and in some cases, primarily) as violence against the male enemy, to emasculate them and show that they cannot even protect "their own" women. Violating "their" women is equivalent to violating the men themselves, emasculating and feminizing the men. Often, far from embracing the women who have been violated by the enemy, the men disdain them since they remind the men of their own sense of shame. Thus there are layers of suffering. War also takes the form of genocide through simultaneous murder of pregnant or potentially pregnant women on the one hand and abduction and forced breeding of virgin girls and women on the other. As an example of this kind of violence, let us consider Numbers 31.

In this passage, Moses, supposedly at the behest of God, enacts violence against the Midianites. (Recall that Moses himself was married to and saved by a Midianite woman, Zipporah.) Numbers 31 opens with these words: "The LORD spoke to Moses, saying, 'Avenge the Israelites on the Midianites.'" Moses, taking along the zealous, murderous Phinehas (more about him later), leads his soldiers to thoroughly exact vengeance. The soldiers kidnap the women and their children at first as "booty." When Moses subsequently learns that they had let the adult Midianite women live, he is furious and commands them to kill all of the nonvirgin women and take all the virgin girls for themselves. "Now therefore, kill every male among the little ones, and kill every woman who has known a man by sleeping with him. But all the young girls [the Greek word in the LXX is *apartian*, "movable goods"] who have not known a man by sleeping with him, keep alive for yourselves" (Num. 31:15–18). The number of girls taken into sexual servitude was thirty-two thousand. They are counted along with the animals, sheep, oxen and donkeys: "The booty remaining from the spoil that the troops had taken totaled six hundred seventy-five thousand sheep, seventy-two thousand oxen, sixty-one thousand donkeys, and thirty-two thousand persons in all, women who had not known a man by sleeping with him" (Num. 31:32–35).

So much is going on here with respect to our topic. Fear of foreign women. Blaming (foreign) women for the choices made by Israelites. Murder of sexually active women. Kidnapping, rape, and sexual enslavement of virgin girls. Not to mention the devastating irony that this whole war is supposedly tied to the problems of "foreign women" infecting Israelite piety, yet now the Israelites are taking foreign women (girls) in rape-marriage.

Gafney addresses the practice of genocide through "religiously sanctioned rape and forced impregnation" (2017, 153). Moses's violence even exceeds that of Pharaoh: he has all the males killed, including infants, toddlers, and those potentially or actually in the womb (all nonvirgin Midianite women are slaughtered by the Israelites in case they are carrying baby Midianites). As Gafney notes: "Moses' genocide is more effective and efficient than that of the pharaoh. He has learned well" (152). By slaughtering all the other Midianites but taking the virgin Midianites and impregnating them with what will be counted as Israelite babies (ancient Israelites, unlike modern Jews, reckoned lineage through the father), the Midianites could be effectively and efficiently exterminated as a people group.

Judges evinces the same values as those found in the Numbers passage. First, the followers of YHWH attack the inhabitants of Jabesh-gilead, slaughtering the men, children, and sexually active women:

> So the congregation sent twelve thousand soldiers there and commanded them, "Go, put the inhabitants of Jabesh-gilead to the sword, including the women and the little ones. This is what you shall do; every male and every woman that has lain with a male you shall devote to destruction." And they found among the inhabitants of Jabesh-gilead four hundred young virgins who had never slept with a man and brought them to the camp at Shiloh, which is in the land of Canaan. (Judg. 21:10–12)

The other tribes had been on bad terms with the Benjaminites and enacted their disdain by using women's bodies politically—they refused to give their women as wives to them (v. 18). It was God's

83

fault, according to the author. The tribes decided to make nice with the Benjaminites and gave them the "booty" from Jabesh-gilead, but that did not suffice. "Then the whole congregation sent word to the Benjaminites who were at the rock of Rimmon, and proclaimed peace to them. Benjamin returned at that time; and they gave them the women whom they had saved alive of the women of Jabesh-gilead; but they did not suffice for them. The people had compassion on Benjamin because the LORD had made a breach in the tribes of Israel" (vv. 13–15).

Even with the gift of the virgin girls, the Benjaminites were experiencing a shortage of women. So the men of God devised another "solution": abducting girls from Shiloh (from among followers of YHWH, not foreigners) and subjecting them to rape-marriage: "And they instructed the Benjaminites, saying, 'Go and lie in wait in the vineyards, and watch; when the young women of Shiloh come out to dance in the dances, then come out of the vineyards and each of you carry off a wife for himself from the young women of Shiloh, and go to the land of Benjamin'" (Judg. 21:16–21). The tribes planned for a negative reaction from the girls' fathers and brothers (notice there is no mention of mothers or sisters—this is typical of the way patriarchy functions):

> Then if their fathers or their brothers come to complain to us, we will say to them, "Be generous and allow us to have them; because we did not capture in battle a wife for each man. But neither did you incur guilt by giving your daughters to them." The Benjaminites did so; they took wives for each of them from the dancers whom they abducted. Then they went and returned to their territory, and rebuilt the towns, and lived in them. (vv. 22–23)

The men who own the bodies of the women are supposed to feel sorry for the Benjaminites because there's a shortage of women, yet they don't have to feel bad about breaking the vow not to give their daughters to Benjaminites. So they can happily, religiously leave their daughters in the hands of their kidnapper-rapists and go to sleep with an easy conscience, knowing they are true promise keepers.

Stories like this demand attention from Christian readers.

> The narrative does not report any resistance from the women of Jabesh-gilead or Shiloh, who never speak. . . .

It is thus incumbent upon readers to read between the lines, look for the unsaid, and imagine the women of Shiloh as speaking out. . . . This story depicts sexual violence in war as sanctioned by the Divinity and executed by male Israelites. . . .

In short, the narratives of Judges 1–21 demonstrate that misogyny, rape, and war are interrelated structures of oppression. In such structures, women are objects, to be used and even abused, murdered, and cut into pieces, trafficked and forced to marriage. They are there for the taking, objects of men, there to fulfill male needs. The problem for readers is what to do with these stories. Shall we be complicit and accept assumptions of phallocentric superiority, or shall we come to recognize the links of misogyny, rape and established hierarchies of sociopolitical and economic life? In the metaphoric language of biblical prose, Judges 19–21 illustrates the misogyny during so-called peacetime and the prevalence of rape during war. The narratives remind readers of the pervasive and persisting problems in androcentric society that include misogyny, gang rape, murder, and war. (Scholz 2012, 126–27)

Of course, the trafficking of women's bodies continues today. Some churches are actively, courageously engaging to combat the lucrative business and minister to its victims, bringing new life, hope, and healing.

Violence against "Foreign [Non-Israelite] Women"

Because of massive global migration today, including refugees fleeing their home countries, contemporary Christians encounter people from other countries, ethnicities, and religious traditions. Our Scriptures can help us navigate this terrain as we decide whether we will embrace or eschew or remain neutral about all of the "mixing." While our texts certainly teach us about radical hospitality and the welcoming and care of the stranger, they also exhibit xenophobia, including ambivalence about intermarriage between Israelite males and foreign women.

Consider the story of Cozbi, for example. So zealous is the priest Phinehas about the marriage issue that he murders the Israelite Zimri and his new wife, Cozbi, a Midianite, in their marriage tent. In a shockingly sexualized scene worthy of the *Game of Thrones* "Red Wedding" episode, Phinehas takes his spear, a phallic

85

symbol to be sure, and after dispensing with his fellow countryman Zimri, specifically penetrates the foreign woman's womb (Num. 25:8). "Cozbi's deathblow is rendered a punch line: the Midianite woman is killed through the violent penetration of her womb and/or vagina—terminating and parodying the conjugal union that Cozbi, Zimri, and his family . . . were gathered in the presence of God to celebrate" (Gafney 2017, 145).

What judgment is God depicted as rendering on this vicious, sexualized attack? The plagues cease, and "God vindicates and rewards Phinehas, with of all things a 'covenant of *shalom*,' superficially a covenant of peace. . . . For the authors, editors, and God in the text, Phinehas has restored the community after its infestation by and infatuation with foreign women; for this, his zealous rage is commended. He is further rewarded in verse 13 with a perpetual priesthood" (Gafney 2017, 145).

As we discussed in the section on violence against women in war, foreign women are depicted as exotic, irresistible temptresses who cause innocent Israelite men to stray into idolatry. With no apparent recognition of the irony, however, this certainly doesn't stop the Israelites from abducting these women, enslaving them, and taking them as secondary wives or sex slaves. The trafficking of women and girls (as well as boys), which currently plagues our globe in astounding numbers, is nothing new. Perceiving "foreigners" as less-than makes it easier to dehumanize them and perpetrate violence against them with a blissfully clear conscience. We Christians are called to disrupt such treatment of God's children, and many communities and individuals are answering that call in creative, faithful ways.

Other Abuses of Female Bodies

In this section I make only brief mention of other passages that exemplify particular aspects of violence against women: male contests using women's bodies as pawns; men protecting themselves by offering up the women in their charge; and women participating in violence against women.

Matriarchs

Recall the commandment in Exodus 20:17 (and Deut. 5:21) not to covet your neighbor's wife (or his other belongings, including his house, his farm animals, and his slaves). Again, the texts are written from a male perspective that assumes a male readership that owns people and other property.

Abraham and Sarah provide material for our topic. They are sister and brother, given that they share a father; in our current context, their marriage would count as incest. Here I draw attention to the ways Sarah's body is used by various men. When Abraham and Sarah go to Egypt, Abraham is worried that Sarah's beauty might cause Egyptian men to covet her in a way that endangers Abraham's own life. Thus, he schemes to present her as his sister (which, technically, she is) but not his wife. In Genesis 12, Pharaoh's men seize Sarah to give to Pharaoh for his sexual use. Abraham stands by, perfectly unaccosted, and watches his wife get abducted into a harem. Abraham is paid with animals and slave women and slave men. Thus, one could calculate exactly the market value of Sarah's body by adding up the money paid by one male to the other. It is fair to assume that Pharaoh used her sexually.

In Genesis 20, King Abimelech decides he wants Sarah for his sexual use, so he takes her (a recurring theme, if one recalls David and Bathsheba), while Abraham remains untouched. This time the text indicates that Sarah's captor does not have sex with her. As a female reader, I am deeply disturbed by the words that God speaks to Abimelech in a dream: "You are about to die because of the woman whom you have taken; for she is a married woman" (v. 3). Apparently, the problem is not that he had abducted a woman into sexual enslavement, but only that she was someone else's property. In the end, Abraham once again receives payment of animals and human slaves, growing even richer. That the money goes to Abraham, not Sarah, is made clear: "To Sarah he said, 'Look, I have given your brother a thousand pieces of silver; it is your exoneration before all who are with you; you are completely vindicated'" (v. 16). Isaac will use this strategy from his father's playbook in Genesis 26 with Abimelech.

While women's bodies are commonly used this way, the fact that even the matriarchs are not immune is noteworthy.

The Levite's *Pîlegeš*

In *Texts of Terror*, Phyllis Trible begins her finely detailed close reading of Judges 19 with this charge: "The betrayal, rape, torture, murder, and dismemberment of an unnamed woman is a story we want to forget but are commanded to speak. It depicts the horrors of male power, brutality, and triumphalism; of female helplessness, abuse, and annihilation. To hear this story is to inhabit a world of unrelenting terror that refuses to let us pass by on the other side" (1984, 65).

In the story a certain Levite takes a *pîlegeš*, a Hebrew term referring to a secondary wife and sometimes translated into English as "concubine." It is customary when discussing the Old Testament to distinguish between a primary wife ('*iššâ*) and a secondary wife (*pîlegeš*) as if their statuses are clearly defined and static and as if children of the former inherit while the children of the latter never do. One can see there is some distinction between the two in a sentence such as 2 Samuel 5:13, "David took more concubines and wives." The distinction does not always remain clear, however, and the subject can quickly become confusing.

The primary issue is the somewhat ambiguous usage of the Hebrew words '*iššâ* and *pîlegeš*. For instance, Bilhah, whose body is used by quite a few people, male and female, old and young, goes from being a slave girl (first of Laban, then of Rachel) to Jacob's *pîlegeš*. Though she's a *pîlegeš*, one could argue that her children inherit, because they get inheritance in the land—allocations in Joshua, for example.

Zilpah's fate appears to follow a similar trajectory as Bilhah's. That is, she too is first Laban's slave girl and then is given as a slave to his daughter Leah. Leah sends her in to get impregnated by Jacob, but the text says she sends her in to be his '*iššâ*, primary wife.

Hagar is an Egyptian slave girl who belongs to Sarah, but in Genesis 16:3 Sarah gives her to Abram to be an '*iššâ*, primary wife, exactly what Sarah herself is called in the same verse. However, Ishmael does not inherit; in fact, inheritance for their sons is part of the crisis that pits Sarah against Hagar: "So she [Sarah] said to Abraham, 'Cast out this slave woman with her son; for the son of this slave woman shall not inherit along with my son Isaac.' The matter was very distressing to Abraham on account of his son [Ishmael]. But God said to Abraham, 'Do not be distressed because of the boy and because of *your slave woman*'" (Gen. 21:10–12; emphasis added). Hagar's designation as an '*iššâ* does not elevate her social status:

The term "wife" is the same term used to describe Sarai's relationship to Abram (16:1; 20:12). Yet, given Sarai's continued
power over Hagar, this new position does not indicate that Hagar
has been liberated from her enslavement or elevated to equal
co-wife status with Sarai. Hagar is only called a "wife" when
the text describes her sexual relationship with Abram in 16:3,
but otherwise she is never referred to explicitly as the wife of
Abram. She is an enslaved woman who serves as a surrogate by
providing Abram with a son. Despite the description of Hagar as
a "wife," the text emphasizes Hagar's enslaved status as a woman
who remains subordinate to Sarai, her "mistress." . . . Similarly,
Bilhah and Zilpah remain "slave women" after becoming "wives."
(Junior 2019, 21–22)

In addition, in the story of the Levite's *pîlegeš*, there is no mention of a primary wife at all. Is she his only woman? In fact, the story
opens by using both words, designating the woman as an *'iššâ pîlegeš*.

All of this is to say that if you are confused, it's understand-
able. To avoid the kinds of confusion I've mentioned, I refer to the
woman with the untranslated Hebrew word *pîlegeš* in what follows.

At some point the *pîlegeš* flees from the Levite back to her
father's house. The Levite comes to get her to take her away to the
hills of Ephraim, where he's from. He and the woman's father spend
five days visiting, eating and drinking. On the night of the fifth day,
the Levite takes his *pîlegeš* and sets out for his home turf. On the
way, they stop to spend the night at Gibeah. An old man takes them
in for the night. In a scene that sounds much like the one from
Sodom, men from the city knock on the door, demanding to have
sexual intercourse with the Levite. The homeowner asks the men to
leave the Levite alone and offers up his own virgin daughter and the
Levite's *pîlegeš*: "No, my brothers, do not act so wickedly. Since this
man is my guest, do not do this vile thing. Here are my virgin daughter and his *pîlegeš*; let me bring them out now. Ravish them and do
whatever you want to them; but against this man do not do such a
vile thing." (Judg. 19:23–24). When the men continue to insist on
the Levite, the Levite throws his *pîlegeš* out to them: "They wantonly
raped her, and abused her all through the night until the morning.
And as the dawn began to break, they let her go" (v. 25).

The woman drags herself to the doorstep of the house where
her husband is and collapses there. How does he respond? "In the

89

morning her master got up, opened the doors of the house, and when he went out to go on his way, there was his *pîlegeš* lying at the door of the house, with her hands on the threshold. 'Get up,' he said to her, 'we are going.' But there was no answer. Then he put her on the donkey; and the man set out for his home" (Judg. 19:27–28). Back at his home, "he took a knife, and grasping his *pîlegeš* he cut her into twelve pieces, limb by limb, and sent her throughout all the territory of Israel" (v. 29). It's not clear when she died and if she was dead before he began chopping her up to make his point about his anger against the Benjaminites.

The layers of violence conducted against this woman are thick, and her isolation and helplessness complete. Her father, her husband, the men who gang-rape her—no one treats her with any regard at all. No other women appear in the narrative.

The *pîlegeš* is not the only one who suffers violence from the man who claims to care for her. Shechem "loves" Dinah and rapes her. Amnon "loves" Tamar and rapes her. The Levite sets out to "speak tenderly" to his *pîlegeš* when he goes to retrieve her from her father, then hands her over for gang rape and personally chops her up. Love and domestic violence do not cohere. Unfortunately, domestic violence remains all too real for women today.

For an excellent resource on walking with victims of domestic violence who, because of their view of the nature and authority of Scripture, find it especially difficult to leave the abuser, read Marie Fortune's *Keeping the Faith*. It is a bit dated in some ways, but the core of it remains exceedingly useful and accessible, in part due to its conciseness.

Revenge Rape

We can also include in this section the practice of "revenge rape," which, according to 2 Samuel 12:11, is the will of God. In that passage, Nathan confronts David about his abduction of Bathsheba for his own sexual use and his murder of her husband Uriah. Nathan prophesies that, as punishment for David's actions, David's own wives will be taken and given to David's neighbor. Tit for tat, rape for rape. While David carried out his rape privately (sort of, anyway), the rape of David's wives will be public: "Thus says the LORD: I will raise up trouble against you from within your own house; and I will take your wives before your eyes, and give them to your neighbor,

90

and he shall lie with your wives in the sight of this very sun. For you did it secretly; but I will do this thing before all Israel, and before the sun" (2 Sam. 12:11–12). Four chapters later (16:22), Absalom, David's son, rapes David's wives as the act of revenge. And, because 2 Samuel 12 portrays God as the one announcing—and thus ordaining—this treatment of women, even God is depicted as one of the males playing twisted games with female bodies.

Women Navigating Patriarchy

What was it like to be a woman in the Bible? It depends, to some degree, on other factors, such as social class and connections. Gender meets social status in the story in which Sarah gives her slave Hagar to Abraham to use for forced breeding. This is the same Sarah who herself was a victim of abduction for sexual use by a male. She and the other matriarchs functioned within a polygynous structure where one man could have multiple wives, though one woman could not have multiple husbands. One could hope to be at the top of the pecking order, though, and to produce children for the husband. If your own body didn't produce a child, you could give your husband one of your slaves to impregnate and count the child as your own (of course, the men were in no way forced to sexually use the women brought to them, though none refuse in our texts).

In her 1993 book *Sisters in the Wilderness: The Challenge of Womanist God-Talk*, womanist theologian Delores Williams draws a connection between the enslaved Hagar and the experiences of African American women. A quarter of a century later, womanist biblical scholar Wil Gafney writes: "I read Hagar's story through the prism of the wholesale enslavement of black peoples in the Americas and elsewhere; Hagar is the mother of Harriet Tubman and the women and men who freed themselves from slavery. I see Hagar as an abused woman" (2017, 44). In her recent *Reimagining Hagar: Blackness and Bible*, biblical scholar Nyasha Junior seeks to answer two questions: "(1) How did Hagar become Black? and (2) what purpose did or does that serve?" (2019, 1).

Rachel and Leah both hand over the bodies of their slaves Bilhah and Zilpah for forced breeding with Jacob. To see how layered these issues of gender become in a patriarchal system that also upholds the economic system of slavery, note that Bilhah first is a slave to

91

Laban, then to Rachel, then she is sexually used and impregnated by Jacob, and then raped by Jacob's son Reuben. Maybe we could have a moment of silence for the Bilhahs of our world.

Metaphorical Violence against Women

Here's something Jesus understood well: thoughts and words lead to action. We might say, "Well, I just *thought* it, I didn't actually *say* it, so what's the harm?" Or, "Oh, those were just *words*; everyone knows I didn't really *mean* anything by it." Jesus isn't buying it; neither should we. Jesus said:

> You have heard that it was said to those of ancient times, "You shall not murder"; and "whoever murders shall be liable to judgment." But I say to you that if you are angry with a brother or sister, you will be liable to judgment; and if you insult a brother or sister, you will be liable to the council; and if you say, "You fool," you will be liable to the hell of fire. (Matt. 5:21–22).

Words matter. Words have power. In the beginning was the Word.

The authors of Ezekiel, Nahum, and Revelation are among those biblical authors who deploy the clichéd yet dangerous trope of a male God punishing feminized followers, including cities (Nineveh, Rome) or people groups (Israel). All of them could learn a thing or two from Jesus. Their chilling gender rhetoric needs to be interrogated and challenged. Their imagined "legitimate" violence against "metaphorical" women easily slips into legitimating violence against actual female bodies. Indulge me for a moment with an academic quotation from cultural theorist Arturo Aldama, whose main purpose is to capture the notion of the way discursive violence ("mere" words) and material violence ("actual" violence on real bodies) relate. He investigates "the relationships between discursive violence—that is, fear-based discourses of otherization and pathologization of subjects whose positions are at the margins and borders of dominant political and cultural apparatuses—and the materiality of violence on these otherized bodies" (Aldama 2003, 5).

Portier-Young serves as a faithful guide as we dip into the prophetic literature and the troubling gendered imagery employed there. In her stunning essay, "Drinking the Cup of Horror and Gnawing on Its Shards: Biblical Theology through Biblical Violence, Not around It," Portier-Young guides us on a close-encounter tour of

92

Ezekiel 16 and 23 as well as Nahum. As a result, we find ourselves again directly confronted as Christians with ethical issues around Scripture and violence, especially gendered violence. I invite you to read Ezekiel 16 and 23, word for word, carefully, before continuing. If you remain undisturbed by it, I'd invite you to read it again. Indeed, "There is . . . a direct correlation between our willingness to attend to the shocking violence in our Scriptures and our willingness to attend to violence and its effects in the world we inhabit" (Portier-Young 2012, 390).

Here's the problem. First, in Ezekiel 16, God is depicted as a male. Samaria and Jerusalem are depicted as females. Ezekiel then marries male God to female Samaria and female Jerusalem, sexualizing the covenantal relationship. Jerusalem's religious infidelity is put into sexualized terms as in repeated language of "whore" and "whoring" (consult esp. vv. 15–43). God is then depicted as sexually abusing Jerusalem, as God hands her over both to other sex partners she has chosen and to sex partners she had attempted to refuse so that they all could pierce her with swords, another sexualized, phallic image (v. 40).

Ezekiel 23 presents much of the same imagery, now addressing both Samaria and Jerusalem as sexually involved with other partners. Ezekiel first portrays God shaming Samaria through sexualized punishment. Next, depicted as a husband in a jealous rage, God "vows to convoke gang rape against his wayward woman," Jerusalem (Portier-Young 2012, 397). Ezekiel's misogyny has been explored at length: "Ezekiel's metaphor relies on and reinforces the notion that a woman or young girl who is sexually promiscuous deserves punishment by being publicly exposed, mutilated, and gang-raped" (399).

Using the same trope, the male prophet Nahum, writing with a male audience in mind, casts the enemy Nineveh in female terms, specifically as a whore. Nahum depicts a male God declaring to female Nineveh that God is going to lift up her skirts and hide her face while exposing her genitalia, publicly shaming her in a sexualized fashion (Nah. 3:5). If you can't see her face and her eyes, it's easier to dehumanize, objectify, and humiliate her.

While Portier-Young sticks to Old Testament texts, one could add Revelation's depiction of the seer's opponent "Jezebel" and the "whore of Babylon." As for Jezebel, Jesus plans to "throw her on a bed" (Rev. 2:22). The image evokes a rape scene, especially given

93

the sexualized context in which she is accused of fornication such that she will presumably get her "just rewards." Later, John relishes his vision of the "whore" experiencing violence against her body: "they will make her desolate and naked; they will devour her flesh and burn her up with fire" (17:16). This is considered part of God's "purpose" (v. 17).

Again, the trope of idolatry is painted with the palette of female sexuality. This in a book that depicts the faithful as 144,000 "who have not defiled themselves with women" (Rev. 14:4). If one doubted that this, like the other biblical books that depend on this imagery, is material written by men with the male imagination in mind, such a statement should settle the issue. This is not to say that the material cannot be useful in some way for contemporary readers. The question becomes, how?

Engaging the Violence, Responding to It

There are many ways to address the issue of women and violence in our sacred texts.

1. Be honest about the both/and. First, we can be honest about the fact that our texts contain both promises and problems, both enduring healing truths and dangerous destructive falsehoods. We can name those features very specifically. We will not hide, pretend, or wring our hands. We will acknowledge that these are part of our sacred Scriptures, take responsibility for them, and have robust conversations about them.

For instance, we can revel in Revelation's call to faithful endurance and critique of imperial practices while lamenting the ways its own rhetoric incites and perpetrates violence. Susan Garrett models this for us when she analyzes gender dynamics in Revelation. On the one hand, she freely grants that John provides Christians an enduring word: "The rehearsal of Babylon's destruction in chap. 18 stands as an important reminder that God is not infinitely tolerant and will indeed judge against the perpetrators of evil: individuals, cities, and entire nations will one day be called to account for their deeds. It is a message that all persons need to hear!" On the other hand, she is honest about scriptural language that promotes violence against women: "And yet one can only regret the misogynist imagery that the author has used to convey this important message.

94

To be sure, the book's imagery is violent from beginning to end. . . . But the author seems especially to delight in describing the gory destruction of the woman Babylon." Finally, she warns us against underestimating or minimizing the power of metaphorical language in our Scriptures: "The objection that 'Babylon' is only a metaphor, a symbol, does not eliminate the problem that the text creates for women readers. The author's exultation over the mutilation, burning, and eating of a woman—even a figurative one—tragically implies that women are sometimes deserving of such violence" (Garrett 1998, 473).

As another example, we can detect the enduring truth from Nahum that war is always full of horrors, while rejecting the "normalizing" of sexualized violence against women. Violence is traumatic. Sometimes violence engenders violence—one fantasizes about doing to the oppressor what has been done to one's self or group. Reading a text like Nahum can fuel such fantasies. On the other hand, one can read the violent desires expressed in Nahum against his enemies and recognize underneath it a cry for justice. One can affirm the call for justice without assuming the violent strategies suggested for achieving it, including the "tit for tat" of sexually attacking women as the "normal" rules of engagement of war. Finally, Portier-Young describes ways that Nahum can be used in the healing process for soldiers who suffered or committed atrocities in war:

> What if pastors can give combat veterans a new kind of assurance: not that the pastor knows what the veteran has experienced and not that all is well, but rather that the horrors the veteran does not dare to speak are ones a prophet already spoke? Our sacred traditions know the horror they know. These horrors come to us in a form that must be engaged and argued with, but their very presence in Scripture suggests that there is no horror we dare not speak before God, no crime we dare not confess, because there is no horror that God does not see and know. (Portier-Young 2012, 407)

Scripture reflects understanding of the complex texture of human existence, often to a stunning degree.

2. Repent, lament, and humanize. Next, we can repent, lament, and humanize. Our authors sometimes use virulent language toward their real or perceived enemies, dehumanizing them and making it appear that the enemy deserves the violence described in the text. One ethical response contemporary readers can employ is to reclaim the practice of lament, mourning for *all* who are caught up in the machinery of war, including our enemies. Instead of villainizing, through the Holy Spirit we have the power to love our enemies and pray for those who persecute us in accordance with Jesus's command. Where the texts glorify violence, we can lament it. Where they dehumanize enemies using misogynistic tropes, we can reject misogyny and try our hardest to remember that we are all human. All. We can repent of the ways we succumb to strategies of violence, revisiting our texts that warn us not to repay evil for evil, lest we fail to attain the mind of Christ and, instead, become morally deformed by the pursuit of violence.

Can we find ways to achieve the justice that Scripture teaches us to value, without the violence? This is the exciting, creative work of those currently committed to *restorative* (or *transformative*) justice rather than the failed practices of *retributive* justice. (For more on mourning for our enemies and humanizing rather than villainizing them, consult Portier-Young 2012, 404–5, and O'Brien 2002, 123–40.)

3. Listen to and with survivors. As part of our commitment to addressing violence and the Bible, our conversations should involve listening to the voices of women who have experienced gender violence. Elaine Heath grounds her book *Healing the Wounds of Sexual Abuse* in two commitments: "First, that the Bible can be a powerful source of healing for survivors of abuse, and second, that survivors who are healing have essential theological wisdom that the whole church needs in order to be the people God has called us to be in this world" (2019, xiv). She notes, however, that though the Bible has healing power for many survivors, for others, the Bible can be wounding, especially if it has been used in the process of the abuse or if the abuser was or is a person with religious authority over the victim. "It is never appropriate to try to force someone to heal by using the Bible" (xv). Each chapter of her book concludes with reflection questions for survivors and those journeying with them, along with activities.

4. Explain but don't explain *away*. We are separated from our texts temporally, geographically, and culturally. Scholars work to bridge the gaps in our knowledge so that we might better understand the original contexts of the authors. This task of historical recovery focuses upon what the text meant in its original context for its earliest audiences. It is an important step in interpreting the texts that involves attention to the biblical languages; literary genres, themes, and techniques; sociopolitical realities; and more. Such studies can help us see beyond the surface of the text, exposing subtleties and richness of meaning that may challenge our assumptions.

The book of Judges provides a case in point. In terms of volume, variety, and severity, Judges ranks high in violence against women. Of the four narratives Trible treats in *Texts of Terror*, two are found in Judges: the rape of the Levite's nameless *pîlegeš* and Jephthah's murder of his nameless daughter. The text never overtly castigates violence against women. Many Judges scholars argue that the text implicitly critiques it, though. In his book *Violence in Scripture*, Jerome Creach represents this trajectory: "Many identify [Judges] as a book that approves of or at least tolerates violence, particularly violence against women. . . . To the contrary . . . the violence against women in the book is a primary sign of how Israel failed to acknowledge and be guided by God's reign" (2013, 13). The book begins with some prominent women who exhibit some amount of agency—such as Achsah, Deborah, and Jael—before moving increasingly to stories of men perpetrating violence on women. Noting the Levite's *pîlegeš*, Creach writes: "As the story subtly communicates, however, the tragic situation is due directly to the Levite's treatment of the woman as one of secondary concern. . . . By the end of the book, Israel traffics in women. . . . In other words, the violent treatment of women in Judges seems the primary illustration of how Israel has lost its way during a time when 'there was no king in Israel'" (129–30).

Such an interpretation of the way individual passages fit into the overall logic of the whole book of Judges can help us teach and preach these passages in a way that overtly critiques and resists violence against women. When Creach uses the phrase "subtly communicates," though, he identifies a potential problem, namely, that it's easy to miss. It certainly does not jump out at a reader, even one reading the book from start to finish. Add to that the fact that readers of the Bible often encounter these stories as isolated individual narratives and the result is that, as Creach notes, the impression is one of acceptance of such violence.

While it's important to consider what ancient texts meant "back then," I want to warn us against some problematic assumptions or

97

tendencies we might harbor. First, we don't want to wave the issue away by thinking, "Well, that was a different time with different values," so we need not engage it because it's no longer a problem in our own time. Violence against women remains an issue.

Second, we don't want to excuse the violence in the Bible by saying, "That's just how they did things back then, and we can't judge by our modern ethical standards." Such logic is problematic on two counts. First, it implies that women "back then" were fine with being handed over as a sex toy or breeder, or with being a *pîlegeš*, or with other aspects of their culture that were "normal." It's "normal" for contemporary American women to make seventy-three cents on the dollar that men make in the same position; it does not mean it is acceptable to women or that they don't notice it and desire a different reality. Second, for Christians biblical interpretation is not simply an exercise in recovering ancient history; for us these texts are foundational and essential to our moral formation. "What the text meant" is part of our query, to be sure, but most importantly, we read the Bible to understand "what the text means" today. How those two aspects relate is the primary work of interpretation, and it's not always obvious. This is why it is imperative for Christians to develop nuanced interpretive skills. Fortunately, many faithful thinkers have provided us strategies and examples of how to use them.

5. Increase our hermeneutical repertoire. In this chapter, we have encountered texts that raise serious questions for those of us who consider the Bible to be a sacred text that informs our ethics. Does God condone or, worse, instigate and relish violence against women? The prophets depict God commanding it. Torah books depict God and Moses commanding the murder and abduction of women. What do we do with this as Scripture?

"Hermeneutics" has to do with interpretive skills and reading strategies. The clearer we can be about articulating what strategies we are using, the better we can understand why we, on the one hand, have arrived at a particular interpretation of a text whereas our neighbor, on the other hand, may have arrived at another. It can allow us to decide as a Christian community which readings we deem to be the most compelling in our context, which will, in turn, help clarify and prioritize our values.

Gafney models this when she overtly states her hermeneutical approach as "womanist midrash" and further defines it:

The expression captures my articulation of a womanist hermeneutic influenced by classical rabbinic and continuing contemporary midrash. Specifically, womanist midrash is a set of
interpretive practices, including translation, exegesis, and biblical
interpretation, that attends to marginalized characters in biblical narratives, especially women and girls, intentionally including and centering on non-Israelite peoples and enslaved persons.
Womanist midrash listens to and for their voices in and through
the Hebrew Bible, while acknowledging that often the text does
not speak, or even intend to speak, to or for them, let alone hear
them. In the tradition of rabbinic midrash and contemporary
feminist biblical scholarship, womanist midrash offers names for
anonymized characters and crafts/listens for/gives voice to those
characters. This particular hermeneutic, womanist midrash, is an
outgrowth of my experience from pulpit and pew with the *sanctified imagination* in black preaching; I have come to recognize the
sanctified imagination as a type of African American indigenous
midrash. (2017, 3; italics in original)

Adele Reinhartz's *Befriending the Beloved Disciple: A Jewish
Reading of the Fourth Gospel* is a good place to start for a reader
who wants to engage hermeneutics. She envisions reading as relationship, an invitation on the part of the author. She provides four
readings of John, which she characterizes as compliant, resistant,
sympathetic, and engaged. In a compliant reading, the reader will
accept and adopt the values of the author and the construal of
reality presented. In a resistant reading, the reader will decline
to do so. Neither of these, according to Reinhartz, requires deep
personal engagement or relationship between reader and author.
A sympathetic reading gets us closer insofar as it requires active
encounter with the Other as we attempt to locate what unites us
with the Other but ignore anything that divides us. The engaged
reading holds the most potential, in her estimation: "[An] infinitely
more challenging possibility, however, is to engage fully with what
separates me from the Other, not in order to persuade him or
her but simply to acknowledge and accept his or her difference.
Although the temptation is to expect reciprocity, this engaged
position cannot demand such reciprocity without compromising
its radical acceptance of the Other's otherness along with one's
own" (2002, 29). Thus, Reinhartz provides a reader four ways to
approach texts.

99

Charles Cosgrove's *Appealing to Scripture in Moral Debate: Five Hermeneutical Rules* remains unparalleled in its ability to instruct us in how to read the Bible ethically as people of faith. Admirably both dense and concise, the book unpacks five "rules" presented in the introduction, using specific biblical texts and moral issues (including treatment of women). A professor of New Testament and Christian ethics, Cosgrove presents what he takes to be five assumptions that appear in moral debate. "My choice of these five particular rules is due to the fact that I find them especially interesting and am more inclined to affirm them than their opposites. My analysis will reveal where I have reservations about some of them. My aim is not so much to recommend the rules as to examine them" (2002, 4). These are his five rules:

1. The Rule of Purpose
2. The Rule of Analogy
3. The Rule of Countercultural Witness
4. The Rule of Nonscientific Scope of Scripture
5. The Rule of Moral-Theological Adjudication

When violence against women is an ethical concern, as in our current chapter, rule 3 often comes into play. Here "there is a presumption in favor of according greater weight to countercultural tendencies in scripture that express the voice of the powerless and the marginalized than to those tendencies that echo the dominant culture of their time" (Cosgrove 2002, 3). For instance, in his treatment of Jeremiah, William Holladay asks "why the pre-exilic prophets, who stood out so sturdily against the prevailing assumptions of their culture in matters of social justice, seem never to have questioned a society in which there was male domination" (Holladay 1995, 282; quoted in Cosgrove, 98). As Cosgrove explains, Holladay answers that for ancient Israelites, "the male/female hierarchy was seen as rooted in the created order" (Cosgrove 2002, 98). It is therefore not particularly surprising that Jeremiah, as a product of his culture, generally accepted this hierarchy. What is noteworthy, though, is Jeremiah 31:22, where he envisions a new creation involving a gender role reversal rather than the patriarchal status quo. "For the LORD has created a *new* thing on the earth: a woman encompasses a man" (emphasis added). That is, the prophets' "acceptance of the priority of male over female is not surprising . . . What is surprising is the ability of Jeremiah, in this curious verse, to envision what had not theretofore been envisioned" (Holladay; quoted in Cosgrove, 98). We will encounter the same kind of countercultural move by Paul—not to mention Jesus—with respect to gender.

The Lectionary

The rapes that occur in David's family are hardly found in the lectionaries. The rape of Tamar is completely absent from the Roman Lectionary (RL), and the Revised Common Lectionary (RCL) includes only a weekday reading of 2 Samuel 13:1–19 during the season after Pentecost of Year B, on Proper 13 (18). Absalom's rape of David's wives in 2 Samuel 16:22 is left out of both lectionaries. Finally, God's declaration of the revenge rape against David's wives in 2 Samuel 12:11–12 is included in the RCL's Sunday reading of 2 Samuel 11:26–12:13a on Proper 13 (18) of Year B, the same week that has Tamar's rape as a weekday reading. God's proclamation in 2 Samuel 12 is also read on a weekday for Proper 12 (17) during Year A in the season after Pentecost. The RL includes only a weekday reading of this passage on the Saturday of Week 3 of Ordinary Time during Year 2. Elsewhere, this passage is skipped in both lectionaries: the RCL calls for a Sunday reading of 2 Samuel 11:26–12:10, 13–15 on Proper 6 (11) during Year C; the RL calls for a Sunday reading of 2 Samuel 12:7–10, 13. Thus, only once is one of these accounts of rape in David's family read on a Sunday for RCL Protestants and never for Catholic Christians. This is, however, more than can be said for the rape of Dinah in Genesis 34:2, which appears nowhere in either lectionary.

Also absent from both lectionaries are the women raped and considered spoils of war in Numbers 31 and Judges 21, the murder of the Midianite woman Cozbi in Numbers 25, and the horrifying story of the Levite's unnamed *pîlegeš* in Judges 19.

The stories of the matriarchs Sarah and Rebekah being offered to foreign rulers by their husbands also receive scant attention in the lectionaries. The RL lacks any references to Genesis 12:10–20; 20:1–18; 26:6–11. The RCL includes no Sunday readings of these stories but has a weekday reading of Genesis 12:10–20 during Proper 11 (16) of the season after Pentecost in Year C and a weekday reading of Genesis 20:1–18 during Proper 22 (27) of the season after Pentecost in Year B. The RCL omits Genesis 26:6–11, despite including Genesis 26:1–5 as a reading during the week of the 6th Sunday after Epiphany in Year A.

The stories of the matriarchs' complicit role in violence against their slaves also appear mostly in weekday readings when they are present at all. Sarah's sending away of Hagar is read, according to the RCL, on Year A, season after Pentecost, Proper 7 (12). Otherwise the RCL calls for parts of Hagar's story, including Sarah's offering of Hagar to Abraham, to be read during weekdays of the following weeks:

Genesis 16: 1–6	Year B, 2nd Sunday in Lent
Genesis 16: 1–14	Year B, 2nd Sunday after the Epiphany
Genesis 16: 1–15	Year A, Proper 5 (10) and Proper 7 (12)
Genesis 16: 7–15	Year B, 2nd Sunday in Lent
Genesis 21: 1–21	Year A, 4th Sunday of Advent

The RL does not include Hagar in any Sunday readings, but two weekday readings during Year 1 include parts of her story: the Thursday of Week 12 of Ordinary Time, Genesis 16:1–12, 15–16 or 16:6b–12, 15–16; the Wednesday of Week 13 of Ordinary Time, Genesis 21:5, 8–20a. As for Bilhah and Zilpah, the slaves of Rachel and Leah respectively, they do not appear at all in the RL and are absent from RCL Sunday readings; however, they appear once during a weekday reading (Gen. 30:1–24) for the 4th Sunday of Advent in Year C.

As for the disturbing language describing God's punishment of wayward cities in sexualized terms in Ezekiel 16 and 23 and Nahum (esp. 3:4–7), these passages are completely absent from RL and RCL Sunday readings and the RCL weekday readings. The RL contains only one verse of the problematic passage in Ezekiel 16:15–43, in a reading of Ezekiel 16:1–15, 60, 63 on the Friday of Week 19 of Ordinary Time, Year 2. Similarly, the RL has a weekday reading of Nahum 3 that omits some problematic verses: Nahum 2:1, 3; 3:1–3, 6–7 is to be read on the Friday of Week 18 of Ordinary Time, Year 2.

The problematic passages in Revelation also receive scant attention, with no Sunday readings in either the RCL or the RL.

The RCL includes weekday readings for Revelation 2:12–29 (Year C, season after Pentecost, Proper 22 [27]), Revelation 14:1–11 (Year A, season after Pentecost, Reign of Christ, Proper 29 [34]), and Revelation 17:1–18 (Year B, season after Pentecost, Proper 24 [29]). The brief reference in Revelation 14:4 to men "who have not defiled themselves with women" is skipped over in a RL weekday reading of Revelation 14:1–3, 4b–5 (Monday of Week 34 of Ordinary Time, Year 2). On the other hand, Matthew 5:21–22, in which Jesus warns about the power of words and thoughts, is a Sunday reading in the RCL during Year A (6th Sunday after the Epiphany) and in the RL during Year A on the 6th Sunday in Ordinary Time.

On the whole, the passages discussed in this chapter that feature violence against women are only occasionally in the RL or the RCL, and most of those occurrences are weekday readings. In fact, the RL does not include a single one of these problematic passages as a Sunday reading, and the RCL only does so twice. In a few instances, some weekday readings skip over problematic portions of passages altogether or in part.

While omitting such passages may signal that the church does not exalt them, it also fails to deal with them properly. In fact, for weekday readings (especially for the Protestant tradition), it leaves the passages open to the lay reader without offering much or any guidance on how to respond to such passages.

Conclusion

In this chapter, we have traversed difficult life-and-death terrain. Regarding the stated goals of the book, we have addressed well-known biblical women, including Sarah, Hagar, Rebekah, and Leah. In addition, we have lifted up ignored women, both individuals (such as the Levite's *pîlegeš*) and groups of women and girls (such as those abducted and trafficked). We have also considered symbolic feminized women. For instance, cities and people groups (e.g., Rome, Israel, Samaria, Nineveh) are often depicted as females, "whores," as a way of metaphorizing idolatry. We have drawn upon social-scientific studies to understand the social structures in which violence against women was (and continues to be) perpetrated. We presented insights from different interpretive voices and perspectives, including women from various social

103

locations. Finally, we have included a rich variety of resources for further study.

I close with an exhortation and invitation to each of us, especially those in the position to teach or preach our biblical texts in ways marked by truth telling, solidarity, and hope. First, I urge us to bring these uncomfortable texts out into broad daylight for communal study and discernment. Second, in doing so, I invite us each to picture a particular woman (or group of women) we know who has suffered gender violence. Say her name; if you don't know it, give her one. Let's say her name is Jane. Then, every time we are preparing an interpretation of a text aimed at the good news (as all Christian interpretation should be), let's ask: "Is this interpretation good news for Jane?" Because if it's not good news for Jane, then it's not good news. If it's not good news, don't preach it. If it is, believe it.

Recommended Resources

Aldama, Arturo, ed. 2003. *Violence and the Body: Race, Gender, and the State*. Bloomington: Indiana University Press.

Cosgrove, Charles H. 2002. *Appealing to Scripture in Moral Debate: Five Hermeneutical Rules*. Grand Rapids: Wm. B. Eerdmans Publishing Co.

Creach, Jerome F. D. 2013. *Violence in Scripture*. Interpretation: Resources for the Use of Scripture in the Church. Louisville, KY: Westminster John Knox Press.

Fortune, Marie M. 1987. *Keeping the Faith: Guidance for Christian Women Facing Abuse*. New York: HarperCollins.

Gafney, Wilda C. 2017. *Womanist Midrash: A Reintroduction to the Women of the Torah and the Throne*. Louisville, KY: Westminster John Knox Press.

Garrett, Susan R. 1998. "Revelation." Pages 469–74 in *Women's Bible Commentary*. Edited by Carol A. Newsom and Sharon H. Ringe. Exp. ed. Louisville, KY: Westminster John Knox Press.

Heath, Elaine A. 2019. *Healing the Wounds of Sexual Abuse: Reading the Bible with Survivors*. Grand Rapids: Brazos Press.

Junior, Nyasha. 2019. *Reimagining Hagar: Blackness and the Bible*. Oxford: Oxford University Press.

O'Brien, Julia. 2002. *Nahum*. Readings: A New Biblical Commentary. London: Sheffield Academic Press.

Portier-Young, Anathea. 2012. "Drinking the Cup of Horror and Gnawing on Its Shards: Biblical Theology through Biblical Violence, Not around It." Pages 387–408 in *Beyond Biblical Theologies*. Edited by Heinrick Assel, Stefan Beyerle, and Christfried Böttrich. Wissenschaftliche Untersuchungen zum Neuen Testament 295. Tübingen: Mohr Siebeck.

Pressler, Carolyn. 1993. *The View of Women Found in Deuteronomic Family Laws*. Berlin: Walter de Gruyter.

Reinhartz, Adele. 2002. *Befriending the Beloved Disciple: A Jewish Reading of the Gospel of John*. New York: Continuum.

Scholz, Susanne. 2010. *Sacred Witness: Rape in the Hebrew Bible*. Minneapolis: Fortress Press.

———. 2012. "Judges." Pages 113–27 in *Women's Bible Commentary*. Edited by Carol A. Newsom, Sharon H. Ringe, and Jacqueline E. Lapsley. 3rd ed. Louisville, KY: Westminster John Knox Press.

Schulte, Leah Rediger. 2017. *The Absence of God in Biblical Rape Narratives*. Emerging Scholars Series. Minneapolis: Fortress Press.

Sharp, Carolyn J. 2021. *Jeremiah 26–52*. International Exegetical Commentary on the Old Testament. Stuttgart: Kohlhammer.

Tracy, Thomas F. 1998. "Why Do the Innocent Suffer?" Pages 40–55 in *Why Are We Here? Everyday Questions and the Christian Life*. Edited by Ronald F. Thiemann and William C. Placher. Harrisburg, PA: Trinity Press International.

Trible, Phyllis. 1984. *Texts of Terror: Literary-Feminist Readings of Biblical Narratives*. Philadelphia: Fortress Press.

Williams, Delores S. 2013. *Sisters in the Wilderness: The Challenge of Womanist God-Talk*. Maryknoll, NY: Orbis Books.

CHAPTER 4

Women Creating

"Against the ruin of the world, there is only one defense—the creative act" (Rexroth 1987, 43). In the preceding chapter, we attended to women and violence, which certainly counts as part of the ruin. As people of faith, however, we know that ruin has neither the first nor the last word: creativity does. Our Scriptures begin and end with the creative act, from Genesis to Revelation.

In this chapter, therefore, we visit some of the women of the Bible who model creativity so that we, too, might be inspired to respond to the ruin of the world with creativity. We lift up Eve, Woman Wisdom and wise women, and prophets. While some New Testament women are mentioned, this chapter focuses primarily on Old Testament figures, since New Testament women are treated at length later in the book. As becomes clear in this chapter, creativity takes many forms. Some women bring forth and sustain biological life, whether human, plant, or animal (Eve, Woman Wisdom). Others proclaim, sing, or dance new life into existence (prophets). Still others ingeniously organize, collaborate, and strategize in politically savvy ways about how to use apparently limited options and resources to make the impossible possible, to make a way out of no way (other wise women in OT narratives), as God continually does as part of God's own creative genius.

Eve Creating: Creat[E]ve

Genesis 1:26–30 provides one account of the creation of human-kind. Genesis 2–3 provides a discrete account, one which eventu-ates in a specifically named female, Eve. It is this story that has held sway (and wreaked some havoc) in the ensuing centuries. Most modern readers have been more influenced by later interpreters of the narrative than by a detailed reading of the passage itself. As Susan Niditch says, "All too often readers come to Genesis weighed down by Augustine's or Milton's interpretation of the story" (1998, 17). I would push that weight all the way back to the New Testa-ment, however. Eve appears by name only twice in the New Testa-ment (2 Cor. 11:3; 1 Tim. 2:13–14), both times negatively as "the one deceived." Paul, who loves to mention Adam regularly, conve-niently makes no mention of him here in 2 Corinthians when he castigates Eve. In contrast, the author of 1 Timothy, in a passage where he robs women of authority and even voice (2:8–15), overtly insists that "Adam was not deceived," a statement which patently contradicts the very Scriptures that the same author declares to be inspired (*theopneustos*, "God-breathed"; 2 Tim. 3:16). Touting one's belief in the inspiration of Scripture does not excuse an inter-preter for egregiously errant interpretations of it.

Near the beginning of her classic essay on Genesis 2–3, "A Love Story Gone Awry," Phyllis Trible addresses "traditional" interpretations that declare that Genesis 2:7–3:24 "proclaims male superiority and female inferiority as the will of God" and "portrays woman as 'temptress' and troublemaker who is dependent upon and dominated by her husband." She lists eleven convictions of this "misogynous reading" and then undermines or refutes them all with her immaculate exegesis. Among those misogynous read-ings she includes, for instance, "Woman tempted man to disobey and thus she is responsible for sin in the world (3:6); she is untrust-worthy, gullible, and simpleminded." And, "A male God creates first man (2:7) and last woman (2:22); first means superior and last means inferior or subordinate." And, "Woman is created for the sake of man: a helpmate to cure his loneliness (2:18–23)" (Trible 1978, 73).

108   Thus, Eve often suffers in a twofold way: first, the part of her story that gets told at all is told incorrectly; second, the whole rest

of her story is ignored. She is actually a rich character whose spirit, choices, and experiences both inspire and instruct. In what follows, I focus on Eve's creativity.

First, Eve herself was the culmination of creation. God created her in God's image (Gen. 1:26); thus, she herself was endowed with the ability to create. This language will be repeated about Woman Wisdom in Proverbs 8, where Woman Wisdom declares that God created her before the world was created and that she in turn cocreated the world with God (Prov. 8:22, 30), bringing forth life. We are not surprised then by distinct references to Eve's creativity.

Genesis 3:20 is the first time the first woman is given a specific name and, like many names in Hebrew, there is a play on words, here with the words for "life" and "living." She is called ḥawwâ (English: Eve) "because she became the mother of all living" (ḥāy); not just people, but everything living. It doesn't get much more creative than that.

In Genesis 4:1, Eve gives birth to Cain and says, "'I have created [qānîtî, first person singular of qānâ] a man with YHWH" (my trans.). The word for "create" used here, qānâ, is used with reference to God's creative acts in a variety of places. Again, Proverbs 8:22 becomes important. There we read that "YHWH created" (qānâ). Clearly, Eve channels God's creative capacity. Eve shows lexical flair by using the verb qānâ in a play on words with the name of her child, Cain (qayin). While some translations lend Eve a more passive role by rendering the verse as "I have gotten . . . with the help of YHWH" (e.g., NASB), one could fairly translate her role more actively as "I have created . . . with YHWH." To be sure, the phrase "the help of" is absent in the Hebrew.

With respect to Eve's creative power, I find Genesis 3:15 particularly interesting because, when cursing the serpent, God speaks not of enmity between the serpent and the man's seed, or between the serpent and the man and woman's seed, but patently between the serpent and *Eve's* seed (zera'; Greek: *sperma*). In antiquity (and today), seed is typically associated with male generative power; yet in Genesis, Eve has seed, conceives, bears, and sustains life.

The presentation of Eve's life-giving creativity speaks into our contemporary lives multifariously. Eve is the mother of mothers who literally incubate and bear children. But I also consider her the mother of scientists and doctors and first responders—all of whom incubate and sustain human lives—and the mother of botanists, zoologists, and ecological activists, those who understand that humans are not the only creatures God created.

It is also the case that Eve is the first theologian, the first academic. She is curious about her world, how it works, and why. She takes advantage of all of her God-given senses to take in new knowledge of her world: sight, smell, hearing, touch, and, yes, taste. She is willing to take risks and push boundaries in order to discover real limits rather than accept merely untested hearsay that others have passively accepted out of fear or lassitude. Phyllis Trible writes of Genesis 3: "The response of the woman to the serpent reveals her as intelligent, informed, and perceptive. Theologian, ethicist, hermeneut, rabbi, she speaks with clarity and authority" (1978, 110).

Eve is a beautifully complex figure, like most of us, I suspect. Above I treated the Hebrew text, but I also love the Septuagint (LXX) version of Genesis 3:20: *kai ekalesen Adam to onoma tēs gynaikos autou Zōē hoti hautē mētēr pantōn tōn zōntōn* ("and [the] earth-creature [*Adam*] named its woman 'Life' because she herself is the mother of all living things"; my trans.). The woman is named Zoe ("Life") because she is the mother of *pantōn tōn zōntōn* ("all living things"). Follow that up with the 135 occurrences of the word *zōē* in the New Testament, and it's a powerful connection, from Zoe in Genesis to Jesus's statement about abundant life in John 10:10 to Revelation 22:17, in which the thirsty are offered "the water of life." From Genesis to Revelation, from beginning to end (not to mention the extensive in-between) the invitation to *life* beckons. Thanks, Mother Zoe, for reminding us.

Woman Wisdom and Wise Women Creating

Woman Wisdom

Anyone who addresses Woman Wisdom in the Bible owes a debt to Claudia Camp's groundbreaking, erudite *Wisdom and the Feminine in the Book of Proverbs* (1985). Though the female character of Wisdom has been sitting in plain sight in Scripture for thousands of years, to my knowledge Camp is the first to popularize the name that most scholars use, Woman Wisdom:

Woman Wisdom is an elusive figure, sought after by scholars, students, and all questioning walkers on the path of life, ancient and modern. Her shape changes: she is as awesome as a goddess, as playful as a small child, as comfortable as a mother's arms, as challenging as a prophet, as satisfying as a table laden with food, as mysterious as a lover hidden among the lilies. She is thus present whenever we are awed or playful, comforted or challenged, satisfied by the earth's bounty or allured by love. She is there in all the experiences of human beings, calling us to her side, waiting to be found and embraced. Yet she resists our efforts to control her, asserting her divine freedom, turning all our answers again to questions. She rules in justice and scorns human folly and deceit. (9)

Proverbs commences and concludes with the figure of Woman Wisdom. As Alyce McKenzie states in *Preaching Biblical Wisdom*, "We have assumed that Proverbs is a hodgepodge of fortune cookies thrown in a bag. In reality, it is carefully constructed, intended to be read as the sayings of Woman Wisdom" (2002, 95). Ḥokmâ, the Hebrew word for wisdom, and *Sophia*, the Greek word for wisdom, are both feminine and are personified (and even hypostasized) as female figures. Chapters 1–9 of Proverbs flesh out what Woman Wisdom is about: instruction, creativity, integrity, judiciousness, resourcefulness, and abundant, full, wholehearted living that comes from living in concert with God's vision for all of creation.

Already in Proverbs 1 we find that Woman Wisdom cares greatly about teaching wisdom to human beings, to whom she refers as her children; however, we tend to resist her offer:

> Wisdom cries out in the street;
> in the squares she raises her voice.
> At the busiest corner she cries out;
> at the entrance of the city gates she speaks:
> "How long, O simple ones, will you love being simple?
> How long will scoffers delight in their scoffing
> and fools hate knowledge?"
>
> *(Prov. 1:20–22)*

The ability to choose wisely is a learned skill that requires the humility to learn from Woman Wisdom. Rejecting her leads to moral and spiritual shallowness (folly), a kind of pallid half-life at best and death at worst.

111

Proverbs 8, in addition to repeating the theme of instruction found in Proverbs 1, is a brilliant, inspiring read about the sheer delight Woman Wisdom takes in cocreating the world with God, with full life in mind for those who will inhabit it. Starting with verse 27, we learn about her role, a role alluded to and assigned to Jesus in the prologue of the Gospel of John.

> When he established the heavens, I was there,
>   when he drew a circle on the face of the deep,
> when he made firm the skies above,
>   when he established the fountains of the deep,
> when he assigned to the sea its limit,
>   so that the waters might not transgress his command,
> when he marked out the foundations of the earth,
>   then I was beside him, like a master worker;
> and I was daily his delight,
>   rejoicing before him always,
> rejoicing in his inhabited world
>   and delighting in the human race.
>
> "And now, my children, listen to me:
>   happy are those who keep my ways.
> Hear instruction and be wise,
>   and do not neglect it.
> Happy is the one who listens to me,
>   watching daily at my gates,
>   waiting beside my doors.
> For whoever finds me finds life
>   and obtains favor from the LORD;
> but those who miss me injure themselves;
>   all who hate me love death."
>
> *(Prov. 8:27–36)*

Woman Wisdom cocreated with God, and she has much to teach us about living fully. She's like the ancient Brené Brown in that way. She wants us to have life and have it more abundantly, but learning about things that truly matter involves humility, vulnerability, and the willingness to learn a thing or two from those who know more than we do—hard-won knowledge that has stood the test of time.

Given her role in the very foundations of the created order, the figure of Wisdom draws us into ecological considerations. Indeed,

112

we refer to our planet as "Mother" Earth. McKenzie has written extensively on the Wisdom literature, especially with respect to preaching. About Woman Wisdom she writes:

> The natural world bears the imprint of the presence of Woman Wisdom. . . . The human community's search for wisdom occurs not apart from but in the context of the natural world in which Wisdom rejoices. These texts provide an early suggestion that ecological and social justice cannot be separated. Neither nature nor other human beings are here to be exploited as mere resources for the projects of those who happen to wield social, political, and economic power. (2002, 31)

What does it look like to live such a life on earth? The woman of Proverbs 31 exemplifies this perfectly. She is wise; physically, intellectually, and morally strong; judicious; and productive. She is an exceptionally gifted businesswoman and manager of those under her. In antiquity, women dominated textile production. No small undertaking, this usually involved coordination and collaboration. The woman in Proverbs 31, then, might be understood as a project manager in today's terms. Proverbs 31:13, 19, 22, and 24 show that, not only does she provide textiles for her own family, but also she runs a profitable business: "She makes linen garments and sells them; she supplies the merchant with sashes" (v. 24). We read of the luxurious crimson and purple clothes that colorize the lives of those in her household: "She is not afraid for her household when it snows, for all her household are clothed in crimson. She makes herself coverings; her clothing is fine linen and purple" (vv. 21–22).

With respect to the garments she makes, the Proverbs 31 woman is the foremother of the New Testament figures Lydia and Dorcas. We meet Lydia in Acts 16: "A certain woman named Lydia, a worshiper of God, was listening to us; she was from the city of Thyatira and a dealer in purple cloth. The Lord opened her heart to listen eagerly to what was said by Paul. When she and her household were baptized, she urged us, saying, 'If you have judged me to be faithful to the Lord, come and stay at my home.' And she prevailed upon us" (Acts 16:14–15). Like the woman of Proverbs 31, Lydia is a textiles businesswoman who also has a penchant for purple. And like the Proverbs 31 woman, she runs her household. When Lydia converts, the household converts. She is depicted as having the same power and role as Cornelius does over his household in

113

Acts 10. (By the way, the Proverbs 31 woman and Lydia are not the only women in the Bible whose households are described in female rather than male terms. Other examples include Rebekah in Gen. 24:28, Ruth and Orpah in Ruth 1:8, and the woman in Song 3:4. In each case, there is reference to the household of each woman's *mother*. For a longer discussion of this phenomenon, consult Carol Meyers, *Rediscovering Eve*, 112–13).

Similarly, Dorcas also follows in the footsteps of the woman of Proverbs 31, a woman who exemplifies a life of wisdom. Such a life, by definition, is characterized by an industriousness that includes care for others. Remember, God and Woman Wisdom *create*. It's what they do. And they create not simply for their own benefit; rather, their joy is made complete when they witness others enjoying what they have produced. Dorcas gets it:

> Now in Joppa there was a disciple whose name was Tabitha, which in Greek is Dorcas. She was devoted to good works and acts of charity. At that time she became ill and died. When they had washed her, they laid her in a room upstairs. Since Lydda was near Joppa, the disciples, who heard that Peter was there, sent two men to him with the request, "Please come to us without delay." So Peter got up and went with them; and when he arrived, they took him to the room upstairs. All the widows stood beside him, weeping and showing tunics and other clothing that Dorcas had made while she was with them. (Acts 9:36–39)

Her creativity, resourcefulness, industriousness, and professional knowledge related to producing textiles is so important to the community, especially those most vulnerable—the widows—that her death is a crisis for the community itself, not just for her friends and family. You probably have a Dorcas or two in your church or community—women who use their textile and managerial skills to improve the lot of other women, from acts of charity to fair-trade businesses to microloans. Reading about what Dorcas does makes a person take stock of their own life, their church, business, or organization. If tomorrow you or your organization were gone, would the community feel a loss? If not, does that signal that it's time to rethink the mission of one's life or organization?

114   According to Exodus 35, the skilled, creative expertise of ancient female textile workers also extended to the creation of the

holy space of the tabernacle, specifically for priestly garments and temple accoutrements (e.g., curtains, hangings): "All the skillful women spun with their hands, and brought what they had spun in blue and purple and crimson yarns and fine linen; all the women whose hearts moved them to use their skill spun the goats' hair" (vv. 25–26). When I read this, I am reminded of and deeply grateful for the countless women in the past and present who devote time and skill in this same way to make worship spaces thoroughly holy ground by their attention to details that allow for space to encounter extraordinary majesty, beauty, transcendence, exquisiteness, awe, and reverence. Men can and do (sometimes) do these things, but the focus here is on celebrating women.

Not only is the woman of Proverbs 31 wise, resourceful, entrepreneurial, industrious, and an excellent project manager, but she also attends to her physical well-being. She works out, if you will. Far from being some kind of meek and mild sidekick to her husband, she readily seeks moral and physical strength: "She girds herself with strength, and makes her arms strong" (v. 17; the Hebrew says she girds her "loins" or "hips" [*motnayim*]—clearly, she's wearing compression shorts, as all serious athletes do!). Creating whole new worlds takes moral and physical strength.

Some interpret the strong woman of Proverbs 31 as a kind of ideal for actual women to strive toward in being a homemaker, but many scholars posit that she is much more: "Surely this woman of worth is Woman Wisdom herself! It sums up the qualities of Wisdom and commends her benefits to potential followers. Woman Wisdom invites [her audience] into her home, a place graced by lovingkindness (31:26), industry, and care for the poor of the community" (McKenzie 2002, 116–17). Surely this ideal is for God-followers of *all* genders.

Woman Wisdom, then, is a wonderfully polyvalent character in the Bible. As Alice Ogden Bellis notes, "In the intertestamental period, Wisdom is an important figure closely allied with God, and in the New Testament Hebrew *ḥokmâ* becomes Greek *sophia* and finally *logos*, the word of God incarnate. For many feminists the female figure Wisdom is therefore extremely important" (2007, 178).

A hymn by Jann Aldredge-Clanton, "Hark! Wisdom's Urgent Cry," expresses Woman Wisdom's creative power:

Hark! Wisdom's urgent cry rings out for all to hear;
though scoffed and scorned She still draws nigh with message strong
and clear.
Awake and heed Her voice; destructive ways now cease;
unite with Wisdom; make a choice to go on paths of peace.

Look, Wisdom's outstretched hands point to long life and love;
Her grace pours forth throughout all lands around us and above.
How long will we refuse Her gifts so rich and free?
How long our bondage will we choose instead of liberty?

Come to the Tree of Life; She honors our embrace.
Her fruit our deepest powers revive; She crowns us with Her grace.
The Tree of Life stands tall; Her beauty fills the earth;
Her radiant flowers never fall; Her fullness brings new birth.
(from Inclusive Hymns for Liberating Christians)

The Wise Woman of 2 Samuel 20 and Other Wise Women

Maybe some readers have read or attended a workshop based upon the best-selling book *Crucial Conversations: Tools for Talking When Stakes Are High*. A "crucial" conversation is marked by three features: opinions vary; stakes are high; and emotions run strong (Patterson et al. 2012, 1–2). The woman who saves the day in 2 Samuel 20 could have taught a course on crucial conversations. She is an ambassador and diplomat for her town. Multiple times the author refers to her as wise. She is another example of those who exhibit the theme of creativity. "Against the ruin of the world, there is only one defense—the creative act" (Rexroth 1987, 43). That act takes many forms, from song and dance, to textile production, to word artistry that staves off death and brings life. This woman does the latter. "When the conflict created by Sheba son of Bichri's presence in Abel Beth-maacah on one hand, and Joab's determination to extricate the rebel at any cost on the other, threatens her city, Abel's wise woman wields not only authority, but also the power of carefully crafted words" (Darr 2009, 102).

In 2 Samuel 20, a man named Sheba rallies people against David. In defense of David, a man named Joab with his troops pursues Sheba, who embeds himself in a town called Abel of

116

Beth-maacah. Joab and his men lay siege to the town and start battering the walls. Enter the wise woman: "Then a wise woman ['iššâ ḥăkāmâ] called from the city, 'Listen! Listen! Tell Joab, "Come here, I want to speak to you"'" (2 Sam. 20:16). Joab comes, and she addresses him directly, fearlessly, and in a manner than commands his undivided attention: "'Are you Joab?' He answered, 'I am.' Then she said to him, 'Listen to the words of your servant.' He answered, 'I am listening'" (v. 17).

She then appeals to the authority of the wisdom of their shared ancestors, a wisdom that precedes them and their present dilemma. "Then she said, 'They used to say in the old days, "Let them inquire at Abel"; and so they would settle a matter'" (v. 18). Hers is no mean city. And she herself is not to be easily dismissed: "'I am one of those who are peaceable and faithful in Israel; you seek to destroy a city that is a mother in Israel; why will you swallow up the heritage of the Lord?'" (v. 19). Her first statement presents an unstated question about Joab's own identity. She knows who she is—one of the peaceable and faithful. Meanwhile, he is warring and, in the process, acting unfaithfully, betraying both a mother and the Lord in one fell swoop. The very lives of her people hang in the balance as she negotiates this delicate, potentially deadly interaction with just the right words. A crucial conversation, indeed.

It works. Now that she has held up a mirror to him, he does not like presenting as a faithless destroyer. "Joab answered, 'Far be it from me, far be it, that I should swallow up or destroy!'" (v. 20). But he still needs to get Sheba, as he was sent to do. She promises to execute diplomacy and compromise. Her people live, and she finds a way to get him Sheba.

She does this by involving "all" (*kol*; 2 Sam. 20:22) of her people as part of the solution. I once heard Jimmy Carter talk about all the peace treaties he and The Elders (an international nongovernmental organization that includes Nina Jilani, Nelson Mandela, and Desmond Tutu, among others) had been part of negotiating. He said the only ones that stick are the ones where women are at the table. They are the glue of the community. They gave birth to the children in the villages, they are connected to others in the community, they collaborate rather than compete. I am reminded of that as I read about the strategy and poise of this woman in 2

117

Samuel 20. The Hebrew declares that she goes to all of her people "with her wisdom" (*bəḥokmātāh*; v. 22). They follow her leadership and execute the plan, and the city is saved.

In the musical *Ragtime*, Lynn Ahrens's lyrics for "Make Them Hear You" contain the line, "Your sword can be a sermon or the power of the pen." Indeed. There are warriors in the Bible like Jael and Deborah who use physical weapons to defend their people. This woman uses words. There are women whose creativity involves liturgical arts (Miriam) or textile production for charity, business, or temple construction. This woman's creativity comes through words. All are essential.

The "wise woman" appears as a theme elsewhere in the Hebrew Bible. The role of the wise woman (*'iššâ ḥăkāmâ*) of Tekoa in 2 Samuel 14 is similar to that of the wise woman of Abel. The woman of Tekoa approaches King David and, by means of careful, creative (even crafty, à la Nathan) rhetoric, impels him to reconcile with his son Absalom. Likewise, there are wise women who have no biological children, such as Deborah the prophet, warrior, and judge, designated with the title "mother in Israel" (Judg. 5:7); they are leaders of all the people, dispensing wisdom and leadership.

Expanding Wisdom

The Wisdom literature honors the knowledge that is gleaned by living life in the "real world" day in and day out. It's the kind of stuff your grandma says: "Fool me once, shame on you; fool me twice, shame on me." "When someone shows you their true colors, believe them. Don't make them show you twice." "You teach others how to treat you by what you tolerate." Grandmas know things. One thing they know is that social location matters and one needs to know how to navigate life based on that social location (even if your grandma doesn't use the phrase "social location").

Postmodernism (an epistemological approach that came on the scene about forty years ago) highlights the importance of social location in interpretation:

What we call objective reality always comes to us by means of someone else's interpretation. What we "see" depends upon our circumstances. We construct our political, psychological and even, to a degree, theological realities. This insight, that theology is contextual, has grown to full flower with the advent, over the past thirty years, of two-thirds world theologies, feminist, womanist and mujerista theologies, and theologies indigenous to other ethnic and cultural groups. (McKenzie 2002, 33)

If we are to have wisdom as a human race, it will have to be pooled wisdom, by definition. Anything else is simply pooled ignorance.

Jesus is depicted in the New Testament as Woman Wisdom incarnate, teaching the same message; sounding the same warnings; inviting us into deeper, more mature relationship with God; and experiencing the same kind of rejection. In the end, of course, Woman Wisdom and Jesus are fully vindicated. It is important to note the recurring emphasis on joy and love that appears in material related to Woman Wisdom and Jesus. Neither aims for us to be stern, dour, or earnest to a fault. Rather, "there is some mysterious delight to the life of Wisdom that involves the love of God, humankind, and Wisdom in a kind of circle dance" (McKenzie 2002, 115). And with this talk of dance we turn to a wise creative prophet named Miriam.

Prophets Creating

If Woman Wisdom speaks creative words to move us to live in accordance with God's will, no less so do the prophets. In fact, McKenzie refers to Woman Wisdom as "this no-nonsense prophetess" (2002, 112). By various means, prophets *seek* the word of God and they *convey* the word of God to the people, then and now. They memorably remind us of the joy and wholeness that can come from a life well lived and warn us about the pitfalls that attend a life poorly lived. Females and males both fulfill the role of prophet in the Bible. Some prophets appear as individuals, some as part of a group. Still others may be in the text but obscured due to the nature of Hebrew and Greek grammar.

The Old Testament specifically identifies five individual female prophets using the Hebrew word *nəbî'â*: Miriam (Exod. 15:20), Deborah (Judg. 4:4), Huldah (after whom gates in Jerusalem are named to this day; 2 Kgs. 22:14; 2 Chr. 34:22), Noadiah (Neh. 6:14), and the prophet with whom Isaiah (also a prophet) produces a child (Isa. 8:3). Wil Gafney, in *Daughters of Miriam*, explains that the Rabbis add to the list of female prophets all the matriarchs, with special emphasis on Sarah, Rachel, and Rahab. They also include Hannah, Abigail, and Esther. The New Testament names Anna (Luke 2:36; named after Hannah, whom the Rabbis name a prophet); the four daughters of Philip (Acts 21:9); the female prophets at Corinth (1 Cor. 11:5); and the rival prophet whom John opposes in Revelation 2:18–28. I say more about a few of the individual prophets below.

Sometimes female prophets appear as part of a group, as in Ezekiel 13:17–23. Joel's glorious, inspiring vision of God's plan celebrates females prophesying: "Then afterward I will pour out my spirit on all flesh; your sons and your daughters shall prophesy, your old men shall dream dreams, and your young men shall see visions. Even on the male and female slaves, in those days, I will pour out my spirit" (Joel 2:28–29). Acts 2:17–18 quotes this passage directly, carrying over into the New Testament the assumption that people of all ages, genders, and socioeconomic classes prophesy and experience divine dreams and visions.

Finally, there are likely female prophets in the text who are obscured by the unfortunate fact that, in both Hebrew and Greek, the male is the "unmarked" grammatical form. An example might clarify the issue. In Greek, one brother is an *adelphos*. One sister is an *adelphē*. If a group of ten brothers gather, they are *adelphoi*. If a group of ten sisters gather, they are *adelphai*. If one sister (or twenty) joins the ten brothers, Greek will still use the masculine plural, *adelphoi*, thus erasing the presence of the women for the reader. If even one brother joins the group of ten sisters, the Greek will change from the feminine plural to the masculine plural, from *adelphai* to *adelphoi*. Thus, if you come across *adelphai*, you can be sure it means only females and there are no males there. However, and this is crucial, if you come across *adelphoi*, there is no way to know from the word whether the group is all male or contains females. It could be either. This is why, for instance, translations like the NRSV accurately render *adelphoi* as "brothers and sisters" rather than just "brothers" in situations where it is reasonable to assume females are there as well.

Thus, when we read of plural prophets who are referred to using the masculine form, we do not know whether the group is all male or is a combination of some males and some females. Given this problem, Gafney treats a number of such passages in *Daughters*

120

of Miriam (2008, 160–65) to argue that there may be even more female prophets than one might assume.

Miriam

Miriam is the first named female prophet in the Bible. She first appears unnamed in Exodus 2. There, her brother Moses is born during the time when Pharaoh has decreed death for all male Israelite babies. Their mother (Jochebed) keeps him until he is three months old and then places him in the famous "ark" in the water. Verse 4 finds Miriam observing the scene. Pharaoh's daughter then finds Moses. In verse 7, Moses's sister offers to find a wet nurse for the child—Moses's actual mother. She nurses him for some time and then hands him over to Pharaoh's daughter.

Miriam's next big appearance comes in Exodus 15:20–21 after the crossing of the Red Sea, where she leads her people in a celebratory song: "Then the prophet Miriam, Aaron's sister, took a tambourine in her hand; and all the women went out after her with tambourines and with dancing. And Miriam sang to them: 'Sing to the LORD, for he has triumphed gloriously; horse and rider he has thrown into the sea.'" Miriam here represents two creative aspects of the prophetic call. First, she responds with embodied creativity—singing and dancing—not with endless propositional statements or banal platitudes; she does not "speechify." Rather, she intuits in that moment, when the miraculous has occurred, when her people have survived against all odds, that *art* is in order, an engagement of the senses: singing, dancing, drums, music. Second, she gets the crowd involved and participating. It's not just about her as an esteemed, courageous leader; rather, it's about her with them, as a people. That is, she evokes the creativity of those around her. Deep calls to deep. The way she inspires others is, to be sure, essential to the genius of her prophetic leadership. Bring on the singers, the dancers, the instrumentalists (especially percussionists, if the Old Testament would have its way), the artists; the mantle of prophecy rests upon them. Worship, liturgy, the arts—all this is essential for the people of God to connect with the God who delivers over and over again. "Against the ruin of the world, there is only one defense— the creative act" (Rexroth 1987, 43).

Miriam is the first woman declared a prophet in the Old Testament. While she is never directly named in the New Testament,

121

one could argue that all those named "Mary" in the New Testament are named after her.

Deborah

Like many modern women of God, some ancient prophets cross (or defy) categories. Deborah is one example of such a prophet. She functions as a prophet, a judge, and a warrior. She is an incredibly rich character, and much has been written about her various leadership roles. Her song in Judges 5 contains some of the oldest material in Scripture. Year after year on my trips to Israel, as we stand on Mount Tabor or Tel Megiddo in the Holy Land, I have (female) students read Deborah's story and words aloud as we celebrate her multifaceted contributions to our faith. I may have an imperfect memory generally speaking, but I assure you that I can name each student, picture them, and tell you why they found reading that Scripture on that spot meaningful to them and their divine call.

Prophet. Warrior. Politician. Poetic composer. As a judge, Deborah "sat" on the bench. Just like Moses. Just like Jesus in John 19:13. Just like judges today. An ancient Ruth Bader Ginsburg. One woman, multiple ways to lead. Space does not permit a thorough treatment of this ancestor of ours, but suffice it to say that "the land had rest forty years" (Judg. 5:31) "because you arose, Deborah, arose as a mother in Israel" (5:7). Deborah effected leadership, in part, through her ability to use words to create and celebrate new worlds, new possibilities, a new way of reconnecting with the old wisdom that perdures over time. Might we?

Other Prophets

Other female prophets occur across the canon—in the Law, the Prophets, and the Writings, and in the New Testament, from the Gospels, to Acts, to the epistles, to Revelation. They will not be silenced, though some of their male counterparts would have it be so. Nehemiah rankles at Noadiah's opposition (Neh. 6:14), and the self-declared prophet John of Revelation can't even bring himself to speak the real name of the female who also prophesies powerfully, so he resorts to derogation through name-calling (Rev. 2:20); presumably her real name is not Jezebel. John, who held out hope for 144,000 (men) who had not "defiled" themselves with women, probably didn't count on us later lady-prophets, we who have been on the receiving end of the slander of "having a Jezebel spirit" because we take up our prophetic mantle, we who recognize and name the fears, biases, and insecurities of those who would silence us. But here we are, following God's call to raise our voices to proclaim the gospel far and wide. In doing so, we certainly follow in the footsteps of Anna the prophet, who, according to Luke, was the first person to announce Jesus publicly as the long-awaited Redeemer (Luke 2:36–38).

However you count or categorize these prophets, they constitute a great cloud of witnesses, inviting us into (or back to) the ways of the God we worship for the sake of the world God loves so dearly. As Gafney writes, "All of these female prophets have an intimate connection with the God of Israel; they express that connection by singing, dancing, drumming, speaking with and for God, waging war, performing miracles, exercising statecraft, and giving birth. Each of them is a daughter of Miriam, the mother of all women-prophets" (2008, x).

The Lectionary

The creation stories in Genesis 1 and Genesis 2–3, as they pertain to Eve, appear as both weekday and Sunday readings for the Revised Common Lectionary (RCL) and Roman Lectionary (RL):

	Revised Common Lectionary	*Roman Lectionary*
Sunday	**Genesis 1:1–2:4a** Year A, season after Pentecost, Trinity Sunday; Years A–C, Easter Vigil	**Genesis 1:1–2:2 or 1:1, 26–31a** Years A–C, Easter Vigil (First Reading)
	Genesis 2:18–24 Year B, season after Pentecost, Proper 22 (27)	**Genesis 2:7–9; 3:1–7** Year A, 1st Sunday of Lent **Genesis 2:18–24** Year B, 27th Sunday in Ordinary Time
	Genesis 3:8–15 Year B, season after Pentecost, Proper 5 (10)	**Genesis 3:9–15** Year B, 10th Sunday in Ordinary Time

123

	Revised Common Lectionary	*Roman Lectionary*
Week-day	**Genesis 1:1–2:4a** Year A, season after Pente-cost, Proper 4 (9)	**Genesis 1:20–2:4a** Year 1, Ordinary Time, Week 5, Tuesday
		Genesis 2:18–25 Year 1, Ordinary Time, Week 5, Thursday
	Genesis 1:20–2:4a Year B, Easter Evening	
	Genesis 2:4b–25 Year A, season after Pente-cost, Proper 4 (9)	**Genesis 3:1–8** Year 1, Ordinary Time, Week 5, Friday
		Genesis 3:9–24 Year 1, Ordinary Time, Week 5, Saturday
	Genesis 3:1–24 Year A, season after Pente-cost, Proper 4 (9)	
	Genesis 3:14–24 Year B, season after Pente-cost, Proper 6 (11)	

These readings provide opportunities to celebrate Eve and reshape the narrative the church often tells about her. Unfortunately, however, Genesis 4:1 only appears as a weekday reading for both lectionaries (RL: Genesis 4:1–15, 25 is to be read during Year 1 on the Friday of Week 5 of Ordinary Time; RCL: Genesis 4:1–16 appears as two weekday readings in Year A—the week of the 1st Sunday in Lent and Proper 4 [9] during the season after Pentecost).

Woman Wisdom appears in both lectionaries and receives slightly more coverage in the RCL. The female personification of wisdom in Proverbs 1 is absent from the RL. The RCL prescribes a Sunday reading of Proverbs 1:20–33 during Year B on Proper 19 (24) of the season after Pentecost. It calls for this passage as a weekday reading (along with Prov. 1:1–7) during Year A, season after Pentecost, Proper 12 (17). As for the treatment of Woman Wisdom in Proverbs 8, the RCL calls for Proverbs 8:1–4, 22–31 to be read during Year C, season after Pentecost, Trinity Sunday. It also calls for five different weekday readings of all or part of the Woman Wisdom passage, spread out in years A, B, and C. The RL calls for Proverbs 8:21–31 to be read during Year C on the Sunday after Pentecost, Holy Trinity, and lacks a weekday reading of this passage. Finally, the woman of Proverbs 31 is called for in the RL only as a Sunday reading: Proverbs 31:10–13, 19–20, 30–31 is to be read on the 33rd Sunday in Ordinary Time of Year A. The RCL also calls for only a Sunday reading: Proverbs 31:10–31 is to be read in Year B, season after Pentecost, on Proper 20 (25).

Some of the other wise women mentioned in this chapter are sparsely represented in the lectionaries. For instance, the wise woman of 2 Samuel 20 appears in neither the RL nor the RCL. The wise woman of 2 Samuel 14 is only present in the RCL and only as weekday readings. Her story is to be read during Year C on three weekdays of Proper 5 (10) during the season after Pentecost and during Year B, season after Pentecost, Proper 14 (19). Otherwise, she is not included in the lectionaries.

Deborah's presence is also limited, especially on Sundays. The RL does not include any reference to Deborah, which is not very surprising since it includes only three readings from Judges as weekday readings and no Judges readings on Sundays. Similarly, the RCL includes only a single Sunday reading from Judges: the introduction to Deborah in Judges 4:1–7 (to be read Year A, season after Pentecost, Proper 28 [33]). The RCL includes several week-day readings from Judges, including six readings from the Deborah passages (all in years A and C).

Similar to its coverage of Deborah, the RL includes no Sunday reading about Miriam. The only reference to Miriam comes as a weekday reading of Exodus 2:1–15a on the Tuesday of Week 15 of Ordinary Time, Year 1. The Song of Miriam in Exodus 15:20–21 is not included in the RL, despite Sunday and weekday readings of the Song of Moses in Exodus 15. The RCL includes the Song of Miriam for Easter Vigil of Years A, B, and C, and on Year A, season after Pentecost, Proper 19 (24), during the week of which it is also a weekday reading. The RCL also includes two weekday readings of the Moses birth story, in which the unnamed Miriam appears. These readings occur on a weekday of Year A, season after Pente-cost, Proper 28 (33), and the day after the Epiphany during Year B.

Conclusion

This chapter relates to every goal stated in the introduction of the book. We have addressed well-known biblical women, such as Eve,

Deborah, and Miriam, from fresh perspectives using a variety of interpretive methods. We have lifted up ignored women, such as the wise women of Abel and Tekoa in 2 Samuel. We have noted Wil Gafney's concern to reinstate women who may have been erased by the vagaries of Hebrew and Greek grammar in which the male is the unmarked grammatical gender. We have considered the symbolic feminized figure of Woman Wisdom. We have explored the ways that the Bible moves across or beyond gender as we considered that Jesus and Woman Wisdom coalesce in the prologue to John (and elsewhere, as I note in chap. 8, "Jesus across Gender"). We have drawn on social-scientific scholarship to place the women in their sociohistorical contexts. We have presented new perspectives that have emerged through the growing participation of women from different social locations in the interpretive conversation. Finally, we have pointed the reader to excellent resources for further study.

As promised at the outset of this chapter, we have canvassed women in the Bible who injected life into their worlds in various arenas of life, from the biological, to the artistic, the economic, and the sociopolitical. The red thread through this chapter, what connects all of the women in the Bible presented here, is *creativity* in the midst of precarity or ruin. Their stories spark our own creative imagination as we dare to believe Joel 2, cited in Acts 2, that God has, indeed, poured out the Spirit on *all* flesh so that we, too, might confront precarity and ruin and replace it with the flourishing of all creation.

Recommended Resources

Aldredge-Clanton, Jann, with composer Larry E. Schultz. 2006. *Inclusive Hymns for Liberating Christians*. Austin, TX: Eakin Press.

Bellis, Alice Ogden. 2007. *Helpmates, Harlots, and Heroes: Women's Stories in the Hebrew Bible*. 2nd ed. Louisville, KY: Westminster John Knox Press.

Camp, Claudia. 1985. *Wisdom and the Feminine in the Book of Proverbs*. Sheffield: Almond Press.

Darr, Katheryn Pfisterer. 2009. "Asking at Abel: A Wise Woman's Proverb Performance in 2 Samuel 20." Pages 102–21 in *From the Margins 1: Women of the Hebrew Bible and Their*

Afterlives. Edited by Peter S. Hawkins and Lesleigh Cushing Stahlberg. The Bible in the Modern World 18. Sheffield: Sheffield Phoenix Press.

Gafney, Wilda C. 2008. *Daughters of Miriam: Women Prophets in Ancient Israel*. Minneapolis: Fortress Press.

McKenzie, Alyce. 2002. *Preaching Biblical Wisdom in a Self-Help Society*. Nashville: Abingdon Press.

Meyers, Carol. 2013. *Rediscovering Eve: Ancient Israelite Women in Context*. Oxford: Oxford University Press.

Niditch, Susan. 1998. "Genesis." Pages 13–29 in *Women's Bible Commentary*. Edited by Carol A. Newsom and Sharon H. Ringe. Exp. ed. Louisville, KY: Westminster John Knox Press.

Trible, Phyllis. 1978. *God and the Rhetoric of Sexuality*. Overtures to Biblical Theology. Philadelphia: Fortress Press.

CHAPTER 5

The Book of Ruth

One of the "Women's Books" in the Bible

It is not uncommon to hear Ruth 1:16–17 at wedding ceremonies: "Where you go, I will go; where you lodge, I will lodge; your people shall be my people, and your God my God." In their original context, the words celebrate the deep bond between two women who are not biologically related, one old and one young.

There are four books in the Bible named after women: Ruth, Esther, Susanna, and Judith, though only the first two appear in the Protestant canon. In this chapter I treat Ruth as an example of one of the "women's books," hoping that the reader will undertake study of the other three books as well.

Like the other "women's books" in Scripture, Ruth is about many things. Throughout this chapter I focus on three aspects of the text. First, I attend to intersectionality, the ways that various aspects of Ruth's social location—gender, ethnicity, and economic status—combine to make life potentially more challenging than if she were in only one precarious category. Ruth is a woman (a frequently disadvantaged gender), she is husbandless (a financially insecure social class), and she is a Moabite (a foreigner/alien whose particular ethnicity puts her in an even more precarious position). Second, I highlight the theme of relationships between women. Third, I focus a lot on the character Naomi. The book of Ruth could be called the book of Naomi and Ruth, since the narrative begins

129

with Naomi's predicament and concludes with a resolution to it, with Ruth serving as a tool to accomplish the solution.

The Story in the Book of Ruth

In a patriarchal system such as ancient Israel's, widows were at risk. That's why the Bible expresses so much concern for the precarity of widows and none for widowers. Right away in the book of Ruth, all three women are widows. In addition, patriarchal cultures value women as child bearers who carry on the name of the male head of household by bearing sons. All three women in Ruth are completely childless, sonless. Ruth and Orpah haven't borne children; Naomi's sons are dead.

Ruth 1:1 introduces the Israelite Elimelech (from Bethlehem in Judah), his unnamed wife, and his two unnamed sons. Again, in patriarchal cultures, the identity of women and children is derived chiefly from their relationship to the male head of the household. So it is no surprise that Elimelech's wife and children only gain names in v. 2, after they are namelessly introduced in relation to him in v. 1. Due to a famine in Judah, Elimelech takes the family to the foreign country of Moab. Then he dies, and Naomi's well-being becomes dependent on her sons, both of whom marry Moabite women, Orpah and Ruth. Next the sons die, catapulting all three women into dire straits. Naomi decides to return to Judah. She advises her Moabite daughters-in-law to go back to "the household of your mother" (1:8, my trans.). This is a relatively infrequent phrase; more typical is "household of your father" (for more information, consult Schipper 2016, 91). Already, then, we see the structures of patriarchy at play but also hints of resisting it or at least working around or within it creatively.

Naomi hopes that Orpah and Ruth each will get a new husband to marry them and thus provide security. The Israelite law of levirate marriage (Deut. 25:5–6) requires the brother of a dead man to take the widow as his own wife and raise up children to honor the dead man (and financially provide for the widow), but since Naomi has no other sons, levirate marriage is not an option in this case.

130   The love and affection and connection among these women is palpable as they repeatedly kiss each other and weep (1:9, 14). Orpah chooses to stay in Moab and salvage her life among her

people. Ruth chooses to become an immigrant. Too many treatments of this book pit Orpah against Ruth and denigrate Orpah in order to celebrate Ruth's choice. The text does not cast Orpah in a negative light for her choice, and interpreters should resist the temptation to pit women against one another, lauding one at the expense of the other (the same move happens with the sisters Mary and Martha in the New Testament, for example). In a patriarchal society where women are at risk of precarity at best, poverty and abuse at worst, different women make different choices. Not better or worse choices, just different choices based on a variety of factors. To remain in one's own country with one's own family, as Orpah did, should not be considered less faithful or exemplary. It is also what Naomi tells her to do, so she could be framed as virtuous for following the instructions of an elder wise woman. Many feminist readers, especially those from minoritized groups, relate far more to Orpah than to Ruth and carefully lift her up as a positive example (e.g., Dube 1999; Donaldson 1999).

Naomi and Ruth travel to Bethlehem. When they arrive, we learn first that "the whole town" is excited, but then specifically that the *women* ask if it could be Naomi (1:19). Naomi repeats her complaint (first lodged at 1:13) that she is bitter and empty because of God, who has "testified" against her and "done evil" (*hiphil* of r") to her.

Chapter 1 concludes by reminding us that Ruth comes from Moab. The possibility of xenophobia based on ethnicity and country of origin arises since Ruth is a Moabite, a group much hated by Israel. Numerous Old Testament books insist that Israelites must stay separate from and must certainly not marry Moabites or fall under their corrupting influence (Num. 25:1–5; Ezra 9:1–10:44; Neh. 13:1–3). Deuteronomy 23:3, for example, minces no words: "No Ammonite or Moabite shall be admitted to the assembly of the LORD. Even to the tenth generation, none of their descendants shall be admitted to the assembly of the LORD." Not only do both of Naomi's sons marry Moabites, Naomi totes one back with her to Judah. The fact of Ruth's immigrant status gets reiterated: in 2:2 she is called Ruth the Moabite.

Chapter 2 introduces us to Boaz, a possible "redeemer" because he was a male relative of Elimelech, Naomi's dead husband. In this context, the redeemer was expected essentially to buy the alienated property of his next of kin, and this likely included financially

131

supporting a widow in the case of the kinsman's death; thus, the language of a kinsman redeemer has a clear financial implication (consult Leslie et. al. 2007, 151; consult also Schipper 2016, 172–73). Scholars debate the implications of Naomi's having "inherited" the property, what the extent of her rights were, and so on. Schipper discusses how she could have been destitute even as the inheritor. One could take a different approach and imagine Naomi as much more secure, since the text ascribes legal agency and financial agency to her (4:3, 5), even if we don't know the exact contours.

Ruth proposes to go and glean in the fields. Gleaning was biblically mandated as a way to care for the poor, by allowing them to pick up what remained after the harvesters did their work. Ruth ends up in Boaz's field, and Boaz wants to know to whom she "belongs." The manager replies to Boaz, emphasizing that Ruth is a Moabite, noting it twice in one sentence (2:6). Notably, Boaz then addresses Ruth as his "daughter" and tells her to stay in his field with "my young women," likely a reference to his female servants (2:8). As Eunny P. Lee articulates in the *Women's Bible Commentary*, "The narrative has already repeatedly underscored Boaz's kinship with Naomi. So it is not surprising that Boaz next speaks directly to Ruth, addressing her as 'my daughter,' much like Naomi" (2012, 236).

Then Boaz assures Ruth that he has "ordered" the young men not to "assault" her (2:9, CEB). How terrifying to think that he must order the young men to keep that from happening. The threat from the young men is repeated throughout the text (2:15, 16, 22), indicating that in the usual order of things the young men would feel free to mistreat her. The threat is kept at bay only if she stays with the other women (safety in numbers) and because Boaz personally ordered it. Ruth prostrates herself, face to the dirt, forced to be grateful for protection, especially because, not only is she a woman, but as she says, "I'm an immigrant" (*nākəriyyâ*; 2:10, CEB) as opposed to a "resident alien." After discussing various implications and the range of meanings associated with the designation *nākəriyyâ* in the Old Testament, Schipper notes: "Ultimately, the use of *nākriyyâ* conveys the multiple nuances and complications of her status within the Bethlehem community that terms such as 'resident alien' or even 'Moabite' would not capture" (2016, 123). As a foreigner, she would not have the same gleaning rights as a resident alien.

Boaz praises Ruth's faithful love of Naomi and mentions seeking refuge under the "wings" of the God of Israel (who is not one of the gods of Moab; 2:12). Ruth thanks him for speaking kindly "to your female servant [*šipḥātekā*]—even though I am not one of your female servants" (2:13; in 3:9, when she is undressed at Boaz's feet, hoping for the best, she will use the word *'āmā*, handmaid). Boaz feeds her and then instructs his "young men" two more times not to mistreat her while she gleans (2:14–16). In 2:15 he orders them not to "humiliate" her and, in verse 16, not to "scold" her (CEB). Clearly, the typical life of the immigrant who has to pick the leftovers is a harsh one.

"Ruth the Moabite" (2:21) tells Naomi about Boaz, and Naomi reiterates how dangerous the young men are for women such that a woman should never be alone: "It's good, my daughter, that you go out with his young women, so that men don't assault you in another field" (2:22 CEB). So Ruth stays with Boaz's "young women." Naomi then encourages Ruth to pretty herself up and go find Boaz on the threshing floor when he's done eating and drinking, and "uncover his feet and lie down" (3:4). Ruth does so. Boaz is pleased and Ruth asks that he cover her with his "wing" (3:9; the Hebrew word also means "robe"), the same word used earlier of taking refuge under God's "wing" (2:12). She lies with Boaz until morning, and then she leaves before anyone can see her. Throughout their exchange, he refers to Ruth as his "daughter." Schipper (2016, 150) notes that Boaz also calls her a "woman of worth" (3:11), which is important because he is identified in 2:1 as a "man of worth"; the phrase also echoes the description of the wise woman of Proverbs 31.

Since there is a relative closer than Boaz, that unnamed man gets first dibs on Elimelech's stuff, along with the responsibility of impregnating Ruth (or possibly Naomi; consult Schipper, 165–67), so that there would be heirs for Elimelech. That man declines (presumably because he does not want to have to split his money with another heir) so Boaz "buys" Ruth, taking her (and Naomi) under his wing, which, in a patriarchal society, means life and security. "Boaz announced to the elders and all the people, 'Today you are witnesses that I've bought from the hand of Naomi all that belonged to Elimelech and all that belonged to Chilion and Mahlon. And also Ruth the Moabite, the wife of Mahlon, I've bought to be my wife, to preserve the dead man's name for his inheritance so that the name of the dead man might not be cut off from his brothers or from the gate of his hometown—today you are witnesses'" (4:9–10 CEB).

Boaz then marries Ruth, and she gives birth to Obed, at which point the narrative turns back to Naomi, with whom the book began. The women say to Naomi (not to Ruth), "'May the LORD be blessed, who today hasn't left you without a redeemer. May his name be proclaimed in Israel. He will restore your life and sustain you in your old age. Your daughter-in-law who loves you has given birth to him. She's better for you than seven sons.' Naomi took the child and held him to her breast, and she became his guardian" (4:14–16 CEB). Next, we learn two striking pieces of information. First, the women, not Ruth or Naomi, name the child: "the women of the neighborhood gave him a name"; second, the women say: "'A son has been born to Naomi.' They named him Obed" (4:17). The son is born to Ruth, though, so why do they say he is born to Naomi? It is important to note that the construction "born to" typically refers to the newborn's father. Subtle, but powerful, material for those looking for footholds when scaling the slippery walls of patriarchy. Additionally, here we find that the book of Ruth is really largely about Naomi, that resourceful wise woman of old, and the resolution of her predicament. Schipper (2016, 183) suggests:

> Despite the elders and people's description of Ruth's marriage to Boaz as her entry to Boaz's household (v. 11), Naomi seems to continue to function as the senior member of the household into which Obed is born. If the birth announcement's reference to Naomi seems to displace Ruth as a Moabite mother in favor of a Judean mother, as some have argued . . . , the announcement's formula would also seem to displace Boaz as the household's paterfamilias. . . . Although Boaz is listed in the final genealogy . . . , he is never mentioned in the narrative portion of the book after he sleeps with Ruth in v. 13.

The birth of this son is celebrated. He is considered a redeemer (gō'ēl; 4:14) who will sustain Naomi in her old age (4:15). The bitter, empty-handed, God-forsaken, hopeless widow now holds abundance and the future in her hands, tenderly. Obed will become the father of Jesse and Jesse the father of David, from whose line Jesus the Messiah, the Redeemer par excellence, will come in the fullness of time.

What to Make of the Book of Ruth?

The history of interpretation of Ruth varies widely. Some consider Naomi and Ruth almost protofeminists because of the subversiveness of their story—two women from different ethnic backgrounds sticking together to survive and thrive in a man's world, taking matters into their own hands. Others see them propping up the status quo, acting in demure, conventional ways to uphold the patriarchal system of levirate marriage to ensure male honor. Between those two lie many other interpretive variants. As Alice Ogden Bellis notes: "How do we evaluate these diverse perspectives? Ruth is a story with many gaps. Depending on how these gaps are filled, different readings result" (2007, 187).

Yet Another Text of Terror?

The reader may experience a variety of reactions to this biblical book. On the one hand, it is disturbing and painful to read how vulnerable females are in a patriarchal society, then and now. Without a husband or sons, a woman's fate often becomes immediately precarious; she is subject to poverty and assault by other males. The fact that Boaz repeatedly has to order the males not to harm Ruth makes the reader's stomach turn. It is similarly troubling that Naomi instructs Ruth to doll herself up with makeup, perfume, and attractive clothing (and then take it off) to snare a man to save them. Better to doll yourself up for a redeemer than end up having to doll yourself up for a customer.

The valuing of sons over daughters also stings. Obed could be a redeemer only because he was male. This "woman's book" ends with a genealogy that takes account only of males, noting who fathers whom.

Perhaps worst of all is how *not* far removed the situation of many women today is from that in the book of Ruth. If our contemporary world were radically different from all of the above, the text might be less disturbing.

A Celebration of Female Ingenuity

On the other hand, the reader may celebrate the ingenuity and determination exhibited by the women in the text. Orpah chooses a path that keeps her loyal to her family and community. Ruth risks leaving her own land to become a stranger in a strange land, away from her family, her culture, and the religion of her people. She boldly cares for Naomi, risking life and limb to glean that they might eat. She does the best she can with what she has in order to secure a future for herself and Naomi, humbly groveling at the "feet" of Boaz, quietly impressing him with her steadfast faithfulness and grit, vocally petitioning the person in power to help them. She wisely uses a multipronged approach and succeeds beyond all expectations, becoming a matriarch of multiple religious traditions down to the present day. In her own way, in her own context, she is "womanish," in the way Alice Walker uses the word:

> From the black folk expression of mothers to female children, "You acting womanish," i.e., like a woman. Usually referring to outrageous, audacious, courageous or *willful* behavior. Wanting to know more and in greater depth than is considered "good" for one. Interested in grown-up doings. Acting grown up. Being grown up. Interchangeable with another black folk expression: "You trying to be grown." Responsible. In charge. *Serious*. (2003, xi)

Not just a shy, pious, quiet, asexual wallflower, Ruth makes history happen.

Consider also Naomi. She, like Job, boldly has it out with God. She does not quietly submit to a life of suffering. She rages and accuses God. She is spirited and spiritual. Like Job, Naomi does not reject God or cease believing in God. On the contrary, God is ever in her sight, and she's fit to be tied; she tells God what it feels like to lose everything, to feel as though God is actively working against one's happiness and well-being. She speaks her truth as she knows it in her life experience. She cannot yet see the surprising, redemptive future that awaits her and, because of her, all the rest of us. (For an excellent treatment of Ruth and especially the parallels between Naomi and Job, consult Lapsley 2005, 89–108.)

In a book so heavy on the importance of husbands and sons, it is striking that the women exclaim to Naomi that Ruth, "who loves you," is "better for you than seven sons" (4:15 CEB)! Now, on the one hand, if I had two named, beloved sons who had died, I would take issue with someone telling me, in effect, "Yeah, you buried two sons, but this other person is better than those two plus more."

136

It is the same resistance I feel when Job gets a "new" family after his original one is holocausted. Children are not interchangeable or replaceable. Period. Ever. No family member is. On the other hand, I appreciate the ways that the women value the woman Ruth, who loves in a way that is magnificent and divine. The women are right to laud Ruth enthusiastically and to remind Naomi what a treasure she is. I just see no reason to do it at the expense of the sons. Much of our trouble could be avoided if we replaced either/ or language with both/and; better/worse with one kind of good / another kind of good.

Women in Relationship with Women

Women working together affected the sociopolitical dynamics of their communities. "The ways in which the connections among women benefited their households and communities are usually overlooked. . . . Gender-sensitive research into traditional societies has corrected the androcentric bias in examining sociopolitical life by recognizing the importance of informal women's alliances, called 'women's networks,' in maintaining community life" (Meyers 2013, 139). Because the women spent a lot of time together in the tasks set before them, they got to know each other, they learned to depend on one another, and they formed relationships. The households depended on mutual assistance in the face of food shortage, illness, death. Thus, "Women's networks were the mechanisms for the mutual aid essential for survival" (142).

The book of Ruth celebrates relationships and community. "Throughout the book the invocation of divine blessing on others, along with the invocation and embodiment of *ḥesed* (covenantal faithfulness) in the attitudes and actions of Ruth and Boaz, function to underscore the way in which the characters' deep faithfulness to God funds their faithfulness to the people around them" (Lapsley 2005, 91). Further, "The narrative offers a portrait of a restored life as a kind of tapestry. Naomi's turmoil is an unraveling of the threads of her family and communal life, and the task of each of the characters (including Naomi herself) is to pick up the threads of that life and weave them back into a restored life in community. . . . What Naomi needs is persons who will take up her narrative and weave her back into the world" (103–4).

137

Naomi, Orpah, and Ruth

The book of Ruth is a study in women in relationship with women. First, there is Naomi in relationship with her daughters-in-law. How did Naomi feel about both of her Israelite sons marrying Moabite women? It is a question asked still today when families emigrate and the children of the immigrants enter the bicultural experience, caught between the expectations of parents who retain the culture of the country of origin and the ways of the country that they currently inhabit. Naomi's sons Mahlon and Chilion were what we would call Third Culture Kids. The text indicates that, regardless of how she may have felt early on (the text does not give us that information), real love developed among these women.

Presumably, they all imagined that Ruth and Orpah would have babies, and there would be a full house of lively family energy as Naomi helped her daughters-in-law raise the next generation. I doubt any of them imagined Elimelech dying before grandchildren were born, let alone one son and then another. But there are readers who will know this experience only too well. Given the structure of the society, it was not possible for the three women simply to create their own family of three women and thrive. In addition, the scene is shot through with barrenness, a terrible lot for women in antiquity. Naomi is too old to bear any more children, and Ruth and Orpah are in a position of "enforced barrenness" since they have no children, and now they have no husbands to produce children. Thus, they tearfully consider their options and do what seems best for each. Orpah chooses well to return to "the house of her mother," another interesting example of women connecting with women. No doubt many readers will resonate with Orpah's choice. One wonders about Ruth's relationship with her own mother, but for whatever reason, Ruth decides her future lies with Naomi. Again, no doubt some modern readers will resonate with Ruth's choice.

The love and faithfulness and even friendship between Ruth and Naomi is appropriately celebrated. As Renita Weems writes: "Naomi and Ruth could never return [to] their former relationship to one another: mother and daughter-in-law. The men they had once shared, the men responsible for bringing them together, were now dead. Their new relationship would have to reflect their new realities. Perhaps they could give friendship a chance" (1988, 28).

Though there is no overt indication in the text of same-sex love between them, queer interpreters find in this story a beautiful example of love and commitment between two people of the same gender operating together against social norms. Mona West treats Ruth in *The Queer Bible Commentary*. Naomi unabashedly brings an outsider, a Moabite, back to Judah, despite the biases clearly recorded in Scripture against loving Moabites, or even liking them, for that matter. The women "cling" to each other with the same language used of Adam and Eve. Boaz uses his privileged position to work in concert with the women to "go above and beyond the law" to provide for those marginalized by the system (2015, 192). Noting the legacy of creativity of Boaz, Ruth, and Naomi with respect to LGBTQIA+ concerns, West declares that "Ruth, Naomi, and Boaz would be proud of the ways we continue to follow their strategies" (194).

The Larger Community of Women

The repeated advice for Ruth to stick with Boaz's female servants in order to stay safe is scary, on the one hand. On the other hand, there is no indication in the text that the women held her immigrant status against her or gave her any trouble. One wishes that women did not have to band together to stay safe from packs of men, but it is encouraging that the group of women chose to include and, therefore, protect Ruth.

The women of Bethlehem feature prominently, functioning almost like a Greek chorus. They first appear in 1:19, wondering if it really is Naomi they are looking at. Had life taken its toll in a way that made her physically unrecognizable? That can happen. Bitterness can be especially disfiguring. The next time the women of Bethlehem appear is when Obed is born (4:14–17). It's as if they met her at the gate in her embittered state and over the course of the narrative integrated her back into the community, helping her to move into her sweet future story with God. They are there when the baby is born, helping Naomi to recognize all her abundance: the relationship with the townspeople, the women, her exceptional daughter-in-law, and now her grandbaby. They even name the child. "The neighborhood women gave him a name, saying, 'A son has been born to Naomi'" (4:17 CEB). As noted earlier, it seems odd to say that a son has been born to Naomi when the *son* has

139

been born to Ruth and the *grandson* to Naomi. In a way, though, the story has been about Naomi all along. She loses her sons, her future, her security at the beginning. Now she will have the benefits she would have had from a son. Naomi pulls him to her breast and becomes his nurse; perhaps she can be a nurse to Obed because these women have been nurses to Naomi. Sometimes it takes a village to restore hope.

It is noteworthy that "all the people who were at the gate, along with the elders," invoke the matriarchs Rachel, Leah, and Tamar as Boaz buys Ruth from Naomi: "May the LORD make the woman who is coming into your house like Rachel and Leah, who together built up the house of Israel. May you produce children in Ephrathah and bestow a name in Bethlehem; and, through the children that the LORD will give you by this young woman, may your house be like the house of Perez, whom Tamar bore to Judah" (4:11–12).

Ruth and Naomi Compared to Other Biblical Figures

Marti Steussey (2016, 323) compares and contrasts Ruth to Abraham: "Both of them left their own lands and people to go places they had never seen, but Abraham did so under direct orders from God, who promised that Abraham would become a 'great nation' (Gen. 12:2). Ruth went to Bethlehem on her own initiative and with no idea that she would become ancestor to both David and Jesus (Ruth 4:17; Matt 1:5)."

Jacqueline Lapsley compellingly compares Naomi to Job. Since both experience profound loss and rail at God on account of it, why is it that people easily recall Job but not Naomi? Lapsley explores this question and the ways that gender (and genre) affects both the telling of each story and the history of interpretation. Surely it is not ladylike to rage against suffering; yet, Naomi does just that. Her story has much to offer contemporary Christians and should be presented more often in its entirety (for more, consult Lapsley 2005, 89–108).

Multiple scholars compare Ruth the Moabite with Tamar the Canaanite (Gen. 38), Canaanites being another group despised by Israel. Indeed, Tamar is one of the three women named in Ruth 4:11–12. Both become widows and both become a crucial part of church history. Tamar is one of the four women in the genealogy at the beginning of Matthew, a Gospel that finds foreign, non-Jewish priests (magi) faithfully worshiping Jesus and that concludes with that same Jesus commissioning his people to make disciples of "all nations" (*ethnē*).

In *Claiming Her Dignity: Female Resistance in the Old Testament*, L. Juliana M. Claassens compares Ruth and Tamar to argue that both stories resist the dehumanization of widows. Each is dehumanized by patriarchy, food insecurity, the threat of violence, and being "invisible." First, they are dehumanized by patriarchy, specifically the need for a male and the need to bear children in order to be more secure. Both Ruth and Tamar are husbandless and childless. Both stories reveal the flawed nature of levirate marriage, especially since males could avoid it. Ruth has no access to other sons of Naomi (since Naomi has no other sons); Judah refuses to give Tamar his third son, forcing her to take extreme risks to survive. Second, Claassens addresses dehumanization by food insecurity. In Ruth, this is raised by the language of famine, gleaning, and the irony of Bethlehem, which literally means "house of bread." For Tamar, "the death of her father would have placed the widowed Tamar in an equally vulnerable situation, causing her to resort perhaps to the same desperate measures of finding food as the widows Ruth and Naomi" (2016, 123). Food insecurity can lead to the need for migration by which one becomes a foreigner. Then as now, food shortages disproportionately affect those who are already in a precarious situation—women and children, and especially those with no male in the picture, such as widows and orphans. Fortunately, many contemporary churches are faithfully responding to the issue of food insecurity and food deserts. How does the theology of "gleaning" play out in our context?

Yet another way by which Ruth and Tamar are dehumanized is the threat of physical violence at the hands of men, men who are happy to assault women in a gleaning field or hire their bodies at a city gate and then are equally happy to instate laws that call for a woman to be burned to death for perceived or real sexual "impropriety." As Claassens notes: "This imminent threat to Tamar's life brings to mind the many women who are killed today by their communities for a variety of sexual infractions" (124). Ruth and Tamar suffer both tragedy and structural injustices that leave male-less women vulnerable. Ruth and Tamar *resist* dehumanization only by cleverness and foresight (if Tamar had not thought ahead to get Judah's items, she would have been executed); they survive and outwit the system in order to gain a future, though each takes great risks to do so—Tamar dressing up and going to the city gate to engage Judah and Ruth dressing up and going to the threshing floor to engage Boaz. In so doing, these women employ a survival strategy of the oppressed: "The genre of the trickster tale is a well-known strategy of resistance of groups who find themselves in situations of oppression" (126).

Claassens also poignantly addresses the fact that one way to dehumanize another person is simply not to "see" them. "It is at the threshing floor that Boaz is finally able to see Ruth as more than a mere foreigner, a needy widow who gleans in his field, but as a 'woman of worth,' a woman whose loyalty inspires him to act in greater loyalty" (131). With respect to Judah finally "seeing" Tamar (which he clearly fails to do while having sex with her, not even recognizing her as his daughter-in-law), Claassens writes:

> It is only when Judah and Tamar meet in the public square—an exceedingly dangerous place for Tamar, who stands to lose her life in a minute—that Judah finally recognizes her righteousness, and her righteousness inspires him to act in greater righteousness. Moreover, it is Tamar's foresight to ask for identification tokens that finally compels Judah to see Tamar's just cause when his eyes are opened by the evidence of his actions (see also the repeated reference to "look," "really look" in Genesis 38:25). It is when Judah truly looks that he recognizes Tamar's true worth as a woman in need who is more righteous than him; not a prostitute but a daughter-in-law who ought to have been protected and provided for by her household and community. There seems to be a connection between really seeing the other and seeing that justice be done. (131)

Ethnicity and Inclusion

Given the staunch, exclusive directives against Moabites in some Old Testament texts, the reader should take note of and perhaps be stunned by the inclusivity of this text. Repeatedly, the text highlights that Ruth is a Moabite, an immigrant, a foreigner, one who has worshiped other gods her whole life. One imagines that if she was already "fair game" as a female alone in the fields with those young men Boaz had to manage, being a foreigner made her even more so. There is no century of human history when that has not been the case, certainly. To have Boaz enact the law of levirate marriage, intended to protect an Israelite male's line, with a Moabite is surprising. To have King David—a centrally important figure for Jews and Christians—descended from the line of a foreigner is no small detail. This also means that the Davidic descendant Jesus— the centrally important figure for Christians—traces his ancestral line back to a foreign immigrant. This fact, of course, is not lost on Matthew, who includes four women in his genealogy (unlike Luke, who includes only males), one of them Ruth.

Repeatedly the text of Ruth indicates that Ruth, the Moabite, exhibits *ḥesed* (covenantal faithfulness), one of the highest virtues for an Israelite. This is unexpected. "It is significant that in both narratives [Ruth and Tamar of Genesis 38], it is the foreigner or the outsider who functions as the revealer, thereby transforming the male leader of the community (perhaps paradigmatically serving as representative of society at large) to a position where the dignity of those who are desolate (females, aliens, and widows) are [*sic*] respected" (Claassens 2016, 132).

Reading Ruth in a global context today has become more common, given the fact of massive migration across the globe. Ruth lends itself perfectly to these important issues. One can easily and advisedly find readings from an Israeli, New Zealand, Native American, South African, and Asian context, to name a few, in which the interpreters see analogies between Ruth's status and people in contemporary contexts. For instance, Judith McKinlay, a white New Zealander, "reads the story of Ruth in the context of the tensions between the dominant *Pakeha/Palagi* (non-South Pacific) culture and the indigenous Maori people" (Bellis 2007, 188; consult also McKinlay 1999).

The Lectionary

In both the Roman Lectionary (RL) and the Revised Common Lectionary (RCL), Ruth gets scant attention on Sundays, with the RL omitting Sunday readings of Ruth altogether. The RCL calls for two readings of Ruth during the season after Pentecost in Year B:

Ruth 1:1–18 is to be read on Proper 26 (31), and Ruth 3:1–5; 4:13–17 is to be read on Proper 27 (32). During these same weeks, the entire book of Ruth is prescribed over twelve RCL weekday readings, a few of which overlap. There is also a weekday reading during Proper 14 (19) of the season after Pentecost during Year B. Five other times, the RCL calls for weekday readings of Ruth, all during Advent and Epiphany of Year A. The RL calls for two weekday readings of Ruth, on the Friday and Saturday of Week 20, Ordinary Time, Year 1. Over these two days, Ruth 1:1, 3–6, 14b–16, 22 and 2:1–3, 8–11; 4:13–17 are read.

Conclusion

This chapter ties in with goals stated in the introduction. Ruth is a well-known biblical woman and counts as exceptional in having a biblical book named after her. We have explored the book from fresh perspectives using a variety of interpretive methods. We have engaged interpreters from different social locations and different parts of the globe. We have exposed the reader to excellent further resources for study. Finally, we have set Ruth's story in its ancient context as part of discerning what meaning it might hold for contemporary readers.

Referring to both Tamar and Ruth, Claassens calls them

> women who, amid very complex and often tragic circumstances, have taken the future into their own hands. Asserting their rights as subjects in their own right, each of these women makes a claim on those in power to acknowledge her worth as a subject who has needs, wants, and desires. The example of women who have taken back their agency, resisting whatever may diminish their worth and dignity, serves as inspiration for women of all ages in their own ongoing struggle against the violence of precarity. (2016, 134)

The book of Ruth may be brief, but it is far from simple or unambiguous. The story is simultaneously horrifying, poignant, suspenseful, and inspiring. There are unexpected twists and turns, characters who are faithful and full of mixed motives, and a God whose redemption comes, if very late sometimes. The story stokes the imagination, the characters come to life, and we are left asking many questions about home and homeland, family, community, social structures, theodicy, and the nature of suffering, faith, hope, and love.

Recommended Resources

Bellis, Alice Ogden. 2007. *Helpmates, Harlots, and Heroes: Women's Stories in the Hebrew Bible*. 2nd ed. Louisville, KY: Westminster John Knox Press.

Claassens, L. Juliana M. 2016. *Claiming Her Dignity: Female Resistance in the Old Testament*. Collegeville, MN: Liturgical Press.

Donaldson, Laura E. 1999. "The Sign of Orpah: Reading Ruth through Native Eyes." Pages 130–44 in *Ruth and Esther.* A Feminist Companion to the Bible 2. Edited by Athalya Brenner. Sheffield: Sheffield Academic Press.

Dube, Musa W. 1999. "The Unpublished Letters of Orpah to Ruth." Pages 145–50 in *Ruth and Esther.* A Feminist Companion to the Bible 2. Edited by Athalya Brenner. Sheffield: Sheffield Academic Press.

Lapsley, Jacqueline E. 2005. *Whispering the Word: Hearing Women's Stories in the Old Testament*. Louisville, KY: Westminster John Knox Press.

Lee, Eunny P. 2012. "Ruth." Pages 142–49 in *Women's Bible Commentary*. Edited by Carol A. Newsom, Sharon H. Ringe, and Jacqueline E. Lapsley. 3rd ed. Louisville, KY: Westminster John Knox Press.

Leslie, Donald Daniel, David Flusser, Alvin J. Reines, Gershom Scholem, and Michael J. Graetz. 2007. "Redemption." Pages 151–55 in vol. 17 of *Encyclopaedia Judaica* Edited by Michael Berenbaum and Fred Skolnik. 2nd ed. Detroit: Macmillan Reference USA.

McKinlay, Judith E. 1999. "A Son Is Born to Naomi: A Harvest for Israel." Pages 151–57 in *Ruth and Esther.* A Feminist Companion to the Bible 2. Edited by Athalya Brenner. Sheffield: Sheffield Academic Press.

Schipper, Jeremy. 2016. *Ruth: A New Translation with Introduction and Commentary*. Anchor Yale Bible 7D. New Haven, CT: Yale University Press.

Steussey, Marti J. 2016. "Ruth." Page 323 in *The CEB Women's Bible*. Edited by Rachel Baughman, Christine Chakoian, Jaime Clark-Soles, Judy Fentress-Williams, and Ginger Gaines-Cirelli. Nashville: Abingdon Press.

Weems, Renita J. 1988. *Just a Sister Away: A Womanist Vision of Women's Relationships in the Bible*. Philadelphia: Innisfree Press.

West, Mona. "Ruth." 2015. Pages 190–94 in *The Queer Bible Commentary*. Edited by Deryn Guest, Robert E. Goss, Mona West, and Thomas Bohache. London: SCM Press.

CHAPTER 6

Magnificent Mary and Her Magnificat

Like Mother, Like Son

Prophet. Student of Scripture. Fresh, young mother pregnant with purpose, vulnerable in a patriarchal system; mournful mother stricken by grief, vulnerable in an imperial system. Moral instructor. Charter church member. Faithful, courageous follower of God.

Apart from Jesus, Mary has inspired more art than any other person from the Bible. Few places are more stunningly beautiful and moving than the Catholic Basilica of the Annunciation in Nazareth. It is huge. Upstairs, including inside and outside, are about fifty large pieces of art depicting Mary, from about fifty countries around the world (pictures of this artwork are online at https://www.biblewalks.com/Annunciation-Mosaics). Some show her with Jesus, some by herself. She is young and old, slim and full figured; she is depicted, for instance, as Japanese, Thai, Cameroonian, Guatemalan, Ukrainian, and American. Downstairs is the traditional site of Mary's childhood home. Outside, a labyrinth winds around a statue of Mary with her hands outstretched, making it nearly impossible to resist holding her hand. If her cold stone hand feels strangely warm in your own, and if her merely carved eyes meet yours in a way that makes you feel deeply seen, you are not alone in your experience.

Whereas Mary finds a central place in the faith of most Christians worldwide, she is largely absent from Protestant piety, save the annual Christmas pageant and the occasional Advent sermon.

147

By sidelining Mary, Protestants miss out on the multitude of meanings she conveys.

Rash would be the scholar who attempted to summarize all that Mary means and has meant to countless people over the millennia. Rather, this chapter attends to Mary's appearances in the Bible. I also include a section on the Protevangelium of James because it has had such a deep influence on later traditions about Mary. A brief list of further resources will lead the interested investigator to myriad others.

Mary in the Gospel of Luke

"The apple doesn't fall far from the tree." "He's a chip off the old block." If you've ever wondered how Jesus could believe what he believed, teach what he taught, live how he lived, and die how he died, you need only look to the mother who raised him, who established his moral compass. At least according to the author of Luke.

One might argue that this chapter should start with Mark, since most scholars consider Mark to be the oldest Gospel and assume that Luke uses Mark as a source. Or one might argue that we should begin with Matthew and treat the subject in canonical order. However, we are going to start with Luke, because Mary looms especially large there.

Luke loves Mary, and we love Luke for loving Mary. The title of Mary's proclamation in Luke 1:46–55, the Magnificat, comes from its first words, "My soul magnifies the Lord," which are *magnificat anima mea* in Latin. We could just as easily refer to it as "Like Mother, Like Son" because, if you understand anything about Mary from this chapter, let it be this: Jesus was just a chip off the old Mary block. She taught him values that he would go on not only to preach, but also to live and die for. As we break that down into specifics, we have to ask if we share these values as individual Christians, as a local church, and as a universal church. Here is where Mary appears in Luke–Acts: Luke 1:27–38; 1:39–55; 2:5–34; 8:19–21; Acts 1:13–14.

The Annunciation (Luke 1:27–38)

> In the sixth month the angel Gabriel was sent by God to a town
> in Galilee called Nazareth, to a virgin engaged to a man whose

name was Joseph, of the house of David. The virgin's name was Mary. And he came to her and said, "Greetings, *favored* one! The Lord is with you." But she was much perplexed by his words and pondered what sort of greeting this might be. The angel said to her, "Do not be afraid, Mary, for you have *found favor* with God. And now, you will conceive in your womb and bear a son, and you will name him Jesus. He will be great, and will be called *the Son of the Most High*, and the Lord God will give to him the throne of his ancestor David. He will reign over the house of Jacob forever, and of his kingdom there will be no end." Mary said to the angel, "How can this be, since I am a virgin?" The angel said to her, "The Holy Spirit will come upon you, and *the power of the Most High will overshadow you*; therefore the child to be born will be holy; he will be called *Son of God*. And now, your relative Elizabeth in her old age has also conceived a son; and this is the sixth month for her who was said to be barren. For nothing will be impossible with God." Then Mary said, "Here am I, the servant of the Lord; let it be with me according to your word." Then the angel departed from her. (Luke 1:26–38, emphasis added)

Let me draw your attention to three features of the annunciation text. First, note that Mary is favored, as indicated in verses 28 and 30. Verse 28 contains a *hapax legomenon*, which means a word that occurs nowhere else in the New Testament. This particular verb, *kecharitōmenē*, occurs in the perfect tense, a special, unusually marked past tense in Greek, used when the author wants to highlight an act that is completed and has ongoing effect into the present. Yes, Mary was favored two thousand years ago, but in a way that will affect all generations after her! In verse 30, Mary is said to have found *charis*, usually translated as "favor" in keeping with the verb in verse 28, but it is also the noun that means "grace." Unlike the verb, which he only uses once, Luke uses this noun twenty-five times. Matthew and Mark never use it. John uses it only three times and only in the prologue. So, whatever is happening with Mary, it is tied to the major theme of grace that Luke regularly replays. She's the Mother of Grace. The next occurrence of the word *charis* comes in Luke 2:40, about Jesus: "The child grew and became strong, filled with wisdom; and the favor [*charis*] of God was upon him." And Luke repeats the sentiment in 2:52. Like Mother, like Son.

Second, every time I lead a group to the Holy Land, we go to the Church of the Transfiguration. Of course, we read the story

149

of the transfiguration while there, but not until after we read the story of the annunciation. Why? In 1:35 Gabriel says to Mary, "The Holy Spirit will come upon you, and the power of the Most High will *overshadow* you; therefore the child to be born will be holy; he will be called Son of God" (emphasis added). The Greek word translated as "overshadow" is *episkiazō*. It occurs in only one other place in Luke—the transfiguration. In Luke 9:34 we read: "While he was saying this, a cloud came and overshadowed [*episkiazō*] them; and they were terrified as they entered the cloud." And, just as we heard in the annunciation that Jesus "will be called the Son of the Most High" (1:32) and "he will be called Son of God" (1:35), so in Luke 9:35 what Mary already knows comes to pass—God calls Jesus God's Son: "Then from the cloud came a voice that said, 'This is my Son, my Chosen; listen to him!'" *Both* Mary and Jesus and *only* Mary and Jesus are divinely overshadowed. They both have access to the divine and have supernatural experiences reminiscent of Moses. Like Mother, like Son. Although there is not an explicit citation, the language of "overshadow" is suggestive of the divine presence as witnessed in the LXX in places such as Exodus 40:35; and Psalms 91:4; 140:7. In ancient rabbinic literature, God's divine presence in the world would come to be referred to as Shekinah, from the Hebrew root *škn*, "to dwell." "Shekinah" is a feminine word and, at least in some later Jewish traditions, would be drawn upon in affirming a feminine aspect of God's person. (Consult Unterman et al., 2007.)

Third, unlike the story in Matthew (in which Joseph alone is told to name Jesus, and Mary has no part in the conversation with the angel or anyone else), in Luke's Gospel Mary names Jesus— Joseph has nothing to do with it. In Luke 1:31 Gabriel declares: "and you [singular] will name him Jesus."

Mary's actions in the annunciation make her a role model for *all* Christians, no matter what their gender. Consider the words of Beverly Roberts Gaventa: "Some traditional interpretations of Mary see in these words the emergence of Mary as a model for all women, but it is difficult to find anything in the text that suggest such an identification between Mary and women in general. With her words of compliance Mary becomes not a model female, but a model disciple who consents to what is not yet fully understood" (1999, 54–55).

150

Mary and Elizabeth (Luke 1:39–45)

Mary visits Elizabeth, and they talk through God's promises and where they fit into the story. When Mary arrives, Elizabeth is filled with the Holy Spirit and exclaims: "Blessed are you among women, and blessed is the fruit of your womb" (Luke 1:42). She then calls Mary "the mother of my Lord" (v. 43). Elizabeth, inspired, makes a proclamation that has served as an anchor of hope for all generations after her: "And blessed is she who believed that there would be a fulfillment of what was spoken to her by the Lord" (v. 45).

In her popular book written for a wide audience, *Showing Mary: How Women Can Share Prayers, Wisdom, and the Blessings of God,* biblical scholar the Rev. Dr. Renita Weems explores Mary's experience in Luke 1:26–56, spending ample time reflecting on the relationship between Mary and Elizabeth. Picking up on Gabriel's words, "Even Elizabeth," Weems writes:

> It's not coincidental that Mary and Elizabeth became pregnant right about the same time. Everything was in God's timing. God knew that Mary would need a confidante, spiritual companion, and wise soul to reach out to. And God knew that Elizabeth would need a friend who would be happy that her prayers were answered, someone else familiar with God's mysterious timing. Each confirmed for the other that with God all things were possible, especially new beginnings. "Synchronicity" is the term the Swiss psychologist Carl Jung used in describing what happens when inner readiness intersects with outer opportunities. It's the curious way in which a person's external reality suddenly clicks into alignment with what's taking place in her inner world. (2005, 81–82)

For those seeking to apply this text to their current lived reality, the text might ask: Who is your Elizabeth? Who is your deepest soul friend with whom you are uncensored and can share your visions and experiences? Who is your safest space when others doubt you?

With both (1) Mary and Elizabeth and (2) ourselves and our world, this text makes us ask about our expectations. Are we dreaming big enough, honestly? Both Elizabeth and Mary experienced being caught up in the scope of the divine, which meant being drawn into a reality far more momentous than any they could have

151

previously imagined. They came to understand that their *experience* of God and God's vision far exceeded any of the theological or intellectual categories they had adopted to date. It leads the rest of us to ask: Do we have any room in ourselves to house the seemingly impossible? What are we on the verge of? Are we willing to take the leap and not count the cost? What promises have already been realized or might very soon be?

Like Ruth with Naomi, and Mary with her sister Martha, here once again we find women in relationship with women, supporting one another, growing together, and modeling deep faith in which the rest of us are invited to join. The examples in Scripture of women helping women could be dramatically multiplied to include Dorcas caring for widows, the midwives who helped Moses's mother, and so on. The larger "takeaways" from such stories are multiplicitous, but at the very least, all Christian readers are invited to meditate upon the call and promise afforded by such texts.

The Magnificat (Luke 1:46–55)

The faith and the legacy of holy women appear often in the Bible. Mary's song is modeled after Hannah's prayer in 1 Samuel 2:1–10. Her song also calls to mind other songs by women in the Old Testament and Apocrypha, including the songs of Miriam (Exod. 15:20–21), Deborah (Judg. 5:1–31), and Judith (Jdt. 16:1–17).

Mary's Magnificat sets the stage for Jesus's own ministry and that which he "learned from his mother's milk," as the expression goes. Augustine uses the expression multifariously, that "[he] sucked in [x] with [his] mother's milk. The [x] we've taken in with our mother's milk." For example, positively we read: "Through your mercy, Lord, my tender little heart had drunk in that name, the name of my Savior and your Son, with my mother's milk, and in my deepest heart I still held on to it" (Augustine, *Confessions* 3.4.8, trans. Boulding). Negatively, in *Exposition of the Psalms* he writes: "Every human being, wherever he or she is born, learns the tongue of that country, or district, or civic community, and is imbued with the customs and way of life proper to the place. How, for instance, could a child born among pagans avoid paying cult to a stone idol, when his parents have trained him in that form of worship? In that milieu he heard his earliest words; he sucked in that falsehood

152

with his mother's milk" (64.6, trans. Boulding). The idea of virtue (or vice) being transmitted from mother to child either literally, through breast milk, or figuratively, through moral training that was in the domain of the mother in the early years, was a given in antiquity. This trope is not lost on Luke.

In the Magnificat, Mary exhibits the passion of the prophets and conveys God's preferential option for the poor. She draws upon her Scriptures (the notes in any good scholarly study Bible will show you the variety of texts she includes), and she announces Luke's primary theme—the Great Reversal (if you have never read Flannery O'Connor's short story "Revelation," now is the time to do so if you want to explore what Luke means by that), which appears throughout the Gospel. The high are brought low, the lowly exalted. Those marginalized in this world are the apple of God's eye. Irony upon irony, throughout the canon.

The Birth, Circumcision, and Presentation (Luke 2:5–34)

Luke tells the story of Jesus's birth in a way that puts a distinctive emphasis on Mary. In Luke 2 we learn that, though they are from Nazareth, Mary and Joseph travel to Bethlehem because of a census that the emperor Augustus ordered, and "while they were there, the time came for her to deliver her child. And she gave birth to her firstborn son and wrapped him in bands of cloth, and laid him in a manger, because there was no place for them in the inn" (Luke 2:5–7). In Matthew, the holy family is from Bethlehem; no census is mentioned. Mary and Joseph only end up in Nazareth because Judea is unsafe for Jesus due to Herod. Matthew and Luke present very different infancy narratives, each told in a way that furthers the theological concerns of each author. They should be respected as separate narratives to be read in the context of each Gospel, not extracted and harmonized.

Given Luke's special concern for the poor and lowly, as evidenced in the Magnificat, it may not be surprising that, according to Luke, soon after Mary and Joseph travel to Bethlehem, they are visited by lowly shepherds (not prestigious magi, as in Matthew) who, like lowly Mary, had been visited by angels. Here I want to draw special attention to the fact that Mary, the one who will shape

153

Jesus, is quite tuned in to what is occurring, and it will affect the child she raises in a very particular way:

> When the angels had left them and gone into heaven, the shepherds said to one another, "Let us go now to Bethlehem and see this thing that has taken place, which the Lord has made known to us." So they went with haste and found Mary and Joseph, and the child lying in the manger. When they saw this, they made known what had been told them about this child; and all who heard it were amazed at what the shepherds told them. *But Mary treasured all these words and pondered them in her heart.* (Luke 2:15–19; emphasis added).

Mary adds this experience to her earlier one and then proceeds to raise this child.

Just as Elizabeth and Zechariah did with John the Baptist, as devout Jews Mary and Joseph have Jesus circumcised on the eighth day, in accordance with Scripture. Next, we find her and Joseph in the temple participating in a purification ritual and offering the sacrifice appropriate for the poor. Clearly, Luke insists that Jesus's relatives are devout Jews.

In the Footsteps of Mary

What does Jesus go on to do, having been morally formed by Mary? Let's look at some of the connections.

1. The temple incident (Luke 2:41–51). Given what the reader knows so far, it should not be surprising that the chapter later finds Jesus in the temple, immersed in Scripture. In 2:41, the family goes to Jerusalem as usual, as they do "every year," being faithful Jews. It takes with Jesus. He stays in the temple debating with the teachers, and, when his mom expresses irritation over the anxiety he caused his parents by staying behind, he indicates that she should have expected as much. He has a point. But the conflict Mary would feel between teaching her child to live in a godly way and the actual ramifications of his practicing what she preached was there from the beginning and was as real as it is for any parent today. As Simeon had already announced to Mary in particular: "This child is destined for the falling and the rising of many in Israel, and to be a sign that will be opposed so that the inner thoughts of many will be revealed—and a sword

154

will pierce your own soul too" (2:34–35). Like the story of Jesus before Simeon, the story of the preteen Jesus in the temple ends thus: *"His mother treasured all these things in her heart"* (v. 51; emphasis added).

Mary, as usual, is spiritually present to the task and mystery of parenting Jesus effectively toward his destiny.

2. Jesus's inaugural synagogue address (Luke 4:16–22). Luke narrates Jesus's first public appearance, where he announces the major themes of his ministry. Again, note that he went to the synagogue "as was his custom." And just like Mary, he frames his morality and vocation by drawing upon the prophets with the same message of the Magnificat, namely the Great Reversal, in which the rich and powerful will be brought low and the poor and powerless exalted:

> He stood up to read, and the scroll of the prophet Isaiah was given to him. He unrolled the scroll and found the place where it was written:
>
> "The Spirit of the Lord is upon me,
>   because he has anointed me
> *to bring good news to the poor.*
> He has sent me to proclaim release to the captives
>   and recovery of sight to the blind,
> *to let the oppressed go free,*
> to proclaim the year of the Lord's favor."
>   *(Luke 4:16b–19; emphasis added)*

He then announces: "Today this scripture has been fulfilled in your hearing" (v. 21). The response? "All spoke well of him and were amazed at the gracious words that came from his mouth" (v. 22). This should sound familiar to the reader who recalls the response when Jesus was in the temple as a boy: "And all who heard him were amazed at his understanding and his answers" (2:47). But the folks in Luke 4 go on to be perplexed, asking, "Is not this Joseph's son?" Fools!! He's Mary's son—that's why he's saying these things. Like Mother, like Son.

3. The Sermon on the Plain (Luke 6:20–26). Jesus's Sermon on the Plain in Luke 6 once again echoes Mary's teaching about the Great Reversal and God's special concern for the poor and oppressed. For example:

Then he looked up at his disciples and said:

"Blessed are you who are poor,
for yours is the kingdom of God.
"Blessed are you who are hungry now,
for you will be filled.
"Blessed are you who weep now,
for you will laugh.

"Blessed are you when people hate you, and when they exclude
you, revile you, and defame you on account of the Son of Man.
Rejoice in that day and leap for joy, for surely your reward is great
in heaven; for that is what their ancestors did to the prophets.

"But woe to you who are rich,
for you have received your consolation.
"Woe to you who are full now,
for you will be hungry.
"Woe to you who are laughing now,
for you will mourn and weep.

"Woe to you when all speak well of you, for that is what their
ancestors did to the false prophets." (Luke 6:20–26)

Jesus absorbed Mary's values regarding the oppressed and down-
trodden.

4. Enlarging the family (Luke 8:19–21). The references to
Jesus's brothers (*adelphoi*) and sisters (*adelphai*) can be a sensitive
one, depending on one's tradition, given particular notions around
the perpetual virginity of Mary. For some, these figures are either
cousins or Joseph's children from another woman. I refrain from
engaging that issue here because it is not central to the goals of
this book.

In Luke 8, Jesus's "mothers and brothers" try to come to him
but are stymied by the multitudes surrounding him. Someone
informs Jesus that his family desires to see him. Jesus, apparently
unstressed, uses the occasion to proclaim: "My mother and my
brothers are those who hear the word of God and do it" (v. 21).
From the moment she appears in the Gospel, Mary is an exceptional model of one who is both a hearer and doer of the word of
God. Thus, in this passage Jesus is not maligning the faithfulness
of his family; rather, he is enlarging the family of faith and adding

156

to the pool of disciples. He is enacting the very inclusive scope of God's call and mercy first voiced by Mary, validated by Simeon and Anna, and expressed throughout the narrative. (For a reading that finds this passage more ambiguous, consult Gaventa 1999, 69–71.)

The harsh nature of Luke's words here may result from the influence of Mark's Gospel, which the author of Luke used as a source. It is, therefore, worth taking a look at Mary in Mark, our earliest Gospel. Mark shows little interest in Mary (or Jesus's other family members, really). She appears in only two places and is named only at Mark 6:3, where Jesus's opponents derogate his authority: "Is not this the carpenter, the son of Mary and brother of James and Joses and Judas and Simon, and are not his sisters here with us?"

However, Mark does include Jesus's family among those who oppose his ministry. In Mark 3:21, we learn that Jesus's family has heard of his exorcism ministry and, in response, they "went out to restrain [*krateō*: seize, grasp, restrain, apprehend] him, for people were saying, 'He has gone out of his mind.'" Presumably, Mary is included in that group, since we learn a few verses later that Jesus's mother and brothers (and sisters?) are asking for him. (I remind the reader that *adelphoi* may mean "brothers," or it may mean "brothers and sisters." The masculine plural is the "unmarked" form. Jesus's sisters are mentioned explicitly in Matt. 13:56 and Mark 6:3.) For a more positive take on the behavior of Jesus's family in Mark 3:21, however, consult Susan Miller, *Women in Mark's Gospel* (2004, 31–38).

Already, we encounter differences between Mark and Luke. First, the context in which the story appears in each Gospel differs, which affects the interpretation of the story itself. The Markan context is one of conflict and controversy. It comes early in Jesus's ministry, right after he calls the disciples and in the midst of conflict with the religious authorities, who are accusing Jesus of being in league with Satan, also called Beelzebul. Luke's version of the story, however, occurs later in his ministry and right after the parable about the soil. A second difference is tone. Luke edits or "softens" the Markan source—there is no indication in Luke that Jesus's family wants to restrain him or that they fear he has lost his mind. Third is the desire of the family. In Mark, the family is there to get Jesus to come out to them—recall that they want to seize him. This is the same word for what the religious authorities want to do to him in Mark 12:12 and what the soldiers do to him

157

in Mark 14. In Luke, on the other hand, there is no talk of Satan or insanity or seizing Jesus in this story; the family aims to go to him to be part of the group of disciples.

This icon of Mary breastfeeding the infant Jesus is on display in the Milk Grotto chapel in Bethlehem.

Photo by Keri Lynn Lucas.

158 **5. The blessed breasts of Mary (Luke 11:27–28).** Mary next appears in an oblique reference made by a woman in a crowd to whom Jesus is teaching: "Blessed is the womb that bore you and

the breasts that nursed you!" (11:27). Review Alicia Myers's ovular (rather than "seminal") work on the role of breast-feeding in moral formation in antiquity in chapter 8, "Jesus across Gender," and the comment makes utter sense. In addition, the careful reader realizes that the woman is echoing the words of Elizabeth to Mary, when Elizabeth was "filled with the Holy Spirit and exclaimed with a loud cry: 'Blessed are you among women, and blessed is the fruit of your womb'" (1:41–42). Again, the connection between nursing and moral formation, getting one's values through the mother's very body/breasts, looms large here. (Consult image on p. 158.)

Jesus takes the comment from the crowd and "grows it," uses it to call people to move into moral adulthood (kind of like what we do with confirmation or believer's baptism). The faith of one's parent is an excellent foundation; one then must move from spiritual milk to spiritual meat, to borrow an image from the apostle Paul. Jesus declares blessed "those who hear the word of God and obey it!" (11:28). Later in the narrative Jesus himself will use the womb-and-breast language to call people again to enacted discipleship even though there will be distress to endure: "For the days are surely coming when they will say, 'Blessed are the barren, and the wombs that never bore, and the breasts that never nursed'" (23:29).

6. Garden of Gethsemane (Luke 22). Jesus in the Garden of Gethsemane is somewhat daunted by the potential path before him. In the process of embracing his call, he first keeps it at arm's length and assesses the situation circumspectly: "Father, if you are willing, remove this cup from me." He goes on, of course, to adopt God's own plan for his life, despite some initial resistance or doubt, and declares boldly and resolutely: "Yet, not my will but yours be done" (22:42). How many of us have pondered this passage, sympathizing with Jesus's desire for a way that involves less sacrifice and being astonished and even inspired by his willingness to serve God in the end? We wonder how on earth he could have willingly trod that road. But if we recall his mother's experience in the opening chapter, we understand that he was spiritually formed by a woman who lived her own life that way. When Gabriel approaches her, like Jesus, she assesses the situation circumspectly: "How can this be?" In the end, though, she declares boldly and resolutely: "Here am I, the servant of the Lord; let it be with me according to your word" (1:38). Like Mother, like Son.

159

7. Jesus's death (Luke 23). Remember Simeon's words to Mary in Luke 2:34–35: "This child is destined for the falling and the rising of many in Israel, and to be a sign that will be opposed so that the inner thoughts of many will be revealed—and a sword will pierce your own soul too." This comes to fruition with the cross. Indeed, Jesus spent his life proclaiming the simultaneously challenging and liberating good news to those in the land of Israel, including Jews and Gentiles. Of course, the prophets constantly worry about how the community is treating the "least of these," the widow, the orphan, the stranger in the land. Luke spends ample literary energy casting Jesus in the role of the prophet and declaring that the pattern of human history shows the penchant for banishing and punishing the prophets who would show us truth. Having read and committed to the message of the prophets, to some degree Jesus and his mom must not have been surprised by the call for and execution of his death. To the end, Jesus lived and died in accordance with the values he was taught by his mother from the start.

8. Jesus's resurrection (Luke 24). Jesus is resurrected, and Mary continues *his* ministry that *she* started before he was born. We encounter her in Acts 1:13–14: "When they had entered the city, they went to the room upstairs where they were staying, Peter, and John, and James, and Andrew, Philip and Thomas, Bartholomew and Matthew, James son of Alphaeus, and Simon the Zealot, and Judas son of James. All these were constantly devoting themselves to prayer, *together with certain women, including Mary the mother of Jesus*, as well as his brothers" (emphasis added). After all, why *wouldn't* she be there?

In contemplating the theme of like Mother, like Son, I invite you to consider this poem:

Liturgy

All the way to Elizabeth
and in the months afterward,
she wove him, pondering,
"This is my body, my blood!"

Beneath the watching eyes
of donkey, ox, and sheep
she rocked him, crooning,
"This is my body, my blood!"

In the moonless desert flight
and the Egypt-days of his growing
she nourished him, singing,
"This is my body, my blood!"

In the search for her young lost boy
and the foreboding day of his leaving
she let him go, knowing,
"This is my body, my blood!"

Under the blood-smeared cross
she rocked his mangled bones,
re-membering him, moaning,
"This is my body, my blood!"

When darkness, stones, and tomb
Bloomed to Easter morning,
She ran to him, shouting,
"This is my body, my blood!"

And no one thought to tell her:
"Woman, it is not fitting
for you to say those words.
You don't resemble him."
    (Irene Zimmerman, "Liturgy")

Mary is a character in her own right in Luke. Far beyond merely bearing children, she is a mother in the sense of the one who starts the child in the process of moral formation, instilling into the child the values of the family. The early Christians would broaden the notion of family beyond biology to include "fictive kin" as they sought to constitute the family of God whose values derived from the life, ministry, death, and resurrection of Jesus of Nazareth.

Mary in the Gospel of Matthew

In the Gospel of Matthew, Mary is depicted primarily as the wife of Joseph (1:16, 19, 20, 24) and mother of Jesus (1:18; 2:11, 13, 14, 20, 21; 12:46, 47, 48; 13:55). Mary, like all of the characters, figures into Matthew's understanding of salvation history and the

161

ways Jesus relates to scriptural fulfillment. For Matthew, God's majestic plan for saving all nations starts with Genesis. So taken is Matthew with Scripture and its fulfillment through Jesus that this Gospel begins with these words: "Book [*biblos*] of the genesis [*genesis*] of Jesus the Christ [*Christos*, Greek for "Messiah"], Son of David, Son of Abraham" (Matt. 1:1, my trans.). In very large letters, Matthew writes: what you are about to read is a continuation of the story of "God with us" (Immanuel) that started with Genesis. It should come as no surprise, then, that every character, including Mary, who appears in the Gospel of Matthew will help Matthew achieve the goal of proclaiming this truth as Matthew perceives it.

Matthew uses "formula citations," in which he narrates an event and then tells the reader that it happened to fulfill a particular Scripture. Matthew also depends heavily on typology in which he patterns characters or the structure of the narrative using Old Testament precedents and frameworks. In Matthew, Jesus is the new Moses, and his birth and infancy mirror Moses's own. Moses is credited with providing the Torah, the first five books in Scripture; in Matthew, and only in Matthew, Jesus delivers five great sermons. One of them, in which he exposits the Torah received on Mount Sinai, takes place on a mountain (in Luke, on the contrary, it occurs on a plain).

Mary is worked into Matthew's strategy of connecting Jesus's life to the Old Testament, though in surprising ways. First, she echoes and connects tightly with Jesus's lineage that links him with David. Second—and here one must appreciate Matthew's love of irony—she shows how God works in mysterious, unexpected ways, against the traditional norms of society. Here is a young woman with no obvious social capital, changing the world by choosing to follow God boldly, come what may, against all expectations and social mores. The irony lies in the fact that it seems like readers of Scripture would eventually learn to "expect the unexpected" and be less surprised by God's surprising ways, to loosen the shackles of "the norm" in order to remain ready to respond to God's movement in an agile fashion. But hard hearts, small expectations, and love for the expedient and the familiar keep our feet heavy and our necks stiff. Enter Matthew, to remind us, once again, that God's pattern is to shake us out of our patterns.

162

Genealogy (Matt. 1)

In Matthew, we first meet Mary in the genealogy: "Joseph the husband of Mary, of whom Jesus was born, who is called the Messiah"
(1:16). Scholars and preachers have long puzzled over the appearance and meaning of the four other women in Matthew's genealogy and how they relate to Mary, the fifth: Tamar (1:3); Rahab
(1:5); Ruth (1:5); wife of Uriah (Bathsheba) (1:6). Is it unusual to
find women in a genealogy? Certainly, Luke does not include any
women in his version of the genealogy (Luke 3:23–38), not even
Mary. (Neither Mark nor John includes a genealogy.)

While the inclusion of women in genealogies is rare in the
Hebrew Bible, it does occur, especially in contexts where the writer
lists all the male descendants of an individual and attempts to distinguish among the sons born to various wives or secondary wives
of the same man (for a longer discussion of the term "secondary
wives," consult chap. 3, "Women and Violence in the Bible"). But
Matthew's genealogy is a linear one, limited to direct paternal
descent, and thus the appearance of women's names is unexpected.
To heighten the startling character of these additions, the women
whose names appear are not Sarah and Rebecca and Rachel, but
women whose stories teem with ambiguity (Gaventa 1999, 33).

From the very start of his narrative, then, Matthew combines
the expected with the surprising. The presence of the women has
generated much scholarly rumination.

Tamar poses as a prostitute as a way to show Judah's true colors.
She is a keeper of the law; he is not. Rahab works as a prostitute
(a common job for women in every century and every place given
that in no century, in no place, have women had equal access to
the "upstanding" jobs that men enjoy). She is hailed as a hero of
the faith by both Jews and Christians, never maligned for being a
prostitute. Ruth, vulnerable as a female and a non-Israelite, uses
the means legally available to her so that she and her mother-in-
law, Naomi, can find protection under the wing of a male, Boaz.
Ruth, too, is celebrated as a heroine of the faith in an ancestral line
that produces King David and Jesus, the Messiah. Bathsheba is not
named in Matthew's genealogy; she is called "the wife of Uriah."
Indeed, this genealogy serves to tell us who Jesus is, namely, the Son
of David, the Messiah. Matthew's choice to call her merely "the wife

163

of Uriah" highlights the unsavory fact that David, as king, desired to possess his subject, Bathsheba, after he saw her bathing. In an act of consummate evil, he intentionally has her husband killed and then procures her for himself to add to his collection of women. But, in God's typical style, God redeems a terrible situation, makes a way out of no way, and brings the Messiah out of this human mess that rivals the most dysfunctional family dynamics to date. Bathsheba is the innocent in the scenario, accused of no wrongdoing.

While no one ever tries to find the thread that binds all of the men of the genealogy together, everyone seems to want to do so with the women. One common explanation for their appearance is that each of them is "sexually suspect" in some way. But this approach quickly fails according to Scripture's own reckoning. In each case, the women are put into awkward (to say the least) positions by a patriarchal system, and then judged to be "sexually suspect" by the very system that creates the categories. The same then happens to Mary. But, as with the others, the text insists *not* that she is a heroine of the faith *despite* being "sexually loose or suspect"; rather, the text insists that she is simply, like the others, a heroine of the faith, without caveat, period. Sex sells, even from the pulpit, but it erases the brilliance of these mothers of the faith.

Another typical approach is to argue that these women foreshadow Jesus's mission beyond the Jews to include the Gentiles. Clearly, the inclusion of the Gentiles in God's salvific plan is a special theme of Matthew's. Already the magi, who are Gentiles, signal this theme that runs throughout Matthew (and is highlighted in the story of the Canaanite woman) and culminates in Jesus's command to "go therefore and make disciples of all nations [*ethnē*]" (Matt. 28:19). This approach fails as well, however. While Rahab and Ruth were Gentiles, Jewish tradition considers them proselytes to Judaism. Tamar and Bathsheba are Israelites, as is Mary.

Much more helpful are the analyses of Amy-Jill Levine and Beverly Gaventa. Levine argues "that the divine plan moves in ways that contravene traditional family values." In addition, each of the women's stories features the theme of a "higher righteousness" (Levine 2012, 467). Judah admits that Tamar is right; Rahab hid the Jewish spies. Ruth is loyal to her mother-in-law, just as Uriah is loyal to his duties as a soldier.

For Gaventa, the women, including Mary, share this in common: "None of them fits in with the way things are 'supposed' to

be. Each of the women is presented as threatening the status quo
in some way, and each is in turn threatened. Each also is shown to
be part of the divine plan, but that goes without saying since each
appears in the genealogy because of the Davidic line" (1999, 39;
consult 32–40 for a fuller, illuminating discussion of the interpretive history).

In sum, I contend that by his inclusion of these women, Matthew heightens the surprise of the ways that God works in history,
bringing disparate parts together to create a whole, and showing
that it was actually meant to be so all the while.

Birth, Visitation, and Flight to Egypt (Matt. 1–2)

In Matthew 1:18–25, in contrast with Luke's version of Jesus's conception and birth, Mary is introduced primarily as Jesus's mother
and Joseph's wife. The narrative focuses on Joseph's character and
actions and only incidentally on Mary:

> Now the birth of Jesus the Messiah took place in this way. When
> *his mother Mary* had been engaged to Joseph, but before they
> lived together, she was found to be with child from the Holy
> Spirit. Her husband Joseph, being a righteous man and unwilling
> to expose her to public disgrace, planned to dismiss her quietly.
> But just when he had resolved to do this, an angel of the Lord
> appeared to him in a dream and said, "Joseph, son of David, do
> not be afraid to take *Mary as your wife*, for the child conceived in
> her is from the Holy Spirit. She will bear a son, and *you* [singular,
> referring only to Joseph] are to name him Jesus, for he will save
> his people from their sins." All this took place to fulfill what had
> been spoken by the Lord through the prophet:
>
> > "Look, *the virgin* shall conceive and bear a son,
> > and they shall name him Emmanuel,"
>
> which means, "God is with us." When Joseph awoke from sleep,
> he did as the angel of the Lord commanded him; *he took her as
> his wife*, but had no marital relations with her until she had borne
> a son; and *he named him* Jesus. (Matt. 1:18–25; emphasis added)

The highlighted material draws attention to four points: First, Mary
is addressed obliquely and draws her identity only from her relationship with Joseph and Jesus—she is virgin, wife, and mother. Second,

she is spoken about but never to. Third, she does not exhibit agency but is depicted as the object of action by the Holy Spirit and by Joseph. Fourth, only Joseph participates in naming Jesus.

Matthew presents Mary as fulfilling Old Testament prophecy. Much ink has been spilled on the virgin/young woman issue related to the original Old Testament context, Isaiah 7:14: "Therefore the Lord himself will give you a sign. Look, the young woman [hā'almâ] is with child and shall bear a son, and shall name him Immanuel." The Hebrew word in question is 'almâ. When Isaiah was translated into Greek sometime around the second century BCE (as part of a larger, if complex, process of translating the OT into Greek, producing a collection commonly referred to as the Septuagint, abbreviated LXX), the Greek word *parthenos*, which can mean "young woman" or "virgin," was used to translate the Hebrew word 'almâ. Thus, Matthew, written about fifty years after the death of Jesus and twenty years after the martyrdom of the apostle Paul, is the earliest evidence of the notion of a *virgin* birth (Luke 1:27 uses this term as well, but does not cite it as an OT prophecy fulfillment), if that is what Matthew meant (consult Gale 2011).

Note that Paul, writing decades earlier, never explicitly mentions Mary at all and does not know of a tradition that makes her a virgin mother. Including admittedly oblique allusions to Mary, the only "evidence" of her existence in Paul's letters is found in these verses:

> But when the fullness of time had come, God sent his Son, born of a woman, born under the law, in order to redeem those who were under the law, so that we might receive adoption as children. (Gal. 4:4–5, written in the 50s)

> The gospel concerning his son, who was descended from David according to the flesh. (Rom. 1:3)

> To them [the Israelites] belong the patriarchs, and from them, according to the flesh, comes the Messiah, who is over all, God blessed forever. Amen. (Rom. 9:5)

The detailed, heated debates and doctrines related to Mary's virginity would come later, and I briefly mention those at the end of the chapter rather than here because they are extrabiblical. As is extremely typical for Matthew, the point in adducing Isaiah is to show that Jesus fulfills Old Testament prophecy, both typologically and in terms of specific quotations. By the former, I refer to the fact that the Old Testament narrates numerous unusual, miraculous births and infancies of founders of the faith, including Isaac, Moses (after whom Jesus is largely modeled in Matthew), and Samson. In this case, Mary appears as part of Jesus's fulfillment of prophecy.

Mary is mentioned again in Matthew 2:11, when the magi appear, but her importance is only as Jesus's mother—the magi are there to see *him*: "On entering the house, they saw the child with Mary *his mother*; and they knelt down and paid *him* homage. Then, opening their treasure chests, they offered *him* gifts of gold, frankincense, and myrrh" (emphasis added). The magi "saw the child" and gave their gifts to him. Mary is present but not the focus of the story.

Finally, Mary's primary role as Jesus's mother and fulfiller of Old Testament promises appears again in 2:13–21, in which an angel instructs Joseph to flee to Egypt and return after Herod dies. Mary is mentioned four times, never by name, but only as the object of what Joseph should do with "the child and his mother." As a parent and a player in salvation history, she shares a common experience with Moses's mother, since Herod, playing the role of Pharaoh (consult the slaughter of the innocents in Exod. 1:16), executes all children under two. Matthew, once again using Old Testament Scripture (Jer. 31:15), ties this to another biblical mother, Rachel, weeping for her children.

Other Occurrences of Mary in Matthew

The last appearance of Mary in Matthew occurs in 12:46–50, in which Matthew takes over Mark's story about Jesus's (nameless) mother and brothers appearing outside and Jesus proclaiming: "Whoever does the will of my Father in heaven is my brother and sister and mother." Matthew's account is softer than Mark's harsh version, but, unlike Luke's version, it does not add strongly to the characterization of Mary. The same is true of Matthew's adoption of Mark's material about Jesus's family: "Is not this the carpenter's son? Is not his mother called Mary? And are not his brothers James and Joseph and Simon and Judas? And are not all his sisters with us? Where then did this man get all this?" (Matt. 13:55–56).

167

Unlike Luke, Matthew does not indicate whether Mary and Jesus enjoyed a close, vital relationship, whether she morally shaped him, or whether she becomes an essential part of the church. In this way, Matthew differs not only from Luke, but also from John.

Mary in the Gospel of John: From Cana to Crucifixion to Church, All in the Family

> But to all who received him, who believed in his name, he gave power to become children of God, who were born, not of blood or of the will of the flesh or of the will of man, but of God. And the Word became flesh and lived among us, and we have seen his glory, the glory as of a father's only son, full of grace and truth. (John 1:12–14)

If those who believe are the "children of God," then Jesus's mother is the matriarch of the family. John depicts the church as one big family living together in the house of God (14:2) here in this world that God (with Jesus) has so lovingly created and sustained. The incarnation trains our eyes on the fact that complete intimacy with God and one another is available here and now, in this world.

Apart from John 6:42—in which the audience asks, "Is not this Jesus, the son of Joseph, whose father and mother we know? How can he now say, 'I have come down from heaven'?"—John includes Mary explicitly in only two places: the wedding at Cana (2:1–12) and the crucifixion (19:25–27). Neither of the stories he includes about Mary appears in any other New Testament source, and he never names Mary; John refers to her only as *Jesus's mother*.

In what follows, I show how Jesus's mother figures into this vision of the church as the family of God. It starts at Cana with a story of a family affair, a wedding. There we behold a woman (*gynē*), the mother (*mētēr*) of Jesus, some wine (*oinos*), Jesus, talk of his "hour" (*hōra*), his glorification (*doxa*), and the overflow from his abundance to those around him that provokes belief and enlarges the family of God. It ends with the scene at the cross. There we behold a woman (*gynē*), the mother (*mētēr*) of Jesus, some wine (*oinos*), the arrival of his hour which is his ultimate glorification, and the overflow from his abundance (blood, water, Spirit) to those around him that provokes belief and enlarges the family of God.

Cana (John 2:1–12)

John depicts Mary as part of Jesus's ministry from the beginning to the end and beyond. In the story of the wedding at Cana, Jesus's mother is mentioned four times (2:1, 3, 5, 12) and is mentioned before anyone else: "On the third day there was a wedding in Cana of Galilee, and the mother of Jesus was there" (v. 1). The story at Cana indicates the closeness between Jesus and his mother. She is confident of Jesus's abilities and expects him to use them for the sake of others. He interacts with her and does, in fact, complete the request.

Jesus and his disciples show up to this wedding, and eventually the wine runs out. Jesus's mother, who is also in attendance, points this out to Jesus. He responds: "Woman [*gynē*], what concern is that to you and to me? My hour [*hōra*] has not yet come" (2:4). To modern ears, or depending upon how one's own family interacts, this may sound harsh and dismissive. Literally, the Greek says, "Woman, what to me and to you?" (Technically speaking, Jesus is correct insofar as this problem fell under the jurisdiction of the bridegroom. But, of course, in Johannine metaphor, Jesus is *the* bridegroom, as indicated in 3:25–30, so it falls to him.) The reader should understand familial, playful banter here. Note that Jesus also addresses the Samaritan woman (4:21) and Mary Magdalene (20:15) with the word "woman," and he clearly does not dismiss them. Obviously, his mother is not at all discomfited and expects him to meet her request, as she immediately tells the servants, "Do whatever he tells you" (2:5). And they do.

As is typical for Johannine passages, there is so much going on here. First, the family of God. This Gospel loves the language of family, and it expands family far beyond the nuclear or biological to include all people as children of God. Consider John 12:32: "And I, when I am lifted up from the earth, will draw *all* people to myself" (emphasis added). As John's narrative progresses, the family expands (consult Clark-Soles 2016, 91–99). Already in John 1, we learn: "He came to what was his own [*eis ta idia*], and his own people did not accept him. But to all who received him, who believed in his name, he gave power to become children of God, who were born, not of blood or of the will of the flesh or of the will of man, but of God" (1:11–13). Based on this very first sign initiated by his mother in John 2, Jesus's initial disciples believe in him such

169

that at the end of the story we already find the expanding of the family described in John 1: "After this he went down to Capernaum with his mother, his brothers and sisters [*adelphoi*; my trans.], and his disciples; and they remained there a few days" (2:12). "Family," for Christians, refers primarily to those connected by faith, not genes; thus, the disciples become family, right along with Jesus's mother and brothers and sisters. This theme is reiterated throughout John. In chapter 20, Jesus will commission a different Mary, Mary Magdalene, to announce to his "brothers and sisters" that he is ascending to "my Father and your [plural] Father, my God and your [plural] God," thus declaring all believers to be brothers and sisters to Jesus and, therefore, to one another.

Second, the narrative serves to pique our curiosity about what Jesus means by his "hour" that has "not yet" come. In John, Jesus's "hour" refers to his passion/crucifixion/exaltation/glorification, which constitute a single moment in the Fourth Gospel. We will also find that, when his hour fully arrives, on the cross, his mother is right there, playing a major role, nurturing and expanding the family of believers that we saw in Cana. To the fulfillment of that hour of glorification, we now turn.

The Cross (John 19:25–27)

We hear no *explicit* mention of Jesus's mother again until we encounter her at the foot of the cross, when his hour has indeed come: "Meanwhile, standing near the cross of Jesus were his mother, and his mother's sister, Mary the wife of Clopas, and Mary Magdalene" (19:25). After referencing these four women, the narrative camera then zooms in on his mother.

The passage echoes the wedding-at-Cana story in which Jesus's mother, his disciples, the language of family, and his addressing his mother as "woman" appeared: "When Jesus saw his mother [*mētēr*] and the disciple whom he loved standing beside her, he said to his mother, 'Woman [*gynē*], here is your son.' Then he said to the disciple, 'Here is your mother.' And from that hour [*hōra*] the disciple took her into his own home [*eis ta idia*]" (19:26–27). Note that just after this we find a jar of wine there. Jesus now receives the wine (and, unlike the wine he himself supplied that was notably called good [*kalon oinon*], his executors provide notably bad, sour wine

170

[*oxos*]). Immediately after, he declares that his mission has been completed (*tetelestai*).

Jesus births the church at the foot of the cross in John, and his mother is foundational in the formation of that community. He gifts her and the Beloved Disciple to one another and shows that church, properly conceived and lived out, is home. Beverly Gaventa notes the intentional ambiguity of "your son" here—does it refer to Jesus or the Beloved Disciple? She argues that this ambiguity helps us observe the process of transition (1999, 94–95). This Gospel loves the language of home and family.

Note that the Beloved Disciple is never named in the Fourth Gospel, an intentional move that allows the reader to assume that role. In doing so, we too find Mary to be our spiritual mother. She is there in the beginning and in the end and, presumably, in between.

Just as promised in John 1, the family of God has been expanded. Jesus's mother is now the mother of the Johannine disciple, which makes Jesus our brother. This point is expressly made again in the resurrection appearances, where we hear Jesus say to another Mary (Magdalene): "But go to my brothers and sisters [*adelphoi*] and say to them, 'I am ascending to my Father and your Father, to my God and your God'" (20:17). Siblings in the family of God.

We noted above the importance of John 1 regarding believers as family with Mary as matriarch. In addition to the maternal theme throughout John, scholars often note the importance of the influence of Genesis on the Gospel of John. Indeed, the Gospel begins in 1:1 by self-consciously citing the opening words of Genesis: "In the beginning" (*en archē*). Mary Coloe traces Mary as an Eve figure in John:

> At both Cana and the cross, only two titles are given to this woman, known in the Synoptics as "Mary." In the Fourth Gospel in both scenes, she is described by the narrator using the title, "Mother" (2:1; 19:25) and spoken to by Jesus, with the title, "Woman" (2:4; 19:26). These two titles were names given to the first woman: "She shall be called Woman" (Gen 2:23). "The man called his wife's name Eve, because she was the *mother* of all the living" (Gen 3:20). These two titles, when considered with other unique features of the Johannine Passion, suggest a deliberate evocation of the primordial Garden of Eden, and a theology of creation.

171

WOMEN IN THE BIBLE

. . . At the cross, there is no need for her to do or say anything. Her presence, her being "Woman and Mother" is suf-
ficient for the theological goal of the narrative to be completed
as disciples become children of God (1:12). Apart from Jesus,
no other character is as important to the ideological point of
view of this Gospel's narrative, than the Mother of Jesus. (2013,
210–11, 213)

Mary is a linchpin in the Gospel's depiction of believers as the true
family of God.

In her book *When Momma Speaks: The Bible and Motherhood
from a Womanist Perspective*, Stephanie Crowder covers a number
of themes related to African American mothering that connect with
my treatment of Mary at the cross. I name four. First, she discusses
the strong role of the mother in the moral formation of her own
children (as I argue Mary does with Jesus). Second, she refers to
"other mothering," in which a woman mothers children apart from
her own. This practice "helped to establish a form of extended family" (2016, 11), as we see at the foot of the cross. Third, "community
and church mothers" work in secular and sacred spaces to fight systemic injustice, especially the interrelated evils of racism, sexism,
and poverty (consult 13–16).

Finally, Crowder gives voice to mothers who weep over the
dead bodies of children murdered by mobs or executed by state-
sanctioned violence. Jesus, an innocent man, was no stranger to
murderous mobs and was himself "legally" hung from a tree for
plenty of onlookers to watch for hours as the life slowly drained
out of him. Too many mothers in Scripture and in our own society
know Mary's pain on this count. Crowder specifically focuses on
the harrowing account of Rizpah's experience in 2 Samuel 21:1–14,
in which the Gibeonites impale her two innocent sons (and five
of Merab's). The bodies are left to decompose out in the open for
months. Daily, Rizpah actively stands vigil over the dead bodies:
"Then Rizpah the daughter of Aiah took sackcloth, and spread it
on a rock for herself, from the beginning of harvest until rain fell
on them from the heavens; she did not allow the birds of the air to
come on the bodies by day, or the wild animals by night" (21:10).

172

Let me make two points here. First, the stories of Mary and
Rizpah remind us of the pain of mothers whose children have died.
Have you ever thought about the fact we have no word for a parent

who has lost a child? We have words for partners losing a partner (widow, widower), children losing parents (orphan), but not for parents losing children. We need language for this so that we can speak our suffering and be in solidarity with such parents. Second, African American mothers today resonate deeply with murderous mobs and state-sanctioned violence that target their children:

> "As knowledge of African American mothers and of their journeys is the root of this project, it helps to elucidate the struggles of Rizpah and her childless death watch. The class dynamic and imperial pressure that forced her to surrender her sons to hanging is not contextually obsolete. Mothers today still watch in agony as their children travel the school-to-prison pipeline. #Blacklivesmatter started from the cries of African American mothers who had to bury their children, like Rizpah." (2016, 107)

Surely Mary experienced such agony as she, too, watched her son impaled and hung at the hands of the state. Mothers who mourn reflect the undying love of our God who mothers and mourns. Mourning mothers grounded in purpose and hope often become midwives of spiritual transformation in the wider world in their own lifetimes and beyond. Like Mary.

Mary and Jesus in the Flesh: Incarnation

I began our treatment of John by citing verses from chapter 1 depicting family language and incarnation language. Jesus is family because he actually became flesh rather than remaining a Platonic ideal of some sort. He had a mother. Some take the "mother" language in John to be an anti-docetic emphasis on the incarnation, a primary theme in John. Docetism, from the Greek word *dokeō*, "to appear or seem," is a theology that claims that Jesus only appeared or seemed to be human but was not. It arose in the first century and flourished in the ensuing centuries. Already we observe the author of 1 John and 2 John (which reflects a later stage of the Johannine community) battling this problem and, with harsh words, rejecting it: "By this you know the Spirit of God: every spirit that confesses that Jesus Christ has come in the flesh is from God, and every spirit that does not confess Jesus is not from God" (1 John 4:2–3); "Many deceivers have gone out into the world, those who do not confess that Jesus Christ has come in the flesh; any such person is

173

the deceiver and the antichrist!" (2 John 7). Gaventa argues that "'the mother of Jesus' underscores the fact—the paradox—that the Johannine Jesus, who comes 'from above,' is at the same time a human being whose earthly father and mother and brothers and geographical origin are known" (1999, 80).

The prologue to John portrays Jesus as the preexistent divine Logos who, like Lady Wisdom, helps God to create the world. As John 1:14b says, "We beheld his glory, the glory of an only-begotten one from the father, full of grace and truth" (my trans.). Such a lofty beginning might encourage the reader to minimize 1:14a: "And the Word became flesh and tabernacled among us." Thus, after the prologue, the author takes pains to speak of Jesus's geographical home, his parents, his family.

An intriguing suggestion by Gaventa on this theme centers on Psalm 22, one of the psalms most alluded to by New Testament authors. For instance, Psalm 22:18 appears in John 19:24: "This was to fulfill what the scripture says, 'They divided my clothes among themselves, and for my clothing they cast lots.'" The quotations and allusions to the Old Testament continue through the crucifixion scene. This makes Gaventa wonder if the author has Psalm 22:9–11 in mind as well: "Yet it was you who took me from the womb; you kept me safe on my mother's breast. On you I was cast from my birth, and since my mother bore me you have been my God. Do not be far from me, for trouble is near and there is no one to help." She explains: "Here the mother serves as a metonym for human life, in that God brings the psalmist safely to life and sustains life itself. God has been near, and God's presence is needed once again in a time of trouble. Certainly any connection between this passage and John 19:25–27 is conjectural, but perhaps the narrator sees Jesus' mother also as his connection with human, physical life" (1999, 92).

The mother of Jesus appears from beginning to end in John. That John intends for us to connect her appearance in chapter 2 with that of chapter 19, the beginning of the Gospel to the end, is clear by (1) the intentional repetition of the cluster of words *one's own, hour, woman, wine,* and *mother,* (2) the broader themes of glorification (*doxa,* tied to the hour), and (3) the Genesis language, especially the language of creation. Like all of the characters in John's Gospel, Jesus's mother serves to teach us something about who Jesus is, what he came to do, and what it might have to do with us. She and her son are tightly connected; she provokes the

174

first sign of his public ministry, and she stands at the cross when he bestows the promised Spirit upon those who are part of the birth of the church at the foot of the cross. (John's cross scene is quite different from the Synoptics, where Jesus is not attended by his followers and in which he utters the "cry of dereliction." That cry would not make sense in John. For further explanation, consult Clark-Soles 2016, 122–31.) Finally, if incarnation is an important theme in John, then the emphasis on Jesus's mother plays a strong role in conveying it.

John calls all readers to become part of the family of God, to be in intimate, authentic relationship with one another in heavily embodied ways, here and now. When one chooses to believe, according to John, one shares a father and mother with Jesus. The proclamation concerning the former ("my Father and your Father") is paralleled in the scene in chapter 19 where Jesus declares his mother to be our mother. All in the family, now and forever.

Mary beyond the Bible

As I teach regularly in churches across a variety of denominations, people ask questions about Marian traditions that do not appear in the Bible but that many Christians consider a vital part of their piety. Thus, it is appropriate, even though this is a book on women in the Bible, to close this chapter with some traditions about Mary that develop postbiblically.

In the chapter titled "Arrival" in the historically informative novel *Our Lady of the Lost and Found*, Mary shows up to the home of an ordinary, not particularly religious Protestant female novelist who lives alone. In the midst of watering her houseplants, the novelist looks up to behold Mary standing there. Mary says to her: "Fear not." The novelist finds herself in stunned silence, so Mary goes on: "It's me, Mary, . . . Mother of God." When that yields no response, she continues: "You know. Mary. Queen of Heaven. Pilgrim of Peace. Daughter of Zion. Sublime Peak of Human Intellect . . . Mother of the Mystical Body." She lists a couple dozen titles and finally the novelist responds: "—Hello, I said" (Schoemperlen 2002, 30).

Later, the protagonist asks Mary why she would appear to her, a non-Catholic. Mary explains that it's because she's a writer and

175

Mary's mother, Saint Anne, teaches Mary to read in this manuscript illumination by Master of Sir John Fastolf found in a medieval French or English book of hours.

Digital image courtesy of the Getty's Open Content Program.

Mary is a bibliophile. This jogs the novelist's memory of an art history course in which they studied numerous paintings of Mary holding a book. The novelist specifically recalls that at the very moment of the angel Gabriel's "big announcement," he finds her reading (60). Indeed, there are two scenes in which one typically finds Mary reading. First, in annunciation scenes. Though most often encountered in paintings, I have experienced it as part of the sculpted statues that appear in the extended nativity display at the Notre Dame Cathedral in Strasbourg. Second, many paintings, often in churches, depict St. Anne (Mary's mother, Jesus's grandma) teaching Mary to read. One of my favorite renderings is in St. Polycarp Church in Izmir (ancient Smyrna), Turkey. Presumably, the book is Scripture.

When I take people to the Church of St. Anne's in Jerusalem, where the Pools of Bethesda mentioned in John 5 are located, Protestants are usually puzzled by hearing about Mary's mother, Anne, and her father, Joachim. Catholic and Orthodox students, on the other hand, are surprised by the Protestants' surprise.

Marian Traditions outside Protestantism

Catholics and Orthodox Christians have enjoyed a much richer set of Marian traditions than Protestants. Protestants, taken by the notion of *sola scriptura*, have been reluctant to accept (some) traditions for which there is no "evidence" in the biblical texts, by which they mean the Old Testament as translated from the Hebrew Bible (as opposed to the LXX) and the New Testament. Not only do most Protestants not consider the deuterocanonical texts (called the Apocrypha in a Protestant study Bible) authoritative, but many have never even heard of them. In addition, they do not typically consider material outside the Protestant canon to be authoritative.

I would challenge some Protestant readers on two counts. First, I typically find that they have not delved deeply into the details and meaning and importance of Mary's presence in the Bible. They know she gave birth to Jesus and they may know she was involved at the wedding in Cana. I hope I have shown that she is a crucial figure in the Bible. Second, in their effort to differentiate themselves from Catholics, many Protestants at best miss out on Mary and at worst denigrate her. They know Mary plays a central role in Catholicism, such as mediatrix and co-redemptrix, and they suspect

177

that Catholics are "mistaken" so they attack Marian traditions. They are the poorer for it. To watch a Protestant soul discover Mary and her importance in the story of "God with us" is a delight.

Protevangelium of James

If Anne and Joachim are not in the Bible, from where does this tradition come? Cue the late-second-century document called the Protevangelium of James. The church fathers, absorbed in their doctrinal theses, were not the only authors developing tradition. Christians composed other Gospels that were not included in the canon in the end (for a brief treatment of the formation of the NT canon, consult Clark-Soles 2010, 89–93). One of the earliest and most important of these is the Protevangelium of James, in which Mary plays a starring role. Here we find the nascent development of Mariology (interest in the theological role of Mary; for more on how Mary has influenced doctrine and Christian cultures, consult Llywelyn 2016). Given the scope of the present volume, we cannot treat the text at length, though it most certainly deserves attention and the reader should read the text in full. Rather, here we pull from it those features that have most widely influenced the tradition, many of them so familiar and meaningful that Christians might assume (incorrectly) that these elements are found in the Bible itself:

- The names of Mary's parents, Anne (or Anna) and Joachim
- Mary's miraculous conception by the childless couple
- The image of Joseph as an elderly widower who marries the young Mary
- Mary being twelve years old when Joseph takes her into his home and sixteen when she becomes pregnant
- Joseph having children with another woman; therefore the brothers and sisters mentioned in the Bible are not Jesus's biological siblings
- Mary's virginity during pregnancy and after Jesus's birth
- The birth of Jesus in a cave

178   (For a standard commentary on the Protevangelium of James, consult Smid 1965. For an accessible introduction and an English translation of the text, consult Elliott 1993, 48–67.)

Developing Marian Traditions

As is the case with Jesus, traditions and texts about Mary continued to develop alongside and after the composition of the New Testament texts. For instance, Revelation 12 does not mention Mary but came to be interpreted as referring to her. It opens: "A great portent appeared in heaven: a woman clothed with the sun, with the moon under her feet, and on her head a crown of twelve stars. She was pregnant and was crying out in birth pangs, in the agony of giving birth" (vv. 1–2). She goes on to give birth to a son. "While this apocalyptic text is more likely to be a reference to the Christian community than to Mary, as early as the fourth century it was interpreted as referring to her, and would centuries later be the source [of] the standard iconography of the Immaculate Conception that emerged in the art of the sixteenth century. It is also the textual referent for the image of the Virgin of Guadalupe" (Llywelyn 2016, 6).

Beverly Gaventa lists four issues that captured the attention of the patristic writers: "Mary's maternity, her virginity, her sinlessness, and her function as the Second Eve" (1999, 101). First, in what way, exactly, was Mary Jesus's mother? Is she merely a container, or does he share in her substance? These christological controversies around the nature of Jesus's conception, his humanity, and his divinity would continue to multiply as councils were convened to debate the subject. By the second century, Mary was called *Theotokos*—"the one giving birth to God." For centuries debate would rage about the meaning and appropriateness of the title. Eastern Christianity has long incorporated the idea into its theology.

Second, we noted above the ambiguity around the language for "young woman" and "virgin" in the Hebrew Bible, the Septuagint, and the infancy narratives of Matthew and Luke. Church leaders would continue to debate the meaning of Isaiah 7:14 and whether Mary is supposed to have been a virgin or not. In addition, debate arose about "the exact nature of Mary's virginity. Was she a virgin when Jesus was conceived (virginity *ante partum*)? Did she remain a virgin even when Jesus was born, as the Protevangelium clearly maintains (virginity *in partu*)? Did she remain a virgin both prior to conception, during birth, and thereafter as well (virginity *post partum*)?" (Gaventa 1999, 103). This topic is referred to as "the perpetual virginity" of Mary. Within it lies the debate over how Jesus is related to his brothers and sisters who are mentioned in the Bible.

179

Third, the sinlessness of Mary is not a notion found in the Bible, nor does it appear in the second century. Protestants have never espoused such a doctrine. For Catholics, the doctrine arose at a later date, though those arguing for it would invoke Gabriel's reference to Mary as "full of grace" in support of her sinlessness. In the East, "The question of Mary's sinlessness . . . was largely accepted . . . in the early centuries. In the West, it was contested for centuries" (Llywelyn 2016, 16). The Immaculate Conception was established as dogma in 1854 for Catholics.

Fourth, the first author to explicitly compare Eve and Mary is Justin Martyr, who contrasts the two. Both virgins, Eve brought forth death and disobedience and Mary brought forth Jesus. Irenaeus pipes in here as well, contrasting Eve as disobedient and Mary as obedient. As Llywelyn (9) notes: "Emerging at the turn of the century, and promoted by Irenaeus of Lyons, 'new Eve' entered into what would become an apparently endless stock of Marian notions, images, and titles. The Eve-Mary contrast would also profoundly affect Christian attitudes to women in the subsequent centuries."

Other traditions and doctrines arose as well. The Dormition of Mary, for example, addresses her death.

Mary's Ongoing Impact

After thousands of years, people continue to encounter and be encountered by Mary, she who cannot be reduced to a single name, trait, image, or interpretation. Mary continues to inspire devotion, affection, healing, imagination, artistic beauty, and faith.

Mary plays an important role throughout Sue Monk Kidd's brilliant novel *The Secret Life of Bees* and the movie based upon it. We meet Lily (and Mary) at the start of the novel in the summer of 1964, when Lily is fourteen. She compares the role of the bees in her life to that of the angel Gabriel in Mary's life. Both the bees and Gabriel are sent to a young woman, reveal important insights, and mark a distinct, memorable moment that launches each woman into an unexpected, unimaginable future as a result. Lily anticipates the reader's potential reluctance to accept her construal—"I know it is presumptuous to compare my small life to hers, but I have reason to believe she wouldn't mind"—and promises to explain further in the story she narrates (2003, 1–2).

180

Early in the story, which is set during the civil rights movement, Lily runs away from the home she shares with her abusive father, T-Ray. She is motherless because, when she was four, her mother tried to leave her father and take Lily with her, but in a scuffle, a gun dropped onto the floor and Lily accidentally killed her mother. Lily, who is white, runs away with the black housekeeper, Rosaleen, to her mother's hometown. At the beginning of the movie, we see Lily going through a box of her mother's things, which include an image of Mary as a black Madonna. She takes the image with her as she runs away. Mary serves to guide and protect. Once Lily makes it to her mother's hometown, she learns that the image is the label of the honey made by the Boatwright sisters, three African American women named May, June, and August. Lily finds the sisters and makes up a story about how she and Rosaleen came to be there. The sisters take her in and apprentice her.

In the living room, she sees the three-foot-tall carved wooden Madonna that inspired the label on the honey. Lily imagines the statue as the figurehead on an old ship, weathered but strong, fiercely leading the way. She decides that black Mary has "a serious look, like she could straighten you out if necessary" (70).

The women become her mothers, as does Mary. Lily describes pressing her own hand upon Mary's heart, saying to her: "*I live in a hive of darkness, and you are my mother . . . You are the mother of thousands*" (164). Mother Mary remains a constant theme throughout the narrative. In the end, menacing T. Ray shows up and, after some creative prompting by the Boatwrights, decides to let her stay with the Boatwright sisters, taking his leave of Lily in a cold, harsh manner. Lily chooses to reinterpret his ugly words as a coded gift instead, as T. Ray knowing that motherless Lily will truly thrive with this community of mothers.

As the story concludes, Lily tells us that she visits Mary daily. Though Mary ages, she never fades in strength. Lily calls her a "muscle of love." She says: "I feel her in unexpected moments, her Assumption into heaven happening in places inside me. She will suddenly rise …she does not go up, up into the sky, but further and further inside me. August says she goes into the holes life has gouged out of us" (302).

The protagonist in *Our Lady of the Lost and Found* suggests that Mary might well be "one of those archetypes that swim in the pool of the collective unconscious that Carl Jung wrote about, a part   181 of that common symbolic inheritance of all humanity. Maybe everyone has some image of Mary in the back of their minds . . . that, like matter, can be neither created nor destroyed" (Schoemperlen 2002, 48).

The Lectionary

Mary mother of Jesus appears or is mentioned repeatedly in all four Gospels, with Luke and Matthew featuring her more often than John and Mark. Mark is the least interested in Mary and includes her in passages (3:21, 31; 6:3) where Jesus's authority and mental health are being questioned, although the depiction of Jesus's family is somewhat ambiguous; however, the other three Gospels feature a distinctly positive and more robust portrayal of Mary. Overall, her impact looms large in the Gospel accounts, and she ought to be celebrated as an inspirational figure today among Christians of all affiliations.

Of the passages about Mary I have treated in this chapter, all are included in the Roman Lectionary (RL), and almost all appear in the Revised Common Lectionary (RCL). For ease of reference, I offer the following chart as an overview of the passages I have treated that appear in either lectionary:

Passage	Roman Lectionary	Revised Common Lectionary
Luke 1:27–38	Year B, 4th Sunday of Advent Years 1 & 2, Advent, Dec. 20	Year B, Advent, 4th Sunday of Advent Years ABC, Lent, Annunciation of the Lord Years BC, Easter, Annunciation of the Lord Year C, Easter, Day of Pentecost, Wed.
Luke 1:39–45	Year C, 4th Sunday of Advent Years 1 & 2, Advent, Dec. 21	Year C, Advent, 4th Sunday of Advent Years AC, Easter, Visitation of Mary to Elizabeth Years BC, season after Pentecost, Visitation of Mary to Elizabeth

Passage	Roman Lectionary	*Revised Common Lectionary*
Luke 1:46–55	Year B, 3rd Sunday of Advent (resp.) Year 1, Ordinary Time, Week 12, Sat. (resp.)	Year C, Advent, 4th Sunday of Advent Years AC, Easter, Visitation of Mary to Elizabeth Years BC, season after Pentecost, Visitation of Mary to Elizabeth Years AB, Advent, 3rd Sunday of Advent Years BC, Advent, 4th Sunday of Advent Year C, season after Pentecost, Proper 25 (30), preceding Sat. Years AC, Dec. 22 Years AC, Dec. 23 Year B, Advent, 4th Sunday of Advent, Mon. Year B, Advent, 4th Sunday of Advent, Tues. Year B, Advent, 4th Sunday of Advent, Wed. Year C, season after Pentecost, Trinity Sunday, Wed. Year C, season after Pentecost, Proper 3 (8)
Luke 2:15–19	Years ABC, Christmas Mass at Dawn Years ABC, Jan. 1: Mary, Mother of God	Years ABC, Christmas, Holy Name of Jesus Years ABC, Christmas, Nativity of the Lord, Proper 1
Luke 8:19–21	Years 1 & 2, Ordinary Time, Week 25, Tues.	Year C, Jan. 3
Luke 11:27–28	Years 1 & 2, Ordinary Time, Week 27, Sat.	Year B, season after Pentecost, Proper 5 (10), Wed. Year C, Epiphany, 6th Sunday after the Epiphany, preceding Sat.

Passage	Roman Lectionary	Revised Common Lectionary
Matt. 1:16	Years ABC, Christmas, Vigil Mass Years 1 & 2, Advent, Dec. 17	Year A, Advent, 4th Sunday of Advent, Wed.
Matt. 1:18–25	Year A, 4th Sunday of Advent Years 1 & 2, Advent, Dec. 18	Year A, Advent, 4th Sunday of Advent
Matt. 12:46–50	Years 1 & 2, Ordinary Time, Week 16, Tues.	Year B, Dec. 29 Year A, season after Pentecost, Reign of Christ, Proper 29 (34), preceding Sat.
Matt. 13:55–56	Years 1 & 2, Ordinary Time, Week 17, Fri.	
John 2:1–12	Year C, 2nd Sunday in Ordinary Time Years 1 & 2, Jan. 7 (if Epiphany is Jan. 8)	Year C, Epiphany, 2nd Sunday after the Epiphany
John 19:25–27	Years ABC, Good Friday of the Lord's Passion	Years ABC, Holy Week, Good Friday
Mark 3:21	Year B, 10th Sunday in Ordinary Time Years 1 & 2, Ordinary Time, Week 2, Sat.	Year B, season after Pentecost, Proper 5 (10)
Mark 6:3	Year B, 14th Sunday in Ordinary Time Years 1 & 2, Ordinary Time, Week 4, Wed.	Year B, season after Pentecost, Proper 9 (14)

It is not surprising that the Catholic tradition has so thoroughly included Mary in lectionary readings, and it is worth noting that the RCL also features her significantly. While several of the readings occur during Advent or at Christmastime, Mary is also featured at several other points in the year. In preaching and teaching Gospel messages, may Mary's frequent presence be a reminder of her instrumental role in shaping Jesus. May we be quick to recognize and quick to proclaim, "Like Mother, like Son."

Conclusion

In keeping with the goals of this book, this chapter has addressed a well-known biblical woman, Mary the mother of Jesus. We considered the ways that Luke, Matthew, and John each present her and the ways that she fits into their particular message. We found that she is a far more robust character in Luke and even John, say, than in Matthew. We also considered some of the reception history of Mary by noting the content of the popular second-century text known as the Protevangelium of James and by considering other doctrinal developments related to Mary and her role in the church. In addition, we presented insights from scholars employing newer interpretive perspectives reflecting the growing body of scholars and scholarship associated with the study of women in the Bible.

Mary. Prophet. Student of Scripture. Fresh, young mother pregnant with purpose, vulnerable in a patriarchal system; mournful mother stricken by grief, vulnerable in an imperial system. Moral instructor. Charter church member. Faithful, courageous follower of God. A woman for the ages, all ages.

Recommended Resources

BibleWalks. 2014. "National Mosaics in the Basilica of Annunciation." Last updated May 5, 2014. https://www.biblewalks.com /Annunciation-Mosaics.

Clark-Soles, Jaime. 2010. *Engaging the Word: The New Testament and the Christian Believer*. Louisville, KY: Westminster John Knox Press.

———. 2016. *Reading John for Dear Life: A Spiritual Walk with the Fourth Gospel*. Louisville, KY: Westminster John Knox Press.

Coloe, Mary. 2013. "The Mother of Jesus: A Woman Possessed." Pages 202–13 in *Character Studies in the Fourth Gospel: Narrative Approaches to Seventy Figures in John*. Edited by Steven A. Hunt, Francois Tolmie, and Ruben Zimmerman. Wissenschaftliche Untersuchungen zum Neuen Testament 314. Tübingen: Mohr Siebeck.

Elliott, J. K. 1993. *Apocryphal New Testament: A Collection of Apocryphal Christian Literature in an English Translation*. New York: Oxford University Press.

Gale, Aaron M. 2011. "The Virgin Birth." Page 4 in *The Jewish Annotated New Testament: New Revised Standard Version*. Edited by Amy-Jill Levine and Marc Zvi Brettler. Oxford: Oxford University Press.

Gaventa, Beverly Roberts. 1999. *Mary: Glimpses of the Mother of Jesus*. Minneapolis: Fortress Press.

Kidd, Sue Monk. 2003. *The Secret Life of Bees*. New York: Penguin.

Levine, Amy-Jill. 2012. "Gospel of Matthew." Pages 465–77 in *Women's Bible Commentary*. Edited by Carol A. Newsom, Sharon H. Ringe, and Jacqueline E. Lapsley. 3rd ed. Louisville, KY: Westminster John Knox Press.

Llywelyn, Dorian, SJ. 2016. "Mary and Mariology." In *Oxford Handbooks Online*. Oxford University Press. Article published June 2016. http://dx.doi.org/10.1093/oxfordhb/9780199935420 .013.62.

O'Connor, Flannery. 1965. "Revelation." Pages 191–218 in *Everything That Rises Must Converge*. New York: Farrar, Straus & Giroux.

Schoemperlen, Diane. 2002. *Our Lady of the Lost and Found: A Novel of Mary, Faith, and Friendship*. New York: Penguin.

Smid, H. R. 1965. *Protoevangelium Jacobi: A Commentary*. Assen: Van Gorcum.

Unterman, Alan, Rivka G. Horwitz, Joseph Dan, and Sharon Faye Koren. 2007. "Shekhinah." Pages 440–44 in vol. 18 of *Encyclopaedia Judaica*. Edited by Michael Berenbaum and Fred Skolnik. 2nd ed. Detroit: Macmillan Reference USA.

Weems, Renita J. 2005. *Showing Mary: How Women Can Share Prayers, Wisdom, and the Blessings of God*. New York: Warner Books.

Zimmerman, Irene. 1992. "Liturgy." Pages 55–56 in *WomenPsalms*. Compiled by Julia Ahlers, Rosemary Broughton, and Carl Koch. Winona, MN: St. Mary's Press.

CHAPTER 7

Women in Jesus's Life and Ministry

Each evangelist writes to influence the reader in some way, having purposes beyond mere conveyance of sterile historical information. The author wants the reader to be affected by the text, to learn, to think, to reconsider, to gain courage and faith (or more of it), to behave according to a certain ethical vision, to be moved, to be comforted, to be challenged and corrected, to be inspired, to receive a commission, to set one's purpose by Jesus of Nazareth, the Christ.

Each Gospel writer uses story as a means to achieve those ends, stories filled with all sorts of characters. Some characters have prominent roles and big personalities, like Mary Magdalene or Mary the mother of Jesus or the Samaritan woman; others appear only briefly. Some have names, and some do not. Some are front and center; some operate in the background until the author or Jesus foregrounds them (e.g., the woman who anoints Jesus in Mark 14 and the widow giving sacrificially in Mark 12). Some are pushy, demanding, and persistent (the Canaanite woman in Matt. 15 and the "persistent widow" in Luke 18:1-8); and some are quiet and prone to remain in the background (the bent-over woman in Luke 13). Some teach us that women's "ways of knowing" are valuable (e.g., Pilate's wife; consult Belenky et al., 197). Some biblical women have had their reputations smeared by later (mis)interpreters (e.g., Mary Magdalene and the Samaritan woman).

Some biblical women belong in more than one of the above categories. Some of them are portrayed differently from Gospel to Gospel (thus, it is crucial for the reader to make use of a Gospel parallels tool when studying the women in the Gospels so that comparisons can be made and conclusions drawn; consult, e.g., Throckmorton, 1992; Aland, 1993). All of these women are depicted in a way that serves each author's desire to affect the reader.

It is also the case that we readers can read "behind" the texts as well to ferret out some of the realities of the lives of our ancient sisters and some of the assumptions that inhere about women in the first-century Roman Empire. For instance, in Matthew's version of the so-called feeding of the five thousand, the last line says: "And those who ate were about five thousand men [*anēr*], *not counting* [!] [*chōris*] women [*gynē*] and children [*paidion*]" (14:21, my trans.; cf. Matt. 15:38). Literally, the author does not count the women and children, and apparently neither do we, since we routinely refer to it as the feeding of the five thousand and, in Matthew 15, the four thousand. (In their commentary [2004, 493], W. D. Davies and Dale C. Allison do not comment on the erasure of the women and children; they simply "entertain the possibility that the concluding words of 14.13–21 were meant to allude to the way the people in the wilderness were counted" [or not!].) If, however, each male had just one female and one child there associated with him (a low estimate), it would mean that Jesus fed fifteen thousand and twelve thousand, respectively. Thus, it is important to note where women are hidden or absent as one reads. Other hidden women include Peter's wife and Jesus's sisters.

Some women are symbolic, such as Rachel weeping for her children in Matthew 2:18 or Lady Wisdom alluded to in Matthew 11:28–30 and the prologue to John. Some women appear in parables (the woman who lost a coin). Some women appear to be missing from parables (does the prodigal son have no sisters or mother?).

In this chapter, I first present a number of adumbrative observations related to my thesis that there are more women doing more things in Jesus's life and ministry than one might think. Then I proceed through his life and ministry, lifting up women and groups of women who exemplify those theses. I consider some of the women who appear before he conducts his public ministry; those who are part of the public ministry; and those who appear in the passion and

188

resurrection. Within the public ministry, I do not adhere to a chronological order. Mark and Matthew tell the story of an unnamed woman who anoints Jesus, after which he declares: "Wherever the good news is proclaimed in the whole world, what she has done will be told in remembrance of her" (Mark 14:9; cf. Matt. 26:13). I have decided to follow his orders and begin with her. Finally, I briefly discuss figurative women in the Gospels before turning to remarks on the dynamic of the portrayal of male and female disciples in the Gospel narratives.

A few caveats. First, it is my usual preference to deal with each Gospel on its own terms, and I commend that approach as best. Given the scope of this series and this volume, however, I am going to take a more thematic approach and pull from the pool of the Gospels. Thus, I address groups of women in Jesus's life (e.g., prophetic women, patrons, foremothers) and individual women whose stories raise questions I invite the reader to ponder (e.g., "the bent-over woman" in Luke; the "woman caught in adultery" in John; the Samaritan woman in John). Second, if I use the names Matthew, Mark, Luke, or John when referring to the author of a Gospel, I am simply following tradition for ease of reference and not arguing for any particular position about the authorship of any Gospel (the Gospels themselves do not state which historical person or people wrote them, and the titles such as "according to Mark" are later additions). Third, my presentation is not meant to be exhaustive, of course, but suggestive in terms of the theses and the characters spotlighted and the conclusions drawn.

Women Galore

There are more women in Jesus's life and ministry than one might realize, and women do a remarkable variety of things. Women are ministers (e.g., Peter's mother-in-law who "ministers to" [*diakaneō*] Jesus, Mark 1:31). Women are prophets (e.g., Mary, mother of Jesus; Anna; the Mark 14 woman who anoints). Women are partners and patrons with Jesus in growing the gospel (e.g., the women of Luke 8:1–3). Women provoke Jesus's ministry (e.g., his mom demanding wine in John 2:3; the Syrophoenician woman; the woman with the nursing comment in Luke 11:27).

189

Women appear as courageous, paradigmatic disciples (e.g., the widow of Mark 12:42–44; the woman healed in Mark 5:25-34). They understand who Jesus is. They have faith. They minister. They show up, and they abide. They are last at the cross and first at the tomb. They are the first to proclaim the resurrected Christ.

Women appear in relationships with other women (e.g., the women of Luke 8; the women at the foot of the cross; Mary and Elizabeth). Women appear as victims of patriarchy. Women are afraid but push forward anyway (e.g., the bleeding woman in Mark 5:33; Mary, mother of Jesus; the women of Mark's shorter ending [16:8]). Women are healed (e.g., Mark 5:29; Luke 13:10–17).

Jesus's Foremothers

Only Matthew and Luke present a genealogy, and Luke does not include any women besides Mary. Mark begins his narrative in Jesus's adulthood. Conversely, the Gospel of John reaches back before creation and depicts Jesus in the role of Woman Wisdom who helps God create the cosmos (for more on Woman Wisdom, consult chap. 4, "Women Creating").

In his genealogy of Jesus, Matthew highlights four women, in addition to Mary, who make possible Jesus's arrival and mission. While I treat this more at length in chapter 6, on Mary the mother of Jesus, here we note the appearance of those four:

> Tamar, daughter-in-law of Judah, in 1:3 (consult Gen. 38)
> Rahab in 1:5 (consult Josh. 2:1–21; 6:2–25)
> Ruth, the Moabite, in 1:5 (consult the book of Ruth)
> The wife of Uriah (Bathsheba) in 1:6 (consult 2 Sam. 11–12;
>   1 Kgs. 15:5)

For some reason, interpreters try to find a common thread that ties the women together. The argument of some that the women all act in sexually suspect ways does not hold, since Tamar is vindicated by her demand for justice from Judah, Ruth does nothing wrong, and we have no reason to think that Bathsheba did anything to ask for David's sexual attention. Likewise, the argument that they are all Gentiles does not cohere. According to A.-J. Levine, what ties these women together is their commitment to (and actions on behalf of)

190

a "higher righteousness" (2012, 467). Each finds herself in a threatened situation given the social constructs of her time and place.
Each acts within the confines of her context to pursue righteousness. As a result, each moves God's salvific plan forward, culminating in the birth of Jesus.

Prophetic Women in Jesus's Early Life

Elizabeth

While Matthew includes women in his genealogy and Luke does
not, Luke depicts numerous important women paving the way for
Jesus's ministry. First, Elizabeth, Mary's cousin. She and Zechariah,
like Abraham and Sarah before them, are beyond their childbearing
years. Yet God, in regular God fashion, decides to make a way out
of no way, and they find themselves pregnant with John the Baptist, the forerunner of Jesus, the Elijah figure in Luke's typological
scheme. Luke loves typology. That is, Luke looks to Old Testament
characters and patterns Lukan characters accordingly. Here Luke
uses the trope of the barren woman who conceives. Reminiscent
of the Abraham and Sarah story, Zechariah does not believe the
angel Gabriel and is chastised by losing his voice. He fades into the
background while Elizabeth takes center stage. Against Zechariah's
muteness, she speaks, then speaks again: "This is what the Lord has
done for me when he looked favorably on me and took away the
disgrace I have endured among my people" (Luke 1:24–25).

Elizabeth speaks again when Mary arrives:

> When Elizabeth heard Mary's greeting, the child leaped in
> her womb. And Elizabeth was filled with the Holy Spirit and
> exclaimed with a loud cry, "Blessed are you among women, and
> blessed is the fruit of your womb. And why has this happened to
> me, that the mother of my Lord comes to me? For as soon as I
> heard the sound of your greeting, the child in my womb leaped
> for joy. And blessed is she who believed that there would be a ful-
> fillment of what was spoken to her by the Lord." (Luke 1:41–45)

Elizabeth's pregnant, profuse declarations speak volumes for   191
the ages. First, she is filled with the Holy Spirit, she is inspired, as
all real prophets are. Luke has a robust pneumatology (that is, role

of the Holy Spirit)—the Holy Spirit looms large in Luke–Acts and directs the action. Elizabeth is caught up in it. She is the first to recognize the special role in salvation history that Mary is playing. Second, she recognizes already and proclaims Jesus to be Lord. Third, she utters one of the most poignant, true, faithful statements in all of Scripture when she declares that the Lord keeps promises. It is a beatitude to women, using the specifically feminine word *makaria* for "blessed" and the feminine participle for "believer" in 1:45. Certainly, this is a verse that has sustained me over the years and caused me to give my daughter the name Elizabeth as her middle name. Raw, direct truth tested over millennia.

Mary

Mary, of course, plays an important role in Jesus's life and ministry. I refer the reader to the full chapter in this book dedicated to Mary. She is the first woman to speak in Luke, and her speech is inspired, prophetic utterance. She lays out one of Luke's primary emphases drawn from the prophets of the Old Testament, namely, God's preferential option for the poor. This is the conviction that the poor and marginalized are especially dear to God. It appears also as the Great Reversal, signified in the Magnificat by the lowly being exalted and the exalted brought low; irony prevails. Jesus himself will echo his mother's prophetic insights when he begins his public ministry:

> He stood up to read, and the scroll of the prophet Isaiah was given to him. He unrolled the scroll and found the place where it was written:
>
> > "The Spirit of the Lord is upon me,
> >   because he has anointed me
> > to bring good news to the poor.
> > He has sent me to proclaim release to the captives
> >   and recovery of sight to the blind,
> > to let the oppressed go free,
> > to proclaim the year of the Lord's favor."
> > > *(Luke 4:16–19)*

192

The ironic themes of reversal and God's preferential option for the poor are repeated again in the Sermon on the Plain, especially the blessings and woes (Luke 6:20–26). Jesus learned his prophetic ways from the first woman in his life, Mary.

Anna

The next woman to appear in the narrative of Jesus's life is Anna, the prophet, who appears at Luke 2:36–38. I spend extra time on Anna here because she seems to be overshadowed by Simeon and his Nunc Dimittis (Luke 2:29–32) in the church's worship life.

I will never forget the time I first preached on Anna. At thirty years old, I was invited to preach at a nursing home to my elders in the faith, the Annas, if you will; the women (and men) who had been tending to the faith for decades before I was even born. The ones who got themselves wheeled in, or hobbled in on walkers, faithfully appeared in the temple to testify to the saving power of Jesus. I was even more awed by the real-life Annas than the Lukan Anna, who herself is quite the luminary. Simeon utters his Nunc Dimittis in the presence of the family and God. But Anna preaches *publicly* to a wide audience. Here is what we know about her from Luke 2:36–38:

She comes from a long line of Jews, many of whom awaited a messiah and knew that God would someday fulfill the promise of a savior.

She is a prophet. What does she prophesy? That this helpless, perhaps pudgy, mewling forty-day-old baby would redeem Israel. Of course, her prophecy was validated.

She is old, especially for a first-century woman.

She lost her husband after only seven years of marriage.

She remained a widow.

Her life consisted of nothing else but living at the temple worshiping God "with fasting and prayer night and day."

She proclaims Jesus publicly as the Redeemer.

That's what we learn *about* Anna, but what do we learn *from* Anna? Why, of all people, did God choose to have her remembered in Scripture? Some might consider her and think: here is this old woman who has nothing left. Her husband has died, and she doesn't appear to have any children, or, if she does, they are not caring for her in their own home; instead she lives in what we might call a denominationally affiliated residence, and she does not seem to get out much. Luke says she did not depart from the temple where she lived, which must mean that she did not belong to a local synagogue congregation. She's out of touch with "the real world," one might charge. Her life just doesn't seem that impressive, and you might feel sorry for her or expect her to feel sorry for herself. Such an assessment ignores Luke's message about the nature of the kingdom of God, who figures prominently in it, and what matters.

But Anna understands which world is real. It is not the world that is obsessed with superficial happiness, staying young, staying healthy, "having it all"; the real world is God's kingdom, and it is concerned with unflinching joy, a faith that perseveres, growing wise in the ways of God, and not "having it all" but having only what matters the most: a sure faith that understands what Luke calls "the kingdom of God."

Women in Jesus's Public Ministry

Prophetic Women: Anointing the Messiah, Foreshadowing his Death

If Mary, Elizabeth, and Anna speak prophetic words, other women in Jesus's ministry perform prophetic acts, including anointing Jesus. (Note that Mary Magdalene never anoints Jesus and is never called a prostitute. These are common, atrocious errors that I hear repeated often, even by pastors in pulpits.) This is the time to consult your Gospel parallels, because each Gospel depicts a woman anointing Jesus, but no two stories are exactly the same. And the differences are important. (For a more detailed discussion, consult Clark-Soles 2010, esp. chap. 3, "Four Gospels: Problem or Gift?")

Mark: An unnamed anointing woman. Not accidentally, Mark 14:3–9, in which an unnamed woman anoints Jesus, falls right between the plot to kill Jesus and Judas's betrayal. As the scene opens, Jesus is in Bethany at the home of Simon the leper. A woman approaches with an alabaster jar of expensive ointment, breaks the jar, and pours the ointment on Jesus's head. This series is suggestive of a prophet coronating a king: in the Old Testament, kings are anointed on the head by a prophet.

194

Mark gives us no other details about the woman. Some unnamed people complain to one another about the waste and then scold her.

Jesus defends her, noting that she, unlike they, understands that Jesus is the Messiah (thus the royal anointing) and that he is going to die. Her action is prophetic; in case that fact is lost on the reader, Jesus declares: "She has done what she could; she has anointed my body beforehand for its burial" (14:8).

Jesus also makes this proclamation: "Truly I tell you, wherever the good news is proclaimed in the whole world, what she has done will be told in remembrance of her" (14:9). This is a weighty statement on many counts. First, the language of "in remembrance of her" may strike a chord with readers who know Jesus's Words of Institution as presented by Luke in Luke 22:19 and by Paul in 1 Corinthians 11:25; each quotes Jesus as saying: "Do this in remembrance of me." In fact, many of us find that quotation on the Communion table in the front of our churches. Second, Jesus clearly expects her story to be preached widely, so when we teach and preach the story of this perceptive disciple, we ourselves perform a faithful, prophetic act in our own time.

Despite Jesus's insistence on the primacy of place this woman was to have in Christian proclamation, few people know of this woman's anointing of Jesus, or they think that Mary Magdalene, whom they imagine to be a sinful and forgiven "whore," did the anointing. We must address this seriously. First, this woman who anoints Jesus's *head* is never named. Mary of Bethany, who is not Mary of Magdala, appears in John and anoints his *feet*, which is not a messianic indicator. Her story is important in John, and we will explore why below, but these are different acts. Second, the woman in Mark is not the woman in Luke 7. They are two very different stories. Luke's story is placed far earlier in Jesus's ministry rather than near the passion and, again, that woman anoints Jesus's *feet*. She is not named, is called a "sinner," and is compared to Simon, the high-status male who comes up short in receiving Jesus correctly. Mary Magdalene is never called a "sinner," much less a "prostitute" (sorry, Pope Gregory of 591 and Dan Brown of today and the producers of *Jesus Christ Superstar*), and she never anoints Jesus anywhere on his body. Unfortunately, popes, Dan Brown, and *Jesus Christ Superstar* have dominated the imaginations of the masses, even the Christian masses, far more deeply than the actual biblical text.

Calling the church to attend to its Scriptures, Harvard New Testament scholar and theologian Elisabeth Schüssler Fiorenza

195

writes: "The woman's prophetic sign-action did not become a part of the gospel knowledge of Christians. Even her name is lost to us. Wherever the gospel is proclaimed and the eucharist celebrated another story is told: the story of the apostle who betrayed Jesus. The name of the betrayer is remembered, but the name of the faithful disciple is forgotten because she was a woman." She further notes: "While Peter had confessed, without truly understanding it, 'you are the anointed one,' the woman anointing Jesus recognizes clearly that Jesus' messiahship means suffering and death." Finally, "the Christian gospel cannot be proclaimed if the women disciples and what they have done are not remembered" (1994, xiii, xiv).

Matthew: A similar account of an unnamed anointing woman. Matthew's version (26:6–13) is similar to Mark's, except it is specifically "the disciples" who scold the woman. This is an example, not uncommon in the Gospels, of an author putting an unnamed female next to Jesus's disciples and having the female actually model good discipleship while the male disciples are in danger of obstructing it.

John: Mary of Bethany anoints Jesus's feet and wipes them with her hair. In John's version of the story (12:3–8), the setting is Bethany, but instead of Simon the leper's house, they are at the home of Mary (not Magdalene), Martha, and Lazarus. So important is it to this Gospel that John alludes to it already at 11:2, a full chapter before it even occurs! Significantly placed, the anointing is done by Mary at the end of Jesus's public ministry, just before the footwashing. Instead of pouring oil on his head (as the royal kingship act), she wipes (*ekmassō*) oil on his feet with her hair.

Mary's act is also prophetic, however. First, as in the story in Mark, Jesus notes that this anointing woman understands that he is going to die and foreshadows it (John 12:7). Second, in the next chapter (John 13:1–15), Jesus wipes (*ekmassō*) the feet of the disciples with a towel and tells them to do the same for one another. The word *ekmassō* occurs only in these two events, which highlights the intentional direct connection. What Jesus overtly teaches the disciples to do in chapter 13 in tending to one another as church, Mary does before he ever mentions it.

In John's version, the woman is named (Mary) and she is put in a scene with a specific individual male disciple (Judas). The woman exemplifies paradigmatic discipleship while the male disciple of Jesus does not. This is a pattern, especially in John and in Mark,

196

and much has been written that explores the significance of the technique (for a treatment of the pattern in Mark, consult Malbon 1983 or 2009).

Luke: An unnamed "sinful" woman bathes and anoints Jesus's feet with tears, oil, and her hair. Luke uses a story of an anointing woman to make different points than the other three Gospels. Luke's anointing woman serves as a paradigm of discipleship for Luke because she exhibits radical, profligate hospitality and love, a key theme in Luke. She also exemplifies another of Luke's favorite themes: *aphesis*, or release, used in its verbal form and translated as "forgive" in 7:48 and 7:49 of the NRSV. All useful lessons, but not at all the same story as we find in the other Gospels.

Notice that the story does not appear anywhere near the end of Jesus's ministry in Luke and is not tied to his burial. The setting is the home of a Pharisee (not Simon the leper and not Mary, Martha, and Lazarus). It is not in Bethany. This is one of those stories where misinterpretation turns this woman into a prostitute and the story into a "here is another sexually loose woman Jesus forgave of her sleazy ways." Luke never identifies her as a prostitute (*pornē*); he calls her a sinner (*hamartōlos*), the same word used for both males and females. In fact, although Jesus is criticized for eating with tax collectors and sinners, there is no story that specifies that sinners are prostitutes.

I teach this passage often, and I always ask what makes people think the woman is a prostitute. Sometimes the answer is that she has expensive ointment. The logic is: how could a woman in antiquity have money unless she was a prostitute? But as we find in the other anointing stories, including that of Mary of Bethany, a woman does not need to be a prostitute to have money to buy oil. At the beginning of Luke 8, soon after this story in Luke 7, we encounter numerous women providing financially for Jesus. They also are not called prostitutes, though, again, I sometimes hear this assumption voiced. Think about Lydia, the seller of purple, and Tabitha who worked in textiles, and Priscilla in Paul's ministry, who worked in tentmaking. Thus, it is important to break the habit of reducing woman after woman in the Bible to a prostitute, which happens especially if a woman appears without a man or with money.

The bulk of commentaries are written by male scholars, so a motivated reader accessing commentaries in a library or pastor's study will encounter male scholars interpreting a text (likely)

197

written by a male author about the assumptions of a male character (here, the Pharisee) when he looks upon a woman who enters
the room and touches a male guest. Many interpreters claim that
the reason we know she is a prostitute is because she is "from the
city." Such interpreters have yet to make this point by adducing
actual evidence from other first-century texts that show a synony-
mous relationship between "from the city" and "prostitute." A lot of
people are from the city but not prostitutes, then and now. Joseph
Fitzmyer is exceptional in this regard, writing in his commentary
about this woman who anoints: "No hint is given of the kind of
sins that she has committed. Many commentators (e.g., J. Ernst,
A. Plummer, J. Schmid, G. Schneider) identify her as the town
harlot, guilty of 'habitual unchastity' (Plummer, *ExpTim* 27 [1915–
1916] 42–43). Possibly this is implied in the Pharisee's thoughts
(v. 39b); but it is at most implied, not being said openly in the text"
(1982, 688–89; consult also Carey 2009).

Women Tended to by Jesus: Not Loose, Just Loosed

In the first three anointing stories above, we find women min-
istering to Jesus's body as they will at his burial. In the last, the
woman both ministers to Jesus and is ministered to by him, as she is
released (*aphiēmi*). That is, we see mutual ministry.

There are numerous examples of this in the New Testament.
In Luke 8:1–3 Jesus cures a number of women. They then become
part of his ministry efforts.

Consider also the story of Peter's mother-in-law (Mark 1:29–31),
in which Jesus ministers to her (curing a fever), and she promptly
ministers to him. I use the word "minister" here advisedly since the
verb *diakoneō* and the noun *diakonos* are behind the English word
"minister." It is what the angels do to Jesus when he is in the wilderness (Mark 1:13; note that the NRSV translates it as "waited on,"
but it is the word *diakoneō*). In Mark 15:40, a host of women (*gyn-
aikes* in 15:40 in addition to the "many other women" [*allai pollai*]
in 15:41) witnesses the crucifixion. Mark then specifically names
three—Mary Magdalene, Mary (mother of James and Joses), and
Salome—and declares that they had ministered (*diēkonoun;* 15:41)
to Jesus during his Galilean period. Finally, and crucially, it is what
Jesus himself does—it is the essence of his ministry according to
Mark 10:45: "For the Son of Man came not to be ministered to but

198

to minister to [*diakoneō*], and to give his life a ransom for many" (my trans.; consult also Luke 22:27).

Thus, we encounter women who minister to Jesus and women in mutual ministry with Jesus. But what about women who find themselves in a desperate, helpless, seemingly hopeless situation, so far gone that they are not even looking for help anymore? One example is the "bent-over woman" or "kyphotic" (from Greek *syg-kyptō*) in Luke 13:10–17.

This passage deserves ample contemplation and exposition that is beyond the scope of our project. Notice, though, that Luke says not that she has an illness (*astheneia*), but rather a "spirit" of illness. Jesus describes her as being held in bondage and names Satan (conceived of as that which opposes God's will) as the one who has bound her. Satan plays a prominent role in Luke's narrative. The religious authorities (all male), the "gatekeepers" of the faith, side with Satan against the woman and Jesus. Same stuff, different century. It is not for no reason that Jesus was opposed by the religious establishment and executed by the state. He was quite serious about living out what Mary and the prophets taught him. Are we?

The story is a microcosm of Lukan theology. One overarching theme of Luke is salvation, and Luke approaches it from a variety of angles. As noted above, one of those has to do with "release" (*aphiēmi*), which is often translated in English as "forgive." We do not want to import our own theology here but rather let Luke speak. When Luke–Acts uses the language of release (the word translated as "loosed"), it can refer to physical, social, and spiritual aspects. All would-be healers know that these are interconnected. (And, for example, in the story of Luke 7, Jesus declares that the woman is "released" [*aphiēmi*], correctly translated as "forgiven" here since "sin" is mentioned.) Whereas the kyphotic woman has a spirit (*pneuma*) of infirmity, Jesus has the "Spirit of the Lord," and for what purpose? "To proclaim release [*aphesis*] to the captives and recovery of sight to the blind, to let the oppressed go free" (Luke 4:18). She is physically released, and she is restored to community insofar as he reminds her and the religious authorities that she is a "daughter of Abraham." She belongs to a specific trajectory of the story of God. The structures of religion (like the Sabbath, on which Jesus heals this woman) are godly when they ground us in specific, concrete, life-giving communities and traditions and

199

practices. When they are used to keep people bound up and bent over, they are nothing less than satanic.

Patrons and Partners in the Gospel: Women Who Minister to and alongside Jesus

Luke introduces us to crucial women in Jesus's ministry who are among the many said to travel with Jesus in this Gospel:

> And soon afterwards he traveled through cities and villages, preaching and proclaiming the good news of the kingdom of God. With him were both the twelve and some women who had been healed of evil spirits [*pneuma*] and illnesses [*astheneia*, meaning illness or weakness]: Mary, called Magdalene, from whom seven demons had gone out, and Joanna, the wife (*gynē*) of Herod's steward Chuza, and Susanna, and many other women, who ministered [*diakoneō*] to them out of their resources [*hyparchō*, property, possessions]. (Luke 8:1–3, my trans.)

Who are all of these women? We learn of "some women," then named women, then "*many* others" who bankrolled not only Jesus, but also his other followers. Which ones were cured of illnesses, and of what kinds of evil spirits and illnesses? Notice that Luke uses some of the same language here as in the story of the bent-over woman. Is it surprising that they are noted as traveling without male companions (except maybe Joanna) but along with male disciples? Who are the "many other women"? The Greek is clear here that these "many others" are all female (*heterai pollai*). Picture the scene of this traveling group!

This passage stokes the imagination in all directions. It reminds one of another passage written by Luke, Acts 1:14 (recall that the same author pens Luke and Acts): "All these were constantly devoting themselves to prayer, together with *certain women*, including Mary the mother of Jesus, as well as his brothers" (emphasis added). Again, who are these "certain women"? In both Luke and Acts, Luke repeatedly indicates that women were a vital, regular part of Jesus's life and ministry who actively participated in and helped to fund the spreading of the gospel.

200   If you were to visit the relatively new Duc et Altum church at Magdala, you would enter first into a round structure called the Women's Atrium (said to honor the feminine, as a womb). Inside

are eight columns. On each of seven columns, you will find the names of women who appear in Jesus's ministry, including Mary Magdalene, Susanna and Joanna, the sisters Mary and Martha, the mother of James and John, the mother-in-law of Peter, and Mary wife of Cleopas, and the many other women in Jesus's ministry (not named individually in the Gospels). The eighth column is an unmarked pillar with no names, for this column honors all of the unnamed women in Jesus's ministry of all times and places. It is my custom to gather together all of the women with me to take a photo by this column. It is always a moving experience.

The fact that women followed Jesus just as the disciples did and supported his ministry financially and otherwise is further attested by Mark's comment in 15:40–41: "There were also women looking on from a distance; among them were Mary Magdalene, and Mary the mother of James the younger and of Joses, and Salome. These used to follow him and provided for [*diakoneō*, ministered to] him when he was in Galilee; and there were many other women who had come up with him to Jerusalem." Matthew's version does not list the exact same women, but it agrees that the women included both followed him (*akoloutheō*, a theologically loaded word that means to be a disciple) and performed ministry (*diakoneō*), just as the angels and Jesus himself did (consult Matt. 27:55–56).

Thus, the Gospels depict women of means and independence who travel with Jesus and fund his ministry. Only once is a husband mentioned. This pattern continues in the book of Acts with leaders such as Tabitha (also known as Dorcas; 9:36–43) and Lydia (16:11–15).

An Unbounded/Unboundaried Woman: John 7:53–8:11

The bent-over woman in Luke 13 was unbound. We now turn to unbounded, unboundaried women, women whose actions and whose bodies in the presence of men raise the issue of boundaries and boundary crossing. The Canaanite woman in Matthew 15:21–28 is important in this vein, and I direct the reader's attention to my fuller treatment of her earlier in this book. Presently, we address the story typically referred to as "the woman caught in adultery," though I hope that by thinking through the story a bit, the reader might ask if there is a better title for it. It is important to note that

201

none of these stories in our Bible comes with titles or subtitles. In fact, the ancient manuscripts that New Testament scholars use to construct the Greek New Testament have no paragraphs, verse numbers, or punctuation. (For a fuller discussion of how we got the Greek text, consult Aland and Aland 1995.) Understand that if you approach a biblical text with a "title" for the story in mind, it will predetermine your interpretation, what you see and what you fail to see.

The story of the woman whom the religious authorities want to stone has an ambiguous textual history. Currently, one finds it at John 7:53–8:11. A study Bible places it in brackets because the best ancient manuscripts show that this story was not originally part of the Gospel of John. Other ancient manuscripts place it after 7:36; 21:25; or Luke 21:38. Thus, its place in the canon is so dubious that one might decide to exclude it from consideration. However, the story has been such a prominent part of the Christian tradition and is retold so often that it makes sense to include it in our treatment of women.

The gifts of this story. This story may be viewed as a text of terror, a text of liberation, or both. As a liberating text, and in light of Jesus's lack of condemnation and concomitant release, the story might help a modern reader suffering from sex-related guilt to move into a future marked by different choices, better choices. Or it might encourage those who have suffered humiliation and judgment at the hands of sanctimonious hypocrites happy to see the speck in the other's eye but never the log in their own; to see Jesus put such haters in their place can be freeing. Or it might just provide a mirror for the reader to realize not that he or she is the victim of graceless judgment (like the woman), but rather a perpetrator of it (like the accusers). Jesus treats the woman exactly as he does the male religious leaders: (1) he pronounces all of them as sinners who need to change their ways; (2) he teaches them; and (3) he reorients their attention from the sinful past to a future way of behaving that starts in the moment of their encounter with him. He levels the playing field in every way, leaving no room for anyone to see themselves as better or worse than the next person.

Getting down on the ground for a closer look: Women as object (lesson?). It is important, however, to tend to the story at a deeper level and explore the gendered interactions in the text as well as gendered interpretations of the text. A closer look raises

202

some disturbing but important observations if we are to grow from encountering the revelatory Word in the text.

If this woman "caught in adultery" is caught in anything, it's a male pissing contest. A pack of male authorities, in this case religious gatekeepers, drag the woman to Jesus, whose religious authority they want to test. She is not there by choice. Next, these men "force her to stand" (*histēmi*) before all, and they ask yet another man to judge her as deserving of extermination. Note the use of the transitive form of *histēmi*, expressly noting that she is the "object," not the subject, of the action (as opposed to the intransitive, which would mean "she stood" and make her the subject rather than the object of the action).

The text is clear that they are using this woman's body merely to "test" Jesus in order to turn their legal accusations and violence upon him as the narrative progresses (which they do). They appear to relish the specificity of her having been caught "in the very act" of adultery. Again, one can speculate about the circumstances, but since neither the men nor the text itself expresses interest in hearing the woman's side of the story, it will remain speculation. But here is a crucial point: If she was caught in the act of adultery, clearly the male was also caught. Yet we hear nothing about him or the desire to kill him. In fact, the sole focus on and animosity toward the female is made even more clear when they generally allude to "the law that Moses" commanded about adultery but only as it relates to "such women." They make two moves here of note. First, just as they seek to kill her, they absolve themselves of the violent act by saying, "Moses made me do it," as it were. Second, they have relegated her to a group they call "such women."

Laws governing sexuality are typically applied more severely to women than to men:

> Men arranged their daughters' marriages with other men; so daughters changed hands from father to husband, the custom curiously still surviving today in the old wedding ritual of fathers giving their daughters away. . . . Male heirs were in most places crucial for ensuring control of property and inheritance. Wives were expected at least to produce sons. An adulterous wife was a huge threat, since she might bring foreign heirs into the family, which could threaten its stability and survival. . . . These social structures ensured that people generally gave much more attention to female sexual behaviour than to male sexual behaviour,

203

except where it, too, could threaten another man's household by adultery, understood as taking what belongs to another man. The unequal focus on women's sexuality still survives in the prominence given to female virginity. (Loader 2010, 4)

And even if the actual biblical law expresses just as much concern for "such men," "the adulterer was in a better position because the adulteress had no free property of her own with which she might redeem herself from her husband's wrath while the adulterer had his labor to pledge" (Derrett 1963, 7).

Famously, and cryptically, Jesus says nothing aloud yet, but he writes on the ground. (Interpreters speculate on what Jesus wrote. For a full scholarly analysis, consult Chris Keith, 2009). They keep coming at him, so he "stands erect" (*anakyptō*), presumably to meet them eye to eye. Jesus confronts them by talking not about the woman and her sin, but about their own sin (one could imagine any number of sins that could be named, but it is for each of those characters, and perhaps the readers themselves, to make an honest moral inventory of motivations and actions). He sends them forth into their future story to make better choices, to avoid sin. Having made this statement, he bends down to write in the sand again. The opponents depart, empty-handed in terms of dirt on Jesus, but perhaps still clutching tightly the stones. The text gives no indication that Jesus's words struck a chord of repentance in the men at all. Given that John 10:31 once again finds Jesus in the temple with opponents who want to stone him, it does not seem likely (consult also 11:57 and 12:10).

The text then indicates specifically that Jesus does three things. (1) He sees that no one else is there except the woman; thus, he knows he is alone with a woman accused of adultery, and what does he do? Does he run away? (2) He stands erect (*anakyptō*) again (same word used with the religious leaders), presumably to meet her eye to eye, as he did with them. She is still standing there, not having said a word or been asked to do so. (3) He engages her as a person and has her voice the fact that she is under no condemnation. None. He sends her forth into her future story to make better choices, to avoid sin, exactly as he had done with the religious leaders who fancied themselves superior to her. Jesus levels the playing field.

Jesus levels the playing field, but the rest of us typically do not. Women's bodies are actually the playing fields of males in power quite often, a fact captured in Susan Brooks Thistlethwaite's fine book *Women's Bodies as Battlefield: Christian Theology and the Global War on Women.* Feminist and postcolonial thinkers know that politics get mapped onto real bodies, especially the bodies of the most vulnerable members of a society. Because the reader may not be familiar with postcolonial analyses and the questions they help us to raise and new angles for viewing a text they may provide, I briefly provide a summary of the insights from two scholars who conduct such analyses.

Engaging the text with Jean K. Kim. In her essay "Adultery or Hybridity? Reading John 7.53–8.11 from a Postcolonial Context," Kim argues two points. First, she argues that this is a story about "the legitimate leadership of Israel in a (de)colonizing context and that the woman caught in adultery may not have been simply a sexually immoral woman but rather a victim used as a site of cultural (im)purity, which is a ground on which competing views of cultural or national identity are debated" (2002, 114–15). Second (and here is the good news), she argues that "the woman can be a site of hybridity which enables a female reader to lay claim to her own subjectivity" (115).

Wondering where the absent male adulterer is, Kim postulates that he may have been a Roman soldier. Kim reminds us that when nations send in their military forces, the soldiers often have sexual intercourse with the native women, even raping them with impunity (because the soldiers are rarely handed over to local authorities but are protected by the colonizing state). The penetrated country often placates the soldiers by offering up its women as "comfort women" but then hates those women for the fact that they are penetrated by the foreign males. "Colonized men who are unable to protect their women tend to feel shame at not being real men, and thus the sexual invasion of their women by foreign men becomes an assault on male and national honor" (122).

In these discourses, a (false) dichotomy is set up between a "good woman," who is a wife and mother and symbolizes the purity of the nation, and a bad woman, the "whore or adulteress" who has contact with other ethnic men. She is the mixed or "hybrid" woman, contaminated and impure. In the case of this woman in John's Gospel, "it was only as a site of (im)purity that she was brought to the debate scene in order that the legitimate authority of the colonized Israel might be contested" (Kim 2002, 126).

There is hope in this reading of the text on at least two counts. First, hope springs forth when those who have been voiceless in the midst of the social systems that oppress them are given voice. One thinks of the "me too." movement where healing and justice emerge when the voices of the formerly voiceless are heard and respected, when patriarchy is contested and all bodies come to matter and be valued. For her part, Kim finds hope in methodologies like the postcolonial feminist reading she provides in which she applies the "social memories of voiceless women to the story of the woman caught in adultery." She writes: "In so doing, I have attempted to release her body from its imprisonment as a site of cultural (im)purity, and to reclaim it as a site of resistant reading (a site of hybridity) to both the internal disease of patriarchal nationalism (Jewish) and the external disease of colonialism (Roman), which have both been influential on the formation of the text as well as on its interpretations" (127).

Second, Jesus himself sometimes appears in the Gospels as the hybrid other who refuses the Caiaphas principle, which declares it is always best to sacrifice the one, even if unjustly, to keep the powers that be—the ruling class, gender, race—on one's side, or at least not against one. The would-be stoners did not count on that; I doubt the woman did either. How will we follow Jesus's lead offered by this narrative?

Engaging the text with Leticia A. Guardiola-Sáenz. In "Border-Crossing and Its Redemptive Power in John 7.53–8.11: A Cultural Reading of Jesus and the *Accused*," Guardiola-Sáenz has two aims: "first, to present a cultural, regional reading of Jn 7.53–8.11 from the hybrid experience of a bicultural Mexican-American subject from the borderlands, living in the diaspora; and second, to begin theorizing and systematizing the elements of a reading strategy aimed at empowering minority readers as agents of historical change in the ongoing process of decolonization and liberation of the Two-Thirds World" (2002, 130–31). There are those who cross borders at great risk, and there are those who patrol borders. Most people prefer to stay in the safe zone. For her part, "As a Mexican woman, born and bred in the bi-cultural, neo-colonialist context of the Rio Grande Valley borderlands, and living now as a resident alien in the US, I read the Accused's story as an encounter between two border-crossers who defy the politico-religious, moral and cultural borders of their time" (135).

In treating the sociohistorical context of the passage within the Gospel of John, Guardiola-Sáenz notes the scholarly consensus that the Johannine community itself was hybrid and border-crossing (containing at least Jews, Gentiles, and Samaritans). Then, she describes the pericope itself as border-crossing since it is not original to this location in John and in some manuscripts appears in different places in John and in Luke, as I have indicated above.

Guardiola-Sáenz argues that both the woman and Jesus transgress the borders set up by the border patrol (here, the religious leaders). Thus, the border patrol wants to get rid of both of them rather than question either (1) the borders themselves or (2) the ways that the leaders police the borders—ways that benefit themselves but oppress and devalue others. They try to trap Jesus in a no-win situation: either he directs them to stone her, which would be usurping Roman authority (Jews under Roman rule did not have the authority to execute death), or he defies Mosaic law (the borders of which the accusers themselves have transgressed by not giving her a proper trial but subjecting her to mob law). Jesus draws a line in the sand, as it were, and invites them to step over into his view of reality, where borders between genders and ethnicities are drawn in ways that create unity-in-diversity. They decline the offer to create new borders that include space for the full personhood and value of the Other and instead depart to plot their murder of him. Left alone, Jesus engages the woman as a person with agency and frees her from the condemnation upon which patriarchy thrives.

In sum, the text shows the precarious situation of any woman in a patriarchal society where a woman is not free to determine her own sexuality apart from a male authority figure, whether father or husband. Jesus skewers the "good old boys" network where "boys will be boys" while women must remain pure. He treats her as an equal to the males. The text also offers the reader the experience of liberation and levity that comes from hearing words of grace from an advocate (*The* Advocate) who defends you and sends you forth repaired, whole, and ready to embrace abundant life.

A Woman Who Dares to Take Matters into Her Own Hands: Mark 5:24–34

207

In some encounters between Jesus and women, Jesus takes the initiative (e.g., Peter's mother-in-law; the Samaritan woman). In others, women provoke the encounter, as in the story of the Canaanite woman who seeks healing of her daughter (and, by extension, herself; consult Matt. 15:21–28). The story of the woman with the incessant flow of blood depicts another who seeks out Jesus for healing.

The woman in Mark 5 appears to be alone and unsupported as she makes her way through a throng of people surrounding Jesus. On a wall in the basement of the Duc et Altum church in Magdala, there is a gigantic painting of this woman touching the hem of Jesus's garment. The floor upon which one stands when viewing the encounter is the first-century road that Jesus himself, not to mention Mary of Magdala, likely walked upon. The viewer does not see the woman's face or that of Jesus; rather one sees the feet of Jesus and the feet of those around him, with the woman's body bent down and her arm reaching through the collection of feet, her finger extended to touch the bottom of his robe.

Many readers will identify with her experience of suffering a disease for which there seems to be no remedy, despite consulting many physicians and spending every last penny. This woman was in a desperate situation. Like many other female characters in the Gospel of Mark, she correctly discerns and has faith in Jesus's ability to heal her. Transgressing social and religious boundaries, she publicly touches a male to whom she is not related, while bleeding. She is not the only one with a flow in this story, however, since her action causes power to flow out of Jesus; in this physical exchange the boundaries of each of their bodies are shown to be porous (for a fuller exploration of this, consult Candida Moss 2017).

The woman knows immediately that something has "happened to her" (5:33) through the touch. Jesus, who is not omniscient or omnipotent in Mark, is curious to discover who has acted upon him, who has drawn from him without his knowledge or consent or initiative. As is typical in Mark, his male disciples are of no help. Courageously, she comes forward and tells Jesus the truth (in a manner similar to the exchange between the Syrophonecian woman and Jesus two chapters later, in Mark 7). The text clearly describes her state as fear and trembling, but, instead of slinking away, she steps forward, owns her experience despite its unorthodox nature, and publicly testifies to the healing she has experienced from Jesus. Far from chastising her or humiliating her in any way, he instead establishes intimate connection with her by calling her "daughter" (Mark

208

5:34)—she is no longer alone but belongs to a family. Jesus praises the woman and her agency—it is her own faith that has saved her. "Saved" (*sōzō*) is a multilayered word, but it refers to a spiritual state of reconciliation. Only secondarily does he pronounce her physically, medically "cured" (*hygiēs*, 5:34) from her affliction.

Mark interweaves the story of the woman bleeding for twelve years with the story of the twelve-year-old daughter who is dead. They are connected by the biblically significant number twelve, which has given rise to many hypotheses that cannot be entertained here. Both are daughters and both have physical contact with Jesus and both are healed.

Women Who Engage Jesus in Theological Conversation or Debate

Jesus was no stranger to engaging women in lively theological dialogue in a period in history when women were generally not regarded as serious thinkers. We discussed in an earlier chapter his encounter with the Canaanite woman in Matthew. Here I draw attention to two more examples: the Samaritan woman, and Mary and Martha.

The Samaritan Woman

Ideal disciple. The story of the Samaritan woman in John 4:1–42 presents a challenge due to incorrect assumptions that people bring to the text. I have heard many a sermon, even from learned preachers, even some women, about this "whore" who was forgiven by Jesus for her loose living. This gives a wrong interpretation of the passage. Nowhere is this woman referred to as a "whore" (*pornē*) and nowhere is she forgiven (*aphiēmi*). John insists she had "husbands," not johns.

The reader focused on the woman's sexual history also misses out on what the story is *actually* about—an exemplar of the faith whom the reader is supposed to imitate. This is clear for at least three reasons: (1) the woman encounters Jesus and engages him in deep theological dialogue, which leads to her experiencing the first theophany (manifestation of God) in the Gospel of John; (2) she moves into her personal story of abundant life in Christ (marked by

209

leaving her water jar behind) that awaits each and every one us; and (3) she immediately shares that abundance with others by testifying about him and inviting them to "come and see" so that they might enjoy a faith based on their own encounter with him instead of one merely derivative of her own. There is so much to be said about this woman whose engagement with Jesus spans forty-two verses, and I have written about her in more detail elsewhere (Clark-Soles 2016, 34–46). Here I raise only a few points for consideration and entreat the reader to dive more deeply into study, preaching, and teaching concerning this woman and her witness.

The Samaritan woman appears only in the Gospel of John. She, along with the man born blind in John 9, serves as an ideal disciple from John's perspective. Jesus seeks her out intentionally; she was not seeking him any more than the man born blind was. The normal route from Jerusalem to Galilee would not involve going into the heart of Samaria, but the text says it was necessary (*dei*) for him to go. He "had" to go because she was there.

He meets her at a well, which readers of the Old Testament will recognize as a betrothal spot (Moses and Zipporah, Rebekah and Isaac, Jacob and Rachel). We already know that Jesus is the Bridegroom from John 2 and 3 (esp. 3:29). So placing the scene there is intentional and rich with allusive meaning. It creates an expectation that a "marriage" of a sort (if between unlikely partners, culturally speaking) will result from their meeting.

It is high noon. Some preachers and teachers often go on about how this woman, with her sexually loose ways, was ostracized by the "other women" in the village, arguing from silence (since nowhere does the text say that) while, ironically, ignoring the glaring theme of light present in this chapter. From John 1 forward, the author insists that Jesus is the true light, the one who is the light of all people, the one coming into the world. In John 3 the narrator, while chastising those who work in the dark, expressly indicates that those tethered to truth work in the light. Here we have a woman who boldly, publicly appears in the brightest light of day to encounter the True Light, and as a result she is enlightened. She is intentionally contrasted with Nicodemus, who comes to Jesus "by night" (John 3:2).

210   Not born yesterday, having endured much, in John 4:9 she appropriately suspects the man who is "out of place": "The Samaritan woman said to him, 'How is it that you, a Jew, ask a drink of

me, a woman of Samaria?' (Jews do not share things in common with Samaritans)." She delineates differences: he is a man, she is a woman; he is a Jew, she is a Samaritan. The narrator heightens the tension for the uninitiated reader with a side comment. Intrepidly, the Samaritan woman engages him and discovers in him a theological conversation partner. She now calls him a prophet (4:19), not because he read her palm or tea leaves, but because Old Testament prophets always critique idolatry, and, as noted further below, Jews considered Samaritans to worship idols in addition to worshiping Israel's God. The woman and Jesus move on to a discussion of proper worship, and Jesus announces that soon all these divisions will be eradicated and unity will prevail—no more fights about worship spaces and places, traditional or contemporary services, and so on, but rather a concern for worship characterized by Spirit and Truth (4:24), the details notwithstanding.

The conversation escalates when the woman moves it from worship to the coming of the Messiah. Then, she receives a theophany when Jesus says to her, "I am" (*egō eimi*, John 4:26). Translations that say "I am he" here do the reader a disservice, as they eclipse the fact that Jesus is claiming *the* title of God that appears when God reveals God's name to Moses as "I AM" (Exod. 3:13–15, esp. v. 14). Our sister the Samaritan woman is the first to behold Jesus as God.

In John 4:27, the disciples reappear and immediately start questioning the breaching of established gender categories that are set in place to benefit males like them. They have no clue about or interest in humbly learning about the transformative exchange that has just occurred. Rather, "They were astonished that he was speaking with a woman, but no one said, 'What do you want?' or, 'Why are you speaking with her?'" For her part, she has no time to be slowed down by their sexist myopia and instead rushes off to proclaim the gospel. She leaves Jesus to deal with their ignorance, and he does. The detail that she "left her water jar" (v. 28) is far from accidental; it is essential to the story. She has not left what is bad for what is good; rather, she has left what is good, a container of water at high noon in a desert, for what is better, the uncontained living water that Jesus provides always and everywhere.

She runs to her community and shares the details of her experience. Far from being an outcast, she is clearly believable enough and authoritative enough for those hearing her to take her seriously 211 enough to want what she has. They, too, come to understand that Jesus is not just the savior of Jews or even of Jews and Samaritans, but in fact, of "the whole cosmos [*kosmos*]" (4:42, my trans.).

Symbolic representation of Samaria itself. The Samaritan woman is also a symbolic character, representing the tension between Israel and Samaria. Jesus, a Jew, represents Israel, which worships on Mount Zion, while the woman represents Samaria, which worships on Mount Gerizim. It is important for the interpreter to understand why Jews and Samaritans are at odds, and to do so one must read 2 Kings 17:13–41 carefully. According to Israel, Samaritans are not fully faithful covenant people because they wed themselves to false gods upon returning after Assyrian captivity: "So they worshiped the LORD but also served their own gods, after the manner of the nations from among whom they had been carried away. To this day they continue to practice their former customs. They do not worship the LORD and they do not follow the statutes or the ordinances or the law or the commandment that the LORD commanded the children of Jacob, whom he named Israel" (2 Kgs. 17:33–34).

So, from Jesus's Jewish perspective, "Samaria's Yahwism was tainted by false worship and therefore even the 'husband' she now has (a reference to her relationship with the God of the covenant) was not really her husband (see v. 18) in the full integrity of the covenantal relationship" (Schneiders 2003, 140). Samaria (which the woman represents) has had five husbands (the false gods of the foreign tribes listed in 2 Kgs. 17:29–31) and is in a "not-quite" relationship with the sixth, the God of Israel. Jesus, the true bridegroom, makes seven, which is, of course, a biblical number for completion and perfection, and abundant life. As Schneiders writes: "In summary, the entire dialogue between Jesus and the woman is the 'wooing' of Samaria to full covenant fidelity in the new Israel by Jesus, the new Bridegroom. It has nothing to do with the women's private moral life but with the covenant life of the community" (141).

Mary and Martha

Luke 10:38–42. In my experience, most people are more familiar with the story of Mary and Martha found in Luke than that in John. In Luke, the two are pitted against one another, with Mary sitting in on Jesus's lectures as an avid disciple, while Martha is, in the words of the NRSV, "distracted by her many tasks" (10:40). Martha complains to Jesus that she feels burdened by the lack of help, and Jesus responds, "Martha, Martha, you are worried and distracted by many things; there is need of only one thing. Mary has chosen the better part, which will not be taken away from her" (vv. 41–42). This creates an unhelpful binary: one either values intellect and study (considered to be a man's game, certainly then, but even now) or one performs traditional female tasks. In the lives of contemporary women, this tension sometimes appears between "women who work" or "career women" and "stay-at-home moms." This language has led to resentment such that now career women are called "women who work outside the home" so as to not demean women who work "inside the home," even though "women who work outside the home" also bear disproportionate duties inside the home compared to their male counterparts, known as "the second shift" (Hochschild and Machung 2012). At times, one hears of churchgoing women referring to themselves as *either* a Mary *or* a Martha.

It is time to lay such dichotomies to rest and not pit women against women. Furthermore, the translation related to Martha is demeaning and wrong; where the NRSV says that she is distracted by "many things" in verse 40, the text literally says she is drawn away into "much ministry [*diakonia*]"! Far from "worrying her pretty little head" over irrelevant minutiae, Martha is a minister who has been on call for too long without a Sabbath. I know many a female (and male) minister in this position, being stretched far too thin, running on fumes, not yet having perfected the practice of what Henri Nouwen calls "the ministry of absence." The ability to carve out time or recognize an unexpected opportunity for spiritual self-care and growth in order to render even better ministry is a learned one that takes much practice and, for most of us, an accountability partner of some sort. Learning to disconnect from the tyranny of the urgent to take advantage of the gift of now is a lifelong practice. As we work toward it, let us try to find a way to do it that neither belittles nor lionizes either Mary or Martha.

John 11. John also knows of a Mary and Martha. Whether or not they are the same women as in Luke 10 is impossible to say and does not really matter, since each Gospel author regularly displays autonomy in using available traditions to make meaning within the context of an individualized narrative. The passage in John 11 can be treated in three major parts.

213

1. The confession of Martha. While some refer to John 11 as "The Raising of Lazarus," in many ways it makes more sense to call it "The Confession of Martha." Jesus arrives at Bethany in 11:17, and we learn that the community has surrounded Mary and Martha to console them. When Martha hears that Jesus is "coming" (remember, in John he is always the one "coming into the world"), she goes to meet him, "while Mary stayed at home" (11:20). The reader of Luke may be confused by the role reversal, which is simply an opportunity to remember that one needs to let each Gospel stand on its own as an integrated whole and not judge according to the criteria of other Gospels.

Martha then engages Jesus in language of deep theological reflection and faith. She believes in Jesus and knows he shares a special relationship with God. Jesus declares a word that applies to each and every one of us who has lost a loved one: "Your brother will rise again." Like most of us, Martha projects Jesus's promise into a distant future, unable to imagine resurrection as a *present* reality (or unpracticed in doing so), not just future, being careful not to dream too big, lest she be disappointed or mocked or taken for a theological simpleton. So Jesus ups the ante, pulls out all the stops, and reveals to her that "I am the resurrection and the life" and directly asks her whether she believes him. And this is the question the Gospel has posed to every reader ever since. Remember that the whole point of John is presented in 20:31: "But these are written so that you may come to believe that Jesus is the Messiah, the Son of God, and that through believing you may have life in his name."

And how does Martha respond? Like a poster child for the whole Gospel of John, she confidently exclaims: "Yes, Lord, I [*egō*] believe that you [*su*] are the Messiah, the Son of God, the one coming into the world" (11:27). In Greek, the pronoun "I" and the pronoun "you" are grammatically unnecessary since the person is contained in the verb conjugation; thus, the use of the pronouns is emphatic, a true "I-Thou" moment where two people are connecting as subjects in a real relationship. Furthermore, the verb "I believe" is in the perfect tense, a special past tense whose force is action completed in the past with ongoing effect into the present. It's an extremely powerful and emphatic declaration of full-fledged, complete belief, without an ounce of hedging her bets.

214

2. Mary's turn. Immediately after her proclamation, Martha retrieves Mary, since Jesus expressly asks to see her (notice that

Mary is gloriously free of judgy male disciples questioning why Jesus would want to meet with her). When she comes out to the very same place where Martha encountered Jesus, she says the same thing that Martha said: "If only." "If only you had been here, my brother would not have died" (11:32). I imagine all of us have played this game with Jesus more than once. "If only ___." The hours, weeks, months, years, lamenting what could have been, as if that has any chance of changing the present facts on the ground. The scene is full of crying: Mary weeps, those with her weep, and Jesus himself begins to weep. The text honors weeping and grieving. Do we?

I'm not a crier. Not long ago I participated in a spiritual formation exercise that took me to deep places, and I found myself crying. In fact, during the course of the experience, I cried more than once, though each instance had a patently different quality to it. In discussing the experience with a close friend over dinner that evening—a friend acquainted with all emotions who can be moved to tears in an instant—I said to her, "You know, there are different kinds of crying," to which she kindly and graciously responded: "Right. And did you know that there are four different canonical Gospels?" Touché. I mention this story because John 11:33 describes Mary and the companions weeping with one word (*klaiō*), while in 11:35 Jesus is weeping with a different word (*dakryō*). They are joined together in grief, but their grieving is not identical. That's important. And Jesus already knows he is going to raise Lazarus; that is, he knows that ultimately the story has a good ending, as do we Christians who know that we come from God and return to God and that death is not ultimate. Yet, he does not don rose-colored glasses in the face of death and pain. He truly exhibits empathy and compassion.

3. Martha's moment. Martha appears one last time in the story. When Jesus commands that the stone be rolled away, Martha, the bold proclaimer of Jesus as Messiah, has a moment to which we can all relate. There's glorious, lofty, real belief, and then there's the reality of decaying bodies that reek. She wants to protect Jesus from the harsh reality of death. It is instructive that the text introduces her here as "Martha, the sister of the dead man." It is one thing to be just Martha (or fill in your own name). It is another to be the relative of a person who is dead or entombed, literally or metaphorically. We are defined by our relationships, finally, whether we like

215

it or not. And there are theologies and practices that "work" when we are only considering ourselves but that are called into question when they are put to the test, that is, are brought out of the private vault and tried out in relationship, in community, in the face of death. We may find, like Martha, that we have the right beliefs and the right theology, and that is a good thing (she is correct in everything she proclaims in v. 27), but, when we bring it to bear in our worst-case scenarios, it takes some work and time for it to "take" or really "stick." It may take multiple experiences until what one believes to be true coheres with one's lived experience.

Women at the Passion and Crucifixion

Women appear prominently in the various passion narratives (but less so in the lectionary selections related to the passion). In what follows, we spotlight significant moments.

Anointing

As discussed above, the unnamed woman in Mark 14:3–9 (and the parallel in Matt. 26:6–13) appears at the beginning of the passion narrative, just after the passage about the plot to kill Jesus and just before Judas's meeting with the priests. The woman anoints Jesus on the head as Messiah and prepares his body for burial, two highly liturgical acts for which Jesus says she will be remembered "wherever the gospel is proclaimed in the whole world." John's story of Mary (not Mary Magdalene), sister of Martha and Lazarus (John 12:1–8), is quite different in details but still serves as a bridge story to the close of Jesus's ministry as he turns toward the passion.

The Woman/Women at Peter's Denial

All four Gospels depict at least one woman involved in Peter's denial. The story of Peter's denial as told in Mark 14:66–72 is precipitated by a servant girl. Peter is in the courtyard when "one of the servant-girls of the high priest came by." After seeing (*horaō*) Peter by the fire, she "fixes her gaze upon" (*emblepō*) Peter and declares, "You also were with Jesus, the man from Nazareth." Who is this girl, how does she serve the priest, and how does she recognize

Peter? Where has she seen him before? Peter denies it and moves to another space. Somehow, she sees him again and announces to the others standing around that Peter is "one of them." Again, he denies it.

In Matthew, two servant girls (neither is said to serve the high priest) each get one of the lines given to Mark's girl. Luke 22:56 has a single otherwise unidentified slave girl making one statement. In John 18:16–17, the slave girl is the high priest's gatekeeper (surely a play on John 10:3) who questions Peter specifically about being a "disciple" of Jesus. The details differ, but Christian history clearly remembers this nameless slave girl as an important catalyst for this part of the passion.

Pilate's Wife

Only Matthew contains the story about Pilate's unnamed wife, and it occurs in a single verse: "While he was sitting on the judgment seat, his wife sent word to him, 'Have nothing to do with that innocent man, for today I have suffered a great deal because of a dream about him'" (Matt. 27:19). Dreams were considered a source of divine communication, as we see from the beginning of Matthew, where Joseph makes many of his moves based on his dreams (taking after the Joseph in the Old Testament, of course). This verse provokes the imagination. Why Pilate's wife? What did she know about Jesus, if anything? Matthew puts the truth of Jesus's innocence in the mouth of this Gentile woman. Why? Where we might expect a response from Pilate, the text immediately turns to the machinations of the chief priests and the elders. Pilate charges ahead with the crucifixion with no evidence of listening to his wife. Sure, he makes a dramatic show of washing his hands of Jesus in verse 24, but he executes him anyway. Only Rome had the power to crucify in Jesus's time.

Matthew (and Mel Gibson, in his 2004 movie *The Passion of the Christ*) may try to convince us that "the people as a whole" called the blood of Jesus down onto themselves and their children (27:25), but do not be fooled. First, "the people as a whole" is clearly Matthean hyperbole, as we see in places like the Sermon on the Mount in the call to chop off one's hand or jab out one's eye or become a "eunuch." One has two options: understand that this is hyperbole or, like Origen, cut off one's actual genitals. Second,

217

we should learn from Pilate—although he did not carry out the execution physically, such that his toga remained white, God is not mocked. The order came from him, and he remains splattered with innocent blood, despite his PR machinations or reputation management maneuvers.

Wailing Women

Only Luke includes the story of the women who wail for Jesus as he carries his cross: "A great number of the people followed him, and among them were women who were beating their breasts and wailing for him" (23:27). Jesus indicates a difficult road ahead for the listeners: "Daughters of Jerusalem, do not weep for me, but weep for yourselves and for your children. For the days are surely coming when they will say, 'Blessed are the barren, and the wombs that never bore, and the breasts that never nursed'" (vv. 28–29). Recall our earlier treatment of women as mourners in antiquity: women's mourning functioned to protest injustice prophetically and express communal lament, and to serve as testimony to trauma. These wailing women have taken up that mantle in their own way.

Women at the Cross

When it comes to the subject of women in the Bible, the scene at the cross is exceedingly important. In Mark, we learn that at Jesus's arrest, just after his praying in the garden while the disciples sleep, "all of them deserted him and fled" (14:50). When the authorities took hold of the young man "wearing nothing but a linen cloth" who was following Jesus, "he left the linen cloth and ran off naked" (vv. 51–52). None of the twelve male disciples ever reappears in the narrative. Many women appear, though, both named and unnamed, starting with the women in Mark 15:40–41: "There were also women looking on from a distance; among them were Mary Magdalene, and Mary the mother of James the younger and of Joses, and Salome. These used to follow him and provided for him when he was in Galilee; and there were many other women who had come up with him to Jerusalem." So many women. Even in the next scene, when Joseph of Arimathea places Jesus's body in a tomb, the author highlights the women's presence: "Mary

Magdalene and Mary the mother of Joses saw where it had been laid" (15:47, my trans.).

Matthew's version is close to Mark's, though he reverses the order and names three women present at the cross: Mary Magdalene, Mary the mother of James and Joseph, and the mother of the sons of Zebedee (Matt. 27:55–56). At 27:61 Mary Magdalene and "the other Mary" sit opposite the tomb as Joseph finishes putting the body in the tomb.

In Luke's version, it is not only women who are at the cross, and none of the women there are named. We hear this instead: "But all his acquaintances, including the women who had followed him from Galilee, stood at a distance, watching these things" (Luke 23:49). Then, we find Joseph laying the body in the tomb, but Luke has two differences: (1) the women are not named: "The women who had come with him from Galilee followed, and they saw the tomb and how his body was laid" (23:55); and (2) they come back to the tomb a second time: "Then they returned, and prepared spices and ointments" (v. 56).

John's passion narrative is quite distinct from the Synoptics. While in the Synoptics women look on "from a distance," in John four women (or three, if you think that Jesus's aunt is also named Mary) are right at the foot of the cross: "Meanwhile, standing near the cross of Jesus were his mother, and his mother's sister, Mary the wife of Clopas, and Mary Magdalene" (19:25). While Mary Magdalene is the constant across the versions, only John has Jesus's mother at the cross, and only John names the other women standing at the cross (the other two women are not named in the other Gospels). Jesus next gives birth to the church as he brings them together as a household of family members: "When Jesus saw his mother and the disciple whom he loved standing beside her, he said to his mother, 'Woman, here is your son.' Then he said to the disciple, 'Here is your mother.' And from that hour the disciple took her into his own home" (19:26–27; actually, the word "home" does not appear in the Greek; the last phrase is "what was his own," mirroring John 1:11). The passage ends with Jesus "bestowing the Spirit" (*paredōken to pneuma*, 19:30; not "gave up the ghost," as the KJV says) upon the church born at the foot of the cross (for a more detailed explanation of this translation choice, consult Clark-Soles 2016, 130). It is John's version of Acts 2, if you like.

As in the Synoptics, Joseph of Arimathea (and, in John only, also Nicodemus) lays Jesus's body in the tomb, but unlike the Synoptics, no women look on, and no one prepares spices.

Women at the Empty Tomb and the Resurrection

Women appear in the resurrection stories in all four Gospels. Because no two of the four accounts are exactly alike, I separate them out by each Gospel to shine a closer light on the details. When one studies each resurrection text in the context of the Gospel in which it is found, one can see that each account furthers the goals of that individual Gospel as it seeks to shape the reader spiritually. That kind of analysis lies beyond the scope of this project, but I honor the fact all the same by breaking them out separately here. Again, the reader will be well served by consulting Aland's *Synopsis of the Four Gospels*. We begin with Mark because it is the basis for Matthew and Luke. John, as usual, takes its own path.

Mark

Mark 16:1–8 describes Mary Magdalene, Mary the mother of James, and Salome going to the tomb to anoint Jesus's dead body with spices. They find the stone rolled away and enter the tomb, where they encounter a young man dressed in a white robe. This young man announces the resurrection and commissions the women to go tell the disciples that Jesus is going ahead of them to meet them in Galilee. The Gospel of Mark concludes by telling us that the women fled the tomb in "terror and amazement" and "they said nothing to anyone, for they were afraid" (16:8).

Scholars have long puzzled over this cryptic ending of Mark. So has the church, apparently, since over time the ending was added to and then added to again (the so-called Shorter Ending of Mark and Longer Ending of Mark, both of which your study Bible marks off with brackets). The ending at 16:8 is most likely a technique used by Mark for rhetorical and theological purposes in keeping with the way he has told the whole narrative (for an accessible treatment of the ending of Mark, consult Rhoads, Dewey, and Michie 2012, esp. 9–11 and 90–96). It is a dramatic, suspenseful ending that disorients the reader as she asks, "Then how did the story get told?" The answer, of course, is that the women did overcome their fear and did tell. And the story has been told and retold ever since.

Mark's community, the original audience, was likely suffering persecution and was tempted, like the women in that moment, to keep silent in the face of fear. Thus, they were faced with a choice as a community and as individuals when they heard this ending— what choice would they make? To continue the story or to save their skin? They are certainly not the last Christians who have had to answer that question.

Matthew

Matthew's version in 28:1–10 is different in a number of ways. First, only two women appear, Mary Magdalene and "the other Mary." Then, there is no mention of plans to anoint the body, as in Mark, and instead of a man there is an angel who is part of a dramatic scene that also involves an earthquake and guards. This radiant angel announces the resurrection but also invites the women to come and see the place where Jesus lay, which is different from Mark. The angel then commissions the women both to tell the disciples to meet Jesus in Galilee and to be the first ones to announce, "He has been raised from the dead."

Unlike the women in Mark, these women joyfully run to tell the disciples. On their way, Jesus meets and greets them. They take hold of his feet, and they worship him. Then Jesus tells them, as the angel already did (Matthew often doubles Mark's material), to send the disciples up to Galilee where they, too, might have the opportunity to see the risen Christ as the women have. These two Marys, the first to see the risen Christ and be entrusted with the proclamation of his resurrection, do go and tell the disciples. The disciples listen to them and proceed to Galilee, where they, too, get to see the risen Christ.

Luke

In Luke, the women (they are unnamed) who had prepared the spices return with them and enter the tomb. They are "perplexed" by the missing body, but soon "two men in dazzling clothes" (not one man nor an angel) appear (24:4). Using different words than

221

those found in Mark and Matthew, they announce that Jesus is risen. Furthermore, they remind the women of what Jesus taught them before in Galilee, thus showing that Luke assumes the women were serious disciples of Jesus taught by him: "Remember how he told you, while he was still in Galilee, that the Son of Man must be handed over to sinners, and be crucified, and on the third day rise again" (vv. 6–7). Luke has repeatedly identified the women as those who had followed Jesus in and from Galilee by now. That they were an established part of his followers, not an occasional exception, is made clear by Luke's repetition in this matter.

Like all good students, when the teacher reminds them, "Then they remembered his words, and returning from the tomb, they told all this to the eleven and to all the rest" (24:8–9). The women announce the resurrection to an audience wider than the disciples, presumably including both males and females, in typical Lukan fashion. Notice that they are not instructed to tell the disciples to meet Jesus in Galilee, because in Luke–Acts the disciples are to stay in Jerusalem for Pentecost, the story that comes to pass in Acts 1–2.

Only at the very end of this story do we get the names of the women who were the first to announce the resurrection, but the named women are not the only ones, according to Luke: "Mary Magdalene, Joanna, Mary the mother of James, and the other women with them (*hai loipai syn autais*)" (24:10). Women and more women. They go and share the news with "the apostles."

Then comes the discouraging experience that I am sure all female pastors, if not all women in general, have experienced when they proclaim what they know to be true: "But these words seemed to them [the apostles] an idle tale, and they did not believe them" (Luke 24:11; for anyone who relates to this experience, I highly recommend Karoline Lewis's book *She: Five Keys to Unlock the Power of Women in Ministry*). Peter insists on running to the tomb to see and finds that he could have just stayed home and believed them. A version of the story is repeated on the road to Emmaus: "Moreover, some women of our group astounded us. They were at the tomb early this morning, and when they did not find his body there, they came back and told us that they had indeed seen a vision of angels who said that he was alive. Some of those who were with us went to the tomb and found it just as the women had said; but they did not see him" (24:22–24). We the readers get to save ourselves the trouble of frantically scurrying about and instead believe

222

the testimony of Luke's original female witnesses to the resurrection who preach the word down to this day every time a reader or congregation reads this Scripture.

John

Mary Magdalene appears as one of the women at the tomb in each of the Synoptics, though she acts in concert with other women in those accounts. In John, she stands alone, a central figure who has profound experiences with angels and Jesus himself and becomes the Apostle to the Apostles. I have written at length about Mary Magdalene elsewhere, and space precludes my providing such detail here (consult Clark-Soles 2019, "In the End: Magdalene"). In 20:1–2 she comes alone to the tomb, sees the stone rolled away, and runs to tell Peter and the Beloved Disciple (who is never named in the Gospel of John). Verses 3–10 recount the race to the tomb by the disciples, who then simply return home. But Mary stays, weeping, reminding us of another Mary lamenting her brother Lazarus, over whom Jesus himself wept. When she looks in the tomb she sees two angels (not one angel, not one man, and not two men), and she speaks with them.

Mary then has a dialogue with Jesus in which he calls her by her name, she recognizes him, and they are reunited. He commissions her to give this message to his "brothers and sisters" (*adelphoi*). Typically the NRSV translates this word inclusively because it is the word one uses when both men and women are present. Here it chooses just to say "brothers." I believe the translator has been overly influenced by reading the Synoptic accounts and has imported "disciples" and "apostles" into the Johannine text inappropriately.

In 20:18 Mary assumes her role as Apostle to the Apostles as she announces: "I have seen [*heōraka*] the Lord." Here, she uses the special past tense in Greek called the perfect, whose force is to mark action completed in the past that has ongoing effect in the present (it is more accurate to say that "John has her say this," since Mary Magdalene would not have spoken Greek, but Aramaic, like Jesus). She has seen in a way that changes her life, its direction, and her legacy, forever. If we hear her well through this gift of Scripture, if the text has its way with us, we too will be able to testify similarly after our encounter with her.

223

Figurative Women

In addition to the actual female characters who appear in the Gospels, we also find figurative women in parables who serve as lessons. For instance, Luke 15:1–7 depicts God as a shepherd who leaves the ninety-nine to go in search of the one who is lost. Luke then switches metaphors to compare God to a woman in search of a lost coin (vv. 8–10) who rejoices when the lost item/person is found. In Luke 18:1–8, Jesus tells a parable in which a widow who has been wronged exemplifies the kind of perseverance and prayerfulness to which Jesus calls his disciples.

Matthew 25, part of Matthew's Apocalyptic Discourse, contains three parables related to being prepared for the return of the Son of Man at the judgment. The first depicts ten virgins whose job it was to await the return of the bridegroom with his new bride. The wise women remained awake and tended to the light, while the foolish ones did not. Matthew 13:33 compares the kingdom of heaven to a baker-woman who mixes a little leaven and leavens the whole dough. She teaches us that a little faith goes a long way.

The Disciples across Gender

In John 16, Jesus associates the disciples with female characteristics, roles, and experiences. First, he depicts them as mourning, a role occupied by females. Second, he compares the disciples to a woman in labor:

> Very truly, I tell you, you will weep and mourn, but the world will rejoice; you will have pain, but your pain will turn into joy. When a woman is in labor, she has pain, because her hour has come. But when her child is born, she no longer remembers the anguish because of the joy of having brought a human being into the world. So you have pain now; but I will see you again, and your hearts will rejoice, and no one will take your joy from you. (16:20–22)

On the one hand, this is shocking for the first-century context where masculinity was clearly defined and pitted against femininity in a way that ridiculed "effeminate" men. On the other hand, it is not surprising insofar as John associates Jesus himself with female characteristics, roles, and experiences, as we will see in the next chapter. In addition, we recall from chapter 2, "God across Gender," that the Scriptures of our authors, the Old Testament, also present God with feminine characteristics.

Not Women *versus* Men, but Women *plus* Men

The fact that the Gospel writers often depict women as more insightful about Jesus than men has interested scholars immensely and generated much commentary (for discussions of this phenomenon in Mark, for instance, consult Malbon 1983; Rhoads, Michie, and Dewey 2012). Here I make only a few comments.

Historical evidence gives no reason to doubt that women were, in fact, leaders and followers in Jesus's ministry (even if one cannot prove the historicity of individual accounts—but that could be said, and indeed has been, of almost everything in the narratives). If the early church could have swept this fact under the rug and thereby made the nascent religion more "respectable," surely they would have. It is likely that the facts were so well known that they had to be included. In Jesus's era and Paul's, there were no church "offices" or ordained clergy. Leadership was charismatic, from the Greek word *charisma*, or gift. People led based on their spiritual giftedness (church offices appear in later New Testament texts and are treated in a later chapter).

From Mark's Suffering Servant to Luke's Justice-Bringing Prophet, each author is writing with a particular agenda to teach the reader about who Jesus is and why the reader should follow him. Each Gospel in its own way challenges our expectations and assumptions. So, for instance, Mark spends the first eight chapters showing us how stunningly powerful and successful Jesus is at every turn, such that we, the readers, are excited to sign on and enjoy him in this illustrious undertaking with all the concomitant status and power. But all of this grinds to a halt after 8:31 and we learn that, although he could have chosen self-aggrandizing power, true power lies in the way of the cross. It is ironic and unexpected. What could be more ironic, in fact, than a crucified Savior? In keeping with Mark's method, one finds that "insiders" (religious leaders,

225

the male disciples) do not understand who Jesus is, while "outsiders" (Gentiles, demons, women, a Roman soldier at the cross) do understand. If one is going to sign on with God, one's expectations, assumptions, and values are going to be turned upside down. Similarly, we have discussed the Great Reversal theme in Luke in which the lowly will be exalted and the exalted brought low; the hungry will be filled and rich sent away empty. Again, notions of power, including those related to gender, get turned on their head.

By focusing on women as exceptionally prominent and perceptive and present to Jesus, neither the Gospel writers nor I seek to "bash" males then or now. The stories that feature women, just like the stories that feature men, are meant to inform and inspire all readers of all genders to deeper discipleship, always keeping an eye out for the unexpected surprises.

The Lectionary

No woman discussed in this chapter is completely absent from either the Revised Common Lectionary (RCL) or the Roman Lectionary (RL). Many of them are included in at least one weekday reading for both traditions. Encouragingly, most of them are included in at least one Sunday reading for both traditions. I focus my comments in this section on the RL and RCL Sunday lectionaries.

Although most of the women in Jesus's ministry are included in the Sunday lectionaries, a few are left out. For example, Jesus's figurative language in which he refers to the disciples as women in John 16:21–22 is not included as a Sunday reading for either the RL or the RCL. The RL does not include the "bent-over woman" from Luke 13:10–17 in Sunday readings, and the RCL does not include Matthew's genealogy of Jesus—and thus the four women mentioned in it—as a Sunday reading. Neither the RL nor the RCL includes a Sunday reading of Matthew's version of the woman who anoints Jesus (26:6–13; in fact, the RL has no weekday reading for this version of the story either), and the RL Sunday schedule also omits John's version of the story, in which it is Mary of Bethany who anoints Jesus (12:1–11).

226   The anointing accounts and the case of the women in Matthew's genealogy raise another issue: optional readings. While the RL lists Matthew 1:1–25 as a reading for Christmas: Vigil Mass of

Years ABC, this longer reading is only optional; some may choose to read only Matthew 1:18–25. A similar but more problematic situation occurs with the anointing accounts told in Mark 14, Matthew 26, John 12, and Luke 7. Recall that neither the RL nor the RCL includes Matthew's version as a Sunday reading. The RL also omits John's version (although the RCL includes it on the Monday of Holy Week for Years ABC and the 5th Sunday in Lent during Year C). Both the RL and the RCL call for Mark's version; however, it is an optional reading for both lectionaries, since both allow for the shorter Mark 15:1–39 to be read. It is in Mark's and Matthew's versions that Jesus calls for the proclamation of the woman's anointing deed, but these are the very two versions that might never be read liturgically. As Marjorie Procter-Smith writes:

> She performs a significant and readily recognizable liturgical act, that of anointing. And Jesus' promise to her is a liturgical one, involving proclamation and remembering. Yet there is no trace of this woman and her liturgical action in our liturgical commemorations of the passion of Jesus. Our lectionaries largely ignore her, our liturgies of anointing do not remember her, our sanctoral cycles confuse her with Mary of Bethany or Mary Magdalene. The church has not kept Jesus' promise to this woman. (2000, 28)

This issue, problematized by omissions and optional readings, is further exacerbated by the fact that both lectionaries call for Luke's anointing woman to be included in a Sunday reading. This means that, unless we choose to proclaim the woman of Mark 14 and Matthew 26, Christians are more likely to be exposed to a version of this story featuring a woman who is a "sinner" than a woman performing a prophetic act upon Jesus. Consider the words of Ruth Fox, who focuses her critique on the RL:

> One might ask if any account of the anointing of Jesus by a woman is familiar to Catholics. Of course, the sinful and penitent woman of Luke 7:36–50, who washes Jesus's feet with her tears, is presented on the 11th Sunday in Ordinary Time in Year C (#94) and every year on Thursday of the 24th week in Ordinary Time (#446). The lectionary does not give us the same familiarity with Mark's and Matthew's versions where a woman, not identified as a sinner, assumes the role of a prophet in anointing Jesus on the head. It is of this woman that Jesus promised (in vain?)

"I assure you, wherever the good news is proclaimed throughout the world, what she did will be spoken of as her memorial."
(1999, 363)

Another optional reading leaves a woman potentially unmen-
tioned in the Catholic Sunday liturgy. The RL and the RCL call for
Mark 5:21–43 on the 13th Sunday in Ordinary Time of Year B and
Proper 8 (13) of the season after Pentecost of Year B, respectively.
The RL allows, however, for the story of the woman with unceas-
ing bleeding to be omitted and for Mark 5:21–24, 35–43 to be read
instead. Fox explains that, if Mark 5:21–43 is not read in Year B,
"it is never heard by the Sunday assembly. Matthew's and Mark's
complete version of this story may be heard on a weekday . . . but
Luke's version is omitted altogether in Year C" (1999, 362). Still
other optional readings may keep certain women from our corporate worship: the RCL calls for Sunday readings including Anna
(Luke 2:36–38), but she is only included in an optional RL reading
during Year B, Sunday in Octave of Christmas: Holy Family. The
high priest's female servant in Mark 14:66–72 is only included in
the RL and RCL as part of lengthy, optional Sunday readings of
Mark 14:1–15:47 (as with Mark's woman who anoints Jesus) and
will be omitted from any reading (Sunday or weekday) in either
lectionary if the choice is not made to read this longer option. The
same situation occurs in the RL and the RCL with regard to the
female servant who questions Peter in Matthew 26 and Luke 22.

This brings up yet another issue: a number of women are
included only in very long readings, and while I recommend that
the longer reading is chosen precisely as a way to include more
women, such long readings have a down side. If a woman is *only*
included in the lectionary as part of a very long reading, it is not
very likely that the woman will receive any sort of extended attention in teaching or preaching. To be sure, her inclusion in the reading is better than her exclusion, and even just exposing parishioners
to the presence of women in these narratives is beneficial; however, it would be better if these women were included in shorter
readings that would allow their presence to be magnified. Thus,
the gate-guarding woman who questions Peter in John 18:16–17
228 is only included in the RCL and RL as Good Friday readings for
Years ABC, but the reading called for in both lectionaries is two
entire chapters: John 18:1–19:42. Pilate's wife (Matt. 27:19) is

included, for both Catholics and Protestants, in a reading of either Matthew 26:14–27:66 or Matthew 27:11–54 (RCL: Year A, Lent, Liturgy of the Passion; RL: Year A, Palm Sunday Mass), both quite long. The wailing women in Luke's account of Jesus's crucifixion face the same plight: their mention in Luke 23:27–29 gets swallowed up in either reading called for by the RCL and the RL: Luke 22:14–23:56 or 23:1–49 (RCL: Year C, Lent, Liturgy of the Passion; RL: Year C, Palm Sunday Mass). The references to Jesus's female followers being present at his cross and tomb in Matthew, Mark, Luke, and John also get included only in very long Sunday or holiday readings of each Gospel. (A shorter RCL Sunday reading of Matt. 27:57–66 references Mary Magdalene and "the other Mary" at Jesus's tomb, but this is only an optional reading on Holy Saturday of Years ABC.)

One final issue pertaining to women from Jesus's ministry in the lectionaries: for some of these women who are included in the lectionaries, parts of their stories are left out. For example, both the RL and the RCL include Mary's visit to Elizabeth (Luke 1:39–45) in the Sunday readings. Both exclude from Sunday readings the angel's reference to Elizabeth in 1:13, Elizabeth's conceiving and proclamation of God's faithfulness in 1:24–25, and Elizabeth giving birth to John in 1:57–66. The RL (Years ABC, 3rd Sunday of Lent) provides an optional Sunday reading of the Samaritan woman's story in John 4:5–42 that includes the entire account, but it also allows the story to be sliced up into 4:5–15, 19b–26, 39a, 40–42. Among other details, this omits the woman's apostolic role in 4:29–30, 39. The RL similarly calls for the story of Mary, Martha, and Lazarus in John to be read either in full on the 5th Sunday of Lent, Years ABC, or to be read only in part (11:3–7, 17, 20–27, 33b–45) on that day.

Conclusion

In this chapter, we have addressed some well-known biblical women. We have reintroduced some of these figures from fresh perspectives using a variety of interpretive methods, exemplifying the potential benefits of reading texts from new angles with new methods and questions. For example, Catholic feminist scholar Sandra Schneiders demonstrates how the Samaritan woman functions not simply as an individual character, but also as symbolic of

229

Samaria itself as it negotiated its relationship to Israel. Moreover, we have presented insights from the growing body of scholars who represent more global voices beyond North America and Europe. We showcased examples from Jean Kim and Leticia Guardiola-Sáenz regarding the woman accused of adultery, thus witnessing how the interpretation of the text might be illuminated by readings placed in conversation with a Korean or Mexican American borderland context. The broader goal is to familiarize ourselves with a variety of scholarly readings available today that help us gain new insights into the texts and how they apply to the life of all Christian discipleship today. We have lifted up women who have been ignored by or inadequately presented in the lectionary.

We have explored the ways that the Bible moves across gender (as when the disciples are depicted as women in labor or God is depicted as a woman diligently and tirelessly seeking that which is lost). We have drawn upon scholarship about the status of women's lives in antiquity and the early church in order to understand more fully the witness of the women in Jesus's life and ministry and the early Christian communities implied by the Gospel texts. Roman Palestine, like the rest of the Roman Empire, functioned according to a system of patriarchy with clear cultural expectations around gender. Knowing such information matters if we are to derive fuller meaning from our Scriptures regarding the ways they reflect or resist their cultural contexts.

I imagine that every reader, regardless of gender, relates to some woman in the Gospels. These women can serve as models for us, and they can help us raise good questions. What do faithfulness and trust look like? What does courage look like? What does justice look like? Fear? Leadership? Hope? Healing? Salvation?

The women in Jesus's ministry defy categorization. One could try to group them in certain categories (mothers, those healed, those who minister, those ministered to), but invariably, the categories are contrived and do not account for all of the women. Or, one could treat the women in each canonical Gospel plus Acts. But some women appear in more than one Gospel, and, besides, they would not all fit into one chapter. We find women behind the scenes, women in the forefront; women operating in traditional roles, women breaking the mold; women barely hanging on, alone and on the margins, and women thriving in community. There is no way to categorize all of the women. Like them, modern women also do not fit into neat categories.

It is a gift to encounter extraordinary women who challenge us to be more, do more, expect more; however, that can also feel exhausting and make one feel like one is not enough. Thus, it is also encouraging to see women going about their daily life without fanfare (like the story of the widow's mite or the woman sweeping her floor). These women had little or no access to power, so they had to improvise to get what they and their children needed. Perhaps *one* faithful way for some contemporary women to honor their legacy and their struggle is to don mantles of leadership and assume positions of power that allow these women to create communal structures dedicated to the flourishing of all people, not just certain groups. These women did not have any such choices; some of us do.

For instance, we might now ask about "missing" women. Does the prodigal son have no mother and no sisters? Where is Peter's wife? We see his mother-in-law, but never his wife. Paul and the Gospels mention that he has a wife. In fact, where are *any* of the male disciples' wives? Were none of the other disciples married? Taking special care to read so closely as to notice the "invisible" women gives us practice in forming skills and habits that may transfer to living as disciples in the world, paying attention to those in danger of remaining invisible and, therefore, excluded or underserved in a variety of ways. This task applies to our teaching and preaching in corporate worship: we must be intentional to include women and emphasize their presence in Jesus's ministry at least by choosing longer readings, choosing optional readings, and choosing to point out the presence of women in these stories.

Some of the women in dire straits in the Gospels appear alone and largely unsupported. On the other hand, women who thrive are in relationship with others. The church does well, then, when it creates opportunities for people to form kinship connections and support one another.

Women minister (*diakoneō*) in the Gospels (and elsewhere in the New Testament, as discussed in other chapters). They are ministers. The only other characters who are said to "minister" in the Gospels besides women are the angels and Jesus. Jesus calls all followers to minister, but in the narratives, no male appears doing

231

so. The women exemplify the leadership to which Jesus calls all disciples.

This leadership is servant leadership. It is strength through vulnerability. It is powerful but not power-hungry. The word that means "to minister," *diakoneō*, also means "to serve." The one noun form in Greek, *diakonos*, is translated with three different English words: deacon, minister, and servant. Do not fall into the trap of thinking that when the word applies to a male it means "minister" or "deacon," but when it applies to a female it must mean "servant" or "deaconess." Beware of anyone who claims such—they are either uninformed or disingenuous in this matter.

Jesus calls all readers to servant leadership, which he knows to be countercultural (then and now): "The kings of the Gentiles lord it over them; and those in authority over them are called benefactors. But not so with you; rather the greatest among you must become like the youngest, and the leader like one who serves" (Luke 22:25–26). He asks them, in effect, to imitate him, declaring, "I am among you as one who serves" (22:27). The women in the Gospels understand and model Christian ministry. They help us to discern our own vocational calls as we align ourselves fully with the gospel of Jesus Christ.

Recommended Resources

Aland, Kurt. 1993. *Synopsis of the Four Gospels*. 10th ed. Stuttgart: United Bible Societies.

Aland, Kurt, and Barbara Aland. 1995. *The Text of the New Testament: An Introduction to the Critical Editions and to the Theory and Practice of Modern Textual Criticism*. Translated by Erroll F. Rhodes. 2nd ed. Grand Rapids: Wm. B. Eerdmans Publishing Co.

Belenky, Mary Field, Blythe McVicker Clinchy, Nancy Rule Goldberger, and Jill Mattuck Tarule. 1997. *Women's Ways of Knowing: The Development of Self, Voice, and Mind*. 10th anniv. ed. New York: Basic Books.

Carey, Greg. 2009. *Sinners: Jesus and His Earliest Followers*. Waco, TX: Baylor University Press.

Chittister, Joan. 2010. *The Gift of Years: Growing Older Gracefully*. New York: BlueBridge.

Clark-Soles, Jaime. 2010. *Engaging the Word: The New Testament and the Christian Believer*. Louisville, KY: Westminster John Knox Press.

———. 2016. *Reading John for Dear Life: A Spiritual Walk with the Fourth Gospel*. Louisville, KY: Westminster John Knox Press.

Davies, W. D., and Dale C. Allison. 2004. *The Gospel according to Saint Matthew*. Volume 2, *Matthew 8–18*. International Critical Commentary. London: T&T Clark.

Derrett, J. Duncan M. 1963. "Law in the New Testament: The Story of the Woman Taken in Adultery." *New Testament Studies* 10:1–26.

Fitzmyer, Joseph A. 1982. *The Gospel according to Luke I–IX*. Anchor Bible 28A. New York: Doubleday.

Fox, Ruth. 1999. "Women in the Bible and the Lectionary." Pages 359–67 in *Remembering the Women*. Compiled and annotated by J. Frank Henderson. Chicago: Liturgy Training Publications.

Guardiola-Sáenz, Leticia A. 2002. "Border-Crossing and Its Redemptive Power in John 7.53–8.11: A Cultural Reading of Jesus and the *Accused*." Pages 129–52 in *John and Postcolonialism: Travel, Space and Power*. Edited by Musa W. Dube and Jeffrey L. Staley. London: Sheffield Academic Press.

Gurian, Michael. 2013. *The Wonder of Aging: A New Approach to Embracing Life after Fifty*. New York: Atria.

Hochschild, Arlie, and Anne Machung. 2012. *The Second Shift: Working Families and the Revolution at Home*. Rev. ed. New York: Penguin Group.

Keith, Chris. 2009. *The Pericope Adulterae, the Gospel of John, and the Literacy of Jesus*. New Testament Tools, Studies, and Documents 38. Leiden: Brill.

Kim, Jean K. 2002. "Adultery or Hybridity? Reading John 7.53–8.11 from a Postcolonial Context." Pages 111–28 in *John and Postcolonialism: Travel, Space and Power*. Edited by Musa W. Dube and Jeffrey L. Staley. London: Sheffield Academic Press.

Levine, Amy-Jill. 2006. *The Misunderstood Jew: The Church and the Scandal of the Jewish Jesus*. New York: HarperOne.

———. 2012. "Gospel of Matthew." Pages 465–77 in *Women's Bible Commentary*. Edited by Carol A. Newsom, Sharon H. Ringe, and Jacqueline E. Lapsley. 3rd ed. Louisville, KY: Westminster John Knox Press.

233

Lewis, Karoline M. 2016. *She: Five Keys to Unlock the Power of Women in Ministry*. Nashville: Abingdon Press.

Loader, William. 2010. *Sexuality in the New Testament: Understanding the Key Texts*. Louisville, KY: Westminster John Knox Press.

Moss, Candida. 2017. "Mark and Matthew." Pages 275–301 in *The Bible and Disability: A Commentary*. Edited by Sarah J. Melcher, Mikeal C. Parsons, and Amos Yong. Waco, TX: Baylor University Press.

Procter-Smith, Marjorie. 2000. *In Her Own Rite: Constructing Feminist Liturgical Tradition*. 2nd ed. Cape May, NJ: OSL Publications.

Rhoads, David, Joanna Dewey, and Donald Michie. 2012. *Mark as Story: An Introduction to the Narrative of a Gospel*. 3rd ed. Minneapolis: Fortress Press.

Rohr, Richard. 2011. *Falling Upward: A Spirituality for the Two Halves of Life*. San Francisco: Jossey-Bass.

Schneiders, Sandra S. 2003. *Written That You May Believe: Encountering Jesus in the Fourth Gospel*. Rev. and exp. ed. New York: Crossroad.

Schüssler Fiorenza, Elisabeth. 1994. *In Memory of Her: A Feminist Theological Reconstruction of Christian Origins*. 10th anniv. ed. New York: Crossroad.

Thistlethwaite, Susan Brooks. 2015. *Women's Bodies as Battlefield: Christian Theology and the Global War on Women*. Basingstoke, UK: Palgrave Macmillan.

Throckmorton, Burton H. 1992. *Gospel Parallels: A Comparison of the Synoptic Gospels, New Revised Standard Version*. 5th ed. Nashville: Thomas Nelson.

CHAPTER 8

Jesus across Gender

The historical Jesus of Nazareth was born a Jew in a tiny strip of
land in the Middle East that Christians now call the Holy Land,
somewhere around 4 BCE. According to our authors, his pronouns
were he, him, and his. He was, though, so much more than a mere
man, and the authors of the New Testament (not to mention postbiblical authors) recruited their imaginations and cultural knowledge and mystical visions and scriptural knowledge and, with the
help of the Holy Spirit, tried to convey to us a little something about
this Jesus who had so captivated them, to the point that nothing else
mattered nearly as much. As part of that effort, they taught us that
the full meaning of who Jesus is cannot be contained by language
tied to a single gender.

In this chapter, I highlight some of the ways the New Testament authors pushed beyond gender in order to introduce us
to a Jesus whose identity will never fully be defined or contained
by human language. In what follows I present Jesus as Woman
Wisdom, Jesus as Mourner, Jesus as Lifebearer, Jesus as Nurser,
and Jesus as Mother Bird. Then, after a discussion of the lectionaries, I conclude with a note on implications for Christian
discipleship.

Jesus as Woman Wisdom

The figure of Wisdom appears prominently in the Old Testament and Apocrypha. If you are unfamiliar with the expanse and depth of Woman Wisdom, I refer you to chapter 4 in this book, "Women Creating," and recommend that you start with the following biblical passages that influenced our Gospel writers: Proverbs 8; Sirach 24:1–9; Wisdom of Solomon 9:1–3; Baruch 3:9–4:4; and Proverbs 1.

Wisdom is a female character. She is the first of all God's creations: "The Lord created me at the beginning of his work, the first of his acts of long ago. Ages ago I was set up, at the first, before the beginning of the earth" (Prov. 8:22–23). She is eternal and exists at creation alongside God: "When he established the heavens, I was there, when he drew a circle on the face of the deep, when he made firm the skies above, when he established the fountains of the deep, when he assigned to the sea its limit, so that the waters might not transgress his command, when he marked out the foundations of the earth, then I was beside him" (Prov. 8:27–30a). Sirach 24:9 also shares the image of preexistent, eternal Wisdom: "From eternity, in the beginning, he created me, and for eternity I shall not cease to exist" (RSV).

In addition to being preexistent, Wisdom helps God create the world, "like a master worker." Finally, she and God dwell in intimate relationship, as Wisdom declares: "I was daily his delight, rejoicing before him always" (Prov. 8:30).

God sends Wisdom to dwell with Israel: "Then the Creator of all things gave me a commandment, and the one who created me assigned a place for my tent [skēnē]. And he said, "Make your dwelling [kataskēnoō] in Jacob, and in Israel receive your inheritance. . . . In the holy tabernacle [skēnē] I ministered before him, and so I was established in Zion" (Sir. 24:8, 10 RSV; emphasis added). Wisdom calls to people: "Wisdom cries out in the street; in the squares she raises her voice. At the busiest corner she cries out; at the entrance of the city gates she speaks: 'How long, O simple ones, will you love being simple?'" (Prov. 1:20–22). Wisdom doesn't just dwell with Israel, she also desires to teach them to live according to her ways. This offer is imagined as food: "She has slaughtered her animals, she has mixed her wine, she has also set her table. . . . 'Come, eat of my bread and drink of the wine I have mixed. Lay aside immaturity, and live, and walk in the way of insight'" (Prov. 9:2, 5–6).

But the people reject her, and because of this, Wisdom turns from them. Woman Wisdom typically suffers this fate: she tries hard to teach human beings, but we tend to love folly and scoff at wisdom and reject what she has to offer, to our own detriment.

> Because I have called and you refused,
>   have stretched out my hand and no one heeded,
> and because you have ignored all my counsel
>   and would have none of my reproof,
> I also will laugh at your calamity;
>   I will mock when panic strikes you,
> when panic strikes you like a storm,
>   and your calamity comes like a whirlwind,
>   when distress and anguish come upon you.
> Then they will call upon me, but I will not answer;
>   they will seek me diligently, but will not find me.
> *(Prov. 1:24–28)*

The rejection of Woman Wisdom is imagined as eating different food: "therefore they shall eat the fruit of their way and be sated with their own devices" (Prov. 1:31).

Anyone familiar with the prologue to the Gospel of John will recognize that Jesus is there depicted as Woman Wisdom. As the Word, he is preexistent and he helps to create the world: "He was in the beginning with God. All things came into being through him, and without him not one thing came into being." (John 1:2–3). Like Wisdom, Jesus comes to his own people, and he dwells and tabernacles among them. John 1:14, echoing Sirach, says that the Word became flesh and *tabernacled (skēnoō)* among us. Sadly, It's rare to find an English translation that translates the word "tabernacled" here; instead, one gets banal words like "dwelled" or "lived." But the author is drawing upon Wisdom imagery to tell us who Jesus is.

Like Wisdom, Jesus offers food. The real goal in discipleship is to hunger and thirst for the metaphorical food and drink—wisdom and the will of God—as Jesus models for the disciples: "But he said to them, 'I have food to eat that you do not know about.' So the disciples said to one another, 'Surely no one has brought him something to eat?' Jesus said to them, 'My food is to do the will of him who sent me and to complete his work'" (John 4:32–34).

Jesus is also rejected like God's Wisdom. John's prologue tells us that Jesus "came unto what was his own, yet his own people did not receive him" (John 1:11, my trans.). Jesus, as the Word of God, tries to reveal God to God's people, yet they continually reject Wisdom, finally to their own detriment: "Yet you refuse to come to me to have life. . . . But I know that you do not have the love of God in you. I have come in my Father's name, and you do not accept me" (John 5:40, 42–43).

In Proverbs 1:28 we found that, as a result of the rejection, Wisdom declares that these people will seek and not find her, words echoed by Jesus, for example, in John 7:32–36:

> The Pharisees heard the crowd muttering such things about him, and the chief priests and Pharisees sent temple police to arrest him. Jesus then said, "I will be with you a little while longer, and then I am going to him who sent me. You will search for me, but you will not find me; and where I am, you cannot come." The Jews said to one another, "Where does this man intend to go that we will not find him? Does he intend to go to the Dispersion among the Greeks and teach the Greeks? What does he mean by saying, 'You will search for me and you will not find me' and 'Where I am, you cannot come'?"

Or consider John 8:21–24:

> Again he said to them, "I am going away, and you will search for me, but you will die in your sin. Where I am going, you cannot come." Then the Jews said, "Is he going to kill himself? Is that what he means by saying, 'Where I am going, you cannot come'?" He said to them, "You are from below, I am from above; you are of this world, I am not of this world. I told you that you would die in your sins, for you will die in your sins unless you believe that I am he."

Like Wisdom, Jesus calls out to people but can be difficult for humans to follow.

Seeing Jesus as Wisdom suggests he has feminine as well as masculine aspects. Focusing upon the Gospel of John, Martin Scott argues, "The point of John's Wisdom Christology is precisely that Jesus Sophia is not mere man, but rather the incarnation of both

238

the male and the female expressions of the divine" (1992, 172). Both masculine and feminine expressions are manifested in Jesus.

Like John, Matthew presents Jesus as Woman Wisdom. In Matthew 11:19, Jesus refers to himself as Woman Wisdom: "The Son of Man came eating and drinking, and they say, 'Look, a glutton and a drunkard, a friend of tax collectors and sinners!' Yet wisdom is vindicated by her deeds." Fools scoff at Wisdom in every century, no matter what form she takes.

Matthew 11:28–30 draws upon many of the themes presented in the verses above—Jesus/Wisdom invites us to come and learn that a life of folly is far more difficult than a life of wisdom: "Come to me, all you that are weary and are carrying heavy burdens, and I will give you rest. Take my yoke upon you, and learn from me; for I am gentle and humble in heart, and you will find rest for your souls. For my yoke is easy, and my burden is light." Jesus's words echo Wisdom's call.

Like any good parent, Wisdom always wants what's best for us, what makes for a life of integrity and wholeness. After all, in Proverbs 8 she tells us that from the beginning she delighted in the human race, and she extends this invitation: "And now, my children, listen to me: happy are those who keep my ways" (8:31–32).

Matthew puts a saying of Wisdom on Jesus's lips. Colleen Conway underscores the association of Jesus with Woman Wisdom in Matthew—which she refers to as a "gender transmutation"—by pointing out that "a saying that is attributed to 'the Wisdom of God' in Luke (11:49) is a direct quote from Jesus in Matthew (23:34)" (2008, 115–16). Compare the two verses:

> Therefore also the Wisdom of God said, "I will send them prophets and apostles, some of whom they will kill and persecute." (Luke 11:49)

> Therefore I send you prophets, sages, and scribes, some of whom you will kill and crucify, and some you will flog in your synagogues and pursue from town to town. (Matt. 23:34)

In both passages, Jesus is critiquing the current religious establishment on a broad range of issues. These verses in particular feature the leaders' rejection of commissioned prophetic agents. In Luke, Jesus quotes the "Wisdom of God" as the commissioning agent. In

239

Matthew, Jesus *is* the commissioning agent, functionally serving the same role as the Wisdom of God.

Scholarship and liturgical resources are now available for those who would introduce congregations to or deepen their knowledge of Woman Wisdom in the Bible, including the ways that Jesus himself is depicted as such. I've included sample resources in the bibliography, and I refer the reader to chapter 4 in this book, "Women Creating," where I discuss Woman Wisdom as well.

Jesus as Mourner

We observed in chapter 2, "God across Gender," that God is associated with lament. Recall that mourning was a job professionally assigned to women and that the role served multiple functions for the community. That is to say, people associated the activity of mourning with women, so God's mourning characterizes God with a female activity.

Jesus, too, is depicted as one who laments. At Bethany, we find Mary crying (*klaiō*; John 11:33) and surrounded by wailers. Laconically, the author tells us: "Jesus wept" (*dakryō*; v. 35).

Jesus laments on the cross: "My God, my God, why have you forsaken me?" (Matt. 27:46). Hebrews recounts Jesus's crying intensely: "In the days of his flesh, Jesus offered up prayers and supplications, with loud cries and tears, to the one who was able to save him from death" (Heb. 5:7). Perhaps the author of Hebrews had in mind Jesus as depicted in Mark and Matthew.

Jesus's cry of dereliction from the cross may associate him with the feminine. Colleen Conway notes that the death of Jesus in the Gospel of Mark "complicates the picture of the manly Markan Jesus. . . . Especially at issue are Jesus' loud cries from the cross" (2008, 100–102). Quite against the ancient ideas of how "manly men" die, Jesus on the cross exemplifies the same witness as the mourning women whom we considered in chapter 2, "God across Gender." In a raw, uncensored, undignified eruption, he testifies to the pain of unjust or inexplicable suffering. He, an innocent person, is murdered by the Roman Empire, and there is no miraculous divine rescue. He cries out not only for himself, but also for all who know this reality, just as the mourning women do.

240

Jesus as Lifebearer

Jesus births life in the Gospel of John. Nicodemus is told that he must be born "from above" or born "again" (John 3:3). The Greek word *anōthen* can mean either, and the author uses that fact to great gain. Jesus means "from above" but Nicodemus understands it as "again," which, as he notes, does not make sense, at least not literally: "Nicodemus said to him, 'How can anyone be born after having grown old? Can one enter a second time into the mother's womb [*koilia*] and be born?'" (3:4). No, but Jesus is the ultimate mother who gives ultimate (eternal, abundant) life.

Furthermore, Jesus possesses a womb (*koilia*), out of which flows "rivers of living water": "On the last day of the festival, the great day, while Jesus was standing there, he cried out, 'Let anyone who is thirsty come to me, and let the one who believes in me drink, as the scripture has said, "Out of his womb [*koilia*] shall flow rivers of living water"'" (John 7:37–38, my trans.). That Jesus is a source of living water should not be surprising since the reader has already read John 4 by now, where Jesus offers the Samaritan living water. "The water that I will give will become in them a spring of water gushing up to eternal life" (4:13–14). What may be surprising is the gender-bending talk of male referents with wombs (leading some translators to erroneously translate *koilia* as "belly" here even though they translate it "womb" in the only other place where *koilia* occurs in John, at 3:4). The connections could not be more direct. In both John 3 and John 7, lifebearing and baptismal imagery go hand in hand.

The physical intermingled with the spiritual is a signature feature of John. In John 3 we read of being born of water and the Spirit. In John 4 we read of water and Spirit, as well as spiritual food ("to do the will of" God). In John 6, the physical and spiritual coalesce again when Jesus gives people physical bread and then identifies himself as the Bread from Heaven: "I am the living bread that came down from heaven. Whoever eats of this bread will live forever; and the bread that I will give for the life of the world is my flesh. . . . Those who eat my flesh and drink my blood abide in me, and I in them. Just as the living Father sent me, and I live because of the Father, so whoever eats me will live because of me" (6:51, 56–57).

241

Three points should be made here. First, nourishment and feeding are associated with women in antiquity. I say more about that below. Second, the passage is eucharistic. Third, there is a blurring of the lines between the body of Jesus and the body of the believer since the believer abides in Jesus and Jesus abides in them; such is the case between a mother and the child she bears.

Indeed, there is a kind of blurring in 7:38 as well. In the clause "out of his womb shall flow rivers of living water," the author indicates that the primary referent for the possessive pronoun *his* is Jesus. However, the pronoun could grammatically refer to "the one who believes," thus indicating that believers bring forth life as well. This blurring occurs over and over in John, since Jesus aims to be one with believers as Jesus and God are one (17:22). In John 16, Jesus depicts the disciples as women in labor (vv. 20–22).

The reader is thus perfectly set up for Jesus birthing the church from the cross in John 19. Notice the language of family and home and the fact that Jesus's own mother who birthed him is standing at the foot of the cross. "When Jesus saw his mother and the disciple whom he loved standing beside her, he said to his mother, 'Woman, here is your son.' Then he said to the disciple, 'Here is your mother.' And from that hour the disciple took her into his own home" (19:26–27). The blood and the water issuing forth from Jesus's side are part of the birth process. John 7:38 set us up for this moment. Now the biology of birth has come to include birth beyond biology as Jesus's biological mother becomes the mother of the Beloved Disciple and all disciples become siblings of Jesus and one another as those who have rooms in the Father's house (cf. John 14:2).

In John 19:30 Jesus "bestowed his Spirit" upon the church, inspiring it, letting it take its first breath, as every newborn must. And birth is wet and messy, with water and blood: "One of the soldiers pierced his side with a spear, and at once blood and water came out" (19:34). That we are supposed to slow down and pay special attention to the statement is signaled by the emphatic parenthetical intrusion on the part of the narrator: "(He who saw this has testified so that you also may believe. His testimony is true, and he knows that he tells the truth)" (vv. 34–35). Blood and water. Wombs and birth. Eucharist and baptism. Lifebearing Jesus birthing believers.

Jesus as Nurser

Just as a good mother doesn't give birth and consider her job done, but also nurses the child physically and spiritually, Jesus, too, does not just birth; he also nurses. We have discussed the ways the Old Testament associates God with a nursing mother, and we will find in the chapter on Paul that he and the apostles identify themselves as wet nurses. Feeding is a female activity, as L. Juliana M. Claassens compellingly argues in *The God Who Provides*: "Ultimately I argue that to think of God as the Mother who feeds may enrich our understanding of God's provision for God's children. My hope is that when worshipers again sing the words, 'Bread of heaven, feed me till I want no more,' they will embrace the richness a female understanding of the God who feeds brings" (2004, xix). Emphasizing that females did the feeding in antiquity and then showing God, Paul, and Jesus as those who feed may help readers gain a more expansive vision of the person and work of each, not to mention embracing more fully female imagery and actual females in ministerial roles.

In her essay "'In the Father's Bosom': Breastfeeding and Identity Formation in John's Gospel," Alicia Myers effectively demonstrates the connection between nursing and moral formation in antiquity. (I highly recommend her recent book, *Blessed among Women? Mothers and Motherhood in the New Testament*, which includes many of the insights from this essay.) Myers argues that in John the movement goes from Jesus nursing at God's bosom, thus imbibing God's virtue, to the disciples nursing at Jesus's breast, thus imbibing Jesus's godly virtue, to the disciples being sent to feed others (John 21) so that they, too, might ingest Jesus/God and thereby be one with them morally and otherwise.

When it comes to the ancients and breastfeeding, *you are what you eat!* Their view of conception, fetal development, and human development (including biological sex formation and moral development) differs considerably from our own. Since ideas of generation and moral development are closely tied, it is important to provide a bit of background, drawing upon Myers's work. According to Aristotle, in reproduction the male supplies seed, whereas the female merely provides menstrual blood. The male's seed "contained the moving spirit [*pneuma*] and pattern [*logos*]" that transformed the female's lifeless blood into life. "Heat from

243

the male seed 'concocted' the menstrual blood, thereby fashioning it into a child and enabling this blood to function as food for the growing fetus" (Myers 2013, 484).

> Since a child was understood to feed on the same substance that s/he did while in utero, s/he also partook of the seed present within the mixture. . . . Since a woman's blood could be made useful for the development and nourishment of a child only when concocted by the male seed, this seed was necessarily present in the milk produced by a woman. Moreover, for Aristotle, the male seed contained the animating [*pneuma*] and patterning [*logos*] that gave both life and form to an embryo. This same [*pneuma*] and [*logos*] continued to be communicated through a woman's breast milk and likewise continued its life-giving and formative functions in an infant. The source of the milk, therefore, necessarily contributed to the identity and character of the infant who nursed and was shaped by this nourishment. (Myers 2013, 486)

Myers notes that the philosopher Favorinus (2nd c. CE) insists that a woman should feed her own child rather than hire a wet nurse. If a wet nurse must be employed, then she must be of the highest virtue, since the breast milk directly shapes the child's moral character:

> Is the blood which is now in the breasts not the same that it was in the womb, merely because it has become white from abundant air and warmth? Is not wisdom of nature evident also in this, that as soon as the blood, the artificer, has fashioned the whole human body within its secret precincts, when the time for birth comes, it rises into the upper parts, is ready to cherish the first beginnings of life and of light, and supplies the newborn children with the familiar and accustomed food? Therefore it is believed not without reason that, just as the power and nature of the seed are able to form likenesses of body and mind, so the qualities and properties of the milk have the same effect. . . . [T]here is no doubt that in forming character the disposition of the nurse and the quality of the milk play a great part; for the milk, although imbued from the beginning with the material of the father's seed, forms the infant offspring from the body and mind of the mother as well. (Aulus Gellius, *Attic Nights* 12.1.12–15, 20)

244   Myers lists thirteen places in the New Testament that mention nursing, but her essay focuses specifically on Jesus in John (consult esp. 492–96). There, Jesus is depicted in terms related to

the ancient assumptions above. Jesus nurses at the father's breast, which also means feeding on the Father's seed, and thus he molded to the virtue of God as both Father and Mother, and he can thus truly reveal God and God's will to all his disciples. Likewise, as nursing bonds child to mother, so the bond between God and Jesus is intimate and complete. The gender-bending depiction of a father who nurses should warn us against dependence upon binary gender categories. The intimate connection and unity between Jesus and God expressed in John 1, where Jesus is in God's (nursing) bosom, is reiterated in John 17, which celebrates the perfect unity between Jesus and God.

In John 1:18, we learn that Jesus is close to the Father's "bosom" (*kolpos*), and, thus, is able to make God known. The word *kolpos* appears in only one other place in John: 13:23, where the (always unnamed) Beloved Disciple reclines upon Jesus's bosom. The Beloved Disciple is shown to have a special relationship with Jesus throughout the Gospel of John. Because the narrator does not name the Beloved Disciple, the reader is able to assume that position of intimacy with Jesus. In John 13:23 the NRSV, sadly, places the Beloved Disciple "next to" Jesus, instead of on Jesus's bosom, thereby destroying the carefully crafted analogy that the author took great pains to engender.

To reiterate, in John 13:23, the Beloved Disciple, who is the representative disciple in John, shares the same position with Jesus as Jesus did with God in 1:18. Thus, the same logic applies. The disciple who suckles at the bosom of Jesus is also morally shaped and formed to have her or his virtues aligned with Jesus's own, thereby being expected and empowered to do Jesus's will. "That this [13:23] is the *first* time the Gospel audience hears of the disciple Jesus 'loved' is also fitting, since breastfeeding traditionally establishes close bonds. Having been nursed by Jesus, the 'beloved' one slips out of view from the narrative until this disciple stands under the cross alongside Jesus' mother in John 19:25–27" (Myers 2013, 495).

The complete intimacy that inheres between disciples and Jesus is highlighted also in Jesus's prayer in John 17, where unity reigns in all forms. It is not surprising, then, that Jesus would command the church to feed the world that God "so loves." In John 21, three times Jesus declares to Peter (and the rest of us overhearing the conversation) that one shows that one loves Jesus by feeding others (vv. 15, 16, 17). The invitation is to be "suckled by

245

a community that has been nursed by the Father's nursling [i.e., Jesus]" (Myers 2013, 497).

Jesus as Mother Bird

Many are familiar with Jesus referring to himself as a mother hen gathering her brood (Matt. 23:37; Luke 13:34), but I imagine fewer know the tradition of Jesus as a mother pelican. Psalm 102 (101 in the Septuagint) has been interpreted as a messianic psalm. Verse 6 refers to a pelican (Greek *pelekan*; sometimes translated "owl" or other creature of the air), and the speaker, taken to be Jesus, laments, "I am like a desert pelican" (my trans.). As Virginia Mollenkott explains, the pelican came to represent "Mother Jesus" for a number of reasons. First, popular belief maintained that the mother pelican fed her young with her own blood:

> In fact, when pelicans are about to feed their brood, they do mac-
> erate small fish in the large bag attached to their under-bill, then
> press the bag against their breast to transfer the macerated food
> into the mouths of the young. Medieval piety saw the pressure
> against the chest as a self-sacrificial bursting of the breastbone in
> order to provide blood for the young to drink. The fact that medi-
> eval medical theory [as with the ancients, as we found above]
> understood breast milk to be processed blood also undergirds the
> pelican image of "Mother Jesus." (Mollenkott 2014, 45)

Second, Christians pick up from an influential twelfth-century Latin bestiary that parent pelicans kill their young and that, three days later, "the mother pierces her breast, opens her side, and lays herself across her young, pouring out her blood over the dead bodies" and they rise again (White 1960, 132). Comparing this idea to Jesus, "That was why he ascended into the height of the cross, and, his side having been pierced, there came from it blood and water for our salvation and eternal life" (133).

In Matthew and Luke, Jesus depicts himself as a mother hen. John portrays Jesus as having a womb and describes water and blood issuing from his side from the cross. Later Christians build upon this foundation to develop a connection between a mother bird and the crucifixion scene in John. All of it invites us to consider afresh the topic of "Jesus across Gender."

246

The Lectionary

The Revised Common Lectionary (RCL) calls for Matthew 11:16–19, 25–30 to be read in Year A during the season after Pentecost, on Proper 9 (14). This combination of verses allows for the connection between Jesus and Woman Wisdom to be featured, especially if one considers Matthew 11:19, 28–30 in combination with Proverbs 1:20–32, for example. Other opportunities to emphasize the connection between Jesus and Woman Wisdom arise when the prologue of John is read on Christmas Day and the 2nd Sunday after Christmas Day in all years for both the RCL and the RL. On these dates one might call attention to the tabernacle language present both in John's prologue and in Sirach 24 as a way to draw associations between Jesus and Woman Wisdom.

Appropriately, John 11, featuring the weeping Jesus, is to be read on the 5th Sunday of Lent according to the RL (all years) and the RCL (Year A; John 11:32–44 is also slated for All Saints' Day in Year B, in the season after Pentecost). Both lectionaries also include Hebrews 5 on the 5th Sunday in Lent in Year B (with the RCL also calling for the reading in Year B, season after Pentecost, Proper 24 [29]). Furthermore, according to the RL, Jesus's lament from the cross is to be read at Palm Sunday Mass in Year A (Matthew's account) and Year B (Mark's account). The RCL calls for Matthew's account of the same for the Liturgy of the Passion in Lent of Year A and for Mark's account for the Liturgy of the Passion in Lent of Year B. Thus, there are ample opportunities during the centrally important season of Lent to recognize the gender-bending lamenting of Jesus in our liturgies.

For those who want to highlight the material related to Jesus's womb, the RCL calls for John 7:37–39 on Year A, Day of Pentecost, and the RL on Pentecost Sunday: Vigil Mass, Years A, B, and C. With respect to the language of bestowing the Spirit at Jesus's death as Jesus gives birth to the church from the cross in John 19, the RL includes John 19:31–37 on the Friday after the 2nd Sunday after Pentecost: Sacred Heart.

Christmas and Easter lectionary readings for Catholics and Protestants also provide other opportunities to draw attention to and celebrate the feminine aspects of God and Jesus, with special attention here to birthing imagery. The aforementioned Christmas Day readings relating to Jesus as Wisdom include John 1:18, in

247

which Jesus is said to be close to God's *kolpos*. The RL includes John 1:18 on the 2nd Sunday after Christmas as well. Then, the recurrence of *kolpos* in John 13:23 could be discussed on the Wednesday of Holy Week in Years A, B, and C (RCL). Both Protestants and Catholics could discuss the infusion of nursing from God to Jesus to disciples on the 3rd Sunday of Easter in Year C, when John 21:1–19 is read. In all, we find opportunities to highlight Jesus across gender at some of the most liturgically significant times of the Christian year: Advent, Christmas, Lent, Easter, and Pentecost.

Conclusion

With respect to the stated goals of the book, this chapter has considered the female figure of Woman Wisdom. Additionally, we have explored the ways the Bible employs feminine imagery and moves across or beyond gender, in this case by depicting Jesus in feminine terms, including as Woman Wisdom. We have drawn upon recent scholarship that addresses the status of women in antiquity and presented insights from new perspectives and methods of interpretation. Finally, we have connected the reader with excellent resources for further study.

What are some implications of "Jesus across Gender" for Christian discipleship? Our treatment of Jesus across gender suggests a variety of touch points. As Lifebearer, Jesus does in fact make us children "who were born, not of blood or of the will of the flesh or of the will of a husband, but of God" (John 1:13, my trans.). We are a community connected not by biology but by common virtues and values that we learned at the breast of Jesus. God and Jesus (and Paul) nurse us, providing spiritual milk. In due time, we grow up and eat solid food, Jesus's own flesh.

Jesus as Lifebearer and Nurser feeds us from and with his own body. In the mystery of the Eucharist (or, in the memorial at the Lord's Supper), Jesus offers us his own flesh and blood as nourishment and, in the eating of it, we become one with him as he is one with God, knowing the will of God and receiving power to effect it. Jesus as Woman Wisdom offers bread and wine as part of our moral formation. Claassens invites us to "look through the maleness of Jesus seeing how Woman Wisdom serves as a legitimate expression of the God who feeds her children" (2004, 103).

248

Exploring Jesus across gender expands our ability to experience God more fully in a way that male-only material does not. It corrects the one-sidedness in our understanding of who God is, giving us access to attributes of God that are present in our Scriptures but missing from our curricula or pulpits or personal repertoire of ways we relate to the triune God. It exposes us to the fuller range of our Scriptures. Sometimes people are quite surprised to discover parts of Scripture that include women in nonstereotypical roles or texts that image God as feminine. I show them that I am not inventing a new category (though I am not opposed to the invention of new categories); I am merely training their attention upon material that has been in their lap the whole time they've been studying Scripture.

Recognizing Jesus across gender has ecclesiological implications. How do we do church? It elevates women and helps us as churches and individual disciples assess how we include or exclude women's bodies, voices, and experiences, on purpose or by accident or both. It helps people across genders explore the fuller spectrum of their own gifts and attributes, those associated with the masculine and those associated with the feminine.

A friend who is an ordained minister shared an encounter she had in her church. "I have been serving this church for approximately five months. Recently, the chair of the church council requested a meeting with my staff parish relations team to voice his concerns. The district superintendent happened to be at the meeting also. During the meeting the chair said that I was too young, too female, and too pregnant to be their pastor. I am the first female pastor this church has had and quite possibly one of the youngest pastors this church has ever had."

Would that this committee person, as well as the rest of us, heed the words of Claassens:

> The sad reality we have to face is that the church has suffered in countless ways from not regularly imaging God in female terms. Nowhere is this poverty of female imagery more evident than in the liturgy, and, particularly, in the celebration of the Eucharist. For centuries, the celebrant of the Eucharist was a male priest or pastor, harking back to the male image of Jesus Christ as host. In some denominations today, this argument is still a vital part of the reason why females are not permitted to the ordained ministry. However, as we have seen earlier, there is actually a strong connection between Jesus and Woman Wisdom, suggesting

249

something of the female dimension of the divine we have seen in this book and raising questions as to how significant Jesus' gender is for the celebration of the Eucharist. (2004, 110)

As we learn from Old Testament texts, Wisdom is the host at the table. When Christians do not understand that Jesus is depicted as Woman Wisdom, the feminine gets wholly subsumed in the masculine, and we have gender trouble. Claassens invites us to correct the problem:

There is something tragic about the many generations of men and women who have never seen a female pastor or priest serving the elements of bread and wine. What a difference it would make to have a female pastor or priest serve as host, acting as an embodied symbol of the God who gives food to all. In light of the emphasis of life . . . how powerful would it be to have a pregnant celebrant whose own body vividly symbolizes the joy of the God who feeds, whose gifts of food and drink provide the ultimate gift—life! (2004, 110)

As we intentionally apply ourselves to attending to every detail of Scripture, we will ever find ourselves surprised, comforted, disciplined, and challenged to expand our understanding and our experience of this God who loves us beyond all telling of it.

Recommended Resources

Aldredge-Clanton, Jann. 2004. *In Search of the Christ-Sophia: An Inclusive Christology for Liberating Christians*. 2nd ed. Woodway, TX: Eakin Press.

———. 2014. *She Lives! Sophia Wisdom Works in the World*. Woodstock, VT: SkyLight Paths.

Allen, Prudence. 1985. *The Concept of Woman: The Aristotelian Revolution, 750 B.C.–A.D. 1250*. Grand Rapids: Wm. B. Eerdmans Publishing Co.

Claassens, L. Juliana M. 2004. *The God Who Provides: Biblical Images of Divine Nourishment*. Nashville: Abingdon Press.

———. 2012. *Mourner, Mother, Midwife: Reimagining God's Delivering Presence in the Old Testament*. Louisville, KY: Westminster John Knox Press.

Conway, Colleen M. 2008. *Behold the Man: Jesus and Greco-Roman Masculinity*. Oxford: Oxford University Press.

Fehribach, Adeline. 2003. "The 'Birthing' Bridegroom: The Portrayal of Jesus in the Fourth Gospel." Pages 104–29 in *A Feminist Companion to John: Volume 2*. Edited by Amy-Jill Levine. New York: Sheffield Academic Press.

Mollenkott, Virginia Ramey. 2014. *The Divine Feminine: The Biblical Imagery of God as Female*. Eugene, OR: Wipf & Stock.

Myers, Alicia. 2013. "'In the Father's Bosom': Breastfeeding and Identity Formation in John's Gospel." *Catholic Biblical Quarterly* 76:481–97.

———. 2017. *Blessed among Women? Mothers and Motherhood in the New Testament*. New York: Oxford University Press.

Sawyer, Deborah. 2003. "John 19:34: From Crucifixion to Birth, or Creation?" Pages 130–39 in *A Feminist Companion to John: Volume 2*. Edited by Amy-Jill Levine. New York: Sheffield Academic Press.

Scott, Martin. 1992. *Sophia and the Johannine Jesus*. Journal for the Study of the New Testament Supplement Series 71. Sheffield: JSOT Press.

White, T. H., ed. and trans. 1960. *The Bestiary: A Book of Beasts*. New York: Putnam.

CHAPTER 9

Women in Paul's Ministry

People have strong opinions about Paul. For some, he is the reason women still struggle for equality in the church (and world); for others, he is a protofeminist. In asking whether Paul was either a male chauvinist pig or a feminist, we may find that Paul is much more complex than either of those categories allows (most of us are). Sometimes called the second founder of Christianity, Paul has been a controversial figure from the moment he showed up, hell-bent on destroying the Way of Jesus—until he decided to live and die for it. I invite us to discard our either/or categories and embrace the both/and: Paul was both a product of his time and ahead of his time.

For our purposes, then, it is best to begin with the undisputed letters of Paul (Romans; 1–2 Corinthians; Galatians; Philippians; 1 Thessalonians; Philemon). Given the goals presented in the introduction, this chapter especially explores the following theses: (1) women were important to Paul's ministry; (2) some women have been overlooked, misinterpreted, or erased; (3) Paul portrayed himself in female terms; and (4) Paul is an innovative thinker about relationships. Because Paul has been influential in Christian history, along the way we note recurring issues that arise in the church about roles of women in church leadership; sexual intimacy between males and females; and whether Paul was/is a friend or enemy to women.

Was Paul married? Not according to 1 Corinthians 9:5: "Do we not have the right to be accompanied by a believing wife, as do the other apostles and the brothers of the Lord and Cephas?" Did he not marry because he didn't like women? What does it mean that, while we hear that other apostles have wives, we never meet these wives? In addition, are the female leaders depicted as married? Some are (such as Prisca and Apphia) and some are not (such as Chloe and Phoebe).

Named Women

That Paul knew of and expected women, like men, to be among both the leaders and the followers in the church is easily observed by attending closely to some of the named women.

Prisca

Prisca (also known as Priscilla) is one of the most prominent leaders in the Pauline trajectory of Christianity. She appears in the undisputed Pauline letters, the deutero-Paulines, and Acts. She leads a house church in Ephesus with her husband, Aquila (1 Cor. 16:19). She and her husband, along with Paul, send greetings to the church at Corinth. By the time Paul writes Romans, the couple has settled there. He calls them "my coworkers [*synergos*] in Christ Jesus" who "risked their necks" for Paul's life (Rom. 16:3–4, my trans.). *Synergos* is the word Paul uses for Urbanus (Rom. 16:9), Timothy (Rom. 16:21), Titus (2 Cor. 8:23), Epaphroditus (Phil. 2:25), Clement (Phil. 4:3), Philemon (Phlm. 1), and Mark, Aristarchus, Demas, and Luke (Phlm. 24). So important are Prisca and her husband that Paul says he—and also all of the Gentiles—owes them a debt of gratitude (Rom. 16:3–4).

It's noteworthy that Prisca is named first in Romans, since normally primacy went to the male. It may mean she is of a higher social status or is a more prominent leader. Acts 18:2–3 indicates she and Aquila left Rome under the edict of Claudius that expelled all Jews from Rome and went to Corinth, where, along with Paul, they plied their tent-making trade and spread the gospel. They then accompanied Paul first to Syria, then to Ephesus, where they remained while he traveled on (Acts 18:18–19). While they were in Ephesus, an Alexandrian Jew named Apollos arrived and began teaching Christian faith in the synagogue. Prisca and her husband (again, she is mentioned first) took him aside and schooled him more fully in Christianity.

Prisca, then, is a prominent leader in the early church who has much in common with Paul: she is a Jew, a tent-maker, and one who travels widely and resides in many of the same places that Paul did, including Corinth, Ephesus, Syria, and Rome, spreading the gospel as she goes. In fact, she was part of the church at Rome before Paul had ever visited even once. By naming her in Romans 16:3, Paul hopes to capitalize on the relationship she already has with the churches in Rome so that he might receive a warm welcome by association. Rarely do we find a coworker of Paul's who appears across two Pauline letters, the book of Acts, and a deutero-Pauline Epistle (2 Tim. 4:19). Prisca was clearly instrumental in the early church.

Prisca is not the only woman mentioned in the closing chapter of Romans. There are nine in all: Prisca, Phoebe, Junia, Julia, Trypheana, Tryphosa, Mary, Rufus's mother, and Nereus's sister. Hence, the church at Rome, not founded by Paul and recipient of his final letter, counts numerous women in its leadership.

Phoebe

Phoebe has been the victim of translational sexism and erasure for centuries now. It is time to end both the willful and the unintentional ignorance. In Romans 16:1 Phoebe is called a *diakonos* of the church in Cenchreae (incidentally, or not, Luke says that this is where Paul got his hair cut when traveling with Prisca and her husband [Acts 18:18]). *Diakonos* is variously rendered in English as "servant" (CSB, KJV, NASB), "deaconess" (NJB, RSV), "deacon" (NRSV), and "minister" (NAB). When Paul uses this word of Phoebe, he does not feminize it (that is, the word is *diakonos*, not *diakonē*), so we can rule out the translation "deaconess" altogether. In fact, *diakonos* is exactly the same word Paul uses in 1 Corinthians 3:5 to speak of himself and Apollos—surely they are not "deaconesses"! This translation displays a political move to belittle Phoebe's role or office. She is a minister, like Paul and Apollos. However you decide to designate them, you need to designate Phoebe.

A further word on translation is in order here. Words do not have meaning on their own; rather, there are a range of usages for a given word. Scholars comb thousands of manuscripts to see how a word was used by different authors in various times and places. They then list those various usages in a lexicon. So, if one were to look up *diakonos* in a lexicon, she would find a multitude of usages. It is used to designate a servant, a minister, and a deacon, among other things. A responsible translator does not simply look in the lexicon, note the list of various usages, and choose the one that she likes the best. Rather, she asks (in our case): how is this word used in all the other places it occurs in Paul? Clearly, no translator has a problem designating Paul, Apollos, and other males as "ministers" when they see the word *diakonos*. So why, when it is applied to Phoebe, do they suddenly decide to choose "servant" or "deaconess"? It may be a politically motivated, gender-biased move used by those who can't imagine a female leader in the church or want to suppress the fact and impose an incorrect interpretation on an unsuspecting reader who does not have access to the original language (hence, the need for the translation in the first place). If the translator comes from a tradition that opposes the ordination of women, he or she is unlikely to render a translation that might be used by opponents to support the ordination of women. From day one in seminary classes, I teach my students to repeat this phrase daily: "All translation is an interpretation."

Not only is Phoebe a *diakonos*, she is also the first interpreter of Romans, since she is the carrier of the letter. Paul recommends her to the congregation in order to validate her authority to read the letter (most people could not read, so the letter was meant for the ear more than the eye). As the deliverer, it seems likely that Phoebe would have been coached by Paul to understand its contents and clarify points of confusion.

Phoebe was clearly a woman of independent financial means and agency, since Paul calls her a "benefactor" or "patron" (*prostatis*) of the church and himself. No husband is mentioned. This may imply that she is an independent woman who travels as she pleases and funds the ministry of the church as she herself personally labors to bring the gospel to the world.

Mary

Phoebe is only one of many women doing their part. We also meet Mary, "who toiled [*kopiaō*] among y'all" in Romans 16:6 (my trans.).

This is the same verb Paul uses of himself (Gal. 4:11; Phil. 2:16; 1 Cor. 15:10), and, in Romans 16:12, of Tryphaena, Tryphosa (both of whom are women), and Persis. And it's the word he uses of other *apostles* as well in one of his most stunning passages of all:

> For I think that God has exhibited *us apostles* as last of all, as though sentenced to death, because we have become a spectacle to the world, to angels and to mortals. We are fools for the sake of Christ, but you are wise in Christ. We are weak, but you are strong. You are held in honor, but we in disrepute. To the present hour we are hungry and thirsty, we are poorly clothed and beaten and homeless, and we grow weary [*kopiaō*] from the work of our own hands. When reviled, we bless; when persecuted, we endure; when slandered, we speak kindly. We have become like the rubbish of the world, the dregs of all things, to this very day. (1 Cor. 4:9–13; emphasis added)

Mary, then, is like other leaders in the Pauline trajectory.

Junia

This leads us to Junia in Romans 16:7, whom Paul specifically calls "outstanding/splendid [*episēmos*] among the apostles" (my trans.). A named female apostle in Paul's ministry? Yes. Why have so many never heard of her? Because an "s" gets added to her name, turning her into a male apostle and thus erasing her from history with a single pen mark (for a full treatment of the issue, consult Epp 2005). Numerous translations (e.g., RSV, NJB, NAS) propagate the error.

Paul refers to himself and others with a variety of terms: coworker (*synergos*), apostle (*apostolos*), and minister (*diakonos*), so the terminology is somewhat fluid. It is unlikely that there were church offices in the modern sense of the word or even to the extent that they were developed by the time of the Pastoral Epistles and other second-century church orders. Be that as it may, one should be on guard and protest whenever someone chooses to translate the terms one way when applied to a male figure and another (lower-status) way when they apply to a female. That's bad scholarship and is ideologically driven by prior patriarchal commitments.

The fact that Paul, in his final, magisterial letter to the church at Rome, names so many women among the leaders there without any fanfare should signal that he found it entirely customary and worthy

257

of no distinction from the males. Paul had never been to Rome, so the fact that he knew them points to their reputation on behalf of the gospel. If you ever thought Romans 16 was just a boring list of names, a throwaway chapter of sorts, think again. It contains volumes of information about our ancient sisters (and brothers).

Apphia

Paul addresses one of his epistles to "Philemon our dear friend and co-worker, to Apphia our sister [adelphē—the same word used of Phoebe], to Archippus our fellow soldier, and to the church in your house" (Phlm. 1–2). As a named figure, Apphia stands out. Early Christians designated one another with the language of fictive kin. Since she is listed with two other male leaders in terms that imply working for the gospel (coworker, fellow soldier), there is reason to assume that she is also a leader, perhaps the second in command in that church.

Chloe

Chloe appears in 1 Corinthians 1:11. Why is she noteworthy? First, she is clearly the leader of a church. In the first century, all churches were house churches. In Corinth, there was a problem with division among the churches, some following Paul, others Apollos, others Cephas (Peter), and, not to be outdone, those following Christ (1:12). It appears that the "saints" (1:2) of antiquity were just as prone to fractiousness and confusion as we are. So the churches at Corinth sent a report to Paul about the *many* problems there. Paul received word of these problems from at least three different avenues. First, he received news from Stephanas and Fortunatus and Achaicus (1 Cor. 16:17). Second, he received a written letter asking about a wide variety of issues. He responds to these issues in turn, starting each new topic with the phrase "now concerning" (*peri de*). Finally, he received an oral report from "Chloe's people." No husband is mentioned (if she had one, he would likely have been mentioned, in accordance with ancient custom; in fact, he would typically be listed first). Most likely Chloe is a woman of independent means who hosts a church in her house and is the leader of it. She has "people."

258

Euodia and Syntyche

In Philippians 4:2–3 we meet two more important women in Paul's ministry: Euodia and Syntyche. We learn much about them in just one clause. They are, like Prisca, Aquila, Urbanus, Timothy, Titus, Clement, Philemon, Mark, Aristarchus, Demas, and Luke, coworkers (*synergos*) with Paul and Clement (and others). They have "struggled along [*synathleō*] with me for the sake of the gospel" (my trans.). Their names are written in the book of life.

However, they are in conflict with one another. Clearly, they have influence and status and power, and as a result, their disagreement has a serious impact on the church. One sees the same dynamic in 3 John, where the tension between the church leaders Diotrephes and the Elder causes serious upheaval. Demetrius comes across as a good guy and Diotrephes as a church leader who is causing division. We also find division around different leaders in 1 Corinthians: "For it has been reported to me by Chloe's people that there are quarrels among you, my brothers and sisters. What I mean is that each of you says, 'I belong to Paul,' or 'I belong to Apollos,' or 'I belong to Cephas,' or 'I belong to Christ.' Has Christ been divided?" (1 Cor. 1:11–13).

Paul commands all of the Philippians: "be of *the same mind*, having the same love, being in full accord and *of one mind*" (Phil. 2:2; emphasis added). What mind is this, exactly? The mind of Christ. "Let the *same mind be in you that was in Christ Jesus*" (2:5). Paul's call to have the same mind that was in Christ Jesus and to "be of the same mind" remains as challenging today as it was in the first century (and maybe every century).

Regardless of their dispute, it is clear that Euodia and Syntyche stand out as important leaders who spread the gospel in mighty ways. One cannot help but wonder if they were able to reconcile or whether, like Paul and Barnabas, two other prominent church leaders in conflict, they decided to part ways: "The disagreement became so sharp that they parted company; Barnabas took Mark with him and sailed away to Cyprus" (Acts 15:39). In short, readers should avoid characterizing the discord as a mere "catfight" (which they would never do if the characters were male) and, rather, see this problem as it is—tension between two effective, prominent leaders in the church.

259

Paul as a Woman in Ministry

In Galatians 3:28, Paul makes this important declaration in a baptismal context: "There is no longer Jew or Greek, there is no longer slave or free, there is no longer male and female; for all of you are one in Christ Jesus." In Christ, the binaries (and inevitable resulting hierarchies) that inhere in the world with respect to race, ethnicity, class, and gender do not apply. Before, Paul would have said that Jew is far better than Greek: "If anyone else has reason to be confident in the flesh, I have more: circumcised on the eighth day, a member of the people of Israel, of the tribe of Benjamin, a Hebrew born of Hebrews; as to the law, a Pharisee; as to zeal, a persecutor of the church; as to righteousness under the law, blameless" (Phil. 3:4–6). On account of Christ, however, he changed in dramatic ways and became, above all, apostle to the Gentiles, though he eagerly evangelized everyone (e.g., 1 Cor. 9:19–22).

Although ancient people considered males superior to females, Paul describes himself with maternal imagery numerous times. In fact, he uses maternal imagery more than paternal. Given his stunning conviction as expressed in Galatians 3:28, we should not be surprised. Given the gender assumptions about male superiority in antiquity and today, however, we are surprised. Some find Paul's maternal imagery so surprising (and unnerving) that they try to hide or at least ignore it. Not on our watch, though. Relevant passages for the theme of Paul as woman include:

> But we were gentle among you, like a nurse tenderly caring for her own children. (1 Thess. 2:7)

> And so, brothers and sisters, I could not speak to you as spiritual people, but rather as people of the flesh, as infants in Christ. I fed you with milk, not solid food, for you were not ready for solid food. (1 Cor. 3:1–2)

> My little children, for whom I am again in the pain of childbirth until Christ is formed in you . . . (Gal. 4:19)

In each of these instances, Paul depicts himself as a female, a woman in labor, and a nursing mother.

Beverly Gaventa has sought to restore this imagery to our understanding of Paul. She makes four observations in her argument that maternal imagery constitutes a theme for Paul (to read her argument in detail, consult Gaventa 2004). First, such passages involve "complex metaphorical movements," what she terms "metaphors squared"; for example, in 1 Corinthians 3:2, "first, [Paul] metaphorizes . . . the gospel as milk, then he squares that by metaphorizing Paul as the mother whose body supplies the milk" (88).

Second, Gaventa critiques those who conflate the paternal image with the maternal. "The distinction between them is an important one, however. At one level, it is important because we have too long neglected any sort of references to women or imagery involving women. Just as we failed to ask about the apostle Junia and the household of Chloe, we failed to notice these astonishing references to the maternity of a male apostle." Moving beyond "this first-level task of *retrieval,*" Gaventa notes that, where paternal imagery is used, it tends to refer to Paul initially ushering people into the faith, whereas the maternal imagery tends to refer to the ongoing nurture and maturing in the faith (89).

A third connection between the maternal texts is that they describe Paul's apostolic office. "Something in Paul's understanding of the apostolic task causes him to turn to this language of maternity" (Gaventa 2004, 91). Gaventa adduces in this context 1 Corinthians 15:8, which does not depict Paul as a mother but does draw upon birth imagery in defining his apostleship: "Now last of all, as to something monstrously born, he appeared to me" (Gaventa's trans.).

Fourth, the maternal texts are connected by their association with apocalyptic contexts. It is not uncommon for the coming of the eschaton to be described in terms of the travails of childbirth (cf. Rom. 8:22). As noted earlier, Paul certainly had an apocalyptic worldview and expected Jesus to return forthwith.

Gaventa concludes the study with the "so-what" question: why bother with this topic? First, reiterating a point made earlier, she wants to "retrieve these texts from their place in the footnotes of Pauline studies" (2004, 95). Second, far from being merely ornamental to the propositional statements, Paul's metaphors convey his theology, in part. "Paul speaks theologically when he says, 'all have sinned and fall short of the glory of God'. He *also* speaks theologically when he says, 'I am in labor until Christ is formed in you'" (96). Third, the study of this imagery contributes to an understanding of the social function of language. We know that early Christians 261 relied on the language of fictive kin to strengthen primary group identity. Certainly, maternal language is among the most intimate.

Finally, Gaventa wonders "whether a study of Paul's use of maternal imagery may have implications for the interrelated and complex sets of questions regarding Paul's understanding of leadership and his attitudes toward women" (96). Is there a way that Paul moves us beyond the binaries of hierarchical and egalitarian? This takes us back to my observations about the importance of Galatians 3:28 as programmatic for Paul's ministry. Not only do Paul's words to others have the potential to shatter oppressive hierarchies, but so do his own words about himself.

Women in 1 Corinthians 7, 11, and 14

First Corinthians 7: Does Paul Hate Sex and Women?

First Corinthians 5–7 is loaded with sex. In chapter 5 a man is having sex with his stepmom; Paul orders the congregation to confront the man. In chapter 6 men are using prostitutes. Again, Paul calls for a halt to the behavior. Interestingly, as Sarah Ruden observes, "Paul blasts men for engaging prostitutes, but he launches no parallel outburst against the female vendors of sex. He would have known that a large number had no choice—many prostitutes were slaves" (2011, 86–87).

Chapter 7 covers a wide array of situations relevant to Paul and women. In broad strokes, Paul is quite surprisingly countercultural for his own Greco-Roman context, treating women as (a) full persons, not defective males, and (b) persons whose desires and needs and vocation are equal to that of males. I am not trying anachronistically to label Paul a feminist or imply that he perfectly transcends his own social location as an educated hellenized Jewish male probably with Roman citizenship. I am claiming, however, that given Paul's transformative experience of Jesus that turned him from killing Christians to becoming one, combined with his views about an imminent return of Jesus, Paul was charting new territory that created opportunities for women in their personal lives and religious communities.

In 1 Corinthians 7, Paul makes a number of points. His overarching point is found in 7:26: "I consider it to be good, on account of the impending distress, for a person to remain as they are" (my trans.). Paul believes that Jesus is returning at any moment. He

262

would like everyone to be single-mindedly focused upon spreading the gospel and not bother changing their relationship status in the little time that is left. Thus, if you are married, stay married. If you are unmarried, stay that way. Had Paul known that two thousand years later the eschaton had still not arrived, would he have advised differently?

So, Paul wants people to remain as they are, not because he is antimarriage, antifemale, or antisex, but because he is extremely proevangelizing. Even he himself chose not to marry. Paul understands that when one has a spouse, part of one's attention must rightfully go to the spouse if one is going to be a good spouse; one cannot be "all things to all people" (1 Cor. 9:22) and still be a good spouse (though many a minister has learned that truth the hard way). Paul says, "Those who marry will experience distress in this life, and I would spare you that" (1 Cor. 7:28).

But Paul notes that not everyone experiences libido the same way. Some have lots of it and welcome it as a gift, not a burden. The word "self-control" appears only twice in 1 Corinthians: at 9:25, about athletes in training, and here in 7:5 where Paul basically says, "If you just can't keep your paws off of each other, get married and get a room." Not exactly a sacramental view of marriage. Paul is able, though, to admit that God has called us to different vocations (7:7). For some, that may entail marriage.

It is important to stop briefly to note how revolutionary Paul's vision is here. Women and men were expected to marry and have children. Women were ideally focused on the household and subject to the rule of males in home and society. Now Paul is advocating that people *not* marry, *not* have children, but devote themselves full-time to evangelism. This was a liberating, revolutionary way to order one's life, especially for a female. To be a full agent of one's destiny (subject only to God), to have the chance *not* to die in childbirth, to travel and participate in work of ultimate significance—this was a vision that many women found attractive. It made Christianity at odds with the host culture, of course, but Paul was in good company, since Jesus had made similar moves. Women took hold of this vision and, in the years ahead, became itinerant preachers, desert mothers, nuns, martyrs, and saints.

So what about those whose vocation (and/or libido) necessitate marriage? Here are the salient points. First, we are quite surprised in 1 Corinthians 7:3 when Paul leads out with the command

263

that "the husband should meet his wife's sexual needs" (CEB). It's hard to say which is more shocking: the recognition that a woman has legitimate sexual needs; the obligation of a man to meet those needs rather than assuming that to do so would warrant an extra pat on the back for going above and beyond; or Paul putting the obligation of the male to meet the female's needs before the obligation for the female to please the male. All of this is highly unusual for Paul's time (and maybe our own as well).

Second, in 7:4 Paul begins by noting that "the wife does not have authority over her own body, but the husband does." No news flash there. But then he drops this bombshell in the same breath: "Likewise, the husband does not have authority over his own body, but the wife does." That is revolutionary and certainly a minority opinion; but that's often the case with the teachings of Jesus and Paul (and other New Testament voices as well). Paul calls the couple to consider the needs of the other, to work together.

The same is true regarding the divorce advice. We would expect a first-century authority to say that a wife should not leave her husband. But Paul makes two further moves. First, he imagines a space where a woman would actually leave. True, he calls her to then remain unmarried or go back to the husband, but that's not at all surprising, given that he wants *everyone* to remain as they are or not get married! It's not because he has it in for women. Second, he enjoins the men not to divorce their wives, which they could do with relative ease and with few negative consequences (which would *not* be as true for the women they were divorcing). Unexpected.

The mutuality continues in verses 12–16. Paul explicitly and almost woodenly addresses the female and male partner in turn, concluding with (notice he mentions the female first): "Wife, for all you know, you might save your husband. Husband, for all you know, you might save your wife" (7:16). Recall Paul's words in chapter 9 that, in every ethical decision he makes, he asks about the saving potential of his action or inaction for the other person. He assumes that all women have the same power that he does as an apostle: the power to save (*sōzō*). Revolutionary.

Here's another reason to find Paul endearing and to defend him against those who readily dismiss him as an arrogant blowhard (I must confess to the reader that I enjoy Paul in all his brilliance, passion, ego, courage, faith, and "rough-around-the-edges-ness"). In 7:10 as he is discussing divorce, he states that he is invoking the

264

word of the Lord (isn't it odd that he doesn't quote words of Jesus there, as Matthew does at 19:8–9 or Mark does at 10:5–12?). But beginning in 1 Cor. 7:12 he addresses the issue of what to do if you are married to an unbeliever. If you become a Christian after marriage, should you remain with a non-Christian? Just like us, Paul has to give his best "now-we-see-through-a-glass-darkly" guess about a contemporary (for him) issue that Jesus never directly addressed. Sound familiar? I appreciate that he owns that fact overtly: "To the rest I say—I and not the Lord . . . " (7:12). He then opines about and adjudicates at length (the chapter goes through v. 40!) numerous issues about the various relationship statuses. But he wants us to understand that, while he's guessing, winging it, doing the best he can with what he's got, it's an *educated* or at least *inspirited* guess, as he concludes the chapter with these words: "And I think that I too have the Spirit of God" (7:40).

One could try to march through 1 Corinthians 7 and make a flow chart of what each person in a given situation, at least those imagined by Paul in the first century, should do, whether they are

an entirely single person not at all contemplating marriage,
a single person who may be considering marriage in the future,
a betrothed person,
a married person,
a divorced person,
a widowed person, or
a person married to a nonbeliever.

All of the advice fits under a few constant themes:

Jesus is coming back soon, and there's a lot of work to be done in preparation.
All Christians are called to do the Lord's work.
You have a *choice* about getting married. That goes for *both* women and men.
If you are not married at present, don't get married, if at all possible.

Far from trying to get women married off and having children, Paul encourages the women *not* to marry, and, therefore, *not* to have children. This definitely undermines the family values of the

Roman Empire, Judaism, and every other system of the period (and, perhaps, our own).

What's good for the goose is good for the gander, and vice versa.

If you do choose to get married, you are not a bad person or lesser disciple in any way. But you have complicated your life by obligating yourself to the needs of another. Those needs may conflict with your sense of your vocational calling to the Lord's work.

In conclusion, far from showing that Paul is opposed to women and sex, 1 Corinthians 7 shows Paul's expansive vision and innovation when it comes to relationships between the sexes in his own time. It is simply stunning that Paul ends the chapter by saying that, if a woman's husband dies, she should feel free to marry whomever she wants, but that Paul would consider her happier (*makarios*) or more blessed to be *unattached* to a male! The word he uses is the same word we find in the Beatitudes (e.g., "Blessed/happy [*makarios*] are the peacemakers" [Matt. 5:9, my trans.]).

A chart may make a stronger impression for the reader when it comes to mutuality in Pauline relationships:

Chart 1: Paul's Commands to Men and Women in 1 Corinthians 7

1 Cor. 7	Instructions to Men	Instructions to Women
v. 2	Each man should have his own wife	and each woman her own husband.
v. 3	The husband should give to his wife her conjugal rights,	and likewise the wife to her husband.
v. 4	For the wife does not have authority over her own body, but the husband does;	likewise the husband does not have authority over his own body, but the wife does.
vv. 10–11	The husband should not divorce his wife.	The wife should not separate from her husband.
vv. 12–13	If any believer has a wife who is an unbeliever, and she consents to live with him, he should not divorce her.	And if any woman has a husband who is an unbeliever, and he consents to live with her, she should not divorce him.

1 Cor. 7	Instructions to Men	Instructions to Women
v. 14	For the unbelieving husband is made holy through his wife,	and the unbelieving wife is made holy through her husband.
v. 16	Husband, for all you know, you might save your wife.	Wife, for all you know, you might save your husband.
vv. 32–34	The unmarried man is anxious about the affairs of the Lord, how to please the Lord; but the married man is anxious about the affairs of the world, how to please his wife, and his interests are divided.	And the unmarried woman and the virgin are anxious about the affairs of the Lord, so that they may be holy in body and spirit; but the married woman is anxious about the affairs of the world, how to please her husband.

First Corinthians 11:1–16: Hair Matters, Then and Now

This part of 1 Corinthians is notoriously difficult to interpret. Wayne Meeks's insight about this passage from decades ago remains true: "These are not the most lucid passages in the Pauline letters. A small mountain of literature about them has by no means relieved their obscurity" (1983, 70). Nevertheless, one must tackle this passage because it still figures so largely in conversations about women in the church today.

Paul begins by exhorting the Corinthians to "be imitators of me, as I am of Christ" (11:1; cf. 4:16). What does he mean by that? Use your authority/rights (*exousia*) to do whatever it takes to spread the gospel in the short time remaining. It's the same argument he uses in 1 Corinthians 9, in which he names the various authorities/rights (*exousia*, 9:12, 18) that he has as an apostle and then declares the crucial *"Nevertheless"* (9:12b). Nevertheless, he willingly forgoes insisting on his particular rights and entitlements for one reason—to share the gospel with as many people as possible. It's the same move Jesus made as celebrated in the Christ hymn of Philippians 2. And, as we shall see later in the passage, Paul goes on to state that, though the Corinthians (in this case some of the women)

267

could stand rigidly in their rights, Paul would like to see them relinquish that legitimate personal *exousia* for a bigger cause—making the gospel of Christ inviting to potential converts.

In 1 Corinthians 11:3–9, Paul appears to subordinate women to men. The salient moves in this section of the argument include: (1) A woman should have long hair and a veil; she should not have short hair or a shaved head; (2) a man should have short hair and no veil; and (3) woman was made from man, not vice versa. One immediately notices that Paul has eclipsed the first creation story, which states, "So God created humankind in his image, in the image of God he created them; male and female he created them" (Gen. 1:27), and invoked only the second creation story.

However, Paul then gives power back to women and levels the playing field. He moves directly to the *exousia* argument, granting that women have authority over their own heads (1 Cor. 11:10), just as Paul has *exousia* associated with being an apostle, the "strong" in chapters 8–10 have *exousia* over food, and so on. He grants that they have authority. Then he says "nevertheless" in verse 11, which indicates a contrast with what has come before. "Nevertheless, in the Lord woman is not independent of man or man independent of woman. For just as woman came from man, so man comes through woman; but all things come from God" (11:11–12). That is, though he has made a number of comments that might lead some to subordinate women, Paul stops that trajectory. In the church (here "in the Lord"), things are done differently.

Like Galatians 3:28, 1 Corinthians 11:11–12 obliterates arguments for female subordination that depend on the second creation story in Genesis 2. The work of Christ on the cross lays waste to our penchant for systems of categorization (usually binary) that lead to domination. In place of domination, we learn that *interdependence* is the key, a theme Paul will warm to greatly in 1 Corinthians 12 with the metaphor of the body in which he overturns conventional wisdom (a head has more honor than a foot) and teaches the logic of the cross, where the less honored is more honored and vice versa. In fact, 1 Corinthians 12 is the only other place that has almost the same quotation as the baptismal formula in Galatians 3:28: "For in the one Spirit we were all baptized into one body—Jews or Greeks, slaves or free—and we were all made to drink of one Spirit" (1 Cor. 12:13).

In 1 Corinthians 11:13–15, Paul argues that nature itself supports the idea of a woman veiling: "Judge for yourselves: is it proper for a woman to pray to God with her head unveiled? Does not nature itself teach you that if a man wears long hair, it is degrading to him, but if a woman has long hair, it is her glory? For her hair is given to her for a covering." Two points should be made. First is the obvious point that nature does not teach this. Culture does. Second, this is not about subordination of women. It's simply about the cultural customs related to head covering while the women are praying in church.

Just as cultural customs related to hair and head coverings existed in Paul's day, so do they today. When I teach 1 Corinthians 11:2–16 in a group, I ask participants to talk to me about hairstyles and how they relate to social class, professional status, and so on. I live in Dallas, Texas, so this is easy. Restricting the conversation to women, one can discern an expensive color job from an inexpensive one, an expensive weave from a cheap one. Hair with purple and orange streaks may work for an artist but not for a Supreme Court judge. Even these few examples highlight that how one wears one's hair (or whether one's hair is even showing) is often a sign of culture and status today. And sometimes our cultural assumptions about hair can be harmful to women. Consider Chris Rock's movie *Good Hair*. He made the movie in response to his four-year-old daughter's question: "Daddy, why don't I have good hair?" Early on she had learned that African American hair is not "good hair." Many interesting, helpful conversations about race, ethnicity, and culture have arisen as groups discuss hair, status, gender, culture, and power gathered around 1 Corinthians 11:2–16, where all of that is at play between Paul and the Corinthians.

Given all that we know from Paul's writings and the women serving in the same capacities as men, including Paul, it should not be surprising to see women leading in church at Corinth through prayer and prophecy. Given Paul's constant concern for and accommodation of potential new converts to the faith, we are also not surprised that he asks the Corinthians to conduct worship with the same stance. In that particular context, that entailed women covering their heads while conducting their part of the worship service, just as it entailed males wearing their hair short and uncovered. Paul concludes the whole section that deals with worship, chapters 11–14, with these summarizing words: "So, my brothers and sisters, be eager to prophesy, and do not forbid speaking in tongues; but all things should be done decently and in order" (1 Cor. 14:39–40).

269

It's the same argument he makes in chapters 8–10 to those who insist on their right to eat meat sacrificed to idols. Paul agrees they have that right and asks them to forgo it for the sake of others. Further, it's the same argument he makes in chapter 14 about speaking in tongues. Yes, some people have that gift and should be able to use it. But Paul asks those with that gift to put it aside when it presents an obstacle to would-be converts.

Thus, it is important to note two main points here: First, Paul never questions whether women are to pray and prophesy in church. How could he, given the female prophets of the Hebrew Bible? "The Talmud counts seven female prophets (Sarah, Miriam, Deborah, Hannah, Abigail, Huldah, and Esther)" (Lander 2011, 304). Second, Paul is asking these particular women in this particular context to operate by his own missionary principle with respect to the host culture. He is not making a timeless statement about all women everywhere. (Note that among Western Christians today—even those who insist on "male headship" on the basis of this very passage—females are not expected to and do not veil.)

First Corinthians 14:33b–36: An Interpolation

First Corinthians 14 concludes the unit beginning at 11:1 that addresses, in part, how the church should behave when gathered for worship. Paul addresses the proper place of speaking in tongues and its relationship to prophesying. The flow of the argument is interrupted by a parenthetical statement about women in 14:33b–36 that contradicts Paul's other material on women in leadership; this is why your study Bible puts it in parentheses as a peculiar intrusion. The passage reads: "(As in all the churches of the saints, women should be silent in the churches. For they are not permitted to speak, but should be subordinate, as the law also says. If there is anything they desire to know, let them ask their husbands at home. For it is shameful for a woman to speak in church. Or did the word of God originate with you? Or are you the only ones it has reached?)." Given the rest of what we know about him and his ministry, this passage is obviously an odd exception to Paul's modus operandi regarding women and does not reflect the apostle's own teaching or practice until his death in 64 CE. The statement directly contradicts what we find not only in the rest of Paul's letters (women leaders in the churches; Gal. 3:28; etc.) but also just

270

three chapters earlier in 1 Corinthians 11, where Paul assumes that women both pray and prophesy in the church. As we saw there, the question has nothing to do with *whether* they speak in church—they clearly do (it doesn't make any sense, of course, to prophesy at home by yourself)—but whether they wear a veil *while doing so.*

Because of these other things we know about Paul, it's not surprising that most scholars think he didn't write this passage. Scholars debate the authenticity of the passage for a number of reasons. First, it interrupts the argument; if one removes it, the passage continues to flow in its discussion of tongues and prophecy. Accordingly, most study Bibles place this section in parentheses.

Second, because the passage sounds strikingly parallel to 1 Timothy 2:11–15, many scholars take 1 Corinthians 14:33b–36 to be a harmonizing scribal interpolation. That is, scribes who copied manuscripts made all kinds of moves that are relevant to understanding our texts. Since scribes knew other texts, at times one text would remind them of another, and they might note that in the margin. Or, in an effort to clarify or deepen the meaning of a passage (in their estimation), they might harmonize one text with another (this is how we came to have numerous endings to the Gospel of Mark, for example). Even though our manuscripts don't omit the passage, they do place some of the verses in different places. This further suggests the scribal gloss theory.

Third, it contradicts the witness of Paul's own ministry as demonstrated across his letters, which shows women as leaders in the churches. If Paul did write the passage, he can't have meant that women should be entirely silent. Or, perhaps more importantly, whatever he meant by them, the way he put these words into practice meant something very different than the way people have interpreted them today to limit women's leadership. Again, we can be confident of this because of the robust witness of Paul's affirmation of women leaders in the church elsewhere in his writings, including the very same letter that contains this passage.

The Implications of Misinterpreting Paul

Unfortunately, many Christians today practice 1 Corinthians 14:33b–36 in a way that would be completely foreign to Paul. "1 Cor. 14:33b–35 . . . speak[s] of women's role in the public

worship service. The main application of [this passage] in the contemporary church is that women are not to exercise those functions in the local congregation which would involve them in the
exercise of authority inherent in the authoritative public teaching
office (i.e., the office of pastor)." These words come from page
38 of "Women in the Church: Scriptural Principles and Ecclesial
Practice," a report produced by the Commission on Theology and
Church Relations of the Lutheran Church–Missouri Synod and
released in September 1985. It is still in effect today. The year
1985 was bad for women with respect to Paul. The Missouri Synod
Lutherans were not alone that year in using a (hotly debated) proof
text to make the apostle do their oppressive work. Notice their
convenient lack of attention to any and all of the material we've
covered in this chapter. The Southern Baptists, who had previously
ordained women—sent them around the world as missionaries and
into hospitals as chaplains—revoked all of those opportunities, citing "Paul." Many women have found their ministries restricted by
this kind of interpretation.

Will Campbell, a Southern Baptist minister from Mississippi,
reacted to this draconian denominational move by writing an essay,
"On Silencing Our Finest," upon the occasion of his daughter
entering seminary. Here is an excerpt:

> Shortly after the spring thaw of 1573 a woman prayed for her
> children: O Holy Father, sanctify the children of Thy hand-
> maiden in Thy truth and keep them from all unrighteousness, for
> Thy holy name's sake. O Almighty Father, I commend them unto
> You, since they are Thy creatures; care for them, for they are Thy
> handiwork; so that they may walk in Thy paths.
>
> She was a cousin to some of us. Her name was Maeyken
> Wens, an Anabaptist woman of Antwerp, who had been arrested
> a few days earlier for proclaiming the Gospel of Christ as she
> understood it from her personal reading of the Scripture, and
> from study and from discussion of it with others of her sisters
> and brothers.
>
> Cousin Maeyken withstood the inquisition of ecclesiastics and
> the bodily torture of those in civil authority. When she would not
> recant after six months of imprisonment and would not promise
> to cease her spreading of the Word, she was sentenced on Octo-
> ber 5 to death. Included in the sentence read by the court was the

instruction to the executioner that her tongue should be screwed fast to the roof of her mouth so that she might not testify along the way to the place of burning.

The next day her teenage son, Adriaen, took his youngest little brother, three-year-old Hans Mattheus, and stood on a bench near the stakes so that her first and last issue might be present at the moment of her death. When it began Adriaen fainted, and was not able to witness her parting. But when it was over and the ashes had cooled he sifted through them and found the screw with which her tongue had been stilled. Three other women and a man died that day of the same offense. The remembrance of them makes me exalt in my heritage.

Four hundred and eleven years later, June 13, 1984, many thousands of Maeyken's spiritual relatives gathered in convention in Kansas City and resolved that women should not be ordained as ministers.

> WHEREAS, while Paul commends women and men in other roles of ministry and service (Titus 2:1–10) he excludes women from pastoral leadership (1 Timothy 2:12) to preserve a submission God requires because the man was first in Creation and the woman was first in the Edenic fall. (1 Timothy 2:13ff.)

The remembrance of that act brings no exultation to many of us that wear the Anabaptist alias, Baptist. I have heard of no 15-year-old sons picking up the paperclips from the discarded resolutions that commended the silencing of their mothers. (Campbell 1985, 340)

I like to laugh as much as the next person and do plenty of it. But when it comes to this issue of women being silenced in the church, or anywhere in social structures, especially power structures, I urge my students to treat this as a matter of life and death where not even gallows humor will do. Subordination of women not only *leads to* violence against women, it *is* violence against women. Not to mention violence against the very God who created male and female in God's image. It is no small thing to deface the very image of God. It is no small thing to screw a woman's tongue to the roof of her mouth, whether literally or figuratively. It is no small thing to destroy the image of God, whether in body or in spirit.

273

The Lectionary

During his ministry, Paul mentions or encounters numerous women, many of whom are in ministry themselves. Such women are often overlooked or forgotten. It is an important act of recovery to name each of these women and to celebrate their presence as well as their specific ministry, when applicable. Thus, in chart 2 I provide a list of women Paul encounters or mentions. Furthermore, in keeping with Paul's own commitment to lifting up the names and work of faithful women, I also include other women in chart 2 whom Paul did not necessarily encounter but who are mentioned in the book of Acts or letters attributed to Paul (including those not likely written by him).

Chart 2: Women in Paul's Ministry, Acts, and Letters Attributed to Paul

Sapphira, property owner and wife of Ananias	Acts 5:1–11
Candace, Ethiopian queen	Acts 8:26–40
Tabitha (Dorcas), social worker	Acts 9:36–42
Rhoda, female servant at Mary's house	Acts 12:13–15
Prominent women from Antioch	Acts 13:50
Lydia, devout cloth merchant, house church host	Acts 16:14–15
A possessed, abused slave woman	Acts 16:16–24
Damaris, new believer	Acts 17:34
Prisca (Priscilla), missionary partner to Paul and married to Aquila	Acts 18:2, 18–19, 26; Rom. 16:3–4; 1 Cor. 16:19; 2 Tim. 4:19
Philip's four daughters	Acts 21:8–9
Paul's sister	Acts 23:16–22
Drusilla, youngest daughter of Agrippa	Acts 24:24
Bernice, eldest daughter of Agrippa	Acts 25:13, 23; 26:30
Phoebe, church leader in Cenchreae	Rom. 16:1

Mary #5, friend of Paul	Rom. 16:6
Junia, a woman "outstanding among the apostles"	Rom. 16:7
Tryphaena and Tryphosa	Rom. 16:12
Rufus's mother	Rom. 16:13
Julia, friend of Paul	Rom. 16:15
Nereus's sister	Rom. 16:15
Chloe	1 Cor. 1:11
Euodia and Syntyche	Phil. 4:2
Nympha	Col. 4:15
Lois, Timothy's grandmother	2 Tim. 1:5
Eunice, mother of Timothy	2 Tim. 1:5
Apphia, Christian at Colossae	Phlm. 2

In this chapter I have discussed several of these women specifically, including Chloe, Euodia and Syntyche, Apphia, and Prisca (Priscilla) and the eight other women mentioned in Romans 16.

The only Sunday reading in the Roman Lectionary (RL) and the Revised Common Lectionary (RCL) for Romans 16 is verses 25–27, meaning that the eight women Paul mentions in Romans 16 who are mentioned nowhere else in the New Testament (Phoebe, Mary, Junia, Tryphaena, Tryphosa, Rufus's mother, Julia, and Nereus's sister) are never included in a lectionary-based Sunday service for Catholics or Protestants. These women are included once in the RCL weekday readings: Year A, season after Pentecost, Proper 20 (25). Only two of them (Junia and Mary) appear in a weekday reading of the RL, on the Saturday of Ordinary Time, Week 31, Year 1. As for Prisca (Priscilla), whom Paul mentions in Romans 16:3–4 but who also appears elsewhere in the New Testament, she is included in both the abovementioned RL and RCL weekday readings but her mention in Romans is not included in Sunday readings for either tradition. Likewise, Acts 18, 1 Corinthians 16, and the mention of Prisca in 2 Timothy 4:19 are omitted from the Sunday RL and RCL readings. This means that, despite receiving mention in four New Testament works, Prisca is never proclaimed in Sunday worship that relies on these lectionaries. She is included, however, in selections from Acts 18 and 1 Corinthians 16 twice in weekday

275

RCL readings and in selections from Acts 18 three times in week-day RL readings (all falling on Week 6 of Easter, Years 1 and 2).

Other named women in Paul's ministry are included in at least one of the Sunday lectionaries, if sparingly. Chloe receives mention on the 3rd Sunday after the Epiphany during Year A (RCL; she also gets included in a single RCL weekday reading) and the 3rd Sunday in Ordinary Time, Year A (RL). Euodia and Syntyche are included in the RCL's Philippians reading on Proper 23 (28) of the season after Pentecost during Year A, although they are omitted from RL Sunday readings altogether. (They are not included as weekday readings for either lectionary.) While not included at all in the RL, Apphia is included in the Sunday RCL readings on Proper 18 (23) of the season after Pentecost, Year C (she is also included in the RCL weekday readings during the week of the 4th Sunday after the Epiphany of Year A).

As for women not discussed specifically in this chapter but otherwise mentioned in Acts or one of Paul's letters (including those letters likely not written by him), consult chart 3 below for a concise overview of their inclusion in the Sunday lectionary:

Chart 3: Select Women in Paul's Ministry, Acts, and Letters Attributed to Paul and Their Inclusion in the Sunday Lectionary

Woman	Mentioned In	Inclusion in Sunday RCL	Inclusion in Sunday RL
Sapphira, property owner and wife of Ananias	Acts 5:1–11	None	None
Candace, Ethiopian queen	Acts 8:26–40	Year B, 5th Sunday of Easter	None
Tabitha (Dorcas), social worker	Acts 9:36–42	Year C, 4th Sunday of Easter	None
Rhoda, female servant at Mary's house	Acts 12:13–15	None	None
Prominent women from Antioch	Acts 13:50	None	Year C, 4th Sunday of Easter

276

Woman	Mentioned In	Inclusion in Sunday RCL	Inclusion in Sunday RL
Lydia, devout cloth merchant, house church host	Acts 16:14–15	Year C, 6th Sunday of Easter	None
A possessed, abused slave woman	Acts 16:16–24	Year C, 7th Sunday of Easter	None
Damaris, new believer	Acts 17:34	None	None
Philip's four daughters	Acts 21:8–9	None	None
Paul's sister	Acts 23:16–22	None	None
Drusilla, youngest daughter of Agrippa	Acts 24:24	None	None
Bernice, eldest daughter of Agrippa	Acts 25:13, 23; 26:30	None	None
Nympha	Col. 4:15	None	None
Lois, Timothy's grandmother	2 Tim. 1:5	Year C, season after Pentecost, Proper 22 (27)	None
Eunice, mother of Timothy	2 Tim. 1:5	Year C, season after Pentecost, Proper 22 (27)	None

Several, though not all, of these women are included in weekday RL and RCL readings, but their scant inclusion in the Sunday lectionaries means worshipers will be far less likely to learn about them in corporate worship.

As for New Testament language in which Paul speaks of himself as a woman in ministry, there are a few opportunities for worshipers to be exposed to these passages on Sundays, and a few weekday readings as well. Galatians 4:19 is only called for as a weekday RCL reading, to be read on two different weekdays: Year A, 4th Sunday of Advent, and Year C, season after Pentecost, Proper 8 (13). The RCL only calls for a Sunday reading of 1 Corinthians 3:1–2: Year

A, 6th Sunday after Epiphany. The RL calls only for a weekday reading of these verses: Wednesday of Week 22 of Ordinary Time during Year 2. Finally, 1 Thessalonians 2:7 is a Sunday RCL reading on Year A, season after Pentecost, Proper 25 (30) (there is no RCL weekday reading for this verse) and a Sunday RL reading on the 31st Sunday in Ordinary Time of Year A (it is a weekday RL reading on the Tuesday of Week 21 of Ordinary Time, Year 1).

As for the passages in 1 Corinthians 7, 11, and 14 that have often been understood to limit women, these passages are included in neither of the Sunday lectionaries. Only 1 Corinthians 7:25–31 is included as a weekday RL reading (Year 2, Ordinary Time, Week 23, Wednesday). The RCL includes at least one weekday reading for each passage. The cumulative effect of this reality is that parishioners are largely on their own to interpret controversial and often misunderstood passages in Paul's letters.

Conclusion

In this chapter, we have engaged a number of the goals stated in the introduction to the book. We have highlighted named women who may have previously been unnoticed or obscured. With Junia the apostle, we have reinstated a woman who has been erased due to certain moves in the transmission of our texts. We have rescued Phoebe from the demoted status inflicted upon her by a sexist translation move that the unsuspecting English reader has little defense against. We have drawn upon sociohistorical scholarship in order to understand the Pauline material in its own social context. Finally, we have explored the ways that the Bible moves across gender as Paul depicts himself and other apostles in feminine terms.

Our investigation of Paul shows that he enthusiastically and unapologetically considers women to be no different from men in value or vocation. He names the women who preceded him in the faith and those whom he worked alongside of (consult chart 2 above). He names women as apostles, ministers, leaders of churches, patrons, and coworkers. He expects them to pray and prophesy and, for those who are called to be partnered, to insist upon relationships that are mutually upbuilding for both participants. In Christ, there is no male and female. Where gender binaries and oppression exist, we can be sure we have yet to attain the

278

full measure of being "in Christ." Fortunately, the gift and power of the Holy Spirit make such attainment just one choice away.

Recommended Resources

Campbell, Will D. 1985. "On Silencing Our Finest." *Christianity and Crisis* 45, no. 14 (September 16): 340–42.

Epp, J. Eldon. 2005. *Junia: The First Woman Apostle*. Minneapolis: Fortress Press.

Gaventa, Beverly Roberts. 2004. "Our Mother Saint Paul: Toward the Recovery of a Neglected Theme." Pages 85–97 in *A Feminist Companion to Paul*. Edited by Amy-Jill Levine. Feminist Companion to the New Testament and Early Christian Writings 6. London: T&T Clark.

Lander, Shira. 2011. Introduction and notes to "The First Letter of Paul to the Corinthians." Pages 287–315 in *The Jewish Annotated New Testament: New Revised Standard Version*. Edited by Amy-Jill Levine and Marc Zvi Brettler. Oxford: Oxford University Press.

Martin, Dale B. 1995. *The Corinthian Body*. New Haven, CT: Yale University Press.

Meeks, Wayne A. 1983. *The First Urban Christians: The Social World of the Apostle Paul*. New Haven, CT: Yale University Press.

———. 2006. *Christ Is the Question*. Louisville, KY: Westminster John Knox Press.

Metzger, Bruce M., and Bart D. Ehrman. 2005. *The Text of the New Testament: Its Transmission, Corruption, and Restoration*. 4th ed. Oxford: Oxford University Press.

Ruden, Sarah. 2011. *Paul among the People: The Apostle Reinterpreted and Reimagined in His Own Time*. New York: Image Books.

Wire, Antoinette Clark. 1990. *The Corinthian Women Prophets: A Reconstruction through Paul's Rhetoric*. Minneapolis: Fortress Press.

CHAPTER 10

The Muting of Paul and His Female Coworkers

Women in the Deutero-Pauline Epistles

The deutero-Pauline epistles comprise five epistles written in the name of Paul but which most scholars consider to have been written by followers of Paul in a later era. In what follows I treat the Pastoral Epistles (1 and 2 Timothy and Titus), which clearly share a literary relationship, and then Colossians and Ephesians, which also share a literary relationship. The focus here remains solely upon the ways these letters relate to the issue of women in the Bible, rather than a general discussion of their contents.

In particular, I address the way the Pastoral Epistles represent a backlash against women who followed Paul's call to renounce marriage and childbearing in order to evangelize. The author is preoccupied with what those outside the church will think if women are not kept "in their place" as dictated by imperial ideals of the home. Widows receive special attention in the Pastorals, with the author concerned to define what a "real" widow is.

I also address the household codes in Ephesians and Colossians. Ancient Greco-Roman political and social theorists, including philosophers, maintained that there was a hierarchical ordering to society that was to be reflected in the household. Thus, for the Romans, Caesar was at the top of the hierarchy, the metaphorical father of the household. I explore how the authors of Ephesians and Colossians interacted with the codes.

281

Before discussing the Pastorals, Ephesians, and Colossians vis-à-vis women, I first offer some introductory comments on the authorship of these five works.

Authorship Issues

I have written at length elsewhere on the issue of Pauline authorship as it relates to the deutero-Pauline material (consult Clark-Soles 2010, chap. 5). Here, I summarize three approaches.

1. Most scholars consider the letters to be pseudonymous and post-Pauline. Paul died circa 64–67 CE, according to tradition. In terms of canonical evidence, Acts depicts Paul under house arrest in Rome in its final chapter. No biblical book narrates Paul's death, which is particularly interesting since all of the Gospels and the book of Acts were composed after his death. Any traditions around Paul's death are extracanonical. Numerous postbiblical sources (such as 1 Clement, Acts of Paul, Tertullian, and Eusebius) take a stab at how Paul died. Many speak of his martyrdom. Some claim he was killed by Nero. Some claim that he was beheaded in Rome. Some combine the two claims. The modern basilica in Rome known as St. Paul Outside the Walls represents this tradition of Paul's martyrdom in Rome.

Most scholars agree that the Pastorals, Ephesians, and Colossians are pseudonymous and written decades after Paul's death. There are at least four different reasons such an argument is made. First, the Pastorals on the one hand and Ephesians and Colossians on the other share language with each other not found elsewhere in the New Testament. Second, the style among them is similar to one another but different from undisputed Paul (e.g., they do not have the varied and rich use of particles that Paul does). Third, the letters differ in their theology when compared to Paul. This is true with respect to faith, the law, righteousness, tradition, and Christology. Fourth, the ethics are different. For instance, gone is the call from 1 Corinthians 7 to live in the world "as though not," given Paul's view of the impending end of the world as we know it. Instead, we find the move to settle in for the long haul and carve out an enduring space in the host society. We find an urge to tone down the edgy, apocalyptic, countercultural energy of Jesus and

282

Paul. In technical sociological terms, we encounter a move from charismatic leadership to the institutionalization of the church.

2. *Occasionally one encounters an argument that Paul had two Roman imprisonments instead of one.* He was released from the first imprisonment in Rome, preached in Spain (which 1 Clement 5:5–7 refers to as "the extreme west"), and was then imprisoned again and martyred. During this "second career," he wrote the Pastorals. This would extend Paul's life and "thought development" and experience in a way that might more reasonably account for the dramatic differences between the undisputed material, all of which would have been written within a more compressed period and completed by 64 CE. The Pastorals are set in the East, however, and there is no evidence to support his going to the East if he did have a second career. The view of multiple imprisonments is not well founded and is not well supported by scholars.

3. *The third approach is to ignore all the problems and just insist they are Pauline because the name Paul appears.* This view is driven by apologetic and dogmatic purposes and does not allow for critical inquiry; thus, it is less convincing. Not only is it driven by defensive motivations, it ignores the prevalent practice of pseudonymity in the ancient world.

The Pastorals and Women

Leadership Models: From Charism to Church Offices—From Paul to the Pastorals

Scholars who question Pauline authorship of the Pastoral Epistles note the stark differences in attitudes about women exhibited by these texts in comparison to the undisputed works of Paul. Certainly Paul's belief that the eschaton would arrive imminently kept him from worrying about systemic reform of society outside the church; however, his undisputed epistles exhibit a profoundly egalitarian visionary insight with respect to gender (among other social relationships), stated concisely in Galatians: "As many of you as were baptized into Christ have clothed yourselves with Christ. There is no longer Jew or Greek, there is no longer slave or free, there is no longer male and female; for all of you are one in Christ Jesus" (Gal. 3:27–28).

283

Here Paul makes it clear that, in God's eyes, distinctions that humans make on the basis of race and religion (such as Jew/ Greek), social class (slave or free), and gender constructs (male and female) are simply that: human constructs that divide and provide hierarchies where God intends unity and equality.

This radical vision appears to have been borne out in his own ministry. At every turn one finds women acting as apostles (Junia, in Rom. 16:7), ministers (Phoebe, in Rom. 16:1–2), prophets (1 Cor. 11), leaders of house churches (the only kind of churches that existed in Paul's day; check out Chloe in 1 Cor. 1:11), and prominent teachers (Priscilla, in Rom. 16:3–4; 1 Cor. 16:19).

In [Paul's ministry], women served the same functions as men since Paul's view of leadership was charismatically based. What do I mean by "charismatically based"? Perhaps it is best described by Paul himself in 1 Corinthians 12 and Romans 12. Here Paul explains that each and every Christian has been gifted by God in some way *for the edification of the church.* Some are called to be teachers, some have the gift of hospitality, some are musicians, and some have a special gift for working with children (cf. Rom. 12:6– 8). *Charisma* is the Greek word for "spiritual gift," and Paul trusts that in any Christian body God has provided the necessary gifts for that community to function for the spread of the gospel, to the glory of God. Gifts are not provided on the basis of gender, race, ethnicity, class, age, and so forth. People, not God, add those limitations and heavy yoke to God's plan. (Clark-Soles 2010, 83–84)

The Pastorals have quite a different view of leadership in the church. Where Paul assumed that the Holy Spirit would call forth in any given community the gifts needed at that time, the Pastorals move into creating particular church offices with specific job qualifications. It is likely that the Pastorals are written in the early second century, when a whole genre of literature called "church orders" was being constructed.

The Pastorals express a concern for church order and conceive of the church as a household of God with a hierarchical ministry of bishops, presbyters, deacons, and, perhaps, orders of deaconesses and widows. The qualifications for bishops are enumerated in 1 Timothy 3:2–7:

Now a bishop must be above reproach, married only once, temperate [*nēphalion*], sensible, respectable, hospitable, an apt teacher, not a drunkard, not violent but gentle, not quarrelsome, and not a lover of money. He must manage his own household well, keeping

284

his children submissive and respectful in every way— for if someone does not know how to manage his own household, how can he
take care of God's church? . . . Moreover, he must be well thought
of by outsiders, so that he may not fall into disgrace and the snare
of the devil [*tou diabolou*].

Notice that the bishop is envisioned as a male head of a household,
a paterfamilias who controls his household, who fits in with and is
palatable to the general non-Christian population.

A concern for institutionalizing the church through the invention of particular offices appears in other documents of this second-
century genre: the Epistles of Ignatius of Antioch (ca. 115 CE), the
Didache, Apostolic Constitutions, and the *Didascalia Apostolorum*,
to name a few. Ignatius was the bishop of Antioch in the early second century. Like Paul, he was martyred; like Paul, he wrote a number of letters along the way to his martyrdom. Part of his concern
was to leave behind a church that was run in an organized, orderly
fashion. Note the following two excerpts, for example. First, in his
letter to the Ephesians he writes: "Now, since Jesus Christ has given
such glory to you, it is only right that you should give glory to Him;
and this, if sanctification is to be yours in full measure, means unit-
ing in a common act of submission and acknowledging the authority
of your bishop and clergy" (*Eph.* 2.2, trans. Staniforth). Second, in
his letter to the Magnesians, Ignatius writes: "For your part, the
becoming thing for you to do is to take no advantage of your bishop's
lack of years, but to show him every possible respect, having regard
to the power God has conferred on him. My information is that the
sacred clergy themselves never think of presuming on the apparent
precocity of his rank; they give precedence to him as a sagacious
man of God—or rather, not so much to him as to the Bishop of us
all, the Father of Jesus Christ" (*Magn.* 3, trans. Staniforth). Similarly, the Pastorals reflect a move away from Paul's commitment to
charismatic leadership, defined by spiritual gifts, to church offices,
centralization of power, and institutionalization. Institutionalization
generally led to a limiting of women's leadership roles.

Pastoral Ambiguities and Inconsistencies regarding Women

The qualifications for deacons in 1 Timothy prompt two interesting
questions vis-à-vis women. We read:

Deacons likewise must be serious [*semnous*], not double-tongued, not indulging in much wine, not greedy for money; they must hold fast to the mystery of the faith with a clear conscience. And let them first be tested; then, if they prove themselves blameless, let them serve as deacons. Women likewise must be serious [*semnas*], not slanderers [*diabolous*], but temperate [*nēphalious*], faithful in all things. Let deacons be married only once, and let them manage their children and their households well; for those who serve well as deacons gain a good standing for themselves and great boldness in the faith that is in Christ Jesus. (1 Tim. 3:8–13)

The first question arises out of verse 12, which indicates that a deacon must be a man of "one woman/wife." Does this mean married only once, or does it mean "not polygamous"? Second, verse 11 says that "women" (*gynaikas*) must have certain qualifications that are among the qualifications for deacons or bishops. Is verse 11, then, referring to female deacons? Or is it referring to wives of deacons? Or, less likely, is it referring to women in general? It intrudes awkwardly in a paragraph on qualifications for the church office. Given that verses 8–9 and 12–13 refer to deacons, it makes the most sense to assume that verse 11 does the same. However, given the author's contention in 1 Timothy 2:12–15 (consult the next section), it is unlikely that women exercised institutional power in this community. (For an excellent, detailed discussion that entertains different viewpoints on this matter, consult Susan Hylen 2015.) Even though it is unlikely that the reference to "women" in 1 Timothy 3:11 is evidence that women exercised institutional power in this community at this time, the requirements given for "women" in 1 Timothy 3:11 *do* parallel expectations placed on bishops and deacons in the same community (3:1–10, 12–13).

The presentation of Lois, Eunice, and Prisca in 2 Timothy makes me wonder if the author is a conflicted soul with regard to the leadership of women. Second Timothy 1:5 says of Lois and Eunice: "I am reminded of your sincere faith, a faith that lived first in your grandmother Lois and your mother Eunice and now, I am sure, lives in you." The verse deserves mention because it attests to the nurturing, guiding faith of two women passed down to the generations following them. Here, within a work that has a very low view of women, we find a passage that speaks of two women so devoted to their faith that they are credited with influencing the faith of those who come after them (including our own generation,

286

thousands of years later). If that is not leadership of utmost importance, I don't know what is.

Another woman is mentioned briefly in the Pastorals who seems to have been a respected leader for this author: "Greet Prisca and Aquila, and the household of Onesiphorus" (2 Tim. 4:19). Although no elaboration is given of who Prisca is (and there is a very good chance she is no longer living by the time this work is written), that she and Aquila can be mentioned so briefly suggests they were well known by the community. Surely their leadership in the early church was unquestioned.

The Pastorals: (Over)Reaction to Thecla, Perpetua, and Felicitas?

The author of the Pastorals has a very low view of women and calls male leaders in the church and household (two sides of the same coin for this author) to manage them at all costs. In this author's construal, left to their own devices, women pose serious problems on a number of counts. Women are especially daft and prone to being led astray: "For among them are those [male teachers] who make their way into households and captivate silly women, overwhelmed by their sins and swayed by *all kinds* of desires, who are *always* being instructed and can *never* arrive at a knowledge of the truth" (2 Tim. 3:6–8; emphasis added). The language is so extreme that it is difficult to emphasize which elements are the harshest.

Lest one hope that this is a momentary anomaly on the author's part, let us (re)turn to another example, 1 Timothy 2:8–15, with a few prefatory comments. First, instead of Paul's urging that women (and men) refrain from marrying if at all possible, this author insists upon the exact opposite. Second, in Romans Paul highlights the transgression of Adam three times in six verses:

> Therefore, just as sin came into the world through one man, and death came through sin, and so death spread to all . . . (Rom. 5:12)

> For if the many died through the one man's trespass . . . (Rom. 5:15)

> If, because of the one man's trespass, death exercised dominion through that one . . . (Rom. 5:17)

287

On the contrary, Eve bears the full burden alone for the author of the Pastorals, and the consequence of Eve's mistake in this author's mind is that women cannot teach or have authority, while men can. Third, where Paul *expects* women to pray and prophesy in church (1 Cor. 11), this author commands women to keep their mouths shut: "Let a woman learn in silence with full submission. I permit no woman to teach or to have authority over a man; she is to shut up" (1 Tim. 2:11–12, my trans.).

In full, 1 Timothy 2:8–15 reads:

> I desire, then, that in every place the men should pray, lifting up holy hands without anger or argument; also that the women should dress themselves modestly and decently in suitable cloth-ing, not with their hair braided, or with gold, pearls, or expensive clothes, but with good works, as is proper for women who profess reverence for God. Let a woman learn in silence with full sub-mission. I permit no woman to teach or to have authority over a man; she is to shut up [*einai en hēsychia*] (1 Tim. 2:11–12, my trans.). For Adam was formed first, then Eve; and Adam was not deceived, but the woman was deceived and became a transgres-sor. Yet she will be saved through childbearing, provided they continue in faith and love and holiness, with modesty.

Are we really to believe that Adam was neither deceived nor a trans-gressor? Further, does it really make sense that this is the rationale for why men can have authority but women cannot? The author of the Pastorals once again communicates his rather low view of women and in so doing takes on a very different attitude than Paul himself.

As I discuss at length in the preceding chapter on women in Paul's ministry, in a countercultural move, Paul implores his fol-lowers to avoid marriage if at all possible and, instead, to use their time to evangelize as many people as possible before Jesus returns (cf. 1 Cor. 7). Some of his earliest female listeners responded to this call, leaving behind traditional roles of wife and mother to become evangelists, martyrs, and saints.

Thecla provides one example. In the Catholic and Episcopal churches, her feast day is September 23. Her story appears in the Acts of Paul and Thecla, whose written composition dates to circa 180 CE. She is engaged to a man named Thamyris. When Paul comes to town, she is convicted by his message and breaks off the

288

engagement with Thamyris to become a traveling missionary. In response, her fiancé and her own mother (Theoclia) call for the town authorities to burn her to death:

> The governor . . . summoned Thecla and said, "Why do you not marry Thamyris, according to the law of the Iconians?" But she stood looking earnestly at Paul. And when she gave no answer Theoclia, her mother, cried out saying, "Burn the wicked one; burn her who will not marry in the midst of the theatre, that all the women who have been taught by this man may be afraid." And the governor was greatly moved, and after scourging Paul he cast him out of the city. But Thecla he condemned to be burned. (Acts of Paul and Thecla 20–21, in Elliott 1993)

Patriarchal societies often try to punish women who opt out of patriarchal structures.

That Paul was remembered as one who encouraged women not to get married and have children, thus upsetting the patriarchal system, is clear. According to the logic of passages such as 2 Timothy 3:6–8, Paul himself could be seen as one who led women astray. Consider the following excerpt from the Acts of Paul and Thecla:

> Theoclia answered, "I have a strange story to tell you, Thamyris. For three days and three nights Thecla does not rise from the window either to eat or to drink; but looking earnestly as if upon some pleasant sight she is devoted to a foreigner teaching deceitful and artful discourses, so that I wonder how a virgin of her great modesty exposes herself to such extreme discomfort. Thamyris, this man will overturn the city of the Iconians and your Thecla too; for all the women and the young men go in to him to be taught by him. He says one must fear only one God and live in chastity." (8–9)

For his part, Thamyris espouses the view set forth by the Pastorals regarding a woman's proper place:

> And Thamyris greeted her with a kiss, but at the same time being afraid of her overpowering emotion said, "Thecla, my betrothed, why do you sit thus? And what sort of feeling holds you distracted? Come back to your Thamyris and be ashamed." . . . And Thamyris, jumping up, went into the street, and watched all who

289

went in to Paul and came out. And he saw two men bitterly quar-
relling with each other and he said to them, "Men, who are you
and tell me who is this man among you, leading astray the souls
of young men and deceiving virgins so that they should not marry
but remain as they are?" (10–11)

Recall this exact exhortation by Paul five different times in
1 Corinthians 7 to "remain" (*menō*) as you are. Thamyris is right
that Paul is telling women not to marry. He is practically a mouth-
piece for the Pastorals as he eschews Paul, though. Not surprisingly, the gatekeepers of patriarchy in the Acts of Paul and Thecla
go after Paul as well, since he is upsetting their apple cart.

The Martyrdom of Perpetua and Felicitas, dated to the late
second or early third century CE, introduces two more women
who leave behind their families in order to testify on behalf of
Christ. They, like Thecla, stand in the tradition of women who
exemplify what it meant for an ancient woman to take 1 Corinthians 7 seriously, prioritizing the spread of the gospel above all else,
even when it contradicts "traditional" (read "patriarchal") norms
and values.

In a society that valued women primarily as keepers of hearth
and home (as many still do), Perpetua's choice to leave her nursing child in order to follow her countercultural vocation has been
inspiring to many who do not fit a traditional mold and whose
choices unleash a cascade of judgments that would not be applied
to males in the same situation (i.e., fathers of young children). Perpetua speaks about her experience:

> Then Hilarianus passed sentence on all of us: we were condemned
> to the beasts, and we returned to prison in high spirits. But my
> baby had got used to being nursed at the breast and to staying
> with me in prison. So I sent the deacon Pomponius straight away
> to my father to ask for the baby. But father refused to give him
> over. But as God willed, the baby had no further desire for the
> breast, nor did I suffer any inflammation; and so I was relieved
> of any anxiety for my child and of any discomfort in my breasts.
> (Martyrdom of Perpetua and Felicitas 6, in Musurillo 1972)

290   Perpetua was not the only woman who defied traditional family
values in the way that stoked the ire of the likes of the author of the

Pastorals. While Perpetua was nursing, Felicitas was pregnant. This did not stop her from embracing a countercultural call:

> As for Felicitas, she too enjoyed the Lord's favour in this wise. She had been pregnant when she was arrested, and was now in her eighth month. As the day of the spectacle drew near she was very distressed that her martyrdom would be postponed because of her pregnancy; for it is against the law for women with child to be executed. Thus she might have to shed her holy, innocent blood afterwards along with others who were common criminals. Her comrades in martyrdom were also saddened; for they were afraid that they would have to leave behind so fine a companion to travel alone on the same road to hope. And so, two days before the contest, they poured forth a prayer to the Lord in one torrent of common grief. And immediately after their prayer the birth pains came upon her. She suffered a good deal in her labour because of the natural difficulty of an eight months' delivery. (15)

I find that this next passage always catches audiences up short. The imagery that combines the blood of childbirth with the blood of martyrdom is poignant:

> The day of their victory dawned, and they marched from the prison to the amphitheatre joyfully as though they were going to heaven, with calm faces, trembling, if at all, with joy rather than fear. Perpetua went along with shining countenance and calm step, as the beloved of God, as a wife of Christ, putting down everyone's stare by her own intense gaze. With them also was Felicitas, glad that she had safely given birth so that now she could fight the beasts, going from one blood bath to another, from the midwife to the gladiator, ready to wash after childbirth in a second baptism. (18)

In moving to the final paragraph under consideration, I note two elements: First, notice the gender aspect—the murderers devoted themselves intentionally to the gender piece, taking special entertainment delight in matching the gender of the victim with the gender of the animal enlisted to murder her. Second, notice that, presented with the opportunity to take a moment to consider the egregious, heinous violence they are about to perpetrate upon

291

a young mother, rather than look in the mirror and be horrified by the depraved reflection of themselves, the crowd is offended not by their murderous ways, but by the victim herself. Thus, rather than the moment leading to repentance and ethical transformation, the crowd takes action to make their depravity appear more civilized by covering the victim's milk-dripping breasts. Our human capacity to justify profound gender violence knows no bounds in any time or place:

> For the young women, however, the Devil had prepared a mad heifer. This was an unusual animal, but it was chosen that their sex might be matched with that of the beast. So they were stripped naked, placed in nets and thus brought out into the arena. Even the crowd was horrified when they saw that one was a delicate young girl and the other was a woman fresh from childbirth with the milk still dripping from her breasts. And so they were brought back again and dressed in unbelted tunics. (20)

While these compositions date to later than the Pastorals, it is not by much and, besides, oral traditions precede written ones. Thus, it is highly likely that the Pastorals are reacting to women who patently follow the preaching of the apostle Paul and who live into the baptismal formula that declares there to be no controlling gender categories (no "male and female") in Christ Jesus. That is to say, the Pastorals may represent a backlash against Paul's view of women and their place in the ministries of the church. By the time the Pastorals were written, Jesus had not returned, and the church moved from charismatic leadership to institutionalization and hierarchies that mirrored the values of the host culture, the Roman Empire.

The author of the Pastorals has no use for the Theclas, Perpetuas, and Felicitases of his world; rather, he wants women to get back into their "proper place" as women who marry, give birth, mother, and take care of the widows in their family (1 Tim. 5:16). This is commensurate with his general concern about being well thought of by those outside the church (1 Tim. 3:7; 5:14; 6:1). In 1 Timothy 2:15, though, the author goes so far as to make salvation dependent upon childbearing. This is a far cry from the Paul who does not want women even to get married, let alone to have children. And it would be awfully difficult to simultaneously pray

292

and prophesy in church (as do the women in 1 Cor. 11) while also "shutting up" (1 Tim. 2:12).

Finally, Titus 2:3–5 enjoins older women to serve as good role models by behaving reverently, not slandering (only he is allowed to do that, apparently), and not abusing alcohol. They are to: "teach what is good, so that they may encourage the young women to love their husbands, to love their children, to be self-controlled, chaste, good managers of the household, kind, being submissive to their husbands, so that the word of God may not be discredited." Why would the young women have to be taught to love their husbands and their children and to be submissive to their husbands? Again, it appears that women such as Thecla, Perpetua, and Felicitas who were convinced by the apostle Paul to live in this world in a radical way provided an attractive model for young women in the second century, and we see, once again, the backlash against them. Additionally, we find once again the anxious concern about "what the neighbors will think." Whereas Paul cared about that insofar as he certainly wanted to make the church inviting to potential converts, this author appears more concerned to blend in with the host culture in a more quietistic fashion.

Most Protestant audiences that I teach have never heard of Thecla, Perpetua, and Felicitas, who so clearly, boldly, and fully live out Paul's call to share the good news far and wide, no matter what the cost or whom they upset—those outside the church or those inside the church for whom "propriety" matters more than passion. These women are just as fully committed as the apostle himself was. (It should not go unsaid that some of the appeal of following Paul's call to celibacy included, for women, not being under the authority and control of a male and not having to risk one's life in childbirth when maternal and infant mortality rates were so high.) I exult in their remembrance! I also wonder what claim, if any, their stories make upon my own life or that of my community. How much are we willing to risk and to what lengths will we go for the sake of the gospel?

Widows—Real or Fake? Total Saints or Satanic Sinners?

293

First Timothy 5:3–16 treats the issue of widows in the church. One might assume that a widow is defined as a woman whose husband

has died and who is now single. For the author of 1 Timothy, however, that does not make her a "real" widow; rather she must be a
woman who

> "has set her hope on God" (5:5),
> "continues in supplications and prayers night and day" (5:5),
> is at least sixty years old (5:9),
> has married only once (or, is the wife of only one husband—the
>   meaning is unclear in Greek; 5:9), and
> is "well attested for her good works, as one who has
> brought up children,
> shown hospitality,
> washed the saints' feet,
> helped the afflicted, and
> devoted herself to doing good in every way." (5:10)

One wonders if anyone actually ever qualified, given this extensive list.

The author goes on to disallow "younger" women (those under
the age of sixty, it would seem) from being put on the list of widows, citing as his "reasons" a host of derogatory descriptions about
a whole group of people:

> But refuse to put younger widows on the list; for when their sen-
> sual desires alienate them from Christ, they want to marry, and
> so they incur condemnation for having violated their first pledge.
> Besides that, they learn to be idle, gadding about from house to
> house; and they are not merely idle, but also gossips and busy-
> bodies, saying what they should not say. So I would have younger
> widows marry, bear children, and manage their households, so
> as to give the adversary no occasion to revile us. For some have
> already turned away to follow Satan. If any believing woman has
> relatives who are really widows, let her assist them; let the church
> not be burdened, so that it can assist those who are real widows.
> (1 Tim. 5:11–16)

The author holds it against women under sixty if they desire
to marry again after their husband dies, going so far as to call this
desire something that alienates them from Christ and causes them
to "incur condemnation." As Hylen notes: "The author ignores the
social and financial factors that were likely to be a woman's calculus

in marriage and opts instead for a negative factor, desire" (2015, 66). Thus, to ensure that these women's sexuality is managed by a male, he insists that they not only remarry but also produce children (consistent with the statement he made in chap. 2). Given that "real" widows are aged sixty and above, one is curious as to how he imagines women, say, over forty managing to have children. Second, he spews slanderous slurs—these women, to a person apparently, are unproductive gadabouts, gossips, and busybodies. One wonders if this author had a wife or close, fond relationships with any females.

The reader would do well to read Joanna Dewey's excellent entry on 1 Timothy in the *Women's Bible Commentary* to sort out the details concisely, confusing as they can be. To wit: "There is thus confusion in the Pastorals between 'widow' as a Christian minister and 'widow' as a welfare recipient" (2012, 600). Dewey recognizes that the author of 1 Timothy is deeply frightened by strong, Spirit-led females. Like those before and after him, he does what he can to impede them.

> The long discussion of widows in 1 Timothy suggests that within the Christian communities the author knows there are independent communities of women with their own discourses, understandings, and practices of Christianity that they are engaged in teaching to other women and perhaps to some men. These alternative communities are perceived as a threat by the author of the Pastorals, and he gives instructions to dismantle them to the extent that he can. (Dewey 2012, 601)

Fortunately, his project is doomed to failure, though it has created havoc over the centuries, including our own, as it marches forward toward its sure demise.

It is important to lift up these texts and deal with them and the ways they have perpetuated sexism. It does not help when scholars bury the offense. Commenting on the Pastorals' treatment of women, Mark Allan Powell (whose work I generally admire and assign in my courses) writes: "It *seems* sexist and unreasonable, and it is expressed in language that *seems* unduly harsh (e.g., 1 Tim. 5:6)" (2018, 424; emphasis added). It doesn't *seem* sexist and harsh, it *is* sexist and harsh. The question before us is not whether it is or isn't but rather how we in the twenty-first century should engage this text as ethical people.

295

Colossians and Ephesians: Household Codes— Accommodating the Host Culture

Colossians 3:18–4:1; Ephesians 5:21–6:9; and 1 Peter 2:13–3:7 contain "household codes" (German: *Haustafeln*), a Greek and Roman philosophical topic that prescribes how each member of a household hierarchy should behave if the household is to accomplish its raison d'être—to replicate and thereby expand the empire. The household is to mirror the structure of the empire, which is best conceived of as a pyramid. In the Roman imperial context, Caesar sits at the pinnacle, followed by the elite, down to the base of the triangle where the masses reside. Likewise, in the home the husband/father/master assumes the top position. Next comes the wife, then the children, then the household slaves. Consider this excerpt from Arius Didymus (1st c. BCE), who writes on the typical subject (*topos*) of "household management": "The man has the rule of this household by nature. For the deliberative faculty in a woman is inferior, in children it does not yet exist, and in the case of slaves, it is completely absent." Didymus also avers that slaves are broken into two groups: those enslaved by being captured in war and those who are slaves "by nature" who are "strong in body for service, but stupid and unable to live by [themselves], for whom slavery is beneficial" (Stobaeus, *Flor.* 2.7.26; trans. Balch 1988, 42).

The paterfamilias usually determined the religion of the household. For women and slaves to adopt a different religion was to undermine the authority of the head of the household. Ephesians 5:22–6:9 (as well as Col. 3:18, 22), quoted ubiquitously in some Christian traditions, enjoins wives to submit to their husbands and slaves to obey their masters. The husband is said to be the "head" of the wife.

The letters to the Ephesians and Colossians are difficult to harmonize with the Paul who proclaimed Galatians 3:27–28 and who named Junia, Phoebe, Chloe, and a host of other women as powerful purveyors of the gospel, independent of husbands. Recall 1 Corinthians 7, where Paul exhorts women to refrain from marriage so that they may devote themselves to serving Christ wholeheartedly, a point not lost on the author of the Acts of Paul and Thecla, which itself was considered scriptural by many early Christians. Is it ironic that Thecla, who clearly upset the "natural" social order, is celebrated as

296

a saint in numerous segments of Christianity, including those that do not ordain women or allow them to serve as priests?

> What appears to have happened in the early church is something like this: Jesus, and Paul after him, brought a message about the reign of God that was countercultural and brought into question, among other things, the justice of contemporary social structures vis-à-vis God's own vision. Both followed a model of charismatic leadership, and both expected the imminent eschaton, the end, when God would set all things right and make good on God's promises of redemption, upon which the hope of all Christians rests.
>
> As it happened, the Parousia did not occur early on. This raised the dilemma referred to as the delay of the Parousia. In a nutshell, the early church discerned that the world might endure rather than end, so they felt compelled to devise strategies of survival for the long haul. As the church became an increasingly centralized institution structured and dependent upon particular offices rather than charismatic leadership, it accommodated and adapted the social structures of its host culture, the Roman Empire. This led to the suppression of women in church leadership and a call for women to get married, get pregnant, and tend to their families—in short, to move from the public to the private sphere. Modern churches have inherited this legacy, and some continue to struggle with the correctness of women as leaders in churches. (Clark-Soles 2010, 85)

One wonders how "strategies of survival" compare to "following the Spirit's lead" when the church determines what its witness should look like in each place and time, including our own.

The Legacy of the Household Codes

The household codes have, of course, been used by those who espouse and starkly profess the supremacy of one group over another or the "rightness" of one group being ordained to rule and another group ordained to submit. Many scholars mask or downplay the real effects of these writings. It is disturbing to find scholars whose work I typically admire soft-stepping around this ethical problem. It is one thing to try to provide a balanced viewpoint on particular matters, but when one group is encouraged to dominate another, it should be identified as a problem and an unacceptable system. ELCA minister and New Testament scholar Mark Allan

297

Powell writes of Ephesians 5:29–6:1: "These directives seem anti-quated and oppressive to many modern readers, who believe that wives are to be equal partners in a marriage, not subjects of the husband's domain; children should be taught respect rather than blind obedience; slaves should be emancipated" (2018, 354). As I have already noted in my critique of Powell with regard to 1 Timothy 5:6, it is not that these directives *seem* antiquated and oppressive—they *are* antiquated and oppressive. Powell goes on:

> The traditional *Haustafel* is set here within a context of *mutual* submission . . . , and the overall focus is shifted toward responsibilities of the more powerful party—this in keeping with the servant ethic encouraged by Jesus in the Gospels. . . . Most notable, perhaps, is the notion that husbands are to love their wives in the same way that Christ loved the church: they are to put their wives' wants and needs ahead of their own, giving of themselves in selfless service. (354)

This kind of interpretation is sometimes referred to as "benevolent patriarchy," an oxymoron if there ever was one. The very lives of women and children, deprived of agency, hang in the balance as the patriarch decides whether he is committed to (or in the mood for) benevolence at any given moment. A deadly game indeed. Surely the cross of Christ calls us to a radically different notion of wielding "power," and a crucified Messiah certainly calls for a reconsideration of imperial business as usual.

Attempts to soften the language of these passages also fail. Richard Hays (Methodist minister and New Testament scholar) argues in reference to the household codes that "the hierarchical structure of the relationships described is tempered by a comprehensive vision of the church as people living in humility and mutual submission. The conventional authority structures of the ancient household are thereby subverted even while they are left in place" (1996, 64). The last sentence is nonsensical. First, the structures are patently those of the ancient Roman pagan household, and as Wayne Meeks notes about the oxymoron, "either they are authoritative or they are not" (1996, 250). Hays further states: "The formal structure of the code is unusual in its pattern of addressing the subordinate persons in the social order (wives, children, slaves) as moral agents who must *choose* to 'be subject'" (1996, 64). Again, Meeks protests: "Hays apparently sees no irony or double entendre in observing that as 'moral agents' the women, slaves, and children '*must* choose to "be subject"'" (1996, 250; Meeks's italics).

This whitewashing of the danger and moral bankruptcy of systems of domination and submission only serves to perpetuate such systems, even if the person explaining away or softening the realities of such a system does not personally subscribe to it. Unintentionally perpetuating unjust systems does not exonerate us morally. One also wonders if scholars writing from a dominant position in society (white, male, ordained, etc.) find such systems of domination less problematic than those on the subordinate side of the system. This is another reason it is imperative to hear the voices of those from the "underside."

Few people are willing to accept the language about the submission of household slaves. I highly recommend Clarice Martin's essay written from a womanist perspective, "The *Haustafeln* (Household Codes) in African American Biblical Interpretation: 'Free Slaves' and 'Subordinate Women,'" which begins with these words: "Few New Testament narratives have exerted as profoundly a malefic and far-reaching impact on the lives of African-Americans as have the *Haustafeln*" (1991, 206). Martin reviews the history of interpretation of the codes, particularly in light of the African American experience of slavery, and then turns to the domination of women. She names particular tensions, including the fact that while black male preachers and theologians insist on a liberationist approach regarding slavery (that is, understanding that the codes are no longer binding and are morally problematic), when it comes to women, many use a literalist approach (thus insisting on keeping women in a subordinate role). She also argues:

> Many African Americans have accepted uncritically a socialization that tolerates and accepts the patriarchal model of male control and supremacy that typifies the Eurocentric, Western, Protestant tradition in general. A patriarchal ethos that inhibits the advancement of women in the socio-political and ecclesiastical spheres has often been mirrored by African American male culture as more normative than exceptional. (227)

Martin calls for a hermeneutic of liberation with respect not only to African Americans in general, but also to African American women in particular.

299

Ethical reading requires us to acknowledge that harm has been done. Wayne Meeks's essay "The 'Haustafeln' and American

Slavery: A Hermeneutical Challenge" is also worth reading in its entirety for those who want to consider the ethics of interpreting material about women in the Bible, as we do. It begins, "Most Christians believe that the Bible ought somehow to play a central role in moral formation and ethical decisions. . . . Yet what are we to make of those cases in which an honest and historically sensitive reading of the New Testament appears to support practices or institutions that Christians now find morally abominable?" (1996, 232). He then analyzes arguments for and against slavery and concludes: "It is not easy to state clearly why the proslavery readers of the Bible were wrong" (245). It is imperative, however, that we develop some interpretive strategies that might minimize "making equally disastrous mistakes" as our proslavery Christian ancestors (245). He ventures some suggestions along with the potential limitations of each. He concludes that "there are no magical rules of historical method or of hermeneutics that will assure that a scripture-based moral judgment will be right and just" (252). Any moral interpretation will necessarily involve communal practices, one of which

> would surely be the habit of listening to the weaker partner in every relationship of power. . . . At least one rule of thumb then emerges for ethical use of the Bible: whenever the Christian community seeks to reform itself, it must take steps to make sure that among the voices interpreting the tradition are those of the ones who have experienced harm from that tradition. "The love command in the New Testament" requires no less, and if the love of neighbor is thus understood, it will not so easily be reduced to the cold and narrow "justice" imposed by the possessors of power. (252–53)

Like Martin, Meeks calls us to a broader conversation about how we as Christians engage texts that have been used to oppress certain populations in a given time and place.

Scripture Has the Power to Interrogate

While we are called to wrestle with the Word and the authors who composed individual texts in a certain time and place, I delight in the fact that Scripture contains such inspiration, sometimes conveyed transcendently through irony. What makes me say this just now? Right on the heels of Ephesians 5:21–6:9—one of the most problematic passages that promotes within the church and within Christian homes power structures of domination and subordination so beloved by the pagan Roman Empire (and any empire of any era)—comes the glorious Ephesians 6:10–17, a passage that calls for spiritual warfare against the powers and principalities! On the one hand, the author is inspired by the Holy Spirit beyond his own historical confines to call out unjust power structures and bequeath us this mighty, eloquent call to arms for every generation. On the other hand, he is a real human being constrained by his own social context of empire where slavery and sexism were the norm. In other words, this passage brilliantly supplies us the tools to see what the original author was not able to see in his own life and thought—his complicity in serving the empire as a model citizen dedicated to upholding the so-called natural order of society as dictated by Aristotle and those after him.

I find this encouraging for a number of reasons. First, we all have this experience in our life of discipleship: on the one hand, we have flashes of insight and we take up the call to make it on earth as it is in heaven, including fighting against powers and principalities; on the other hand, we allow the flashes of insight to fade away, we find it easy to abandon the work of making heaven a reality on earth, and, truth be told, it is always tempting (and certainly tangibly rewarded) to work with or for the powers and principalities. To some degree, we are all products of the societies and cultures into which we are born and raised and taught to perpetuate indefinitely, so I sympathize with our author.

Second, however, salvation is always at hand, every minute of every day. We do not have to live as mere cogs in an unhealthy system (whether a family system, a religious system, or a societal system). As often as we immerse ourselves in Scripture, in the believing community, in relationship with God in Christ, we are met moment by moment with the offer of real power that empowers real relationships that are truly mutual and have real meaning for our precious lives. We don the belt of truth, the breastplate of righteousness, the shield of faith, the helmet of salvation, and "the sword of the Spirit, which is the word of God" (Eph. 6:17). Indeed, we have absolutely everything we need "to proclaim the gospel of peace" (6:15). Thanks be to God!

301

The Lectionary

The passages in 1–2 Timothy that seem to suggest positive involvement of women in ministry are hardly found in the Revised Common Lectionary (RCL) and the Roman Lectionary (RL). Thus, 1 Timothy 3:11 is not in the RCL as a Sunday or weekday reading (there is a weekday reading of 1 Tim. 3:1–9 during the week of the 5th Sunday after Epiphany in Year C), nor is it included as a Sunday RL reading. It is read on the Tuesday of Ordinary Time, Week 24, according to the RL. Although corporate worship provides little opportunity for interacting with this passage, Christians who wish to engage in creative application might read this passage with a focus on the mention of women among other groups of leaders (whether this was the author's intention or not). According to the RCL, 2 Timothy 1:1–14, containing mention of Eunice and Lois, is read on Year C in the season after Pentecost, on Proper 22 (27), and 2 Timothy 1:3–7 is prescribed as a weekday reading during the week of the 2nd Sunday in Lent of Year A. The Sunday and weekday readings in the RL include 2 Timothy 1 but omit 1:5, which mentions Eunice and Lois. Neither lectionary includes the reference to Prisca in 2 Timothy 4:19 (for a discussion of Prisca's presence elsewhere in the lectionary, consult the previous chapter in this book, "Women in Paul's Ministry").

The RCL conspicuously omits the controversial passages about women in 1 Timothy 2:8–15 and 2 Timothy 3:6–8 from Sunday readings, though the latter is included as a weekday reading during Proper 25 (30) of the season after Pentecost during Year C. The RL completely omits both of these passages from Sunday and weekday readings. Relatedly, Titus 2:3–5 and 1 Timothy 5:3–16, two passages that provide instructions to women and have rather critical tones, are only included as weekday lectionary readings. Titus 2:3–5 is altogether absent from the RCL but included in the RL during Year 2, on Tuesday of Ordinary Time, Week 32. First Timothy 5:3–16 is not included in the RL but appears as a weekday reading for the RCL during Year B, season after Pentecost, Proper 27 (32).

While the RCL omits Sunday readings of the household code passages as they pertain to women, the RL includes Ephesians 5:21–32 as an option on the 21st Sunday in Ordinary Time, Year B. The RL calls for a weekday reading of Ephesians 5:21–33 on Tuesday of Ordinary Time, Week 30, Year 2. The RCL also lists weekday readings for the codes: Colossians 3:18–4:1 is to be read during Proper 13 (18) of the season after Pentecost of Year C; Ephesians 5:21–6:9 is to be read during Proper 16 (21) of the season after Pentecost of Year B. (Both lectionaries include a portion of the 1 Peter code—the part pertaining to slaves—as Sunday readings. The RCL also includes this portion of 1 Peter 2 as a single weekday reading, and the RL does the same for the portion of the Ephesians code relating to slaves.)

On the one hand, perhaps the essential omission of several of these harsh passages from the lectionaries lessens opportunities for such patriarchal passages to be lifted up in churches. On the other hand, we should not forget that they exist as long as they are given power to oppress women (or other groups). Finally, when Ephesians 6:10–20 is read during Year B, season after Pentecost, Proper 16 (21) (per the RCL) or on the Thursday of Ordinary Time, Week 23 (per the RL), Christians have an opportunity to emphasize the liberative nature of Ephesians 6 even though Ephesians 5 fails to be liberative. Such proclamation reminds Christians that, while we must wrestle with Ephesians 5, it is not the only perspective to be heard, nor is it the final perspective in Ephesians.

Conclusion

In this chapter, we have explored the path that led away from the egalitarian, gender-bending, charismatically based models of leadership embraced by Jesus and Paul in the first century and toward the systematic (because it was systematic, organized, and institutionalized in turn) silencing of women and "putting them in their place" that the church unveiled in the second century. That path travels, in part, through the deutero-Pauline corpus.

Our investigation has intersected a number of the goals presented in the introduction. We have highlighted active though perhaps obscured early women of the faith, including Lois and Eunice and "the widows" of the Pastorals. We drew upon sociohistorical knowledge of first- and second-century realities to set the texts in context as we witnessed both the evolution of the church into an era of institutionalization and the rise of the genre of literature known as "church orders." We encountered women in the early church who took Paul at his word about forsaking traditional gender and

303

family mores when one's vocation calls for it. Thecla, Perpetua, and Felicitas serve as named examples, but the fact that other unnamed sisters already acted thusly in the community that generated the Pastorals is evident by the reactionary response of the author who anxiously spends considerable energy trying to get these women back in line. In addition, attending to the work of such womanist scholars as Clarice Martin and others, we learn to ask more profound questions about the nature and practice of ethical interpretation of our sacred texts.

Recommended Resources

Balch, David L. 1988. "Household Codes." Pages 25–50 in *Greco-Roman Literature and the New Testament*. Edited by David E. Aune. Society of Biblical Literature Sources for Biblical Study 21. Atlanta: Scholars Press.

Bassler, Jouette M. 1996. *1 Timothy, 2 Timothy, Titus*. Abingdon New Testament Commentaries. Nashville: Abingdon Press.

Clark-Soles, Jaime. 2010. *Engaging the Word: The New Testament and the Christian Believer*. Louisville, KY: Westminster John Knox Press.

Dewey, Joanna. 2012. "1 Timothy." Pages 595–601 in *Women's Bible Commentary*. Edited by Carol A. Newsom, Sharon H. Ringe, and Jacqueline E. Lapsley. 3rd ed. Louisville, KY: Westminster John Knox Press.

Hylen, Susan. 2015. *A Modest Apostle: Thecla and the History of Women in the Early Church*. Oxford: Oxford University Press.

Kittredge, Cynthia Briggs, and Claire Miller Colombo. 2002. "Colossians." Pages 123–200 in *Philippians, Colossians, Philemon*. Edited by Mary Ann Beavis. Wisdom Commentary series 51. Collegeville, MN: Liturgical Press.

Martin, Clarice J. 1991. "The *Haustafeln* (Household Codes) in African American Biblical Interpretation: 'Free Slaves' and 'Subordinate Women.'" Pages 206–31 in *Stony the Road We Trod: African American Biblical Interpretation*. Edited by Cain Hope Felder. Minneapolis: Augsburg Fortress Press.

Meeks, Wayne A. 1996. "The 'Haustafeln' and American Slavery: A Hermeneutical Challenge." Pages 232–53 in *Theology and Ethics in Paul and His Interpreters: Essays in Honor of Victor*

Paul Furnish. Edited by Eugene H. Lovering Jr. and Jerry L. Sumney. Nashville: Abingdon Press.

Tamez, Elsa. 2007. *Struggles for Power in Early Christianity: A Study of the First Letter to Timothy*. Maryknoll, NY: Orbis Books.

Thurston, Bonnie Bowman. 1973. *The Widows: A Women's Ministry in the Early Church*. Minneapolis: Fortress Press.

In the End,
Toward *the* End (Goal)

Truth, with Hope

Women strong. Women vulnerable. Women eclipsed. Women strategic. Woman created, women creating. Woman Wisdom, wise women. They are all there in Scripture, ready to teach, inspire, move, question, and challenge us. A grand invitation has been extended to us. How will we respond?

We began this journey on a note of celebration and end on a note of celebration for the witness of faithful women from antiquity until now. We noted ongoing challenges within Christianity with respect to women as well as our construals of God. We laid out eight specific goals aimed at equipping the reader with more knowledge in the service of their own faith as well as the faith of others. We committed to an honest conversation about the promises and pitfalls of the biblical texts under consideration with respect to ancient audiences and later interpreters, including us. We asked, "In what ways does the text have liberative potential, and in what ways does it present potential obstacles for those seeking abundant life?" (John 10:10). We then devoted chapter upon chapter to delving into the specifics of our Scriptures.

I conclude not only with celebration, but also with thanksgiving for what may be termed a veritable feast. The table is exceedingly large, even infinite. It includes at least four groups, all guests of honor.

307

First, I give thanks for all the women in the Bible, my ancestors in the faith, each of whom has instructed me in her/their own way, as I hope this book has manifested.

Second, I give thanks for later interpreters from across time and space. Writing this book, for instance, provoked me to reread Elizabeth Cady Stanton's groundbreaking work *The Woman's Bible*. I'm not going to lie—I take pleasure in the connection between the title of her work and the title of mine. I hope she would find that my book faithfully carries forward the work that hers accomplished. Tough as she was (and I fancy myself the same), something tells me she'd take special pleasure in the fact that my daughter, Chloe, named after the church leader in 1 Corinthians 1:11, gave me a rare copy of Stanton's book. Strength and tenderness are not opposing virtues, it turns out. I hope I have introduced you to some new conversation partners and maybe even new topics of conversation.

Third, I give thanks for a *living* tradition, a living faith in which God and Jesus and the Holy Spirit continue to astonish me with new facets of truth, grace, faith, hope, and love. The table is set, and it is endless. I trust you will continue to invite others, pass the food down, feel free to try everything at least once, and come back for seconds whenever you find a particularly nourishing dish. We recall that women typically provided nourishment in antiquity, working together to provide bread. God continually provides the Bread from Heaven to satisfy our hunger. Jesus said, "My food is to do the will of the one who sent me." We can never go wrong with the Bread from Heaven, divine nourishment, spiritual milk from the bosom of God, and living water from the womb of Jesus (John 7:38). Taste and see that the Lord is good, indeed.

Kenneth Rexroth reminded us: "Against the ruin of the world, there is only one defense—the creative act" (1987, 43). Recall how Miriam drew upon creativity to lead her people. She created a song with meaningful lyrics that inspired her people in their own context, and she invited their very bodies (not just their analytical minds) into the mix. While she could have very easily made it so, it wasn't the "Miriam show"; rather, she drew out of her people their *own* creativity! Through this book, I have audaciously attempted to follow in my sister Miriam's footsteps. If this project has been successful, then, far from being the "Jaime show," it will be a creative act whose power is displayed most splendidly by inspiring the creativity of the readers themselves so that the singing and the dancing

308

is so vibrant, pulsing, and contagious that the question becomes not "Who started it?" but "How could we begin to map the effect of the throng devoted to 'turning the world upside down'?" as the author of Acts puts it in 17:6. I know I'm dreaming big, but why not? Creative audaciousness seems to describe Jesus himself; the same Jesus who emphatically declared that we would do greater works than he himself did!

But how? If Scripture teaches us anything, it's the power of a compelling story to transform us. Think of your favorite story from the Bible. Then ponder this: what are the compelling features of that story that make it so dear to you, so true? Storyteller Tobias Wolff, in the introduction to *The Vintage Book of Contemporary American Short Stories* (1994, xiii), writes:

> That sense of kinship is what makes stories important to us. The pleasure we take in cleverness and technical virtuosity soon exhausts itself in the absence of any recognizable human landscape. We need to feel ourselves acted upon by a story, outraged, exposed, in danger of heartbreak and change. Those are the stories that endure in our memories, to the point where they take on the nature of memory itself. In this way the experience of something read can form us no less than the experience of something lived through.

What he avers of short stories, we know to be true of Scripture. The question then becomes: "How does the story of my life and the life of my community fit into the story of all stories—the story of God with Us (Immanuel)?"

I fervently hope that through this book you have not only gained knowledge, but also feel inspired, equipped, and encouraged to work for the flourishing of all of God's beautiful, if complicated, creation. Remember the women who have gone before us, who have given us wisdom and faith. May we join them at the table and share our stories for the sake of those who will come after us.

WORKS CITED

Ahrens, Lynn, lyricist. 1996. "Make Them Hear You." In *Ragtime: The Musical*. Performed by Brian Stokes Mitchell. Music by Stephen Flaherty. Musical cast recording. BMG Music. Released February 11, 1996.

Aland, Kurt. 1993. *Synopsis of the Four Gospels*. 10th ed. Stuttgart: United Bible Societies.

Aland, Kurt, and Barbara Aland. 1995. *The Text of the New Testament: An Introduction to the Critical Editions and to the Theory and Practice of Modern Textual Criticism*. Translated by Erroll F. Rhodes. 2nd ed. Grand Rapids: Wm. B. Eerdmans Publishing Co.

Aldama, Arturo, ed. 2003. *Violence and the Body: Race, Gender, and the State*. Bloomington: Indiana University Press.

Aldredge-Clanton, Jann. 2004. *In Search of the Christ-Sophia: An Inclusive Christology for Liberating Christians*. 2nd ed. Woodway, TX: Eakin Press.

———. 2014. *She Lives! Sophia Wisdom Works in the World*. Woodstock, VT: SkyLight Paths.

Aldredge-Clanton, Jann, with composer Larry E. Schultz. 2006. *Inclusive Hymns for Liberating Christians*. Austin, TX: Eakin Press.

Allen, Prudence. 1985. *The Concept of Woman: The Aristotelian Revolution, 750 B.C.–A.D. 1250*. Grand Rapids: Wm. B. Eerdmans Publishing Co.

Alonso, Pablo. 2011. *The Woman Who Changed Jesus: Crossing Boundaries in Mk 7,24–30*. Biblical Tools and Studies 11. Leuven: Peeters.

Anderson, Janice Capel, and Stephen D. Moore, eds. 2008. *Mark & Method: New Approaches to Biblical Studies*. 2nd ed. Minneapolis: Fortress Press.

Augustine. 1997. *The Confessions*. Introduction, translation and notes by Maria Boulding, OSB. Vol. 1/1 of *The Works of Saint Augustine*. Hyde Park, NY: New City Press.

————. 2001. *Expositions of the Psalms, 51–72.* Translation and notes by Maria Boulding. Vol. 3/17 of *The Works of Saint Augustine.* Hyde Park, NY: New City Press.

Balch, David L. 1988. "Household Codes." Pages 25–50 in *Greco-Roman Literature and the New Testament.* Edited by David E. Aune. Society of Biblical Literature Sources for Biblical Study 21. Atlanta: Scholars Press.

Bassler, Jouette M. 1996. *1 Timothy, 2 Timothy, Titus.* Abingdon New Testament Commentaries. Nashville: Abingdon Press.

Baughman, Rachel, Christine Chakoian, Jaime Clark-Soles, Judy Fentress-Williams, and Ginger Gaines-Cirelli, eds. 2016. *The CEB Women's Bible.* Nashville: Abingdon Press.

Belenky, Mary Field, Blythe McVicker Clinchy, Nancy Rule Goldberger, and Jill Mattuck Tarule. 1997. *Women's Ways of Knowing: The Development of Self, Voice, and Mind.* 10th anniv. ed. New York: Basic Books.

Bellis, Alice Ogden. 2007. *Helpmates, Harlots, and Heroes: Women's Stories in the Hebrew Bible.* 2nd ed. Louisville, KY: Westminster John Knox Press.

BibleWalks. 2014. "National Mosaics in the Basilica of Annunciation." Last updated May 5, 2014. https://www.biblewalks.com/Annunciation-Mosaics.

Black, Kathy. 1996. *A Healing Homiletic: Preaching and Disability.* Nashville: Abingdon Press.

Bohache, Thomas. 2006. "Matthew." Pages 487–516 in *The Queer Bible Commentary.* Edited by Deryn Guest, Robert E. Goss, Mona West, and Thomas Bohache. London: SCM Press.

Camp, Claudia. 1985. *Wisdom and the Feminine in the Book of Proverbs.* Sheffield: Almond Press.

Campbell, Will D. 1985. "On Silencing Our Finest." *Christianity and Crisis* 45, no. 14 (September 16): 340–42.

Carey, Greg. 2009. *Sinners: Jesus and His Earliest Followers.* Waco, TX: Baylor University Press.

Carter, Warren. 2001. *Matthew and Empire: Initial Explorations.* Harrisburg, PA: Trinity Press International.

————. 2006. *The Roman Empire and the New Testament: An Essential Guide.* Nashville: Abingdon Press.

Chittister, Joan. *The Gift of Years: Growing Older Gracefully.* New York: BlueBridge, 2010.

Claassens, L. Juliana M. 2004. *The God Who Provides: Biblical Images of Divine Nourishment*. Nashville: Abingdon Press.

———. 2012. *Mourner, Mother, Midwife: Reimagining God's Delivering Presence in the Old Testament*. Louisville, KY: Westminster John Knox Press.

———. 2016. *Claiming Her Dignity: Female Resistance in the Old Testament*. Collegeville, MN: Liturgical Press.

Clark-Soles, Jaime. 2010. *Engaging the Word: The New Testament and the Christian Believer*. Louisville, KY: Westminster John Knox Press.

———. 2016. *Reading John for Dear Life: A Spiritual Walk with the Fourth Gospel*. Louisville, KY: Westminster John Knox Press.

Collaborative on Faith and Disabilities. https://faithanddisability.org.

Coloe, Mary. 2013. "The Mother of Jesus: A Woman Possessed." Pages 202–13 in *Character Studies in the Fourth Gospel: Narrative Approaches to Seventy Figures in John*. Edited by Steven A. Hunt, Francois Tolmie, and Ruben Zimmerman. Wissenschaftliche Untersuchungen zum Neuen Testament 314. Tübingen: Mohr Siebeck.

Commission on Theology and Church Relations of the Lutheran Church–Missouri Synod. 1985. "Women in the Church: Scriptural Principles and Ecclesial Practice."

Conway, Colleen M. 2008. *Behold the Man: Jesus and Greco-Roman Masculinity*. Oxford: Oxford University Press.

Cosgrove, Charles H. 2002. *Appealing to Scripture in Moral Debate: Five Hermeneutical Rules*. Grand Rapids: Wm. B. Eerdmans Publishing Co.

Creach, Jerome F. D. 2013. *Violence in Scripture*. Interpretation: Resources for the Use of Scripture in the Church. Louisville, KY: Westminster John Knox Press.

Crowder, Stephanie Buckhanon. 2016. *When Momma Speaks: The Bible and Motherhood from a Womanist Perspective*. Louisville, KY: Westminster John Knox Press.

Daly, Mary. 1973. *Beyond God the Father: Toward a Philosophy of Women's Liberation*. Boston: Beacon Press.

Darr, Katheryn Pfisterer. 2009. "Asking at Abel: A Wise Woman's Proverb Performance in 2 Samuel 20." Pages 102–21 in *From the Margins 1: Women of the Hebrew Bible and Their Afterlives*. Edited by Peter S. Hawkins and Lesleigh Cushing

313

Stahlberg. The Bible in the Modern World 18. Sheffield: Sheffield Phoenix Press.

Davies, W. D., and Dale C. Allison. 2004. *The Gospel according to Saint Matthew*. Volume 2, *Matthew 8–18*. International Critical Commentary. London: T&T Clark.

Dean-Jones, Lesley. 1991. "The Cultural Construct of the Female Body in Classical Greek Science." Pages 111–37 in *Women's History and Ancient History*. Edited by Sarah B. Pomeroy. Chapel Hill: University of North Carolina Press.

Derrett, J. Duncan M. 1963. "Law in the New Testament: The Story of the Woman Taken in Adultery." *New Testament Studies* 10:1–26.

deSilva, David A. 2000. *Honor, Patronage, Kinship and Purity: Unlocking New Testament Culture*. Downers Grove, IL: InterVarsity Press.

Dewey, Joanna. 2012. "1 Timothy." Pages 595–601 in *Women's Bible Commentary*. Edited by Carol A. Newsom, Sharon H. Ringe, and Jacqueline E. Lapsley. 3rd ed. Louisville, KY: Westminster John Knox Press.

Donaldson, Laura E. 1999. "The Sign of Orpah: Reading Ruth through Native Eyes." Pages 130–44 in *Ruth and Esther*. A Feminist Companion to the Bible 2. Edited by Athalya Brenner. Sheffield: Sheffield Academic Press.

Dube, Musa W. 1999. "The Unpublished Letters of Orpah to Ruth." Pages 145–50 in *Ruth and Esther*. A Feminist Companion to the Bible 2. Edited by Athalya Brenner. Sheffield: Sheffield Academic Press.

Elliott, J. K. 1993. *Apocryphal New Testament: A Collection of Apocryphal Christian Literature in an English Translation*. New York: Oxford University Press.

Emerson, Ralph Waldo. 2017. *Self-Reliance*. Scotts Valley, CA: CreateSpace Independent Publishing Platform.

Epp, J. Eldon. 2005. *Junia: The First Woman Apostle*. Minneapolis: Fortress Press.

Fehribach, Adeline. 2003. "The 'Birthing' Bridegroom: The Portrayal of Jesus in the Fourth Gospel." Pages 104–29 in *A Feminist Companion to John: Volume 2*. Edited by Amy-Jill Levine. New York: Sheffield Academic Press.

Fitzmyer, Joseph A. 1982. *The Gospel according to Luke I–IX*. Anchor Bible 28A. New York: Doubleday.

314

Fortune, Marie M. 1987. *Keeping the Faith: Guidance for Christian Women Facing Abuse*. New York: HarperCollins.

Fox, Ruth. 1999. "Women in the Bible and the Lectionary." Pages 359–67 in *Remembering the Women*. Compiled and annotated by J. Frank Henderson. Chicago: Liturgy Training Publications.

Gafney, Wilda C. 2008. *Daughters of Miriam: Women Prophets in Ancient Israel*. Minneapolis: Fortress Press.

———. 2017. *Womanist Midrash: A Reintroduction to the Women of the Torah and the Throne*. Louisville, KY: Westminster John Knox Press.

Gale, Aaron M. 2011. "The Virgin Birth." Page 4 in *The Jewish Annotated New Testament: New Revised Standard Version*. Edited by Amy-Jill Levine and Marc Zvi Brettler. Oxford: Oxford University Press.

Garrett, Susan R. 1998. "Revelation." Pages 469–74 in *Women's Bible Commentary*. Edited by Carol A. Newsom and Sharon H. Ringe. Exp. ed. Louisville, KY: Westminster John Knox Press.

Gaventa, Beverly Roberts. 1999. *Mary: Glimpses of the Mother of Jesus*. Minneapolis: Fortress Press.

———. 2004. "Our Mother Saint Paul: Toward the Recovery of a Neglected Theme." Pages 85–97 in *A Feminist Companion to Paul*. Edited by Amy-Jill Levine. Feminist Companion to the New Testament and Early Christian Writings 6. London: T&T Clark.

Gellius. 1927. *Attic Nights, Volume II: Books 6–13*. Translated by J. C. Rolfe. Loeb Classical Library 200. Cambridge, MA: Harvard University Press.

Gnadt, Martina. 2012. "Gospel of Matthew: Jewish-Christian in Opposition to the Pax Romana." Pages 607–25 in *Feminist Biblical Interpretation: A Compendium of Critical Commentary on the Books of the Bible and Related Literature*. Edited by Luise Schottroff and Marie-Theres Wacker. Grand Rapids: Wm. B. Eerdmans Publishing Co.

Guardiola-Sáenz, Leticia A. 2002. "Border-Crossing and Its Redemptive Power in John 7.53–8.11: A Cultural Reading of Jesus and the *Accused*." Pages 129–52 in *John and Postcolonialism: Travel, Space and Power*. Edited by Musa W. Dube and Jeffrey L. Staley. London: Sheffield Academic Press.

Gurian, Michael. 2013. *The Wonder of Aging: A New Approach to Embracing Life after Fifty*. New York: Atria.

315

Haught, Kaylin. 1995. "God Says Yes to Me." Page 6 in *In the Palm of Your Hand: The Poet's Portable Workshop*. Edited by Steve Kowit. Thomaston, ME: Tilbury House.

Hays, Richard B. 1996. *The Moral Vision of the New Testament: A Contemporary Introduction to New Testament Ethics*. New York: HarperOne.

Heath, Elaine A. 2019. *Healing the Wounds of Sexual Abuse: Reading the Bible with Survivors*. Grand Rapids: Brazos Press.

Henderson, J. Frank, compiler. 1998. *Remembering the Women: Women's Stories from Scripture for Sundays and Festivals*. 2nd ed. Chicago: Liturgy Training Publications.

Hochschild, Arlie, and Anne Machung. 2012. *The Second Shift: Working Families and the Revolution at Home*. Rev. ed. New York: Penguin Group.

Holladay, William L. 1995. *Long Ago God Spoke: How Christians May Hear the Old Testament Today*. Minneapolis: Augsburg Fortress Press.

Hylen, Susan. 2015. *A Modest Apostle: Thecla and the History of Women in the Early Church*. Oxford: Oxford University Press.

———. 2019. *Women in the New Testament World*. Essentials of Biblical Studies. Oxford: Oxford University Press.

Ignatius. 1987. *Letters. To the Ephesians*. Translated by Maxwell Staniforth. Pages 59–68 in *Early Christian Writings: The Apostolic Fathers*. Edited by Andrew Louth. New York: Penguin.

———. 1987. *Letters. To the Magnesians*. Translated by Maxwell Staniforth. Pages 69–76 in *Early Christian Writings: The Apostolic Fathers*. Edited by Andrew Louth. New York: Penguin.

Johnson, Elizabeth A. 2002. *She Who Is: The Mystery of God in Feminist Theological Discourse*. Anniv. ed. New York: Crossroad.

Junior, Nyasha. 2019. *Reimagining Hagar: Blackness and the Bible*. Oxford: Oxford University Press.

Keener, Craig S. 2009. *The Gospel of Matthew: A Socio-Rhetorical Commentary*. Grand Rapids: Wm. B. Eerdmans Publishing Co.

Keith, Chris. 2009. *The Pericope Adulterae, the Gospel of John, and the Literacy of Jesus*. New Testament Tools, Studies, and Documents 38. Leiden: Brill.

Kidd, Sue Monk. 2003. *The Secret Life of Bees*. New York: Penguin.

Kim, Jean K. 2002. "Adultery or Hybridity? Reading John 7.53–8.11 from a Postcolonial Context." Pages 111–28 in *John and Postcolonialism: Travel, Space and Power.* Edited by Musa W. Dube and Jeffrey L. Staley. London: Sheffield Academic Press.

Kittredge, Cynthia Briggs, and Claire Miller Colombo. 2002. "Colossians." Pages 123–200 in *Philippians, Colossians, Philemon.* Edited by Mary Ann Beavis. Wisdom Commentary series 51. Collegeville, MN: Liturgical Press.

Lander, Shira. 2011. Introduction and notes to "The First Letter of Paul to the Corinthians." Pages 287–315 in *The Jewish Annotated New Testament: New Revised Standard Version.* Edited by Amy-Jill Levine and Marc Zvi Brettler. Oxford: Oxford University Press.

Lapsley, Jacqueline E. 2005. *Whispering the Word: Hearing Women's Stories in the Old Testament.* Louisville, KY: Westminster John Knox Press.

Lee, Eunny P. 2012. "Ruth." Pages 142–49 in *Women's Bible Commentary.* Edited by Carol A. Newsom, Sharon H. Ringe, and Jacqueline E. Lapsley. 3rd ed. Louisville, KY: Westminster John Knox Press.

Leslie, Donald Daniel, David Flusser, Alvin J. Reines, Gershom Scholem, and Michael J. Graetz. 2007. "Redemption." Pages 151–55 in vol. 17 of *Encyclopaedia Judaica.* Edited by Michael Berenbaum and Fred Skolnik. 2nd ed. Detroit: Macmillan Reference USA.

Levine, Amy-Jill. 2001. "Matthew's Advice to a Divided Readership." Pages 22–41 in *The Gospel of Matthew in Current Study.* Edited by David E. Aune. Grand Rapids: Wm. B. Eerdmans Publishing Co.

———. 2006. *The Misunderstood Jew: The Church and the Scandal of the Jewish Jesus.* New York: HarperOne.

———. 2012. "Gospel of Matthew." Pages 465–77 in *Women's Bible Commentary.* Edited by Carol A. Newsom, Sharon H. Ringe, and Jacqueline E. Lapsley. 3rd ed. Louisville, KY: Westminster John Knox Press.

Lewis, Karoline M. 2016. *She: Five Keys to Unlock the Power of Women in Ministry.* Nashville: Abingdon Press.

Llywelyn, Dorian, SJ. 2016. "Mary and Mariology." *Oxford Handbooks Online.* Oxford University Press. Article published June 2016. http://dx.doi.org/10.1093/oxfordhb/9780199935420.013.62.

Loader, William. 2010. *Sexuality in the New Testament: Understanding the Key Texts*. Louisville, KY: Westminster John Knox Press.

Love, Stuart L. 2009. *Jesus and Marginal Women: The Gospel of Matthew in Social-Scientific Perspective*. Eugene, OR: Cascade Books.

Malbon, Elizabeth Struthers. 1983. "Fallible Followers: Women and Men in the Gospel of Mark." *Semeia* 28:29–48.

———. 2009. *Mark's Jesus: Characterization as Narrative Christology*. Waco, TX: Baylor University Press.

Martin, Clarice J. 1991. "The *Haustafeln* (Household Codes) in African American Biblical Interpretation: 'Free Slaves' and 'Subordinate Women.'" Pages 206–31 in *Stony the Road We Trod: African American Biblical Interpretation*. Edited by Cain Hope Felder. Minneapolis: Augsburg Fortress Press.

Martin, Dale B. 1995. *The Corinthian Body*. New Haven, CT: Yale University Press.

McKenna, Megan. 1994. *Not Counting Women and Children: Neglected Stories from the Bible*. Maryknoll, NY: Orbis Books.

McKenzie, Alyce. 2002. *Preaching Biblical Wisdom in a Self-Help Society*. Nashville: Abingdon Press.

McKinlay, Judith E. 1999. "A Son Is Born to Naomi: A Harvest for Israel." Pages 151–57 in *Ruth and Esther*. Edited by Athalya Brenner. A Feminist Companion to the Bible 2. Sheffield: Sheffield Academic Press.

Meeks, Wayne A. 1983. *The First Urban Christians: The Social World of the Apostle Paul*. New Haven, CT: Yale University Press.

———. 1996. "The 'Haustafeln' and American Slavery: A Hermeneutical Challenge." Pages 232–53 in *Theology and Ethics in Paul and His Interpreters: Essays in Honor of Victor Paul Furnish*. Edited by Eugene H. Lovering Jr. and Jerry L. Sumney. Nashville: Abingdon Press.

———. 2006. *Christ Is the Question*. Louisville, KY: Westminster John Knox Press.

Melcher, Sarah J., Mikeal C. Parsons, and Amos Yong, eds. 2017. *The Bible and Disability: A Commentary*. Waco, TX: Baylor University Press.

Metzger, Bruce M., and Bart D. Ehrman. 2005. *The Text of the New Testament: Its Transmission, Corruption, and Restoration*. 4th ed. Oxford: Oxford University Press.

Meyers, Carol. 2013. *Rediscovering Eve: Ancient Israelite Women in Context*. Oxford: Oxford University Press.

Miller, Susan. 2004. *Women in Mark's Gospel*. Journal for the Study of the New Testament Supplement Series 259. New York: T&T Clark International.

Mollenkott, Virginia Ramey. 2014. *The Divine Feminine: The Biblical Imagery of God as Female*. Eugene, OR: Wipf & Stock.

Moss, Candida. 2017. "Mark and Matthew." Pages 275–301 in *The Bible and Disability: A Commentary*. Edited by Sarah J. Melcher, Mikeal C. Parsons, and Amos Yong. Waco, TX: Baylor University Press.

Musurillo, H. M., introduction, texts, and translation. 1972. *The Acts of the Christian Martyrs*. Oxford Early Christian Texts. Oxford: Clarendon.

Myers, Alicia. 2013. "'In the Father's Bosom': Breastfeeding and Identity Formation in John's Gospel." *Catholic Biblical Quarterly* 76:481–97.

———. 2017. *Blessed among Women? Mothers and Motherhood in the New Testament*. New York: Oxford University Press.

Niditch, Susan. 1998. "Genesis." Pages 13–29 in *Women's Bible Commentary*. Edited by Carol A. Newsom and Sharon H. Ringe. Exp. ed. Louisville, KY: Westminster John Knox Press.

O'Brien, Julia. 2002. *Nahum*. Readings: A New Biblical Commentary. London: Sheffield Academic Press.

O'Connor, Flannery. 1965. "Revelation." Pages 191–218 in *Everything That Rises Must Converge*. New York: Farrar, Straus & Giroux.

O'Day, Gail. 2001. "Surprised by Faith: Jesus and the Canaanite Woman." Pages 114–25 in *A Feminist Companion to Matthew*. Edited by Amy-Jill Levine with Marianne Blickenstaff. Sheffield: Sheffield Academic Press.

Patterson, Kerry, Joseph Grenny, Ron McMillan, and Al Switzler. 2012. *Crucial Conversations: Tools for Talking When Stakes Are High*. 2nd ed. New York: McGraw-Hill.

Portier-Young, Anathea. 2012. "Drinking the Cup of Horror and Gnawing on Its Shards: Biblical Theology through Biblical Violence, Not around It." Pages 387–408 in *Beyond Biblical Theologies*. Edited by Heinrick Assel, Stefan Beyerle, and Christfried Böttrich. Wissenschaftliche Untersuchungen zum Neuen Testament 295. Tübingen: Mohr Siebeck.

319

Powell, Mark Allan. 2018. *Introducing the New Testament: A Historical, Literary and Theological Survey*. Grand Rapids: Baker Academic.

Pressler, Carolyn. 1993. *The View of Women Found in Deuteronomic Family Laws*. Berlin: Walter de Gruyter.

Procter-Smith, Marjorie. 2013. *In Her Own Rite: Constructing Feminist Liturgical Tradition*. 2nd ed. Cape May, NJ: OSL Publications.

Reid, Barbara E., ed. 2015–. Wisdom Commentary series. Collegeville, MN: Liturgical Press.

Reinhartz, Adele. 2002. *Befriending the Beloved Disciple: A Jewish Reading of the Gospel of John*. New York: Continuum.

Rexroth, Kenneth. 1987. "Disengagement: The Art of the Beat Generation." Pages 41–56 in *World outside the Window: The Selected Essays of Kenneth Rexroth*. Edited by Bradford Morrow. New York: New Directions.

Rhoads, David, Joanna Dewey, and Donald Michie. 2012. *Mark as Story: An Introduction to the Narrative of a Gospel*. 3rd ed. Minneapolis: Fortress Press.

Rohr, Richard. 2011. *Falling Upward: A Spirituality for the Two Halves of Life*. San Francisco: Jossey-Bass.

Ruden, Sarah. 2011. *Paul among the People: The Apostle Reinterpreted and Reimagined in His Own Time*. New York: Image Books.

Sanders, Cody J. 2017. *A Brief Guide to Ministry with LGBTQIA Youth*. Louisville, KY: Westminster John Knox Press.

Sawyer, Deborah. 2003. "John 19:34: From Crucifixion to Birth, or Creation?" Pages 130–39 in *A Feminist Companion to John: Volume 2*. Edited by Amy-Jill Levine. New York: Sheffield Academic Press.

Schipper, Jeremy. 2016. *Ruth: A New Translation with Introduction and Commentary*. Anchor Yale Bible 7D. New Haven, CT: Yale University Press.

Schneiders, Sandra S. 2003. *Written That You May Believe: Encountering Jesus in the Fourth Gospel*. Rev. and exp. ed. New York: Crossroad.

Schoemperlen, Diane. 2002. *Our Lady of the Lost and Found: A Novel of Mary, Faith, and Friendship*. New York: Penguin.

Scholz, Susanne. 2010. *Sacred Witness: Rape in the Hebrew Bible*. Minneapolis: Fortress Press.

———. 2012. "Judges." Pages 113–27 in *Women's Bible Commentary*. Edited by Carol A. Newsom, Sharon H. Ringe, and Jacqueline E. Lapsley. 3rd ed. Louisville, KY: Westminster John Knox Press.

Schuller, Eileen. 1999. "Women in the Lectionary." Pages 368–74 in *Remembering the Women*. Compiled and annotated by J. Frank Henderson. Chicago: Liturgy Training Publications.

Schulte, Leah Rediger. 2017. *The Absence of God in Biblical Rape Narratives*. Emerging Scholars Series. Minneapolis: Fortress Press.

Schüssler Fiorenza, Elisabeth. 1994. *In Memory of Her: A Feminist Theological Reconstruction of Christian Origins*. 10th anniv. ed. New York: Crossroad.

Scott, Martin. 1992. *Sophia and the Johannine Jesus*. Journal for the Study of the New Testament Supplement Series 71. Sheffield: JSOT Press.

Sechrest, Love L. 2015. "Enemies, Romans, Pigs, and Dogs: Loving the Other in the Gospel of Matthew." *Ex Auditu* 31:71–105.

Sharp, Carolyn J. 2021. *Jeremiah 26–52*. International Exegetical Commentary on the Old Testament. Stuttgart: Kohlhammer.

Smid, H. R. 1965. *Protoevangelium Jacobi: A Commentary*. Assen: Van Gorcum.

Smith, Paul R. 1993. *Is It Okay to Call God "Mother"? Considering the Feminine Face of God*. Ada, MI: Baker Academic.

Steussey, Marti J. 2016. "Ruth." Page 323 in *The CEB Women's Bible*. Edited by Rachel Baughman, Christine Chakoian, Jaime Clark-Soles, Judy Fentress-Williams, and Ginger Gaines-Cirelli. Nashville: Abingdon Press.

Swidler, Leonard. 1979. *Biblical Affirmations of Women*. Philadelphia: Westminster Press.

Tamez, Elsa. 2007. *Struggles for Power in Early Christianity: A Study of the First Letter to Timothy*. Maryknoll, NY: Orbis Books.

Tavard, George H. 1973. *Woman in Christian Tradition*. Notre Dame, IN: University of Notre Dame Press.

Thistlethwaite, Susan Brooks. 2015. *Women's Bodies as Battlefield: Christian Theology and the Global War on Women*. Basingstoke, UK: Palgrave Macmillan.

Throckmorton, Burton H. 1992. *Gospel Parallels: A Comparison of the Synoptic Gospels, New Revised Standard Version*. 5th ed. Nashville: Thomas Nelson.

Thurston, Bonnie Bowman. 1973. *The Widows: A Women's Ministry in the Early Church*. Minneapolis: Fortress Press.

Tracy, Thomas F. 1998. "Why Do the Innocent Suffer?" Pages 40–55 in *Why Are We Here? Everyday Questions and the Christian Life*. Edited by Ronald F. Thiemann and William C. Placher. Harrisburg, PA: Trinity Press International.

Trible, Phyllis. 1978. *God and the Rhetoric of Sexuality*. Overtures to Biblical Theology. Philadelphia: Fortress Press.

———. 1984. *Texts of Terror: Literary-Feminist Readings of Biblical Narratives*. Philadelphia: Fortress Press.

Unterman, Alan, Rivka G. Horwitz, Joseph Dan, and Sharon Faye Koren. 2007. "Shekhinah." Pages 440–44 in vol. 18 of *Encyclopaedia Judaica*. Edited by Michael Berenbaum and Fred Skolnik. 2nd ed. Detroit: Macmillan Reference USA.

Wainwright, Elaine M. 1997. "The Gospel of Matthew." Pages 635–77 in *Searching the Scriptures*. Vol. 2, *A Feminist Commentary*. Edited by Elisabeth Schüssler Fiorenza. New York: Crossroad.

———. 1998. *Shall We Look for Another? A Feminist Rereading of the Matthean Jesus*. Maryknoll, NY: Orbis Books.

———. 2001. "Not Without My Daughter: Gender and Demon Possession in Matthew 15.21–28." Pages 126–37 in *A Feminist Companion to Matthew*. Edited by Amy-Jill Levine with Marianne Blickenstaff. Sheffield: Sheffield Academic Press.

Walker, Alice. 2003. *In Search of Our Mothers' Gardens: Womanist Prose*. Boston: Mariner Books.

Weems, Renita J. 1988. *Just a Sister Away: A Womanist Vision of Women's Relationships in the Bible*. Philadelphia: Innisfree Press.

———. 2005. *Showing Mary: How Women Can Share Prayers, Wisdom, and the Blessings of God*. New York: Warner Books.

West, Mona. 2015. "Ruth." Pages 190–94 in *The Queer Bible Commentary*. Edited by Deryn Guest, Robert E. Goss, Mona West, and Thomas Bohache. London: SCM Press.

White, T. H., ed. and trans. 1960. *The Bestiary: A Book of Beasts*. New York: Putnam.

Williams, Delores S. 2013. *Sisters in the Wilderness: The Challenge of Womanist God-Talk*. Maryknoll, NY: Orbis.

Wire, Antoinette Clark. 1990. *The Corinthian Women Prophets: A Reconstruction through Paul's Rhetoric*. Minneapolis: Fortress Press.

Wittgenstein, Ludwig. 1922. *Tractatus Logico-Philosophicus*. New York: Harcourt, Brace & Co.

Wolff, Tobias, ed. 1994. *The Vintage Book of Contemporary American Short Stories*. New York: Penguin Random House.

Wynn, Kerry H. 2007. "Johannine Healings and the Otherness of Disability." *Perspectives in Religious Studies* 34:61–75.

Zimmerman, Irene. 1992. "Liturgy." Pages 55–56 in *WomenPsalms*. Compiled by Julia Ahlers, Rosemary Broughton, and Carl Koch. Winona, MN: St. Mary's Press.

Zusak, Markus. 2005. *The Book Thief*. Sydney: Picador.

INDEX OF SCRIPTURE
AND OTHER ANCIENT SOURCES

INDEX OF SUBJECTS

331

335

Isaiah (book of), maternal imagery in,
60–66
Isaiah (prophet), 58
Ishmael, 88
Israel. *See also* Judaism/Jews
enemies of, 18, 23, 37, 131, 212
femininity of, 92–93
violence, gender-based, in, 97
Woman Wisdom in, 236–37

Jabesh-gilead, 83–84
Jacob, 88, 91
Jael, 50, 97
Jeremiah (book of)
Holladay on, 100
mourning imagery in, 54–57
Jerome, 28
Jerusalem, 31, 48, 53, 62, 93, 154, 177
Jesus Christ. *See also* Jesus, gender and;
ministry of Jesus, women in
anointment of (*see* anointment of
Jesus)
birth and infancy of, 158–59, 158i,
243–45 (*see also under* birth)
as bread, 47, 241–42
breastfeeding of, 244–45
as bridegroom, 169, 210, 212
burial of, 218–20
and Canaanite woman, 17–22, 33–34
circumcision of, 154
crucifixion of, 160 (*see also* crucifixion)
crying of, 58
on defilement, 18
disciples of (*see* disciples of Jesus)
divinity of, 174
family of (*see* family, of Jesus)
humanity of, 173–75
Jezebel and, 93–94
as lifebearer, 241–42
lineage of (*see* genealogies, biblical)
on murder, 92
naming of, 150, 166
as nurser, 243–45, 248
race and, 36–39
as rejected, 238
resurrection of, 168, 170, 174, 221–23
as savior of Israelites, 20, 22–23, 27–28,
30, 33
Second Coming of, Paul on, 262–63,
265
similarities to Mary (Blessed Mother),
148
as Son of David, 18–19
suffering, as example of, 76
as swayed by Canaanite woman, 24,
26–27, 30, 33–34
touching of, by sick woman, 208

as unmarried, 4
values of, as taught by Mary (Blessed
Mother), 148, 152–54, 159
as Woman Wisdom (*see* Woman
Wisdom)
as Word of God, 237
Jesus Christ and gender, 235–50
and birth of church, 68
lectionary for, 247–48
as lifebearer, 248
as mother bird, 246
as mourner, 240
as nurser, 243–46, 248
as Woman Wisdom, 236–40
Jezebel, 78, 93–94, 122–23
Jilani, Nina, 117
Joab, 116–18
Joachim (father of Mary (Blessed
Mother)), 177
Joanna, 200, 222
Job, 136–37, 140
Jochebed (mother of Moses), 121, 167
Joel, 120
Johannine community, as bi-cultures,
207
John (Gospel of), Mary (Blessed
Mother) in
at crucifixion of Christ, 170–73
incarnation and, 173–75
as mother of the church, 168, 171
at wedding at Cana, 168–70
John the Baptist, 154
Jonadab, 81
Joppa, 114
Joseph (husband of Mary (Blessed
Mother)), 149–50, 165
Joseph of Arimathea, 218, 220
Josephus, 2
joy, Woman Wisdom as, 119
Judaism/Jews
anti-Semitism and, 23, 36
chosenness and, 30
ethnocentrism of, 23, 36
feminists on Canaanite woman, 30
and Gentiles, relationship with, 18, 20,
22–23
hermeneutics and, 99
Holocaust and, 57
Jesus as savior for, 20, 22
Joseph and Mary as, 154
lament of, 27–28
in Matthean church, 23, 31–32,
36–37
under Roman rule, 31
wisdom tradition of, 29–30
judge, Deborah as, 122
Judges, violence in, 97

CPSIA information can be obtained
at www.ICGtesting.com
Printed in the USA
BVHW070039230821
614959BV00001B/22